# EUROPEAN MORALS.

VOL. II.

# HISTORY

OF

# EUROPEAN MORALS

FROM

*AUGUSTUS TO CHARLEMAGNE.*

BY

WILLIAM EDWARD HARTPOLE LECKY, M.A.

IN TWO VOLUMES.

VOL. II.

NEW YORK:
D. APPLETON AND COMPANY,
90, 92 & 94 GRAND STREET.
1870.

# CONTENTS

OF

# THE SECOND VOLUME.

## CHAPTER IV.

### FROM CONSTANTINE TO CHARLEMAGNE.

## CHAPTER V.

### THE POSITION OF WOMEN.

# HISTORY

OF

# EUROPEAN MORALS.

## CHAPTER IV.

### FROM CONSTANTINE TO CHARLEMAGNE.

HAVING in the last chapter given a brief, but I trust not altogether indistinct account of the causes that ensured the triumph of Christianity in Rome, and of the character of the opposition it overcame, I proceed to examine the nature of the moral ideal the new religion introduced, and also the methods by which it attempted to realise it. And at the very outset of this enquiry it is necessary to guard against a serious error. It is common with many persons to establish a comparison between Christianity and Paganism, by placing the teaching of the Christians in juxtaposition with corresponding passages from the writings of Marcus Aurelius or Seneca, and to regard the superiority of the Christian over the philosophical teaching as a complete measure of the moral advance that was effected by Christianity. But a moment's reflection is sufficient to display the injustice of such a conclusion. The ethics of Paganism were part of a philosophy. The ethics of Christianity were part of a religion. The first were the speculations of a few highly cultivated individuals, and neither had nor could have had any direct influence upon the masses of mankind. The second were indissolubly connected with the worship, hopes, and fears of a vast religious system, that acts at least as powerfully on the most ignorant as on the most educated. The objects of the Pagan systems were to foretell the future, to explain the universe, to avert calamity, to obtain the assistance of the gods. They contained no instruments of moral teaching analogous to our institution of preaching, or to the moral preparation for the reception of the sacrament, or to confession, or to the reading of the Bible, or to religious education, or to united prayer for spiritual benefits. To make men virtuous was no more the function of the priest than of the physician. On the other hand, the philosophic expositions of duty were wholly unconnected with the religious ceremonies of the temple. To amalgamate these two spheres, to incorporate moral culture with religion, and thus to enlist in its behalf that desire to enter, by means of ceremonial observances, into direct communication with Heaven, which experience has shown to be one of the most universal and powerful passions of mankind, was among the most important achievements of Christianity. Something had no doubt been already attempted in this direction. Philosophy, in the hands of the rhetoricians, had become more popular. The Pythagoreans enjoined religious ceremonies for the purpose of purifying the mind, and expiatory rites were common, especially in the Oriental religions. But it was the distinguishing characteristic of Christianity, that its moral influence was not indirect, casual, remote, or spasmodic. Unlike all Pagan religions, it made moral teaching a main function of its clergy, moral discipline the leading object of its services, moral dispositions the necessary condition of the due performance of its rites. By the pulpit, by its ceremonies, by all the agencies of power it possessed, it laboured systematically and perseveringly for the regeneration of mankind. Under its influence, doctrines concerning the nature of God, the immortality of the soul, and the duties of men, which the noblest intellects of antiquity could barely grasp, have become the truisms of the village school, the proverbs of the cottage and of the alley.

But neither the beauty of its sacred writings, nor the perfection of its religious services, could have achieved this great result without the introduction of new motives to virtue. These may be either interested or disinterested, and in both spheres the influence of Christianity was very great. In the first, it effected a complete revolution by its teaching concerning the future world and concerning the nature of sin. The doctrine of a future life was far too vague among the Pagans to exercise any powerful general influence, and among the philosophers, who clung to it most ardently, it was regarded solely in the light of a consolation. Christianity made it a deterrent influence of the strongest kind. In addition to the doctrines of eternal suffering, and the lost condition of the human race, the notion of a minute personal retribution must be regarded as profoundly original. That the commission of great crimes, or the omission of great duties, may be expiated hereafter, was indeed an idea familiar to the Pagans, though it exercised little influence over their lives, and seldom or never produced, even in the case of the worst criminals, those scenes of deathbed repentance which are so conspicuous in Christian biographies. But the Christian notion of the enormity of little sins, the belief that all the details of life will be scrutinised hereafter, that weaknesses of character and petty infractions of duty, of which the historian and the biographer take no note, which have no perceptible influence upon society, and which scarcely elicit a comment among mankind, may be made the grounds of eternal condemnation beyond the grave, was altogether unknown to the ancients, and at a time when it possessed all the freshness of novelty, it was well fitted to transform the character. The eye of the Pagan philosopher was ever fixed upon virtue, the eye of the Christian teacher upon sin. The first sought to amend men by extolling the beauty of holiness; the second, by awakening the sentiment of remorse. Each method had its excellencies and its defects. Philosophy was admirably fitted to dignify and ennoble, but altogether impotent to regenerate mankind. It did much to encourage virtue, but little or nothing to restrain vice. A relish and taste for virtue was formed and cultivated, which attracted many to its practice; but in this, as in the case of all our other higher tastes, a nature that was once thoroughly vitiated became altogether incapable of appreciating it, and the transformation of such a nature, which was continually effected by Christianity, was confessedly beyond the power of philosophy.[1] Experience has abundantly shown that men who are wholly insensible to the beauty and dignity of virtue, can be convulsed by the fear of judgment, can be even awakened to such a genuine remorse for sin, as to reverse the current of their dispositions, detach them from the most inveterate habits, and renew the whole tenor of their lives.

But the habit of dilating chiefly on the darker side ot human nature, while it has contributed much to the regenerating efficacy of Christian teaching, has not been

[1] There is a remarkable passage of Celsus, on the impossibility of restoring a nature once thoroughly depraved, quoted by Origen in his answer to him

without its disadvantages. Habitually measuring character by its aberrations, theologians, in their estimates of those strong and passionate natures in which great virtues are balanced by great failings, have usually fallen into a signal injustice, which is the more inexcusable, because in their own writings the psalms of David are a conspicuous proof of what a noble, tender, and passionate nature could survive, even in an adulterer and a murderer. Partly, too, through this habit of operating through the sense of sin, and partly from a desire to show that man is in an abnormal and dislocated condition, they have continually propounded distorted and degrading views of human nature, have represented it as altogether under the empire of evil, and have sometimes risen to such a height of extravagance as to pronounce the very virtues of the heathen to be of the nature of sin. But nothing can be more certain than that that which is exceptional and distinctive in human nature is not its vice, but its excellence. It is not the sensuality, cruelty, selfishness, passion, or envy, which are all displayed in equal or greater degrees in different departments of the animal world; it is that moral nature which enables man apparently, alone of all created beings, to classify his emotions, to oppose the current of his desires, and to aspire after moral perfection. Nor is it less certain that in civilised, and therefore developed man, the good greatly preponderates over the evil. Benevolence is more common than cruelty; the sight of suffering more readily produces pity than joy; gratitude, not ingratitude, is the normal result of a conferred benefit. The sympathies of man naturally follow heroism and goodness, and vice itself is usually but an exaggeration or distortion of tendencies that are in their own nature perfectly innocent.

But these exaggerations of human depravity, which

have attained their extreme limits in some Protestant sects, do not appear in the Church of the first three centuries. The sense of the sin was not yet accompanied by a denial of the goodness that exists in man. Christianity was regarded rather as a redemption from error than from sin,[1] and it is a significant fact that the epithet 'well deserving,' which the Pagans usually put upon their tombs, was also the favourite inscription in the Christian catacombs. The Pelagian controversy, the teaching of St. Augustine, and the progress of asceticism, gradually introduced the doctrine of the utter depravity of man, which has proved in later times the fertile source of degrading superstition.

In sustaining and defining the notion of sin, the early Church employed the machinery of an elaborate legislation. Constant communion with the Church was regarded as of the very highest importance. Participation in the Sacrament was believed to be essential to eternal life. At a very early period it was given to infants, and at least as early as the time of St. Cyprian we find the practice universal in the Church, and pronounced by at least some of the Fathers to be ordinarily necessary to their salvation.[2] Among the adults it was customary to receive the Sacrament daily, in some churches four times a week.[3] Even

[1] This is well shown by Pressensé in his *Hist. des trois premiers Siècles.*

[2] See a great deal of information on this subject in Bingham's *Antiquities of the Christian Church* (Oxford, 1853), vol. v. pp. 370–378. It is curious that those very noisy contemporary divines who profess to resuscitate the manners of the primitive Church, and who lay so much stress on the minutest ceremonial observances, have left unpractised what was undoubtedly one of the most universal, and was believed to be one of the most important, of the institutions of early Christianity. Bingham shows that the administration of the Eucharist to infants continued in France till the twelfth century.

[3] See Cave's *Primitive Christianity*, part i. ch. xi. At first the Sacrament was usually received every day; but this custom soon declined in the Eastern Church, and at last passed away in the West.

in the days of persecution the only part of their service Christians consented to omit was the half secular agape.[1] The clergy had power to accord or withhold access to the ceremonies, and the reverence with which they were regarded was so great that they were able to dictate their own conditions of communion.

From these circumstances there very naturally arose a vast system of moral discipline. It was always acknowledged that men could only rightly approach the sacred table in certain moral dispositions, and it was very soon added that the commission of crimes should be expiated by a period of penance, before access to the communion was granted. A multitude of offences, of very various degrees of magnitude, such as prolonged abstinence from religious services, prenuptial unchastity, prostitution, adultery, the adoption of the profession of gladiator or actor, idolatry, the betrayal of Christians to persecutors, and paideristia or unnatural love, were specified, to each of which a definite spiritual penalty was annexed. The lowest penalty consisted of deprivation of the Eucharist for a few weeks. More serious offenders were deprived of it for a year, or for ten years, or until the hour of death, while in some cases the sentence amounted to the greater excommunication, or the deprivation of the Eucharist for ever. During the period of penance the penitent was compelled to abstain from the marriage bed, and from all other pleasures, and to spend his time chiefly in religious exercises. Before he was readmitted to communion, he was accustomed publicly, before the assembled Christians, to appear clad in sackcloth, with ashes strewn upon his head, with his hair shaven off, and thus to throw himself at the feet of the minister, to confess

[1] Plin. *Ep.* x. 97.

aloud his sins, and to implore the favour of absolution. The excommunicated man was not only cut off for ever from the Christian rites; he was severed also from all intercourse with his former friends. No Christian, on pain of being himself excommunicated, might eat with him or speak with him. He must live hated and alone in this world, and be prepared for damnation in the next.[1]

This system of legislation, resting upon religious terrorism, forms one of the most important parts of early ecclesiastical history, and a leading object of the Councils was to develope or modify it. Although confession was not yet an habitual and universally obligatory rite, although it was only exacted in cases of notorious sins, it is manifest that we have in this system, not potentially or in germ, but in full developed activity, an ecclesiastical despotism of the most crushing order. But although this recognition of the right of the clergy to withhold from men what was believed to be essential to their salvation, laid the foundation of the worst superstitions of Rome, it had, on the other hand, a very valuable moral effect. Every system of law is a system of education, for it fixes in the minds of men certain conceptions of right and wrong, and of the proportionate enormity of different crimes; and no legislation was enforced with more solemnity, or appealed more directly to the religious feelings, than the penitential discipline of the Church. More than, perhaps, any other single agency, it confirmed that conviction of the enormity of sin, and of the retribution that follows it, which was one of the two great levers by which Christianity acted upon mankind.

[1] The whole subject of the penitential discipline is treated minutely in Marshall's *Penitential Discipline of the Primitive Church* (first published in 1714, and reprinted in the library of Anglo-Catholic Theology), and also in Bingham, vol. vii. Tertullian gives a graphic description of the public penances, *De Pudicit.* v. 13.

But if Christianity was remarkable for its appeals to the selfish or interested side of our nature, it was far more remarkable for the empire it attained over disinterested enthusiasm. The Platonist exhorted men to imitate God, the Stoic, to follow reason, the Christian, to the love of Christ. The later Stoics had often united their notions of excellence in an ideal sage, and Epictetus had even urged his disciples to set before them some man of surpassing excellence, and to imagine him continually near them; but the utmost the Stoic ideal could become was a model for imitation, and the admiration it inspired could never deepen into affection. It was reserved for Christianity to present to the world an ideal character, which through all the changes of eighteen centuries has inspired the hearts of men with an impassioned love, has shown itself capable of acting on all ages, nations, temperaments, and conditions, has been not only the highest pattern of virtue but the strongest incentive to its practice, and has exercised so deep an influence that it may be truly said that the simple record of three short years of active life has done more to regenerate and to soften mankind than all the disquisitions of philosophers and all the exhortations of moralists. This has indeed been the wellspring of whatever is best and purest in the Christian life. Amid all the sins and failings, amid all the priestcraft and persecution and fanaticism that have defaced the Church, it has preserved, in the character and example of its Founder, an enduring principle of regeneration. Perfect love knows no rights. It creates a boundless, uncalculating self-abnegation that transforms the character, and is the parent of every virtue. Side by side with the terrorism and the superstitions of dogmatism, there have ever existed in Christianity those who would echo the wish of St. Theresa, that she could blot out both heaven and hell, to serve God for Himself alone; and the power of the love of Christ has been displayed alike in the most heroic pages of Christian martyrdom, in the most pathetic pages of Christian resignation, in the tenderest pages of Christian charity. It was shown by the martyrs who sank beneath the fangs of wild beasts, extending to the last moment their arms in the form of the cross they loved;[2] who ordered their chains to be buried with them as the insignia of their warfare;[2] who looked with joy upon their ghastly wounds, because they had been received for Christ;[3] who welcomed death as the bridegroom welcomes the bride, because it would bring them near to Him. St. Felicitas was seized with the pangs of childbirth as she lay in prison awaiting the hour of martyrdom, and as her sufferings extorted from her a cry, one who stood by said, 'If you now suffer so much, what will it be when you are thrown to wild beasts?' 'What I now suffer,' she answered, 'concerns myself alone; but then another will suffer for me, for I will then suffer for Him.'[4] When St. Melania had lost both her husband and her two sons, kneeling by the bed where the remains of those she loved were laid, the childless widow exclaimed, 'Lord, I shall serve thee more humbly and readily for being eased of the weight thou hast taken from me.'[5]

Christian virtue was described by St. Augustine as 'the

[1] Eusebius, *H. E.* viii. 7.

[2] St. Chrysostom tells this of St. Babylas. See Tillemont, *Mém. pour servir à l'Hist. eccl.* tome iii. p. 403.

[3] In the preface to a very ancient Milanese missal it is said of St. Agatha, that as she lay in the prison cell, torn by the instruments of torture, St. Peter came to her in the form of a Christian physician, and offered to dress her wounds; but she refused, saying that she wished for no physician but Christ. St. Peter, in the name of that Celestial Physician, commanded her wounds to close, and her body became whole as before. (Tillemont, tome iii. p. 412.)

[4] See her acts in Ruinart.

[5] St. Jerome, *Ep.* xxxix.

order of love.'[1] Those who know how imperfectly the simple sense of duty can with most men resist the energy of the passions; who have observed how barren Mahommedanism has been in all the higher and more tender virtues, because its noble morality and its pure theism have been united with no living example; who, above all, have traced through the history of the Christian Church the influence of the love of Christ, will be at no loss to estimate the value of this purest and most distinctive source of Christian enthusiasm. In one respect we can scarcely realise its effects upon the early Church. The sense of the fixity of natural laws is now so deeply implanted in the minds of men, that no truly educated person, whatever may be his religious opinions, seriously believes that all the more startling phenomena around him—storms, earthquakes, invasions, or famines—are results of isolated acts of supernatural power, and are intended to affect some human interest. But by the early Christians all these things were directly traced to the Master they so dearly loved. The result of this conviction was a state of feeling we can now barely understand. A great poet, in lines which are among the noblest in English literature, has spoken of one who had died as united to the all-pervading soul of nature, the grandeur and the tenderness, the beauty and the passion of his being blending with the kindred elements of the universe, his voice heard in all its melodies, his spirit a presence to be felt and known, a part of the one plastic energy that permeates and animates the globe. Something of this kind, but of a far more vivid and real character, was the belief of the early Christian world. The universe, to them, was transfigured by love. All its phenomena, all its catastrophes were

[1] 'Definitio brevis et vera virtutis; ordo est amoris.'—*De Civ. Dei*, xv. 22.

read in a new light, were endued with a new significance, acquired a religious sanctity. Christianity offered a deeper consolation than any prospect of endless life, or of millennial glories. It taught the weary, the sorrowing, and the lonely, to look up to heaven and to say, 'Thou, God, carest for me.'

It is not surprising that a religious system, which made it a main object to inculcate moral excellence, and which, by its doctrine of future retribution, by its organisation, and by its capacity of producing a disinterested enthusiasm, acquired an unexampled supremacy over the human mind, should have raised its disciples to a very high condition of sanctity. There can indeed be little doubt that, for nearly two hundred years after its establishment in Europe, the Christian community exhibited a moral purity which, if it has been equalled, has never for any long period been surpassed. Completely separated from the Roman world that was around them, abstaining alike from political life, from appeals to the tribunals, and from military occupations; looking forward continually to the immediate advent of their Master, and the destruction of the empire in which they dwelt, and animated by all the fervour of a young religion, the Christians found within themselves a whole order of ideas and feelings sufficiently powerful to guard them from the contamination of their age. In their general bearing towards society, and in the nature and minuteness of their scruples, they probably bore a greater resemblance to the Quakers than to any other existing sect.[1] Some serious signs of moral deca-

[1] Besides the obvious points of resemblance in the common, though not universal, belief that Christians should abstain from all weapons and from all oaths, the whole teaching of the early Christians about the duty of simplicity, and the wickedness of ornaments in dress (see especially the writings of Tertullian, Clemens Alexandrinus, and Chrysostom, on this subject), is exceedingly like that of the Quakers. The scruple of Ter-

dence might indeed be detected even before the Decian persecution ; and it was obvious that the triumph of the Church, by introducing numerous nominal Christians into its pale, by exposing it to the temptations of wealth and prosperity, and by forcing it into connection with secular politics, must have damped its zeal and impaired its purity ; yet few persons, I think, who had contemplated Christianity as it existed in the first three centuries would have imagined it possible that it should completely supersede the Pagan worship around it ; that its teachers should bend the mightiest monarchs to their will, and stamp their influence on every page of legislation, and direct the whole course of civilisation for a thousand years, and yet that the period in which they were so supreme should have been one of the most contemptible in history.

The leading features of that period may be shortly told. From the death of Marcus Aurelius, about which time Christianity assumed an important influence in the Roman world, the decadence of the empire was rapid and almost uninterrupted. The first Christian emperor transferred his capital to a new city, uncontaminated by the traditions and the glories of Paganism ; and he there founded an empire which derived all its ethics from Christian sources, and which continued in existence for about eleven hundred years. Of that Byzantine Empire the universal verdict of history is that it constitutes, without a single exception, the most thoroughly base and despicable form that civilisation has yet assumed. Though very cruel and very sensual, there have been times when cruelty assumed

tullian (*De Coronâ*) about Christians wearing, in military festivals, laurel wreaths, because laurel was called after Daphne, the lover of Apollo, was much of the same kind as that of the Quakers about recognising the gods Tuesco or Woden by speaking of Tuesday or Wednesday. On the other hand, the ecclesiastical aspects and the sacramental doctrines of the Church were the extreme opposites of Quakerism.

more ruthless, and sensuality more extravagant aspects; but there has been no other enduring civilisation so absolutely destitute of all the forms and elements of greatness, and none to which the epithet *mean* may be so emphatically applied. The Byzantine Empire was pre-eminently the age of treachery. Its vices were the vices of men who had ceased to be brave without learning to be virtuous. Without patriotism, without the fruition or desire of liberty, after the first paroxysms of religious agitation, without genius or intellectual activity; slaves, and willing slaves, in both their actions and their thoughts immersed in sensuality and in the most frivolous pleasures, the people only emerged from their listlessness when some theological subtlety, or some rivalry in the chariot races, stimulated them into frantic riots. They exhibited all the externals of advanced civilisation. They possessed knowledge; they had continually before them the noble literature of ancient Greece, instinct with the loftiest heroism; but that literature, which afterwards did so much to revivify Europe, could fire the degenerate Greeks with no spark or semblance of nobility. The history of the empire is a monotonous story of the intrigues of priests, eunuchs, and women, of poisonings, of conspiracies, of uniform ingratitude, of perpetual fratricides. After the conversion of Constantine there was no prince in any section of the Roman Empire altogether so depraved, or at least so shameless, as Nero or Heliogabalus; but the Byzantine Empire can show none bearing the faintest resemblance to Antonine or Marcus Aurelius, while the nearest approximation to that character at Rome was furnished by the emperor Julian, who contemptuously abandoned the Christian faith. At last the Mahommedan invasion terminated the long decrepitude of the Eastern Empire. Constantinople sank beneath the Crescent, its inhabitants wrangling about theological differences to the very moment of their fall.

The Asiatic churches had already perished. The Christian faith, planted in the dissolute cities of Asia Minor, had produced many fanatical ascetics and a few illustrious theologians, but it had no renovating effect upon the people at large. It introduced among them a principle of interminable and implacable dissension, but it scarcely tempered in any appreciable degree their luxury or their sensuality. The frenzy of pleasure continued unabated, and in a great part of the empire it seemed indeed only to have attained its climax after the triumph of Christianity.

The condition of the Western Empire was somewhat different. Not quite a century after the conversion of Constantine, the Imperial city was captured by Alaric, and a long series of barbarian invasions at last dissolved the whole framework of Roman society, while the barbarians themselves, having adopted the Christian faith and submitted absolutely to the Christian priests, the Church, which remained the guardian of all the treasures of antiquity, was left with a virgin soil to realise her ideal of human excellence. Nor did she fall short of what might be expected. She exercised for many centuries an almost absolute empire over the thoughts and actions of mankind, and created a civilisation which was permeated in every part with ecclesiastical influence. And the dark ages, as the period of Catholic ascendancy is justly called, do undoubtedly display many features of great and genuine excellence. In active benevolence, in the spirit of reverence, in loyalty, in co-operative habits, they far transcend the noblest ages of Pagan antiquity, while in that humanity which shrinks from the infliction of suffering, they were superior to Roman, and in their respect for chastity, to Greek civilisation. On the other hand, they rank immeasurably below the best Pagan civilisations in civic and patriotic virtues, in the love of liberty, in the number and splendour of the great characters they produced, in the dignity and beauty of the type of character they formed. They had their full share of tumult, anarchy, injustice, and war, and they should probably be placed, in all intellectual virtues, lower than any other period in the history of mankind. A boundless intolerance of all divergence of opinion was united with an equally boundless toleration of all falsehood and deliberate fraud that could favour received opinions. Credulity being taught as a virtue, and all conclusions dictated by authority, a deadly torpor sank upon the human mind, which for many centuries almost suspended its action, and was only broken by the scrutinising, innovating, and free-thinking habits that accompanied the rise of the industrial republics in Italy. Few men who are not either priests or monks would not have preferred to live in the best days of the Athenian or of the Roman republics, in the age of Augustus or in the age of the Antonines, rather than in any period that elapsed between the triumph of Christianity and the fourteenth century.

It is indeed difficult to conceive any clearer proof than was furnished by the history of the twelve hundred years after the conversion of Constantine, that while theology has undoubtedly introduced into the world certain elements and principles of good, scarcely if at all known to antiquity, while its value as a tincture or modifying influence in society can hardly be overrated, it is by no means for the advantage of mankind that in the form which the Greek and Catholic Churches present, it should become a controlling arbiter of civilisation. It is often said that the Roman world before Constantine was in a period of rapid decay, that the traditions and vitality of half-suppressed Paganism account for many of the aberrations of later times; that the influence of the Church was often rather nominal and superficial than supreme; and that, in judging the ignorance of the dark ages, we must make large allowance for the dislocations of society by the barbarians. In all this there is much truth; but when we remember that in the Byzantine Empire the renovating power of theology was tried in a new capital free from Pagan traditions, and for more than one thousand years unsubdued by barbarians, and that in the West the Church, for at least seven hundred years after the shocks of the invasions had subsided, exercised a control more absolute than any other moral or intellectual agency has ever attained, it will appear, I think, that the experiment was very sufficiently tried. It is easy to make a catalogue of the glaring vices of antiquity, and to contrast them with the pure morality of Christian writings; but if we desire to form a just estimate of the realised improvement, we must compare the classical and ecclesiastical civilisations as wholes, and must observe in each case not only the vices that were repressed, but also the degree and variety of positive excellence attained. In the first two centuries of the Christian Church the moral elevation was extremely high, and was continually appealed to as a proof of the divinity of the creed. In the century before the conversion of Constantine, a marked depression was already manifest. The two centuries after Constantine are uniformly represented by the Fathers as a period of general and scandalous vice. The ecclesiastical civilisation that followed, though not without its distinctive merits, assuredly supplies no justification of the common boast about the regeneration of society by the Church. That the civilisation of the last three centuries has risen in most respects to a higher level than any that had preceded it, I at least firmly believe; but theological ethics, though very important, form but one of the many and complex elements of its excellence. Mechanical inventions, the habits of industrialism, the discoveries of physical science, the improvements of government, the expansion of literature, the traditions of Pagan antiquity, have all a distinguished place, while, the more fully its history is investigated, the more clearly two capital truths are disclosed. The first is that the influence of theology having for centuries numbed and paralysed the whole intellect of Christian Europe, the revival, which forms the starting-point of our modern civilisation, was mainly due to the fact that two spheres of intellect still remained uncontrolled by the sceptre of Catholicism. The Pagan literature of antiquity, and the Mahommedan schools of science, were the chief agencies in resuscitating the dormant energies of Christendom. The second fact, which I have elsewhere endeavoured to establish in detail, is that during more than three centuries the decadence of theological influence has been one of the most invariable signs and measures of our progress. In medicine, physical science, commercial interests, politics, and even ethics, the reformer has been confronted with theological affirmations which barred his way, which were all defended as of vital importance, and were all in turn compelled to yield before the secularising influence of civilisation.

We have here, then, a problem of deep interest and importance, which I propose to investigate in the present chapter. We have to inquire why it was that a religion which was not more remarkable for the beauty of its moral teaching than for the power with which it acted upon mankind, and which during the last few centuries has been the source of countless blessings to the world, should have proved itself for so long a period, and under such a variety of conditions, altogether unable to regenerate Europe. The question is not one of languid or imperfect action, but of conflicting agencies. In the vast and complex organism of Catholicity there were some parts which acted with admirable force in improving and elevating mankind. There were others which had a directly opposite effect.

The first aspect in which Christianity presented itself to the world was as a declaration of the fraternity of men in Christ. Considered as immortal beings, destined for the extremes of happiness or of misery, and united to one another by a special community of redemption, the first and most manifest duty of a Christian man was to look upon his fellow-men as sacred beings, and from this notion grew up the eminently Christian idea of the sanctity of all human life. I have already endeavoured to show—and the fact is of such capital importance in meeting the common objections to the reality of natural moral perceptions, that I venture, at the risk of tediousness, to recur to it—that nature does not tell man that it is wrong to slay without provocation his fellow-men. Not to dwell upon those early stages of barbarism in which the higher faculties of human nature are still undeveloped, and almost in the condition of embryo, it is an historical fact, beyond all dispute, that refined, and even moral societies, have existed, in which the slaughter of men of some particular class or nation has been regarded with no more compunction than the slaughter of animals in the chase. The early Greeks, in their dealings with the barbarians; the Romans, in their dealings with gladiators, and, in some periods of their history, with slaves; the Spaniards, in their dealings with Indians;

nearly all colonists removed from European supervision, in their dealings with an inferior race; an immense proportion of the nations of antiquity, in their dealings with new-born infants, display this complete and absolute callousness, and we may discover traces of it even in our own islands and within the last three hundred years.[1] And difficult as it may be to realise it in our day, when the atrocity of all wanton slaughter of men has become an essential part of our moral feelings, it is nevertheless an incontestable fact that this callousness has been continually shown by good men, by men who in all other respects would be regarded in any age as conspicuous for their humanity. In the days of the Tudors, the best Englishmen delighted in what we should now deem the most barbarous sports, and it is absolutely certain that in antiquity men of genuine humanity—tender relations, loving friends, charitable neighbours—men in whose eyes the murder of a fellow-citizen would have appeared as atrocious as in our own, frequented, instituted, and applauded gladiatorial games, or counselled without a scruple the exposition of infants. But it is, as I conceive, a complete confusion of thought to imagine, as is so commonly done, that any accumulation of facts of this nature throws the smallest doubt upon the reality of innate moral perceptions. All that the intuitive moralist asserts is that we know by nature that there is a distinction between humanity and cruelty, that the first belongs to the higher or better part of our nature, and that it is our duty to cultivate it. The standard of the age, which is itself determined by the general condition of society, con-

[1] See the masterly description of the relations of the English to the Irish in the reign of Queen Elizabeth, in Froude's *History of England*, ch. xxiv.; and also Lord Macaulay's description of the feelings of the Master of Stair towards the Highlanders. (*Hist. of England*, ch. xviii.)

stitutes the natural line of duty; for he who falls below it contributes to depress it. Now, there is no fact more absolutely certain, than that nations and ages which have differed most widely as to the standard have been perfectly unanimous as to the excellence of humanity. Plato, who recommended infanticide; Cato, who sold his aged slaves; Pliny, who applauded the games of the arena; the old generals, who made their prisoners slaves or gladiators, as well as the modern generals, who refuse to impose upon them any degrading labour; the old legislators, who filled their codes with sentences of torture, mutilation, and hideous forms of death, as well as the modern legislators, who are continually seeking to abridge the punishment of the most guilty; the old disciplinarian, who governed by force, as well as the modern educationalist, who governs by sympathy; the Spanish girl, whose dark eye glows with rapture as she watches the frantic bull, while the fire streams from the explosive dart that quivers in its neck; the English lady, whose sensitive humanity shudders at the chase; the reformers we sometimes meet, who are scandalised by all field sports, or by the sacrifice of animal life for food; or who will eat only the larger animals, in order to reduce the sacrifice of life to a minimum; or who are continually inventing new methods of quickening animal death—all these persons, widely as they differ in their acts and in their judgments of what things should be called 'brutal,' and what things should be called 'fantastic,' agree in believing humanity to be better than cruelty, and in attaching a definite condemnation to acts that fall below the standard of their country and their time. Now, it was one of the most important services of Christianity, that besides quickening greatly our benevolent affections, it definitely and dogmatically asserted the sinfulness of all destruction of human life as a matter of amusement, or of simple convenience, and thereby formed a new standard higher than any which then existed in the world.

The influence of Christianity in this respect began with the very earliest stage of human life. The practice of abortion was one to which few persons in antiquity attached any deep feeling of condemnation. I have noticed in a former chapter that the physiological theory that the fœtus did not become a living creature till the hour of birth, had some influence on the judgments passed upon this practice; and even where this theory was not generally held, it is easy to account for the prevalence of the act. The death of an unborn child does not appeal very powerfully to the feeling of compassion, and men who had not yet attained any strong sense of the sanctity of human life, who believed that they might regulate their conduct on these matters by utilitarian views, according to the general interest of the community, might very readily conclude that the prevention of birth was in many cases an act of mercy. In Greece, Aristotle not only countenanced the practice, but even desired that it should be enforced by law, when population had exceeded certain assigned limits.[1] No law in Greece, or in the Roman Republic, or during the greater part of the Empire, condemned it;[2] and if, as has been thought, some measure was adopted condemnatory of it in the latter days of the Pagan Empire, that measure was altogether inoperative. A long chain of writers, both Pagan and Christian, represent the practice as avowed and almost universal. They describe it as resulting, not simply from licentiousness or from poverty, but even from so slight a motive as

[1] See on the views of Aristotle, Labourt, *Recherches historiques sur les Enfants trouvés* (Paris, 1848), p. 9.

[2] See Gravina, *De Ortu et Progressu Juris Civilis*, lib. i. 44.

vanity, which made mothers shrink from the disfigurement of childbirth. They speak of a mother who had never destroyed her unborn offspring as deserving of signal praise, and they assure us that the frequency of the crime was such that it gave rise to a regular profession. At the same time, while Ovid, Seneca, Favorinus the Stoic of Arles, Plutarch, and Juvenal, all speak of abortion as general and notorious, they all speak of it as unquestionably criminal.[1] It was probably regarded by the average Romans of the later days of Paganism much as Englishmen in the last century regarded convivial excesses, as certainly wrong, but so venial as scarcely to deserve censure.

The language of the Christians from the very beginning was very different. With unwavering consistency and with

1 'Nunc uterum vitiat quæ vult formosa videri,
Raraque in hoc ævo est, quæ velit esse parens.'
Ovid, *De Nuce*, lines 22–23.

The same writer has devoted one of his elegies (ii. 14) to reproaching his mistress Corinna with having been guilty of this act. It was not without dangers, and Ovid says,

'Sæpe suos utero quæ necat ipsa perit.'

A niece of Domitian is said to have died in consequence of having, at the command of the emperor, practised it (Sueton. *Domit.* xxii.). Plutarch notices the custom (*De Sanitate Tuenda*), and Seneca eulogises Helvia (*Ad Helv.* xvi.) for being exempt from vanity and having never destroyed her unborn offspring. Favorinus, in a remarkable passage (Aulus Gellius, *Noct. Att.* xii. 1), speaks of the act as 'publica detestatione communique odio dignum,' and proceeds to argue that it is only a degree less criminal for mothers to put out their children to nurse. Juvenal has some well-known and emphatic lines on the subject:—

'Sed jacet aurato vix nulla puerpera lecto;
Tantum artes hujus, tantum medicamina possunt,
Quæ steriles facit, atque homines in ventre necandos
Conducit.' *Sat.* vi. lines 592–595.

There are also many allusions to it in the Christian writers. Thus Minucius Felix (*Octavius*, xxx.): 'Vos enim video procreatos filios nunc feris et avibus exponere, nunc adstrangulatos misero mortis genere elidere. Sunt quæ in ipsis visceribus medicaminibus epotis, originem futuri hominis extinguant et parricidium faciant antequam pariant.'

the strongest emphasis, they denounced the practice, not simply as inhuman, but as definitely murder. In the penitential discipline of the Church, abortion was placed in the same category as infanticide, and the stern sentences to which the guilty person was subject imprinted on the minds of Christians, more deeply than any mere exhortations, a sense of the enormity of the crime. By the Council of Ancyra the guilty mother was excluded from the Sacrament till the very hour of death, and though this penalty was soon reduced, first to ten and afterwards to seven years' penitence,[1] the offence still ranked among the gravest in the legislation of the Church. In one very remarkable way the reforms of Christianity in this sphere were powerfully sustained by a doctrine which is perhaps the most revolting in the whole theology of the Fathers. To the Pagans, even when condemning abortion and infanticide, these crimes appeared comparatively trivial, because the victims seemed very insignificant and their sufferings very slight. The death of an adult man who is struck down in the midst of his enterprise and his hopes, who is united by ties of love or friendship to multitudes around him, and whose departure causes a perturbation and a pang to the society in which he has moved, excites feelings very different from any produced by the painless extinction of a new-born infant, which, having scarcely touched the earth, has known none of its cares and very little of its love. But to the theologian this infant life possessed a fearful significance. The moment, they taught, the fœtus in the womb acquired animation, it became an immortal being, destined, even if it died unborn, to be raised again on the last day, responsible for the sin of Adam, and doomed, if it perished without baptism, to be excluded for ever from heaven

[1] See Labourt, *Recherches sur les Enfans trouvés*, p. 25.

and to be cast, as the Greeks taught, into a painless and joyless limbo, or, as the Latins taught, into the abyss of hell. It is probably, in a considerable degree, to this doctrine that we owe in the first instance the healthy sense of the value and sanctity of infant life which so broadly distinguishes Christian from Pagan societies, and which is now so thoroughly incorporated with our moral feelings as to be independent of all doctrinal changes. That which appealed so powerfully to the compassion of the early and mediæval Christians, in the fate of the murdered infants, was not that they died, but that they commonly died unbaptised; and the criminality of abortion was immeasurably aggravated when it was believed to involve, not only the extinction of a transient life, but also the damnation of an immortal soul.[1] In the 'Lives of the Saints' there is a

[1] Among the barbarian laws there is a very curious one about a daily compensation to the parents of children who had been killed in the womb on account of the daily suffering of those children in hell. 'Propterea diuturnam judicaverunt antecessores nostri compositionem et judices postquam religio Christianitatis inolevit in mundo. Quia diuturnam postquam incarnationem suscepit anima quamvis ad nativitatis lucem minime pervenisset, patitur pœnam, quia sine sacramento regenerationis abortivo modo tradita est ad inferos.'—*Leges Bajuvariorum*, tit. vii. cap. xx. in Canciani, *Leges Barbar.* vol. ii. p. 374. The first foundling hospital of which we have undoubted record is that founded at Milan, by a man named Datheus, in A.D. 789. Muratori has preserved (*Antich. Ital.* Diss. xxxvii.) the charter embodying the motives of the founder, in which the following sentences occur:—'Quia frequenter per luxuriam hominum genus decipitur, et exinde malum homicidii generatur, dum concipientes ex adulterio ne prodantur in publico, fetos teneros necant, *et absque Baptismatis lavacro parvulos ad Tartara mittunt,* quia nullum reperiunt locum, quo servare vivos valeant,' &c. Henry II. of France, 1556, made a long law against women who, 'advenant le temps de leur part et délivrance de leur enfant, occultement s'en délivrent, puis le suffoquent et autrement suppriment *sans leur avoir fait empartir le Saint Sacrement du Baptême.*'—Labourt, *Recherches sur les Enf. trouvés*, p. 47. There is a story told of a Queen of Portugal (sister to Henry V. of England, and mother of St. Ferdinand) that, being in childbirth, her life was despaired of unless she took a medicine which would accelerate the birth but probably sacrifice the life of the child. She answered that 'she would not purchase her temporal life by the eternal salvation of her son.'—Bollandists, *Act. Sanctor.*, June 5th.

curious legend of a man who, being desirous of ascertaining the condition of a child before birth, slew a pregnant woman, committing thereby a double murder, that of the mother and of the child in her womb. Stung by remorse, the murderer fled to the desert, and passed the remainder of his life in constant penance and prayer. At last, after many years, the voice of God told him that he had been forgiven the murder of the woman. But yet his end was a clouded one. He never could obtain an assurance that he had been forgiven the death of the child.[1]

If we pass to the next stage of human life, that of the new-born infant, we find ourselves in presence of that practice of infanticide which was one of the deepest stains of the ancient civilisation. The natural history of this crime is somewhat peculiar.[2] Among savages, whose feelings of compassion are very faint, and whose warlike and nomadic habits are eminently unfavourable to infant life, it is, as might be expected, the usual custom for the parent to decide whether he desires to preserve the child he has called into existence, and if he does not, to expose or slay it. In nations that have passed out of the stage of barbarism, but are still rude and simple in their habits, the practice of infanticide is usually rare; but unlike

[1] Tillemont, *Mémoires pour servir à l'Histoire ecclésiastique* (Paris, 1701) tome x. p. 41. St. Clem. Alexand. says that infants in the womb and exposed infants have guardian angels to watch over them. (*Strom.* v.)

[2] There is an extremely large literature devoted to the subject of infanticide, exposition, foundlings, &c. The books I have chiefly followed are Terme et Monfalcon, *Histoire des Enfans trouvés* (Paris, 1840); Remacle, *Des Hospices d'Enfans trouvés* (1838); Labourt, *Recherches historiques sur les Enfans trouvés* (Paris, 1848); Kœnigswarter, *Essai sur la Législation des Peuples anciens et modernes relative aux Enfans nés hors Mariage* (Paris, 1842). There are also many details on the subject in Godefroy's Commentary to the laws about children in the Theodosian Code, in Malthus *On Population,* in Edward's tract *On the State of Slavery in the Early and Middle Ages of Christianity,* and in most ecclesiastical histories.

other crimes of violence, it is not naturally diminished by the progress of civilisation, for after the period of savage life is passed, its prevalence is influenced much more by the sensuality than by the barbarity of a people.[1] We may trace, too, in many countries and ages, the notion that children, as the fruit, representatives, and dearest possessions of their parents, are acceptable sacrifices to the gods.[2] Infanticide, as is well known, was almost universally admitted among the Greeks, being sanctioned, and in some cases enjoined, upon what we should now call 'the greatest happiness principle,' by the ideal legislations of Plato and Aristotle, and by the actual legislations of Lycurgus and Solon. Regarding the community as a whole, they clearly saw that it is in the highest degree for the interests of society that the increase of population should be very jealously restricted, and that the State should be as far as possible free from helpless and unproductive members; and they therefore concluded that the

[1] It must not, however, be inferred from this that infanticide increases in direct proportion to the unchastity of a nation. Probably the condition of civilised society in which it is most common, is where a large amount of actual unchastity coexists with very strong social condemnation of the sinner, and where, in consequence, there is an intense anxiety to conceal the fall. A recent writer on Spain has noticed the almost complete absence of infanticide in that country, and has ascribed it to the great leniency of public opinion towards female frailty. Foundling hospitals, also, greatly influence the history of infanticide; but the mortality in them was long so great that it may be questioned whether they have diminished the number of the deaths, though they have, as I believe, greatly diminished the number of the murders of children. Lord Kames, writing in the last half of the eighteenth century, says, 'In Wales, even at present, and in the Highlands of Scotland, it is scarce a disgrace for a young woman to have a bastard. In the country last mentioned, the first instance known of a bastard child being destroyed by its mother through shame is a late one. The virtue of chastity appears to be thus gaining ground, as the only temptation a woman can have to destroy her child is to conceal her frailty.'—*Sketches of the History of Man—On the Progress of the Female Sex.* The last clause is clearly inaccurate, but there seems reason for believing that maternal affection is generally stronger than want, but weaker than shame.

[2] See Warburton's *Divine Legation*, vii. 2.

painless destruction of infant life, and especially of those infants who were so deformed or diseased that their lives, if prolonged, would probably have been a burden to themselves, was on the whole a benefit. The very sensual tone of Greek life rendered the modern notion of prolonged continence wholly alien to their thoughts, and the extremely low social and intellectual condition of Greek mothers, who exercised no appreciable influence over the habits of thought of the nation should also, I think, be taken into account, for it has always been observed that mothers are much more distinguished than fathers for their affection for infants that have not yet manifested the first dawning of reason. Even in Greece, however, infanticide and exposition were not universally permitted. In Thebes these offences were punished by death.[1]

The power of life and death, which in Rome was originally conceded to the father over his children, would appear to involve an unlimited permission of infanticide; but a very old law, popularly ascribed to Romulus, in this respect restricted the parental rights, enjoining the father to bring up all his male children, and at least his eldest female child, forbidding him to destroy any well-formed child till it had completed its third year, when the affections of the parent might be supposed to be developed, but permitting the exposition of deformed or maimed children with the consent of their five nearest relations.[2] The Roman policy was

[1] Ælian. *Varia Hist.* ii. 7. Passages from the Greek imaginative writers, representing exposition as the avowed and habitual practice of poor parents, are collected by Terme et Monfalcon, *Hist. des Enfans trouvés,* pp. 39–45. Tacitus notices with praise (*Germania,* xix.) that the Germans did not allow infanticide. He also notices (*Hist.* v. 5) the prohibition of infanticide among the Jews, and ascribes it to their desire to increase the population.

[2] Dion. Halic. ii.

always to encourage, while the Greek policy was rather to restrain population, and infanticide never appears to have been common in Rome till the corrupt and sensual days of the Empire. The legislators then absolutely condemned it, and it was indirectly discouraged by laws which accorded special privileges to the fathers of many children, exempted poor parents from most of the burden of taxation, and in some degree provided for the security of exposed infants. Public opinion probably differed little from that of our own day as to the fact, though it differed from it much as to the degree, of its criminality. It was, as will be remembered, one of the charges most frequently brought against the Christians, and it was one that never failed to arouse popular indignation. Pagan and Christian authorities are, however, united in speaking of infanticide as a crying vice of the Empire, and Tertullian observed that no laws were more easily or more constantly evaded than those which condemned it.[1] A broad distinction was popularly drawn between infanticide and exposition. The latter, though probably condemned, was certainly not punished by law;[2] it was practised on a

[1] *Ad Nat.* i. 15.

[2] The well-known jurisconsult Paulus had laid down the proposition, 'Necare videtur non tantum is qui partum perfocat sed et is qui abjicit et qui alimonia denegat et qui publicis locis misericordiæ causa exponit quam ipse non habet.' (*Dig.* lib. xxv. tit. iii. l. 4.) These words have given rise to a famous controversy between two Dutch professors, named Noodt and Bynkershoek, conducted on both sides with great learning, and on the side of Noodt with great passion. Noodt maintained that these words are simply the expression of a moral truth, not a judicial decision, and that exposition was never illegal in Rome till some time after the establishment of Christianity. His opponent argued that exposition was legally identical with infanticide, and became, therefore, illegal when the power of life and death was withdrawn from the father. (See the works of Noodt (Cologne, 1763) and of Bynkershoek (Cologne, 1761). It is at least certain that exposition was notorious and avowed, and the law against it, if it existed, inoperative. Gibbon (*Decline and Fall,* ch. xliv.) thinks the law censured but did not punish exposition. See, too, Troplong, *Influence du Christianisme sur le Droit*, p. 271.

gigantic scale and with absolute impunity, noticed by writers with the most frigid indifference, and at least, in the case of destitute parents, considered a very venial offence.[1] Often, no doubt, the exposed children perished, but more frequently the very extent of the practice saved the lives of the victims. They were brought systematically to a column near the Velabrum, and there taken by speculators who educated them as slaves, or very frequently as prostitutes.[2]

[1] Quintilian speaks in a tone of apology, if not justification, of the exposition of the children of destitute parents (*Decl.* cccvi.), and even Plutarch speaks of it without censure. (*De Amor. Prolis.*) There are several curious illustrations in Latin literature of the different feelings of fathers and mothers on this matter. Terence (*Heauton,* Act. iii. Scene 5) represents Chremes as having, as a matter of course, charged his pregnant wife to have her child killed provided it was a girl. The mother, overcome by pity, shrank from doing so, and secretly gave it to an old woman to expose it, in hopes that it might be preserved. Chremes, on hearing what had been done, reproached his wife for her womanly pity, and told her she had been not only disobedient but irrational, for she was only consigning her daughter to the life of a prostitute. In Apuleius (*Metam.* lib. x.) we have a similar picture of a father starting for a journey, leaving his wife in childbirth, and giving her his parting command to kill her child if it should be a girl, which she could not bring herself to do. The girl was brought up secretly. In the case of weak or deformed infants infanticide seems to have been habitual. 'Portentos fœtus extinguimus, liberos quoque si debiles monstrosique editi sunt, mergimus. Non ira sed ratio est a sanis inutilia secernere.'—Seneca, *De Ira,* i. 15. Terence has introduced a picture of the exposition of an infant into his *Andria,* Act iv. Scene 5. See, too, Suet. *August.* lxv. According to Suetonius (*Calig.* v.), on the death of Germanicus, women exposed their new-born children in sign of grief. Ovid had dwelt with much feeling on the barbarity of these practices. It is a very curious fact, which has been noticed by Warburton, that Chremes, whose sentiments about infants we have just seen, is the very personage into whose mouth Terence has put the famous sentiment, 'Homo sum humani nihil a me alienum puto.'

[2] That these were the usual fates of exposed infants is noticed by several writers. Some, too, both Pagan and Christian (Quintilian, *Decl.* cccvi.; Lactantius, *Div. Inst.* vi. 20, &c.), speak of the liability to incestuous marriages resulting from frequent exposition. In the Greek poets there are several allusions to rich childless men adopting foundlings, and Juvenal says it was common for Roman wives to palm off foundlings on their husbands for their sons. (*Sat.* vi. 603.) There is an extremely horrible declamation in Seneca the Rhetorician (*Controvers.* lib. v. 33) about exposed children

On the whole, what was demanded on this subject was not any clearer moral teaching, but rather a stronger enforcement of the condemnation long since passed upon infanticide, and an increased protection for exposed infants. By the penitential sentences, by the dogmatic considerations I have enumerated, and by the earnest exhortations both of her preachers and writers, the Church laboured to deepen the sense of the enormity of the act, and especially to convince men that the guilt of abandoning their children to the precarious and doubtful mercy of the stranger was scarcely less than that of simple infanticide.[1] In the civil law her influence was also displayed, though not, I think, very advantageously. By the counsel, it is said, of Lactantius, Constantine, in the very year of his conversion, in order to prevent the frequent instances of infanticide by destitute parents, issued a decree applicable in the first instance to Italy, but extended in A.D. 322 to Africa, in which he ordered that those children whom their parents were unable to support should be clothed and fed at the expense of the State,[2] a policy which had already been pursued on a large scale under the Antonines. In A.D. 331, a law intended to multiply the chances of the exposed child being taken charge of by some charitable or interested person, provided that the foundling should remain the absolute property of its saviour, whether he adopted it as a son or employed it as a slave, and that the parent should not have power at any future time to reclaim it.[3] By another

who were said to have been maimed and mutilated, either to prevent their recognition by their parents, or that they might gain money as beggars for their masters.

[1] See passages on this point cited by Godefroy in his *Commentary to the Law De Expositis*, *Codex Theod.* lib. v. tit. 7.

[2] *Codex Theod.* lib. xi. tit. 27.

[3] Ibid. lib. v. tit. 7, lex 1.

law, which had been issued in A.D. 329, it had been provided that children who had been not exposed but sold, might be reclaimed upon payment by the father.[1]

The two last laws cannot be regarded with unmingled satisfaction. That regulating the condition of exposed children, though undoubtedly enacted with the most benevolent intentions, was in some degree a retrograde step, the Pagan laws having provided that the father might always withdraw the child he had exposed from servitude, by payment of the expenses incurred in supporting it,[2] while Trajan had even decided that the exposed child could not become under any circumstance a slave.[3] The law of Constantine, on the other hand, doomed it to an irrevocable servitude, and this law continued in force till A.D. 529, when Justinian, reverting to the principle of Trajan, decreed that not only the father lost all legitimate authority over his child by exposing it, but also that the person who had saved it could not by that act deprive it of its natural liberty. But this law applied only to the Eastern Empire; and in part at least of the West[4] the servitude of exposed infants continued for centuries, and appears only to have terminated with the general extinction of slavery in Europe. The law of Constantine concerning the sale of children was also a step, though perhaps a necessary step, of retrogression. A series of emperors, among whom Caracalla was conspicuous, had denounced and endeavoured to abolish as 'shameful,' the traffic in free children, and Diocletian had expressly and absolutely condemned it.[5] The extreme misery, however, resulting from the civil wars under Constantine, had

[1] *Codex Theod.* lib. v. tit. 8, lex 1.

[2] See Godefroy's *Commentary to the Law.*

[3] In a letter to the younger Pliny. (*Ep.* x. 72.)

[4] See on this point Muratori, *Antich. Italian.* Diss. xxxvii.

[5] See on these laws, Wallon, *Hist. de l'Esclavage*, tome iii. pp. 52–53.

rendered it necessary to authorise the old practice of selling children in the case of absolute destitution, which, though it had been condemned, had probably never altogether ceased. Theodosius the Great attempted to take a step in advance, by decreeing that the children thus sold might regain their freedom without the repayment of the purchase-money, a temporary service being a sufficient compensation for the purchase;[1] but this measure was repealed by Valentinian III. The sale of children in case of great necessity, though denounced by the Fathers,[2] continued long after the time of Theodosius, nor does any Christian emperor appear to have enforced the humane enactment of Diocletian.

Together with these measures for the protection of exposed children, there were laws directly condemnatory of infanticide. This branch of the subject is obscured by much ambiguity and controversy; but it appears most probable that the Pagan legislature reckoned infanticide as a form of homicide, though, being deemed less atrocious than other forms of homicide, it was punished, not by death, but by banishment.[3] A law of Constantine, intended principally, and perhaps exclusively, for Africa, where the sacrifices of children to Saturn were very common, assimilated to parricide the murder of a child by its father;[4] and finally, Valentinian, in A.D. 374, made all infanticide a capital offence,[5] and especially enjoined the

[1] See *Cod. Theod.* lib. iii. tit. 3, lex 1, and the Commentary.

[2] On the very persistent denunciation of this practice by the Fathers, see many examples in Terme et Monfalcon.

[3] This is a mere question of definition, upon which lawyers have expended much learning and discussion. Cujas thought the Romans considered infanticide a crime, but a crime generically different from homicide. Godefroy maintains that it was classified as homicide, but that, being esteemed less heinous than the other forms of homicide, it was only punished by exile. See the Commentary to *Cod. Theod.* lib. ix. tit. 14, l. 1.

[4] *Cod. Theod.* lib. ix. tit. 15.

[5] *Ibid.* lib. ix. tit. 14, lex 1.

punishment of exposition.[1] A law of the Spanish Visigoths, in the seventh century, punished infanticide and abortion with death or blindness.[2] In the Capitularies of Charlemagne the former crime was punished as homicide.[3]

It is not possible to ascertain, with any degree of accuracy what diminution of infanticide resulted from these measures. It may, however, be safely asserted that the publicity of the trade in exposed children became impossible under the influence of Christianity, and that the sense of the serious nature of the crime was very considerably increased. The extreme destitution, which was one of its most fertile causes, was met by Christian charity. Many exposed children appear to have been educated by individual Christians.[4] Brephotrophia and Orphanotrophia are among the earliest recorded charitable institutions of the Church; but it is not certain that exposed children were admitted into them, and we find no trace for several centuries of Christian foundling hospitals. This form of charity grew up gradually in the early part of the middle ages. It is said that one existed at Treves in the sixth, and at Angers in the seventh century, and it is certain that one existed at Milan in the eighth century.[5] The Council of Rouen, in the ninth century, invited women who had secretly borne children to place them at the door of the church, and undertook to provide for them if they

[1] *Corp. Juris*, lib. viii. tit. 52, lex 2.

[2] *Leges Wisigothorum* (lib. vi. tit. 3, lex 7) and other laws (lib. iv. tit. 4) condemned exposition.

[3] 'Si quis infantem necaverit ut homicida teneatur.'—*Capit.* vii. 168.

[4] It appears from a passage of St. Augustine, that Christian virgins were accustomed to collect exposed children and to have them brought into the church. See Terme et Monfalcon, *Hist. des Enfans trouvés*, p. 74.

[5] Compare Labourt, *Rech. sur les Enfans trouvés*, pp. 32–33; Muratori, *Antichità Italiane*, Dissert. xxxvii. Muratori has also briefly noticed the history of these charities in his *Carità Christiana*, cap. xxvii.

were not reclaimed. It is probable that they were brought up among the numerous slaves or serfs attached to the ecclesiastical properties, for a decree of the Council of Arles, in the fifth century, and afterwards a law of Charlemagne, had echoed the enactment of Constantine, declaring that exposed children should be the slaves of their protectors. As slavery declined, the memorials of many sins, like many other of the discordant elements of mediæval society, were doubtless absorbed and consecrated in the monastic societies. The strong sense always evinced in the Church of the enormity of unchastity probably rendered the ecclesiastics more cautious in this than in other forms of charity, for institutions especially intended for deserted children advanced but slowly. Even Rome, the mother of many charities, could boast of none till the beginning of the thirteenth century.[1] About the middle of the twelfth century we find societies at Milan charged, among other functions, with seeking for exposed children. Towards the close of the same century, a monk of Montpellier, whose very name is doubtful, but who is commonly spoken of as Brother Guy, founded a confraternity called by the name of the Holy Ghost, and devoted to the protection and education of children; and this society in the two following centuries ramified over a great part of Europe.[2] Though principally, and at first,

[1] The first seems to have been that of Sta. Maria in Sassia—a hospital which had existed with various changes from the eighth century, but which was made a foundling hospital and confided to the care of Guy of Montpellier in A.D. 1204. According to one tradition, Pope Innocent III. had been shocked at hearing of infants drawn in the nets of fishermen from the Tiber. According to another, he was inspired by an angel. Compare Remacle, *Hospices d'Enfans trouvés*, pp. 36–37, and Amydenus, *Pietas Romana* (a book written A.D. 1624, and translated in part into English in A.D. 1687), Eng. trans. pp. 2–3.

[2] For the little that is known about this missionary of charity, compare Remacle, *Hospices d'Enfans trouvés*, pp. 34-44, and Labourt, *Recherches historiques sur les Enfans trouvés*, pp. 38-41.

perhaps, exclusively intended for the care of the orphans of legitimate marriages, though in the fifteenth century the Hospital of the Holy Ghost at Paris even refused to admit deserted children, yet the care of foundlings soon passed in a great measure into its hands. At last, after many complaints of the frequency of infanticide, St. Vincent de Paul arose, and gave so great an impulse to that branch of charity, that he may be regarded as its second author, and his influence was felt not only in private charities, but in legislative enactments. Into the effects of these measures—the encouragement of the vice of incontinence by institutions that were designed to suppress the crime of infanticide, and the serious moral controversies suggested by this apparent conflict between the interests of humanity and of chastity—it is not necessary for me to enter. We are at present concerned with the principles that actuated, not with the wisdom of the organisations, of Christian charity. Whatever mistakes may have been made, the entire movement I have traced displays an anxiety not only for the life, but also for the moral wellbeing of the castaways of society, such as the most humane nations of antiquity had never reached. This minute and scrupulous care for human life and human virtue in the humblest forms, in the slave, the gladiator, the savage, or the infant, was indeed wholly foreign to the genius of Paganism. It was produced by the Christian doctrine of the inestimable value of each immortal soul. It is the distinguishing and transcendent characteristic of every society into which the spirit of Christianity has passed.

The influence of Christianity in the protection of infant-life, though very real, may be, and I think often has been, exaggerated. It would be difficult to overrate its influence in the sphere we have next to examine. There is scarcely any other single reform so important in the moral history of mankind as the suppression of the gladiatorial shows, and this feat must be almost exclusively ascribed to the Christian Church. When we remember how extremely few of the best and greatest men of the Roman world had absolutely condemned the games of the amphitheatre, it is impossible to regard, without the deepest admiration, the unwavering and uncompromising consistency of the patristic denunciations. And even comparing the Fathers with the most enlightened Pagan moralists in their treatment of this matter, we shall usually find one most significant difference. The Pagan, in the spirit of philosophy, denounced these games as inhuman, or demoralising, or degrading, or brutal. The Christian, in the spirit of the Church, represented them as a definite sin, the sin of murder, for which the spectators as well as the actors were directly responsible before Heaven. In the very latest days of the Pagan Empire, magnificent amphitheatres were still arising,[1] and Constantine himself had condemned numerous barbarian captives to combat with wild beasts.[2] It was in A.D. 365, immediately after the convocation of the Council of Nice, that the first Christian emperor issued the first edict in the Roman Empire condemnatory of the gladiatorial games.[3] It was issued in Berytus in Syria, and is believed by some to have been only applicable to the province of Phœnicia;[4] but even in this province it was suffered to be inoperative, for, only four years later, Libanius speaks of the

[1] E.g. the amphitheatre of Verona was only built under Diocletian.

[2] 'Quid hoc triumpho pulchrius? . . . Tantam captivorum multitudinem bestiis objicit ut ingrati et perfidi non minus doloris ex ludibrio sui quam ex ipsa morte patiantur.'—Incerti *Panegyricus Constant.* 'Puberes qui in manus venerunt, quorum nec perfidia erat apta militiæ, nec ferocia servituti ad pœnas spectaculo dati sævientes bestias multitudine sua fatigarunt.'—Eumenius, *Paneg. Constant.* xi.

[3] *Cod. Theod.* lib. xv. tit. 12, lex 1. Sozomen, i. 8.

[4] This, at least, is the opinion of Godefroy, who has discussed the subject very fully. (*Cod. Theod.* lib. xv. tit. 12.)

shows as habitually celebrated at Antioch.[1] In the Western Empire their continuance was fully recognised, though a few infinitesimal restrictions were imposed upon them. Constantine, in A.D. 357, forbade the lanistæ, or purveyors of gladiators, bribing servants of the palace to enroll themselves as combatants.[2] Valentinian, in A.D. 365, forbade any Christian criminal,[3] and in A.D. 367, anyone connected with the Palatine,[4] being condemned to fight. Honorius prohibited any slave who had been a gladiator passing into the service of a senator; but the real object of this last measure was, I imagine, not so much to stigmatise the gladiator, as to guard against the danger of an armed nobility.[5] A much more important fact is, that the spectacles were never introduced into the new capital of Constantine. At Rome, though they became less numerous, they do not appear to have been suspended until their final suppression. The passion for gladiators was the worst, while religious liberty was probably the best feature of the old Pagan society; and it is a melancholy fact, that of these two it was the nobler part that in the Christian Empire was first destroyed. Theodosius the Great, who suppressed all diversity of worship throughout the empire, and who showed himself on many occasions the docile slave of the clergy, won the applause of the Pagan Symmachus by compelling his barbarian prisoners to fight as gladiators.[6] Besides this occasion, we have special knowledge of gladiatorial games that were celebrated in A.D. 385, in A.D. 391, and afterwards in the reign of Honorius, and the practice of condemning criminals to the arena still continued.[7]

[1] Libanius, *De Vita Sua*, 3.

[2] *Cod. Theod.* lib. xv. tit. 12, l. 2.

[3] *Cod. Theod.* lib. ix. tit. 40, l. 8.

[4] Ibid. lib. ix. tit. 40, l. 11.

[5] Ibid. lib. xv. tit. 12, l. 3.

[6] Symmach. *Ep.* x. 61.

[7] M. Wallon has traced these last shows with much learning. (*Hist. de l'Esclavage*, tome iii. pp. 421–429.)

But although the suppression of the gladiatorial shows was not effected in the metropolis of the empire till nearly ninety years after Christianity had been the State religion, the distinction between the teaching of the Christians and Pagans on the subject remained unimpaired. To the last, the most estimable of the Pagans appear to have regarded them with favour or indifference. Julian, it is true, with a rare magnanimity worthy of his most noble nature, refused persistently, in his conflict with Christianity, to avail himself, as he might most easily have done, of the popular passion for games which the Church condemned; but Libanius has noticed them with some approbation,[1] and Symmachus, as we have already seen, both instituted and applauded them. But the Christians steadily refused to admit any professional gladiator to baptism till he had pledged himself to abandon his calling, and every Christian who attended the games was excluded from communion. The preachers and writers of the Church denounced them with the most unqualified vehemence, and the poet Prudentius made a direct and earnest appeal to the emperor to suppress them. In the East, where they had never taken very firm root, they appear to have ceased about the time of Theodosius, and a passion for chariot races, which rose to the most extravagant height at Constantinople and in many other cities, took their place. In the West, the last gladiatorial show was celebrated at Rome, under Honorius, in A.D. 404, in honour of the triumph of Stilicho, when an Asiatic monk, named Telemachus, animated by the noblest heroism of philanthropy, rushed into the amphitheatre and attempted to part the combatants. He

[1] He wavered, however, on the subject, and on one occasion condemned them. See Wallon, tome iii. p. 423.

perished beneath a shower of stones flung by the angry spectators; but his death led to the final abolition of the games.[1] Combats of men with wild beasts continued, however, much later, and were especially popular in the East. The difficulty of procuring wild animals, amid the general poverty, contributed, with other causes, to their decline. They sank, at last, into games of cruelty to animals, but of little danger to men, and were finally condemned, at the end of the seventh century, by the Council of Trullo.[2] In Italy, the custom of sham fights, which continued through the whole of the middle ages, and which Petrarch declares were in his day sometimes attended with considerable bloodshed, may perhaps be traced in some degree to the traditions of the amphitheatre.[3]

The extinction of the gladiatorial spectacles is, of all the results of early Christian influence, that upon which the historian can look with the deepest and most unmingled satisfaction. Horrible as was the bloodshed they directly caused, these games were perhaps still more pernicious on account of the callousness of feeling they diffused through all classes, the fatal obstacle they presented to any general elevation of the standard of humanity. Yet the attitude of the Pagans decisively proves that no progress of philosophy or social civilisation was likely, for a very long period, to have extirpated them, and it can hardly be doubted that, had they been flourishing unchallenged as in the days of Trajan, when the rude warriors of the North obtained the empire of Italy, they would have been eagerly adopted by the conquerors, would have taken deep root in mediæval life, and have indefi-

[1] Theodoret, v. 26.

[2] Muller, *De Genio Ævi Theodosiani* (1797), vol. ii. p. 88; Milman, *Hist. of Early Christianity*, vol. iii. pp. 343–347.

[3] See on these fights Ozanam's *Civilisation in the Fifth Century* (Eng. trans.), vol. i. p. 130.

nitely retarded the progress of humanity. Christianity alone was powerful enough to tear this evil plant from the Roman soil. The Christian custom of legacies for the relief of the indigent and suffering replaced the Pagan custom of bequeathing sums of money for games in honour of the dead, and the month of December, which was looked forward to with eagerness through all the Roman world, as the special season of the gladiatorial spectacles, was consecrated in the Church by another festival commemorative of the advent of Christ.

The notion of the sanctity of human life, which led the early Christians to combat and at last to overthrow the gladiatorial games, was carried by some of them to an extent altogether irreconcilable with national independence, and with the prevailing penal system. Many of them taught that no Christian might lawfully take away life, either as a soldier or by bringing a capital charge, or by acting as an executioner. The first of these questions it will be convenient to reserve for a later period of this chapter, when I propose to examine the relations of Christianity to the military spirit, and a very few words will be sufficient to dispose of the others. The notion that there is something impure and defiling, even in a just execution, is one which may be traced through many ages, and executioners, as the ministers of the law, have been from very ancient times regarded as unholy. In both Greece and Rome the law compelled them to live outside the walls, and at Rhodes they were never permitted even to enter the city.[1] Notions of this kind were very strongly held in the early Church; and a decree of the penitential discipline which was enforced, even against emperors and generals, forbade anyone whose hands had been imbrued

[1] Nieupoort, *De Ritibus Romanorum*, p. 169.

in blood, even when that blood was shed in a war which was recognised as righteous, approaching the altar without a preparatory period of penance. The opinions of the Christians of the first three centuries were usually formed without any regard to the necessities of civil or political life; but when the Church obtained an ascendancy, it was found necessary speedily to modify them; and although Lactantius, in the fourth century, maintained the unlawfulness of all bloodshed,[1] as strongly as Origen in the third, and Tertullian in the second, the common doctrine was simply that no priest or bishop must take any part in a capital charge. From this exceptional position of the clergy they speedily acquired the position of official intercessors for criminals, ambassadors of mercy, when, from some act of sedition or other cause, their city or neighbourhood was menaced with a bloody invasion. The right of sanctuary, which was before possessed by the Imperial statues and by the Pagan temples, was accorded to the Churches. During the holy seasons of Lent and Easter, no criminal trials could be held, and no criminal could be tortured or executed.[2] Miracles, it was said, were sometimes wrought to attest the innocence of accused or condemned men, but were never wrought to consign criminals to execution by the civil power.[3]

All this had an importance much beyond its imme-

[1] See a very unequivocal passage, *Inst. Div.* vi. 20. Several earlier testimonies on the subject are given by Barbeyrac, *Morale des Pères,* and in many other books.

[2] See two laws enacted in A.D. 380 (*Cod. Theod.* ix. tit. 35, l. 4) and A.D. 389 (*Cod. Theod.* ix. tit. 35, l. 5). Theodosius the Younger made a law (ix. tit. 35, l. 7) excepting the Isaurian robbers from the privileges of these laws.

[3] There are, of course, innumerable miracles punishing guilty men, but I know none assisting the civil power in doing so. As an example of the miracles in defence of the innocent, I may cite one by St. Macarius. An innocent man, accused of a murder, fled to him. He brought both the accused and accusers to the tomb of the murdered man, and asked him whether

diate effect, in tempering the administration of the law. It contributed largely to associate in the popular imagination the ideas of sanctity and of mercy, and to increase the reverence for human life. It had also another remarkable effect, to which I have adverted in another work. The belief that it was wrong for a priest to bring any charge that could give rise to a capital sentence, caused the leading clergy to shrink from persecuting heresy to death, at a time when in all other respects the theory of persecution had been fully matured. When it was readily admitted that heresy was in the highest degree criminal, and ought to be made penal, when laws banishing, fining, or imprisoning heretics filled the statute-book, and when every vestige of religious liberty was suppressed at the instigation of the clergy, these still shrank from the last and inevitable step, not because it was an atrocious violation of the rights of conscience, but because it was contrary to the ecclesiastical discipline for a bishop, under any circumstances, to countenance bloodshed. It was on this ground that St. Augustine, while eagerly advocating the persecution of the Donatists, more than once expressed a wish that they should not be punished with death, and that St. Ambrose, and St. Martin of Tours, who were both energetic persecutors, expressed their abhorrence of the Spanish bishops, who had caused some Priscillianists to be executed. I have elsewhere noticed the odious evasion of the later inquisitors, who relegated the execution of the sentence to the civil power, with a prayer that the heretics should be punished without the 'effusion of blood,'[1] or, in other words, by the death of fire; but I

the prisoner was the murderer. The corpse answered in the negative; the bystanders implored St. Macarius to ask it to reveal the real culprit, but St. Macarius refused to do so. (*Vitæ Patrum,* lib. ii. cap. xxviii.)

[1] 'Ut quam clementissime et ultra sanguinis effusionem puniretur.'

may here add, that this hideous mockery is not unique in the history of religion. Plutarch suggests, that one of the reasons for burying unchaste vestals alive, was that they were so sacred that it was unlawful to lay violent hands upon them,[1] and among the Donatists the Circumcelliones were for a time accustomed to abstain, in obedience to the evangelical command, from the use of the sword, while they beat to death those who differed from their theological opinions with massive clubs, to which they gave the very significant name of Israelites.[2]

The time came when the Christian priests shed blood enough. The extreme scrupulosity, however, which they at first displayed, is not only exceedingly curious when contrasted with their later history; it was also, by the association of ideas which it promoted, very favourable to humanity. It is remarkable, however, that while some of the early Fathers were the undoubted precursors of Beccaria, their teaching, unlike that of the philosophers in the eighteenth century, had little or no appreciable influence in mitigating the severity of the penal code. Indeed, the more carefully the Christian legislation of the empire is examined, and the more fully it is compared with what had been done under the influence of Stoicism by the Pagan legislators, the more evident, I think, it will appear that the golden age of Roman law was not Christian, but Pagan. Great works of codification were accomplished under the younger Theodosius, and under Justinian, but it was in the reign of Pagan emperors, and especially of Hadrian and Alexander Severus, that nearly all the most important measures were taken redressing injustice,

[1] *Quæst. Romanæ*, xcvi.

[2] Tillemont, *Mém. d'Hist. ecclés.* tome vi. pp. 88-98. The Donatists after a time, however, are said to have overcome their scruples, and used swords.

elevating oppressed classes, and making the doctrine of the natural equality and fraternity of mankind the basis of legal enactments. Receiving the heritage of these laws, the Christians no doubt added something; but a careful examination will show that it was surprisingly little. In no respect is the greatness of the Stoic philosophers more conspicuous than in the contrast between the gigantic steps of legal reform made in a few years under their influence, and the almost insignificant steps taken when Christianity had obtained an ascendancy in the empire, not to speak of the long period of decrepitude that followed. In the way of mitigating the severity of punishments, Constantine made, it is true, three important laws prohibiting the custom of branding criminals upon the face, the condemnation of criminals as gladiators, and the continuance of the once degrading but now sacred punishment of crucifixion, which had been very commonly employed; but these measures were more than counterbalanced by the extreme severity with which the Christian emperors punished infanticide, adultery, seduction, rape, and several other crimes, and the number of capital offences became considerably greater than before.[1] The most prominent evidence, indeed, of ecclesiastical influence in the Theodosian code, is that which must be most lamented. It is in the immense

[1] Under the Christian kings, the barbarians multiplied the number of capital offences, but this has usually been regarded as an improvement. The Abbé Mably says: 'Quoiqu'il nous reste peu d'ordonnances faites sous les premiers Mérovingiens, nous voyons qu'avant la fin du sixième siècle, les François avoient déjà adopté la doctrine salutaire des Romains au sujet de la prescription; et que renonçant à cette humanité cruelle qui les enhardissoit au mal, ils infligèrent peine de mort contre l'inceste, le vol et le meurtre qui jusques-là n'avoient été punis que par l'exil, ou dont on se rachetoit par une composition. Les François, en réformant quelques-unes de leurs lois civiles, portèrent la sévérité aussi loin que leurs pères avoient poussé l'indulgence.'—Mably, *Observ. sur l'Hist. des François*, liv. i. ch. iii. See, too, Gibbon's *Decline and Fall*, ch. xxxviii.

mass of legislation, intended on the one hand to elevate the clergy into a separate and sacred caste, and on the other to persecute in every form, and with every degree of violence, all who deviated from the fine line of Catholic orthodoxy.[1]

The last consequence of the Christian estimate of human life was a very emphatic condemnation of suicide. We have already seen that the arguments of the Pagan moralists, who were opposed to this act, were of four kinds. The religious argument of Pythagoras and Plato was, that we are all soldiers of God, placed in an appointed post of duty, which it is a rebellion against our Maker to desert. The civic argument of Aristotle and the Greek legislators was that we owe our services to the State, and that therefore voluntarily to abandon life is to abandon our duty to our country. The argument which Plutarch and other writers derived from human dignity was that true courage is shown in the manful endurance of suffering, while suicide, being an act of flight, is an act of cowardice, and therefore unworthy of man. The mystical or Quietist argument of the Neo-platonists was that all perturbation is a pollution of the soul; that the act of suicide is accompanied by and springs from perturbation, and that therefore the perpetrator ends his days by a crime. Of these four arguments, the last cannot, I think, be said to have had any place among the Christian dissuasives from suicide, and the influence of the second was almost imperceptible. The notion of patriotism being a moral duty was habitually discouraged in the early Church, and it was impossible to urge the civic argument against suicide without at the same time condemning the hermit life, which in the third century

[1] The whole of the sixth volume of Godefroy's edition (folio) of the Theodosian Code is taken up with laws of these kinds.

became the ideal of the Church. The duty a man owes to his family, which a modern moralist would deem the most obvious and perhaps the most conclusive proof of the general criminality of suicide, and which may be said to have replaced the civic argument, was scarcely noticed either by the Pagans or the early Christians. The first were accustomed to lay so much stress upon the authority, that they scarcely recognised the duties of the father, and the latter were too anxious to attach all their ethics to the interests of another world, to do much to supply the omission. The Christian estimate of the duty of humility, and of the degradation of man, rendered appeals to human dignity somewhat uncongenial to the patristic writers, yet these writers frequently dilated upon the true courage of patience, in language to which their own heroism under persecution gave a noble emphasis. To the example of Cato they opposed those of Regulus and Job, the courage that endures suffering to the courage that confronts death. The Platonic doctrine, that we are servants of the Deity, placed upon earth to perform our allotted task in His sight, with His assistance, and by His will, they continually enforced and most deeply realised; and this doctrine was in itself in most cases a sufficient preventive; for, as a great writer has said, 'Though there are many crimes of a deeper dye than suicide, there is no other by which men appear so formally to renounce the protection of God.'[1]

But in addition to this general teaching, the Christian theologians introduced into the sphere we are considering new elements both of terrorism and of persuasion, which have had a decisive influence upon the judgments of mankind. They carried their doctrine of the sanctity of

[1] Mme. de Staël, *Réflexions sur le Suicide.*

human life to such a point that they maintained dogmatically that a man who destroys his own life has committed a crime similar both in kind and magnitude to that of an ordinary murderer,[1] and they at the same time gave a new character to death by their doctrines concerning its penal nature and concerning the future destinies of the soul. On the other hand, the high position assigned to resignation in the moral scale, the hope of future happiness, which casts a ray of light upon the darkest calamities of life, the deeper and more subtle consolations arising from the feeling of trust and from the outpouring of prayer, and above all, the Christian doctrine of the remedial and providential character of suffering, have proved sufficient protection against despair. The Christian doctrine that pain is a good, had in this respect an influence that was never attained by the Pagan doctrine, that pain is not an evil.

There were, however, two forms of suicide which were regarded in the early Church with some tolerance or hesitation. During the frenzy excited by persecution, and under the influence of the belief that martyrdom effaced in a moment the sins of a life, and introduced the sufferer at once into celestial joys, it was not uncommon for men, in a transport of enthusiasm, to rush before the Pagan judges, imploring or provoking martyrdom, and some of the ecclesiastical writers have spoken of them with considerable admiration,[2] though the general

[1] The following became the theological doctrine on the subject:—'Est vere homicida et reus homicidii qui se interficiendo innocentem hominem interfecerit.'—Lisle, *Du Suicide*, p. 400. St. Augustine has much in this strain. Lucretia, he says, either consented to the act of Sextius, or she did not. In the first case she was an adulteress, and should therefore not be admired. In the second case she was a murderess, because in killing herself she killed an innocent and virtuous woman. (*De Civ. Dei*, i. 19.)

[2] Justin Martyr, Tertullian, and Cyprian, are especially ardent in this respect; but their language is, I think, in their circumstances, extremely

tone of the patristic writings and the councils of the Church condemned them. A more serious difficulty arose about Christian women who committed suicide to guard their chastity when menaced by the infamous sentences of their persecutors, or more frequently by the lust of emperors, or by barbarian invaders. St. Pelagia, a girl of only fifteen, who has been canonised by the Church, and who was warmly eulogised by St. Ambrose and St. Chrysostom, having been captured by the soldiery, obtained permission to retire to her room for the purpose of robing herself, mounted to the roof of the house, and, flinging herself down, perished by the fall.[1] A Christian lady of Antioch, named Domnina, had two daughters renowned alike for their beauty and their piety. Being captured during the Diocletian persecution, and fearing the loss of their chastity, they agreed by one bold act to free themselves from the danger, and, casting themselves into a river by the way, mother and daughters sank unsullied in the wave.[2] The tyrant Maxentius was fascinated by the beauty of a Christian lady, the wife of the Prefect of Rome. Having sought in vain to elude his addresses, having been dragged from her house by the minions of the tyrant, the faithful wife obtained permission, before yielding to her master's embraces, to retire for a moment into her chamber, and she there, with true Roman courage, stabbed herself to the heart.[3] Some Protestant controversialists

excusable. Compare Barbeyrac, *Morale des Pères*, ch. ii. § 8; ch. viii. §§ 34–39. Donne's *Biathanatos* (ed. 1644), pp. 58–67. Cromaziano, *Istoria critica e filosofica del Suicidio ragionato* (Venezia, 1788), pp. 135–140. The true name of the author of this last book (which was first published at Lucca in 1761, and is still, perhaps, the best history of suicide) was Buonafede. He was a Celestine monk, and died at Rome in 1793. His book on suicide was translated into French in 1841.

[1] Ambrose, *De Virginibus*, iii. 7.

[2] Eusebius, *Eccles. Hist.* viii. 12.

[3] Eusebius, *Eccles. Hist.* viii. 14. Bayle, in his article upon Sophronia,

have been scandalised,[1] and some Catholic controversialists perplexed, by the undisguised admiration with which the early ecclesiastical writers narrate these histories. To those who have not suffered theological opinions to destroy all their natural sense of nobility it will need no defence.

This was the only form of avowed suicide which was in any degree permitted in the early Church. St. Ambrose rather timidly, and St. Jerome more strongly, commended it; but at the time when the capture of Rome by the soldiers of Attila made the question one of pressing interest, St. Augustine devoted an elaborate examination to the subject, and while expressing his pitying admiration for the virgin suicides, decidedly condemned their act.[2] His opinion of the absolute sinfulness of suicide has since been generally adopted by the Catholic theologians, who pretend that Pelagia and Domnina acted under the impulse of a special revelation.[3] At the same time, by a

appears to be greatly scandalised at this act, and it seems that among the Catholics it is not considered right to admire this poor lady as much as her sister suicides. Tillemont remarks, 'Comme on ne voit pas que l'église romaine l'ait jamais honorée, nous n'avons pas le mesme droit de justifier son action.'—*Hist. ecclés.* tome v. pp. 404–405.

[1] Especially Barbeyrac, in his *Morale des Pères.* He was answered by Ceillier, Cromaziano, and others. Mathew of Westminster relates of Ebba, the abbess of a Yorkshire convent which was besieged by the Danes, that she and all the other nuns, to save their chastity, deformed themselves by cutting off their noses and upper lips. (A.D. 870.)

[2] *De Civ. Dei*, i. 22–27.

[3] This had been suggested by St. Augustine. In the case of Pelagia, Tillemont finds a strong argument in support of this view in the astounding, if not miraculous fact, that having thrown herself from the top of the house, she was actually killed by the fall! 'Estant montée tout au haut de sa maison, fortifiée par le mouvement que J.-C. formoit dans son cœur et par le courage qu'il luy inspiroit, elle se précipita de là du haut en bas, et échapa ainsi à tous les piéges de ses ennemis. Son corps en tombant à terre frapa, dit S. Chrysostome, les yeux du démon plus vivement qu'un éclair . . . . . Ce qui marque encore que Dieu agissoit en tout ceci c'est qu'au lieu que ces chutes ne sont pas toujours mortelles, ou que souvent

glaring though very natural inconsistency, no characters were more enthusiastically extolled than those anchorites who habitually deprived their bodies of the sustenance that was absolutely necessary to health, and thus manifestly abridged their lives. St. Jerome has preserved a curious illustration of the feeling with which these slow suicides were regarded by the outer world, in his account of the life and death of a young nun named Blesilla. This lady had been guilty of what, according to the religious notions of the fourth century, was, at least, the frivolity of marrying, but was left a widow seven months after, having thus 'lost at once the crown of virginity and the pleasure of marriage.'[1] An attack of illness inspired her with strong religious feelings. At the age of twenty she retired to a convent. She attained such a height of devotion, that, according to the very characteristic eulogy of her biographer, 'she was more sorry for the loss of her virginity than for the decease of her husband;'[2] and a long succession of atrocious penances preceded, if they did not produce, her death.[3] The conviction that she had been killed by fasting, and the spectacle of the uncontrollable grief of her mother, filled the populace with indignation, and the funeral was disturbed by tumultuous cries, that the 'accursed race of monks should be banished from the city, stoned, or drowned.'[4] In the Church itself, however, we find very few traces of any condem-

ne brisant que quelques membres, elles n'ostent la vie que longtemps après, ni l'un ni l'autre n'arriva en cette rencontre; mais Dieu retira aussitost l'âme de la sainte, en sorte que sa mort parut autant l'effet de la volonté divine que de sa chute.'—*Hist. ecclés.* tome v. pp. 401–402.

[1] 'Et virginitatis coronam et nuptiarum perdidit voluptatem.'—*Ep.* xxii.

[2] 'Quis enim siccis oculis recordetur viginti annorum adolescentulam tam ardenti fide crucis levasse vexillum ut magis amissam virginitatem quam mariti doleret interitum?'—*Ep.* xxxix.

[3] For a description of these penances, see *Ep.* xxxviii.

[4] Ep. xxxix.

nation of the custom of undermining the constitution by austerities,[1] and if we may believe but a small part of what is related of the habits of the early and mediæval monks, great numbers must have thus shortened their days. There is a touching story told by St. Bonaventura, of St. Francis Assisi, who was one of these victims to asceticism. As the dying saint sank back exhausted with spitting blood, he avowed, as he looked upon his emaciated body, that 'he had sinned against his brother, the ass;' and then the feeling of his mind taking, as was usual with him, the form of an hallucination, he imagined that when at prayer during the night, he heard a voice saying, 'Francis, there is no sinner in the world whom, if he be converted, God will not pardon; but he who kills himself by hard penances will find no mercy in eternity.' He attributed the voice to the devil.[2]

Direct and deliberate suicide, which occupies so prominent a place in the moral history of antiquity, almost absolutely disappeared within the Church; but beyond its pale the Circumcelliones, in the fourth century, constituted themselves the apostles of death, and not only carried to the highest point the custom of provoking martyrdom, by challenging and insulting the assemblies of the Pagans, but even killed themselves in great numbers, imagining, it would seem, that this was a form of martyrdom, and would secure for them eternal salvation. Assembling in hundreds, St. Augustine says even in thousands, they leaped with paroxysms of frantic joy from the brows of overhanging cliffs, till the rocks below were reddened with their blood.[3] At a much later period, we find among the

[1] St. Jerome gave some sensible advice on this point to one of his admirers. (*Ep.* cxxv.)

[2] Hase, *St. François d'Assise*, pp. 137–138. St. Palæmon is said to have died of his austerities. (*Vit. S. Pachomii.*)

[3] St. Augustine and St. Optatus have given accounts of these suicides in their works against the Donatists.

Albigenses a practice, known by the name of Endura, of accelerating death, in the case of dangerous illness, by fasting, and sometimes by bleeding.[1] The wretched Jews, stung to madness by the persecutions of the Catholics, furnish the most numerous examples of suicide during the middle ages. A multitude perished by their own hands, to avoid torture, in France, in 1095; five hundred, it is said, on a single occasion at York; five hundred in 1320, when besieged by the Shepherds. The old Pagan legislation on this subject remained unaltered in the Theodosian and Justinian codes, but a Council of Arles, in the fifth century, having pronounced suicide to be the effect of diabolical inspiration, a Council of Bragues, in the following century, ordained that no religious rites should be celebrated at the tomb of the culprit, and that no masses should be said for his soul; and these provisions, which were repeated by later Councils, were gradually introduced into the laws of the barbarians and of Charlemagne. St. Lewis originated the custom of confiscating the property of the dead man, and the corpse was soon subjected to gross and various outrages. In some countries it could only be removed from the house through a perforation specially made for the occasion in the wall; it was dragged upon a hurdle through the streets, hung up with the head downwards, and at last thrown into the public sewer, or burnt, or buried in the sand below high-water mark, or transfixed by a stake on the public highway.[2]

[1] See Todd's *Life of St. Patrick*, p. 462.

[2] The whole history of suicide in the dark ages has been most minutely and carefully examined by M. Bourquelot, in a very interesting series of memoirs in the third and fourth volume of the *Bibliothèque de l'École des Chartes.* I am much indebted to these memoirs in the following pages. See, too, Lisle, *Du Suicide, Statistique, Médecine, Histoire et Législation.* (Paris, 1856.) The ferocious laws here recounted contrast remarkably with a law in the Capitularies (lib. vi. lex 70), which provides that though mass may not be celebrated for a suicide, any private person may, through charity,

These singularly hideous and at the same time grotesque customs, and also the extreme injustice of reducing to beggary the unhappy relations of the dead, had the very natural effect of exciting, in the eighteenth century, a strong spirit of reaction. Suicide is indeed one of those acts which may be condemned by moralists as a sin, but which, in modern times at least, cannot be regarded as within the legitimate sphere of law; for a society which accords to its members perfect liberty of emigration, cannot reasonably pronounce the simple renunciation of life to be an offence against itself. When, however, Beccaria and his followers went further, and maintained that the mediæval laws on the subject were as useless as they were revolting, they fell, I think, into a serious error. The outrages lavished upon the corpse of the suicide, though in the first instance an expression of the popular horror of his act, contributed by the associations they formed, to strengthen the feeling that produced them, and they were also peculiarly fitted to scare the diseased, excited, and over sensitive imaginations that are most prone to suicide. In the rare occasions when the act was deliberately contemplated, the knowledge that religious, legislative, and social influences would combine to aggravate to the utmost the agony of the surviving relatives, must have had great weight. The activity of the legislature shows the continuance of the act; but we have every reason to believe that within the pale of Catholicism it was for many centuries extremely rare. It is said to have been somewhat prevalent in Spain in the last and most corrupt period of the Gothic kingdom,[1] and many instances occurred during a great pestilence which raged in England

cause prayer to be offered up for his soul. 'Quia incomprehensibilia sunt judicia Dei, et profunditatem consilii ejus nemo potest investigare.'

[1] See the very interesting work of the Abbé Bourret, *l'École chrétienne de Séville sous la monarchie des Visigoths* (Paris, 1855), p. 196.

during the seventh century,[1] and also during the Black Death of the fourteenth century.[2] When the wives of priests were separated in vast numbers from their husbands by Hildebrand, and driven into the world blasted, heart-broken, and hopeless, not a few of them shortened their agony by suicide.[3] Among women it was in general especially rare, and a learned historian of suicide has even asserted that a Spanish lady, who, being separated from her husband, and finding herself unable to resist the energy of her passions, killed herself to preserve her chastity, is the only instance of female suicide during several centuries.[4] In the romances of chivalry, however, this mode of death is frequently pourtrayed without horror,[5] and its criminality was discussed at considerable length by Abelard and St. Thomas Aquinas, while Dante has devoted some fine lines to painting the condition of suicides in hell, where they are also frequently represented on the bas-reliefs of cathedrals. A melancholy leading to desperation, and known to theologians under the name of 'acedia,' was not uncommon in monasteries, and most of the recorded instances of mediæval suicides in Catholicism were by monks. The frequent suicides of monks, sometimes to escape the world, sometimes through despair at their inability to quell the propensities of the flesh,

[1] Roger of Wendover, A.D. 665.

[2] Esquirol, *Maladies mentales*, tome i. p. 591.

[3] Lea's *History of Sacerdotal Celibacy* (Philadelphia, 1867), p. 248.

[4] 'Per lo corso di molti secoli abbiamo questo solo suicidio donnesco, e buona cosa è non averne più d' uno; perchè io non credo che la impudicizia istessa sia peggiore di questa disperata castità.'—Cromaziano, *Ist. del Suicidio*, p. 126. Mariana, who, under the frock of a Jesuit, bore the heart of an ancient Roman, treats the case in a very different manner. 'Ejus uxor Maria Coronelia cum mariti absentiam non ferret, ne pravis cupiditatibus cederet, vitam posuit, ardentem forte libidinem igne extinguens adacto per muliebria titione; dignam meliori seculo fœminam, insigne studium castitatis.'—*De Rebus Hispan.* xvi. 17.

[5] A number of passages are cited by Bourquelot.

sometimes through insanity produced by their mode of life, and by their dread of surrounding dæmons, were noticed in the early Church,[1] and a few examples have been gleaned from the mediæval chronicles [2] of suicides produced by the bitterness of hopeless love, or by the derangement that follows extreme austerity. These are, however, but few, and it is probable that the monasteries, by providing a refuge for the disappointed and the broken-hearted, have prevented more suicides than they have caused, and that, during the whole period of Catholic ascendancy, the act was more rare than before or after. The influence of Catholicism was seconded by Mahommedanism, which on this as on many other points borrowed its teaching from the Christian Church, and even intensified it; for suicide, which is never expressly condemned in the Bible, is more than once forbidden in the Koran, and the Christian duty of resignation was exaggerated by the Moslem into a complete fatalism. Under the empire of Catholicism and Mahommedanism, suicide, during many centuries, almost absolutely ceased in all the civilised, active, and progressive part of mankind. When we recollect how warmly it was applauded, or how faintly it was condemned in the civilisations of Greece and Rome; when we remember, too, that there was scarcely a barbarous tribe, from Denmark to Spain, who did not habitually

[1] This is noticed by St. Gregory Nazianzen in a little poem which is given in Migne's edition of *The Greek Fathers*, tome xxxvii. p. 1459. St. Nilus and the biographer of St. Pachomius speak of these suicides, and St. Chrysostom wrote a letter of consolation to a young monk, named Stagirius, which is still extant, encouraging him to resist the temptation. See Neander, *Ecclesiastical Hist.* vol. iii. pp. 319-320.

[2] Bourquelot. Pinel notices (*Traité médico-philosophique sur l'Aliénation mentale* (2nd ed.), pp. 44–46) the numerous cases of insanity still produced by strong religious feeling, and the history of the movements called 'revivals, in the present century, supplies much evidence to the same effect. Pinel says, religious insanity tends peculiarly to suicide (p. 265).

practise it,[1] we may realise the complete revolution which was effected in this sphere by the influence of Christianity.

A few words may be added on the later phases of this mournful history. The Reformation does not seem to have had any immediate effect in multiplying suicide, for Protestants and Catholics held with equal intensity the religious sentiments which are most fitted to prevent it, and in none of the persecutions was impatience of life largely displayed. The history at this period passes chiefly into the new world, where the unhappy Indians, reduced to slavery, and treated with atrocious cruelty by their conquerors, killed themselves in great numbers, till the Spaniards, it is said, discovered an ingenious method of deterring them, by declaring that the master also would commit suicide, and would pursue his victims into the world of spirits.[2] In Europe the act was very common among the witches, who underwent all the sufferings with none of the consolations of martyrdom. Without enthusiasm, without hope, without even the consciousness of innocence, decrepit in body, and distracted in mind,

[1] Orosius notices (*Hist.* v. 14) that of all the Gauls conquered by Q. Marcius there were none who did not prefer death to slavery. The Spaniards were famous for their suicides, to avoid old age as well as slavery. Odin, who, under different names, was the supreme divinity of most of the Northern tribes, is said to have ended his earthly life by suicide. Boadicea, the grandest figure of early British history, and Cordeilla, or Cordelia, the most pathetic figure of early British romance, were both suicides. (See on the first, Tacitus, *Ann.* xiv. 35–37, and on the second Geoffrey of Monmouth, ii. 15—a version from which Shakspeare has considerably diverged, but which is faithfully followed by Spenser. (*Faery Queen*, book ii. canto 10.)

[2] 'In our age, when the Spaniards extended that law which was made only against the cannibals, that they who would not accept Christian religion should incur bondage, the Indians in infinite numbers escaped this by killing themselves, and never ceased till the Spaniards, by some counterfeitings, made them think that they also would kill themselves, and follow them with the same severity into the next life.'—Donne's *Biathanatos*, p. 56 (ed. 1644). On the evidence of the early travellers on this point, see the essay on 'England's Forgotten Worthies,' in Mr. Froude's *Short Studies*.

compelled in this world to endure tortures, before which the most impassioned heroism might quail, and doomed, as they often believed, to eternal damnation in the next, they not unfrequently killed themselves in the agony of their despair. A French judge named Remy tells us that he knew no less than fifteen witches commit suicide in a single year.[1] In these cases, fear and madness combined in urging the victims to the deed. Epidemics of purely insane suicide have also not unfrequently occurred. Both the women of Marseilles and the women of Lyons were afflicted with an epidemic not unlike that which, in antiquity, had been noticed among the girls of Miletus.[2] In that strange mania which raged in the Neapolitan districts from the end of the fifteenth to the end of the seventeenth century, and which was attributed to the bite of the tarantula, the patients thronged in multitudes towards the sea, and often, as the blue waters opened to their view, they chaunted a wild hymn of welcome, and rushed with passion into the waves.[3] But together with these cases, which belong rather to the history of medicine than to that of morals, we find many facts exhibiting a startling increase of deliberate suicide, and a no less startling modification of the sentiments with which it was

[1] Lisle, pp. 427–434. Sprenger has noticed the same tendency among the witches he tried. See Calmeil, *De la Folie* (Paris, 1845), tome i. pp. 161, 303–305.

[2] On modern suicides the reader may consult Winslow's *Anatomy of Suicide*; as well as the work of M. Lisle, and also Esquirol, *Maladies mentales* (Paris, 1838), tome i. pp. 526–676.

[3] Hecker's *Epidemics of the Middle Ages* (London, 1844), p. 121. Hecker, in his very curious essay on this mania, has preserved a verse of their song:—

'Allu mari mi portati
Se voleti che mi sanati,
Allu mari, alla via,
Così m' ama la donna mia,
Allu mari, allu mari,
Mentre campo, t' aggio amari.'

regarded. The revival of classical learning, and the growing custom of regarding Greek and Roman heroes as ideals, necessarily brought the subject into prominence. The Catholic casusists, and at a later period philosophers of the school of Grotius and Puffendorf, began to distinguish certain cases of legitimate suicide, such as that committed to avoid dishonour or probable sin, or that of the soldier who fires a mine, knowing he must inevitably perish by the explosion, or that of a condemned person who saves himself from torture by anticipating an inevitable fate, or that of a man who offers himself to death for his friend.[1] The effect of the Pagan examples may frequently be detected in the last words or writings of the suicides. Philip Strozzi, when accused of the assassination of Alexander I. of Tuscany, killed himself through fear that torture might extort from him revelations injurious to his friends, and he left behind him a paper in which, among other things, he commended his soul to God, with the prayer that if no higher boon could be granted, he might at least be permitted to have his place with Cato of Utica and the other great suicides of antiquity.[2] In England, the act appears in the seventeenth and in the first half of the eighteenth centuries to have been more common than upon the Continent,[3] and several partial or even unqualified apologies for it were written. Sir Thomas More, in his 'Utopia,' represented the priests and magistrates of his ideal republic permitting or even

[1] Cromaziano, *Ist. del Suicidio*, caps. viii. ix.

[2] Ibid., pp. 92-93.

[3] Montesquieu, and many continental writers, have noticed this, and most English writers of the eighteenth century seem to admit the charge. There do not appear, however, to have been any accurate statistics, and the general statements are very untrustworthy. Suicides were supposed to be especially numerous under the depressing influence of English winter fogs. The statistics made in the present century prove beyond question that they are most numerous in summer.

enjoining those who were afflicted with incurable disease to kill themselves, but depriving of burial those who had done so without authorisation.[1] Dr. Donne, the learned and pious Dean of St. Paul's, had in his youth written an extremely curious, subtle, and learned, but at the same time feeble and involved work, in defence of suicide, which on his deathbed he commanded his son neither to publish nor destroy, and which his son published in 1644. Two or three English suicides left behind them elaborate defences, as did also a Swede named Robeck, who drowned himself in 1735, and whose treatise, published in the following year, acquired considerable celebrity.[2] But the most influential writings about suicide were those of the French philosophers and revolutionists. Montaigne, without discussing its abstract lawfulness, recounts with much admiration many of the instances in antiquity.[3] Montesquieu, in a youthful work, defended it with ardent enthusiasm.[4] Rousseau devoted to the subject two letters of a burning and passionate eloquence,[5] in the first of which he presented with matchless power the

[1] *Utopia,* book ii. ch. vi.

[2] A sketch of his life, which was rather curious, is given by Cromaziano, pp. 148–151. There is a long note on the early literature in defence of suicide, in Dumas, *Traité du Suicide* (Amsterdam, 1723), pp. 148–149. Dumas was a Protestant minister who wrote against suicide. Amongst the English apologists for suicide (which he himself committed) was Blount, the translator of the *Life of Apollonius of Tyana,* and Creech, an editor of Lucretius. Concerning the former there is a note in Bayle's *Dict.* art. 'Apollonius.' The latter is noticed by Voltaire in his *Lettres philos.* He wrote as a memorandum on the margin of his 'Lucretius,' 'N.B. When I have finished my Commentary I must kill myself;' which he accordingly did—Voltaire says, to imitate his favourite author. (Voltaire, *Dict. phil.* art. 'Caton.')

[3] *Essais,* liv. ii. ch. xiii.

[4] *Lettres persanes,* lxxvi.

[5] *Nouvelle Héloïse,* partie iii. let. 21–22. Esquirol gives a curious illustration of the way the influence of Rousseau penetrated through all classes. A little child of thirteen committed suicide, leaving a writing beginning, 'Je lègue mon âme à Rousseau, mon corps à la terre.'—*Maladies mentales,* tome i. p. 588.

arguments in its favour, while in the second he denounced those arguments as sophistical, dilated upon the impiety of abandoning the post of duty, and upon the cowardice of despair, and with a deep knowledge of the human heart revealed the selfishness that lies at the root of most suicide, exhorting all who felt impelled to it to set about some work for the good of others, in which they would assuredly find relief. Voltaire, in the best known couplet he ever wrote, defends the act on occasions of extreme necessity.[1] Among the atheistical party it was warmly eulogised, and Holbach and Deslandes were prominent as its defenders. The rapid decomposition of religious opinions weakened the popular sense of its enormity, and at the same time the humanity of the age, and also a clearer sense of the true limits of legislation, produced a reaction against the horrible laws on the subject. Grotius had defended them. Montesquieu at first denounced them with unqualified energy, but in his later years in some degree modified his opinions. Beccaria, who was, more than any other writer, the representative of the opinions of the French school on such matters, condemned them partly as unjust to the innocent survivors, partly as incapable of deterring any man who was resolved upon the act. Even in 1749, in the full blaze of the philosophic movement, we find a suicide named Portier dragged through the streets of Paris with his face to the ground, hung from a gallows by his feet, and then thrown into the sewers;[2] and the laws were not abrogated till the Revolution, which, having founded so many other forms of freedom, accorded the liberty of death. Amid the dramatic vicissitudes, and the fierce enthusiasm of that

[1] In general, however, Voltaire was extremely opposed to the philosophy of despair, but he certainly approved of some forms of suicide. See the articles 'Caton' and 'Suicide,' in his *Dict. philos.*

[2] Lisle, *Du Suicide*, pp. 411–412.

period of convulsions, suicides immediately multiplied. 'The world,' it was said, had been 'empty since the Romans.'[1] For a brief period, and in this one country, the action of Christianity appeared suspended. Men seemed to be transported again into the age of Paganism, and the suicides, though more theatrical, were perpetrated with no less deliberation, and eulogised with no less enthusiasm than among the Stoics. But the tide of revolution passed away, and with some qualifications the old opinions resumed their authority. The laws against suicide were, indeed, for the most part abolished. In France and several other lands there exists no legislation on the subject. In other countries the law simply enjoins burial without religious ceremonies. In England, the burial in a highway and the mutilation by a stake were abolished under George IV.; but the monstrous injustice of confiscating to the Crown the entire property of the deliberate suicide still disgraces the statute-book, though the force of public opinion and the charitable perjury of juries render it inoperative. The common sentiment of Christendom has, however, ratified the judgment which the Christian teachers pronounced upon the act, though it has somewhat modified the severity of the old censure, and has abandoned some of the old arguments. It was reserved for Madame de Staël, who, in a youthful work upon the Passions, had commended suicide, to reconstruct this department of ethics, which had been somewhat disturbed by the Revolution, and she did so in a little treatise which is a model of calm, candid, and philosophic piety. Frankly abandoning the old theological notions that the deed was of the nature of murder, that it was the worst of crimes, and that it was always, or even generally, the offspring of cowardice; abandoning, too, all

[1] 'Le monde est vide depuis les Romains.'—St.-Just, *Procès de Danton.*

attempts to scare men by religious terrorism, she proceeded, not so much to meet in detail the isolated arguments of its defenders, as to sketch the ideal of a truly virtuous man, and to show how such a character would secure men against all temptation to suicide. In pages of the most tender beauty, she traced the influence of suffering in softening, purifying, and deepening the character, and showed how a frame of habitual and submissive resignation was not only the highest duty, but also the source of the purest consolation, and at the same time the appointed condition of moral amelioration. Having examined in detail the Biblical aspect of the question, she proceeded to show how the true measure of the dignity of man is his unselfishness. She contrasted the martyr with the suicide—the death which springs from devotion to duty with the death that springs from rebellion against circumstances. The suicide of Cato, which had been absurdly denounced by a crowd of ecclesiastics as an act of cowardice, and as absurdly alleged by many suicides as a justification for flying from pain or poverty, she represented as an act of martyrdom—a death like that of Curtius, accepted nobly for the benefit of Rome. The eye of the good man should be for ever fixed upon the interest of others. For them he should be prepared to relinquish life with all its blessings. For them he should be prepared to tolerate life, even when it seemed to him a curse.

Sentiments of this kind have, through the influence of Christianity, thoroughly pervaded European society, and suicide, in modern times, is almost always found to have sprung either from absolute insanity, from diseases which, though not amounting to insanity, are yet sufficient to discolour our judgments, or from that last excess of sorrow, when resignation and hope are both extinct. Considering it in this light, I know few things more fitted to qualify the optimism we so often hear, than the fact that statistics show it to be rapidly increasing, and to be peculiarly characteristic of those nations which rank most high in intellectual development and in general civilisation.[1] In one or two countries, strong religious feeling has counteracted the tendency, but the comparison of town and country, of different countries, of different provinces of the same country, and of different periods in history, proves conclusively its reality. Many reasons may be alleged to explain it. Mental occupations are peculiarly fitted to produce insanity,[2] and the blaze of publicity, which in modern times encircles an act of suicide, to draw weak minds to its imitation. It is probable, too, if we put aside the condition of absolutely savage life, a highly developed civilisation, while it raises the average of well-being, is accompanied by more extreme misery and acute sufferings than the simpler stages that had preceded it. Nomadic habits, the vast agglomeration of men in cities, the pressure of a fierce competition, and the sudden fluctuations to which manufactures are peculiarly liable, are the conditions of great prosperity, but also the causes of the most profound misery. Civilisation makes many of what once were superfluities, necessaries of life, so that their loss inflicts a pang long after their possession had ceased to be a pleasure. It also, by softening the character, renders it peculiarly sensitive to

[1] This fact has been often noticed. The reader may find many statistics on the subject in Lisle, *Du Suicide,* and Winslow's *Anatomy of Suicide.*

[2] 'There seems good reason to believe, that with the progress of mental development through the ages, there is, as in the case with other forms of organic development, a correlative degeneration going on, and that an increase of insanity is a penalty which an increase of our present civilisation necessarily pays.'—Maudsley's *Physiology of Mind,* p. 201.

pain, and it brings with it a long train of antipathies, passions, and diseased imaginations, which rarely or never cross the thoughts or torture the nerves of the simple peasant. The advance of religious scepticism, and the relaxation of religious discipline, have weakened and sometimes destroyed the horror of suicide and the habits of self-assertion; the eager and restless ambitions which political liberty, intellectual activity, and manufacturing enterprise, all in their different ways, conspire to foster, while they are the very principles and conditions of the progress of our age, render the virtue of content in all its forms extremely rare, and are peculiarly unpropitious to the formation of that spirit of humble and submissive resignation which alone can mitigate the agony of hopeless suffering.

From examining the effect of Christianity in promoting a sense of the sanctity of human life, we may now pass to an adjoining field, and examine its influence in promoting a fraternal and philanthropic sentiment among mankind. And first of all we may notice its effects upon slavery.

The reader will remember the general position this institution occupied in the eyes of the Stoic moralists, and under the legislation which they had in a great measure inspired. The legitimacy of slavery was fully recognised; but Seneca and other moralists had asserted, in the very strongest terms, the natural equality of mankind, the superficial character of the differences between the slave and his master, and the duty of the most scrupulous humanity to the former. Instances of a very warm sympathy between master and slave were of frequent occurrence; but they may unfortunately be paralleled by not a few examples of the most atrocious cruelty. To guard against such cruelty, a long series of enactments, based avowedly upon the Stoical principle of the essential equality of mankind, had been made under Hadrian, the Antonines, and Alexander Severus. Not to recapitulate at length what has been mentioned in a former chapter, it is sufficient to remind the reader that the right of life and death had been definitely withdrawn from the master, and that the murder of a slave was stigmatised and punished by the law. It had, however, been laid down by the great lawyer Paul, that homicide implies an intention to kill, and that therefore the master was not guilty of that crime if his slave died under chastisement which was not administered with this intention. But the licence of punishment which this decision might give was checked by laws which forbade excessive cruelty to slaves, provided that, when it was proved, they should be sold to another master, suppressed the private prisons in which they had been immured, and appointed special officers to receive their complaints.

In the field of legislation, for about two hundred years after the conversion of Constantine, the progress was extremely slight. The Christian emperors, in A.D. 319 and 326, adverted in two elaborate laws to the subject of the murder of slaves,[1] but beyond reiterating in very emphatic terms the previous enactments, it is not easy to see in what way they improved the condition of the class.[2] They provided that any master who applied to his slave certain atrocious tortures, that are enumerated, with the object of killing him, should be deemed a homicide, but

[1] *Cod. Theod.* lib. ix. tit. 12.

[2] Some commentators imagine (see Muratori, *Antich. Ital.* Diss. xiv.) that among the Pagans the murder of a man's own slave was only assimilated to the crime of murdering the slave of another man, while in the Christian law it was defined as homicide, equivalent to the murder of a freeman. I confess, however, this point does not appear to me at all clear.

if the slave died under moderate punishment, or under any punishment not intended to kill him, the master should be blameless; no charge whatever, it was emphatically said, should be brought against him. It has been supposed, though I think without evidence, by commentators[1] that this law accorded immunity to the master only when the slave perished under the application of 'appropriate' or servile punishments—that is to say, scourging, irons, or imprisonment; but the use of torture not intended to kill was in no degree restricted, nor is there anything in the law to make it appear either that the master was liable to punishment, if contrary to his intention his slave succumbed beneath torture, or that Constantine proposed any penalty for excessive cruelty short of death. It is perhaps not out of place to remark, that this law was in remarkable harmony with the well-known article of the Jewish code, which provided that if a slave, wounded to death by his master, linger for a day or two, the master should not be punished, for the slave was his money.[2]

The two features that were most revolting in the slave system, as it passed from the Pagan to the Christian emperors, were the absolute want of legal recognition of slave marriage, and the licence for torturing still conceded to the master. The Christian emperors before Justinian took no serious steps to remedy either of these evils, and the measures that were taken against adultery still continued inapplicable to slave unions, because 'the vileness of their condition makes them unworthy of the observation of the law.'[3] The abolition of the punish-

[1] See Godefroy's *Commentary* on these laws. [2] Exodus xxi. 21.

[3] 'Quas vilitates vitæ dignas legum observatione non credidit.'—*Cod. Theod.* lib. ix. tit. 7. See on this law, Wallon, tome iii. pp. 417, 418.

Dean Milman observes, 'In the old Roman society in the Eastern empire this distinction between the marriage of the freeman and the con-ment of crucifixion had, however, a special value to the slave class, and a very merciful law of Constantine forbade the separation of the families of the slaves.[1] Another law, which in its effects was perhaps still more important, imparted a sacred character to manumission, ordaining that the ceremony should be celebrated in the Church,[2] and permitted it on Sundays. Some measures were also taken, providing for the freedom of the Christian slaves of Jewish masters, and, in two or three cases, freedom was offered as a bribe to slaves, to induce them to inform against criminals. Intermarriage between the free and slave classes was still strictly forbidden, and if a free woman had improper intercourse with her slave, Constantine ordered that the woman should be executed and the slave burnt alive.[3] By the Pagan law, the woman had been simply reduced to slavery. The laws against fugitive slaves were also rendered more severe.[4]

This legislation may on the whole be looked upon as a progress, but it certainly does not deserve the enthusiasm which ecclesiastical writers have sometimes bestowed upon it. For about two hundred years, there was an almost absolute pause in the legislation on this subject. Some slight restrictions were, however, imposed upon the use of torture in trials; some slight additional facilities of manumission were given, and some very atrocious enactments made to prevent slaves accusing their masters. According to that of Gratian, any slave who accused his

cubinage of the slave was long recognised by Christianity itself. These unions were not blessed, as the marriages of their superiors had soon begun to be, by the Church. Basil the Macedonian (A.D. 867–886) first enacted that the priestly benediction should hallow the marriage of the slave; but the authority of the emperor was counteracted by the deep-rooted prejudices of centuries.'—*Hist. of Latin Christianity*, vol. ii. p. 15.

[1] *Cod. Theod.* lib. ii. tit. 25.

[2] Ibid. lib. iv. tit. 7.

[3] Ibid. lib. ix. tit. 9.

[4] *Corpus Juris*, vi. 1.

master of any offence, except high treason, should immediately be burnt alive, without any investigation of the justice of the charge.[1]

Under Justinian, however, new and very important measures were taken. In no other sphere were the laws of this emperor so indisputably an advance upon those of his predecessors. The measures of Justinian may be comprised under three heads. In the first place, all the restrictions upon enfranchisement which had accumulated under the Pagan legislation were abolished; the legislator proclaimed in emphatic language, and by the provisions of many laws, his desire to encourage manumission, and free scope was thus given to the action of the Church. In the second place, the freedmen, or intermediate class between the slave and the citizen, were virtually abolished, all or nearly all the privileges accorded to the citizen being granted to the emancipated slave. This was the most important contribution of the Christian emperors to that great amalgamation of nations and classes which had been advancing since the days of Augustus, and one of its effects was, that any person, even of senatorial rank, might marry a slave when he had first emancipated her. In the third place, a slave was permitted to marry a free woman with the authorisation of the master of the former, and children born in slavery became the legal heirs of their emancipated father. The rape of a slave woman was also in this reign punished like that of a free woman, by death.[2]

But, important as were these measures, it is not in the field of legislation that we must chiefly look for the influence of Christianity upon slavery. This influence was indeed very great, but it is necessary carefully to define its nature. The prohibition of all slavery, which was one

[1] *Cod. Theod.* lib. vi. tit. 2.

[2] See on all this legislation, Wallon, tome iii.; Champagny, *Charité chrétienne*, pp. 214–224.

of the peculiarities of the Jewish Essenes, and the elligitimacy of hereditary slavery, which was one of the speculations of the Stoic Dion Chrysostom, had no place in the ecclesiastical teaching. Slavery was distinctly and formally recognised by Christianity,[1] and no religion ever laboured more to encourage a habit of docility and passive obedience. Much was indeed said by the Fathers about the natural equality of mankind, about the duty of regarding slaves as brothers or companions, and about the heinousness of cruelty to them; but all this had been said with at least equal force, though it had not been disseminated over an equally wide area, by Seneca and Epictetus, and the principle of the original freedom of all men was repeatedly averred by the Pagan lawyers. The services of Christianity in this sphere were of three kinds. It supplied a new order of relations, in which the distinction of classes was unknown. It imparted a moral dignity to the servile classes, and it gave an unexampled impetus to the movement of enfranchisement.

The first of these services was effected by the Church ceremonies and the penitential discipline. In these spheres, from which the Christian mind derived its earliest, its deepest, and its most enduring impressions, the difference between the master and his slave was unknown. They received the sacred elements together, they sat side by side at the agape, they mingled in the public prayers. In the penal system of the Church, the distinction between wrongs done to a freeman, and wrongs done to a slave, which lay at the very root of the whole civil legislation, was repudiated. At a time when, by the civil law,

[1] It is worthy of notice, too, that the justice of slavery was frequently based by the Fathers, as by modern defenders of slavery, on the curse of Ham. See a number of passages noticed by Moehler, *Le Christianisme et l'Esclavage* (trad. franç.), pp. 151–152.

a master, whose slave died as a consequence of excessive scourging, was absolutely unpunished, the Council of Illiberis excluded that master for ever from the communion.[1] The chastity of female slaves, for the protection of which the civil law made but little provision, was sedulously guarded by the legislation of the Church. Slave birth, moreover, was no disqualification for entering into the priesthood, and an emancipated slave, regarded as the dispenser of spiritual life and death, often saw the greatest and the most wealthy kneeling humbly at his feet, imploring his absolution or his benediction.[2]

In the next place, Christianity imparted a moral dignity to the servile class. It did this not only by associating poverty and labour with that monastic life which was so profoundly revered, but also by introducing new modifications into the ideal type of morals. There is no fact more prominent in the Roman writers than the profound contempt with which they regarded slaves, not so much on account of their position, as on account of the character which that position had formed. A servile character was a synonym for vice. Cicero had declared that nothing great or noble could exist in a slave, and the plays of Plautus exhibit the same estimate in every scene. There were, it is true, some exceptions. Epictetus had

[1] The penalty, however, appears to have been reduced to two years' exclusion from communion. Muratori says, 'In più consili si truova decretato, "excommunicatione vel pœnitentiæ biennii esse subjiciendum qui servum proprium sine conscientia judicis occiderit."'—*Antich. Ital.* Diss. xiv.

Besides the works which treat generally of the penitential discipline, the reader may consult with fruit Wright's letter *On the Political Condition of the English Peasantry*, and Moehler, p. 186.

[2] On the great multitude of emancipated slaves who entered, and at one time almost monopolised, the ecclesiastical offices, compare Moehler, *Le Christianisme et l'Esclavage*, pp. 177–178. Leo the Great tried to prevent slaves being raised to the priestly office, because it would degrade the latter.

not only been, but had been recognised as one of the noblest characters of Rome. The fidelity of slaves to their masters had been frequently extolled, and Seneca in this, as in other respects, had been the defender of the oppressed. Still, there can be no doubt that this contempt was general, and also that in the Pagan world it was to a great extent just. Every age has its own moral ideal, to which all virtuous men aspire. Every sphere of life has also a tendency to produce a distinctive type being specially favourable to some particular class of virtues, and specially unfavourable to others. The popular estimate, and even the real moral condition, of each class depends chiefly upon the degree in which the type of character its position naturally developes coincides with the ideal type of the age. Now, if we remember that magnanimity, self-reliance, dignity, independence, and, in a word, elevation of character, constituted the Roman ideal of perfection, it will appear evident that this was pre-eminently the type of freemen, and that the condition of slavery was in the very highest degree unfavourable to its development. Christianity for the first time gave the servile virtues the foremost place in the moral type. Humility, obedience, gentleness, patience, resignation, are all cardinal or rudimentary virtues in the Christian character; they were all neglected or underrated by the Pagans, they can all expand and flourish in a servile position.

The influence of Christianity upon slavery, by inclining the moral type to the servile classes, though less obvious and less discussed than some others, is, I believe, in the very highest degree important. There is, I imagine, scarcely any other single circumstance that exercises so profound an influence upon the social and political relations of a religion, as the class type with which it can most readily assimilate; or, in other words, the group or variety of virtues to which it gives the foremost place. The virtues that are most suited to the servile position were in general so little honoured by antiquity, that they were not even cultivated in their appropriate sphere. The aspirations of good men were in a different direction. The virtue of the Stoic, which rose triumphantly under adversity, nearly always withered under degradation. For the first time, under the influence of Christianity, a great moral movement passed through the servile class. The multitude of slaves who embraced the new faith was one of the reproaches of the Pagans, and the names of Blandina, Potamiæna, Eutyches, Victorinus, and Nereus show how fully they shared in the sufferings and in the glory of martyrdom.[1] The first and grandest edifice of Byzantine architecture in Italy—the noble church of St. Vital, at Ravenna—was dedicated by Justinian to the memory of a martyred slave.

While Christianity thus broke down the contempt with which the master had regarded his slaves, and planted among the latter a principle of moral regeneration which expanded in no other sphere with an equal perfection, its action in procuring the freedom of the slave was unceasing. The law of Constantine, which placed the ceremony under the superintendence of the clergy, and the many laws that gave special facilities of manumission to those who desired to enter the monasteries or the priesthood, symbolised the religious character the act had assumed. It was celebrated on Church festivals, especially on Easter, and although it was not proclaimed a matter of duty or necessity, it was always regarded as one of the most acceptable modes of expiating past sins. St. Melania was

[1] See a most admirable dissertation on this subject in Le Blant, *Inscriptions chrétiennes de la Gaule*, tome ii. pp. 284–299; Gibbon's *Decline and Fall*, ch. xxxviii.

said to have emancipated 8,000 slaves, St. Ovidius, a rich martyr of Gaul, 5,000, Chromatius, a Roman prefect under Diocletian, 1,400, Hermes, a prefect in the reign of Trajan, 1,250,[1] Pope St. Gregory, and many of the clergy at Hippo, under the rule of St. Augustine, and great numbers of private individuals, freed their slaves as an act of piety.[2] It became customary to do so on occasions of national or personal thanskgiving, on recovery from sickness, on the birth of a child, at the hour of death, and above all, in testamentary bequests.[3] Numerous charters and epitaphs still record the gift of liberty to slaves throughout the middle ages, 'for the benefit of the soul' of the donor or testator. In the thirteenth century, when there were no slaves to emancipate in France, it was usual in many churches to release caged pigeons on the ecclesiastical festivals, in memory of the ancient charity, and that prisoners might still be freed in the name of Christ.[4]

Slavery, however, lasted in Europe for about 800 years after Constantine, and during the period with which alone this volume is concerned, although its character was mitigated, the number of men who were subject to it was probably greater than in the Pagan Empire. In the West the barbarian conquests modified the conditions of labour in

[1] Champagny, *Charité chrétienne*, p. 210. These numbers are no doubt exaggerated; see Wallon, *Hist. de l'Esclavage*, tome iii. p. 38.

[2] See Schmidt, *La Société civile dans le Monde romain*, pp. 246-248.

[3] Muratori has devoted two valuable dissertations (*Antich. Ital.* xiv. xv.) to mediæval slavery.

[4] Ozanam's *Hist. of Civilisation in the Fifth Century* (Eng. trans.), vol. ii. p. 43. St. Adelbert, Archbishop of Prague at the end of the tenth century, was especially famous for his opposition to the slave trade. In Sweden, the abolition of slavery in the thirteenth century was avowedly accomplished in obedience to Christian principles. (Moehler, *Le Christianisme et l'Esclavage*, pp. 194-196; Ryan's *History of the Effects of Religion upon Mankind*, pp. 142-143.)

two directions. The cessation of the stream of barbarian captives, the empoverishment of great families, who had been surrounded by vast retinues of slaves, the general diminution of town life, and the barbarian habits of personal independence, checked the old form of slavery, while the misery and the precarious condition of the free peasants induced them in great numbers to barter their liberty for protection to the neighbouring lord.[1] In the East, the destruction of great fortunes through excessive taxation diminished the number of superfluous slaves, and the fiscal system of the Byzantine Empire, by which agricultural slaves were taxed according to their employments,[2] as well as the desire of emperors to encourage agriculture, led the legislators to attach the slaves permanently to the soil. In the course of time, almost the entire free peasantry, and the greater number of the old slaves, had sunk or risen into the qualified slavery called serfdom, which formed the basis of the great edifice of feudalism. Towards the end of the eighth century, the sale of slaves beyond their native provinces was in most countries prohibited.[3] The creation of the free cities of Italy, the custom of emancipating slaves who were enrolled in the army, and economical changes which made free labour more profitable than slave labour, conspired with religious motives in effecting the ultimate freedom of labour. The practice of manumitting, as an

[1] Salvian, in a famous passage (*De Gubernatione Dei*, lib. v.), notices the multitudes of poor who voluntarily became 'coloni' for the sake of protection and a livelihood. The coloni who were attached to the soil were much the same as the mediæval serfs. We have already noticed them coming into being apparently when the Roman emperors settled barbarian prisoners to cultivate the desert lands of Italy; and before the barbarian invasions their numbers seem to have much increased. M. Guizot has devoted two chapters to this subject. (*Hist. de la Civilisation en France*, vii. viii.)

[2] See Finlay's *Hist. of Greece*, vol. i. p. 241.

[3] Moehler, p. 181.

act of devotion, continued to the end; but the ecclesiastics, probably through the feeling that they had no right to alienate corporate property, in which they had only a life interest, were among the last to follow the counsels they so liberally bestowed upon the laity.[1] In the twelfth century, however, slaves in Europe were very rare. In the fourteenth century, slavery was almost unknown.[2]

Closely connected with the influence of the Church in destroying hereditary slavery, was its influence in redeeming captives from servitude. In no other form of charity was its beneficial character more continually and more splendidly displayed. During the long and dreary trials of the barbarian invasions, when the whole structure of society was dislocated, when vast districts and mighty cities were in a few months almost depopulated, and when the flower of the youth of Italy were mowed down by the sword or carried away into captivity, the bishops never desisted from their efforts to alleviate the sufferings of the prisoners. St. Ambrose, disregarding the outcries of the Arians, who denounced his act as atrocious sacrilege, sold the rich church ornaments of Milan to rescue some captives who had fallen into the hands of the Goths, and this practice—which was afterwards formally sanctioned by St. Gregory the Great—became speedily general. When the Roman army had captured, but refused to sup-

[1] 'Non v' era anticamente signor secolare, vescovo, abbate, capitolo di canonici e monastero che non avesse al suo servigio molti servi. Molto frequentemente solevano i secolari manometterli. Non così le chiese, e i monasteri, non per altra cagione, a mio credere, se non perchè la manumissione è una spezie di alienazione, ed era dai canoni proibito l' alienare i beni delle chiese.'—Muratori, *Dissert.* xv. Some Councils, however, recognised the right of bishops to emancipate church slaves. Moehler, *Le Christianisme et l'Esclavage*, p. 187. Many peasants placed themselves under the dominion of the monks, as being the best masters, and also to obtain the benefit of their prayers.

[2] Muratori; Hallam's *Middle Ages*, ch. ii. part ii.

port, seven thousand Persian prisoners, Acacius, Bishop of Amida, undeterred by the bitter hostility of the Persians to Christianity, and declaring that 'God had no need of plates or dishes,' sold all the rich church ornaments of his diocese, rescued the unbelieving prisoners, and sent them back unharmed to their king. During the horrors of the Vandal invasion, Deogratias, Bishop of Carthage, took a similar step to ransom the Roman prisoners. St. Augustine, St. Gregory the Great, St. Cæsarius of Arles, St. Exuperius of Toulouse, St. Hilary, St. Remi, all melted down or sold their church vases to free prisoners. St. Cyprian sent a large sum for the same purpose to the Bishop of Nicomedia. St. Epiphanius and St. Avitus, in conjunction with a rich Gaulish lady named Syagria, are said to have rescued thousands. St. Eloi devoted to this object his entire fortune. St. Paulinus of Nola displayed a similar generosity, and the legends even assert, though untruly, that he, like St. Peter Teleonarius and St. Serapion, having exhausted all other forms of charity, as a last gift sold himself for slavery. When, long afterwards, the Mahommedan conquests in a measure reproduced the calamities of the barbarian invasions, the same unwearied charity was displayed. The Trinitarian monks, founded by John of Matha in the twelfth century, were devoted to the release of Christian captives, and another society was founded with the same object by Peter Nolasco, in the following century.[1]

The different branches of the subject I am examining are so closely intertwined, that it is difficult to investigate one without in a measure anticipating the others. While discussing the influence of the Church in protecting

[1] See on this subject, Ryan, pp. 151–152; Cibrario, *Economica politica del Medio Evo,* lib. iii. cap. ii., and especially Le Blant, *Inscriptions chrétiennes de la Gaule,* tome ii. pp. 284–299.

infancy, in raising the estimate of human life, and in alleviating slavery, I have trenched largely upon the last application of the doctrine of Christian fraternity I must examine—I mean the foundation of charity. The difference between Pagan and Christian societies in this matter is very profound; but a great part of it must be ascribed to causes other than religious opinions. Charity finds an extended scope for action only where there exists a large class of men at once independent and impoverished. In the ancient societies slavery in a great measure replaced pauperism, and by securing the subsistence of a very large proportion of the poor, contracted the sphere of charity. And what slavery did at Rome for the very poor, the system of clientage did for those of a somewhat higher rank. The existence of these two institutions is sufficient to show the injustice of judging the two societies by a simple comparison of their charitable institutions, and we must also remember that among the ancients the relief of the indigent was one of the most important functions of the State. Not to dwell upon the many measures taken with this object in ancient Greece, in considering the condition of the Roman poor, we are at once met by the simple fact that for several centuries the immense majority of these were habitually supported by gratuitous distributions of corn. In a very early period of Roman history we find occasional instances of distribution; but it was not till A.U.C. 630, that Caius Gracchus caused a law to be made, supplying the poorer classes with corn at a price that was little more than nominal; and although two years after the Patricians succeeded in revoking this law, it was after several fluctuations finally re-enacted in A.U.C. 679. The Cassia-Terentia law, as it was called, from the consuls under whom it was at last established, was largely extended in its operation, or, as some think, revived from neglect in A.U.C. 691, by Cato of Utica, who desired by this means to divert popularity from the cause of Cæsar, under whom multitudes of the poor were enrolling themselves. Four years later, Clodius Pulcher, abolishing the small payment which had been demanded, made the distribution entirely gratuitous. It took place once a month, and consisted of five modii[1] a head. In the time of Julius Cæsar no less than 320,000 persons were inscribed as recipients; but Cæsar reduced the number by one half. Under Augustus it had risen to 200,000. This emperor desired to restrict the distribution of corn to three or four times a year, but, yielding to the popular wish, he at last consented that it should continue monthly. It soon became the leading fact of Roman life. Numerous officers were appointed to provide for it. A severe legislation controlled their acts, and, to secure a regular and abundant supply of corn for the capital became the principal object of the provincial governors. Under the Antonines the number of the recipients had considerably increased, having sometimes, it is said, exceeded 500,000. Septimus Severus added to the corn a ration of oil. Aurelian replaced the monthly distribution of unground corn by a daily distribution of bread, and added, moreover, a portion of pork. Gratuitous distributions were afterwards extended to Constantinople, Alexandria, and Antioch, and were probably not altogether unknown in smaller towns.[2]

We have already seen that this gratuitous distribu-

[1] About $\frac{5}{6}$ths of a bushel. See Hume's *Essay on the Populousness of Ancient Nations.*

[2] The history of these distributions is traced with admirable learning by M. Naudet in his *Mémoire sur les Secours publics dans l'Antiquité* (*Mém. de l'Académie des Inscrip. et Belles-lettres*, tome xiii.), an essay to which I am much indebted. See, too, Monnier, *Hist. de l'Assistance publique*; B. Dumas, *Des Secours publics chez les Anciens*; and Schmidt, *Essai sur la Société civile dans le Monde romain et sur sa Transformation par le Christianisme.*

tion of corn ranked, with the institution of slavery and the gladiatorial exhibitions, as one of the chief demoralising influences of the empire. The most injudicious charity, however pernicious to the classes it is intended to relieve, has commonly a beneficial and softening influence upon the donor, and through him upon society at large. But the Roman distribution of corn being merely a political device, had no humanising influence upon the people, while, being regulated simply by the indigence, and not at all by the infirmities or character of the recipient, it was a direct and overwhelming encouragement to idleness. With a provision of the necessities of life, and with an abundant supply of amusements, the poor Romans readily gave up honourable labour, all trades in the city languished, every interruption in the distribution of corn was followed by fearful sufferings, free gifts of land were often insufficient to divert the citizens to honest labour, and the multiplication of children, which rendered the public relief inadequate, was checked by abortion, exposition, or infanticide.

When we remember that the population of Rome probably never exceeded a million and a half, that a large proportion of indigent were provided for as slaves, and that more than 200,000 freemen were habitually supplied with the first necessary of life, we cannot, I think, charge the Pagan society of the metropolis, at least, with an excessive parsimony in relieving poverty. But besides the distribution of corn, several other measures were taken. Salt, which was very largely used by the Roman poor, had during the republic been made a monopoly of the State, and was sold by it at a price that was little more than nominal.[1] The distribution of land, which was the subject of the agrarian laws, was under a new

[1] Livy, ii. 9; Pliny, *Hist. Nat.* xxxi. 41.

form practised by Julius Cæsar,[1] Nerva,[2] and Septimus Severus,[3] who bought land to divide it among the poor citizens. Large legacies were left to the people by Julius Cæsar, Augustus, and others, and considerable, though irregular, donations made on occasions of great rejoicings. Numerous public baths were established, to which, when they were not absolutely gratuitous, the smallest coin in use gave admission, and which were in consequence habitually employed by the poor. Vespasian instituted, and the Antonines extended, a system of popular education, and the movement I have already noticed, for the support of the children of poor parents, acquired very considerable dimensions. The first trace of it at Rome may be found under Augustus, who gave money and corn for the support of young children, who had previously not been included in the public distributions.[4] This appears, however, to have been but an act of isolated benevolence, and the honour of first instituting a systematic effort in this direction belongs to Nerva, who enjoined the support of poor children, not only in Rome, but in all the cities of Italy.[5] Trajan greatly extended the system. In his reign 5,000 poor children were supported by the Government in Rome alone,[6] and similar measures, though we know not on what scale, were taken in the other Italian and even African cities. At the little town of Velleia, we find a charity instituted by Trajan, for the partial

[1] Dion Cassius, xxxviii. 1–7.

[2] Xiphilin, lxviii. 2; Pliny, *Ep.* vii. 31.

[3] Spartian. *Sept. Severus.*

[4] Suet. *August.* 41; Dion Cassius, li. 21.

[5] 'Afflictos civitatis relevavit; puellas puerosque natos parentibus egestosis sumptu publico per Italiæ oppida ali jussit.'—Sext. Aurelius Victor, *Epitome*, 'Nerva.' This measure of Nerva, though not mentioned by any other writer, is confirmed by the evidence of medals. (Naudet, p. 75.)

[6] Plin. *Panegyr.* xxvi. xxviii.

support of 270 children.[1] Private benevolence followed in the same direction, and several inscriptions which still remain, though they do not enable us to write its history, sufficiently attest its activity. The younger Pliny, besides warmly encouraging schools, devoted a small property to the support of poor children in his native city of Como.[2] The name of Cælia Macrina is preserved as the foundress of a charity for 100 children at Terracina.[3] Hadrian increased the supplies of corn allotted to these charities, and he was also distinguished for his bounty to poor women.[4] Antoninus was accustomed to lend money to the poor at four per cent., which was much below the normal rate of interest,[5] and both he and Marcus Aurelius dedicated to the memory of their wives institutions for the support of girls.[6] Alexander Severus in like manner dedicated an institution for the support of children to the memory of his mother.[7] Public hospitals were probably unknown before Christianity; but there were private infirmaries for slaves, and also, it is believed, military hospitals.[8] Provincial towns were occasionally assisted by the Government in seasons of great distress, and there are some recorded instances of private legacies for their benefit.[9]

These various measures are by no means inconsiderable, and it is not unreasonable to suppose that many similar

[1] We know of this charity from an extant bronze tablet. See Schmidt, *Essai historique sur la Société romaine*, p. 428.

[2] Plin. *Ep.* i. 8; iv. 13.

[3] Schmidt, p. 428.

[4] Spartianus, *Hadrian.*

[5] Capitolinus, *Antoninus.*

[6] Capitolinus, *Anton.*, *Marc. Aurel.*

[7] Lampridius, *A. Severus.*

[8] Seneca (*De Ira*, lib. 1, cap. 16) speaks of institutions called valetudinaria, which most writers think were private infirmaries in rich men's houses. The opinion that the Romans had public hospitals is maintained in a very learned and valuable, but little-known work, called *Collections relative to the Systematic Relief of the Poor.* (London, 1815.)

[9] See Tacit. *Annal.* xii. 58; Pliny, v. 7; x. 79.

steps were taken, of which all record has been lost. The history of charity presents so few salient features, so little that can strike the imagination or arrest the attention, that it is usually almost wholly neglected by historians; and it is easy to conceive what inadequate notions of our existing charities could be gleaned from the casual allusions in plays or poems, in political histories or court memoirs. There can, however, be no question that neither in practice nor in theory, neither in the institutions that were founded nor in the place that was assigned to it in the scale of duties, did charity in antiquity occupy a position at all comparable to that which it has obtained by Christianity. Nearly all relief was a State measure, dictated much more by policy than by benevolence, and the habit of selling young children, the innumerable expositions, the readiness of the poor to enroll themselves as gladiators, and the frequent famines, show how large was the measure of unrelieved distress. A very few Pagan examples of charity have, indeed, descended to us. Among the Greeks, Epaminondas was accustomed to ransom captives and collect dowers for poor girls;[1] Cimon, to feed the hungry and clothe the naked;[2] Bias, to purchase, emancipate, and furnish with dowers the captive girls of Messina.[3] Tacitus has described with enthusiasm how, after a catastrophe near Rome, the rich threw open their houses and taxed all their resources to relieve the sufferers.[4] There existed, too, among the poor, both of Greece and Rome, mutual insurance societies, which undertook to provide for their sick and infirm members.[5] The very frequent reference

[1] Cornelius Nepos, *Epaminondas*, cap. 3.

[2] Lactantius, *Div. Inst.* vi. 9.

[3] Diog. Laërt. *Bias.*

[4] Tac. *Annal.* iv. 63.

[5] See Pliny, *Ep.* x. 94, and the remarks of Naudet, pp. 38–39.

to mendicancy in the Latin writers show that beggars, and therefore those who relieved beggars, were numerous. The duty of hospitality was also strongly enjoined, and was placed under the special protection of the supreme Deity. But the active, habitual, and detailed charity of private persons, which is so conspicuous a feature in all Christian societies, was scarcely known in antiquity, and there are not more than two or three moralists who have even noticed it. Of these, the chief rank belongs to Cicero, who devoted two very judicious but somewhat cold chapters to the subject. Nothing, he said, is more suitable to the nature of man than beneficence and liberality, but there are many cautions to be urged in practising it. We must take care that our bounty is a real blessing to the person we relieve; that it does not exceed our own means; that it is not, as was the case with Sylla and Cæsar, derived from the spoliation of others; that it springs from the heart and not from ostentation; that the claims of gratitude are preferred to the mere impulses of compassion, and that due regard is paid both to the character and to the wants of the recipient.[1]

Christianity for the first time made charity a rudimentary virtue, giving it the foremost place in the moral type, and in the exhortations of its teachers. Besides its general influence in stimulating the affections, it effected a complete revolution in this sphere, by representing the poor as the special representatives of the Christian Founder, and thus making the love of Christ rather than the love of man the principle of charity. Even in the days of persecution, collections for the relief of the poor were made at the Sunday meetings. The Agapæ or feasts of love were intended mainly for the poor, and food

[1] *De Offic.* i. 14–15.

that was saved by the fasts was devoted to their benefit. A vast organisation of charity, presided over by the bishops, and actively directed by the deacons, soon ramified over Christendom, till the bond of charity became the bond of unity, and the most distant sections of the Christian Church corresponded by the interchange of mercy. Long before the era of Constantine, it was observed that the charities of the Christians were so extensive—it may, perhaps, be said so excessive—that they drew very many impostors to the Church,[1] and when the victory of Christianity was achieved, the enthusiasm for charity displayed itself in the erection of numerous institutions that were altogether unknown to the Pagan world.

A Roman lady, named Fabiola, in the fourth century, founded at Rome, as an act of penance, the first public hospital, and the charity planted by that woman's hand overspread the world, and will alleviate, to the end of time, the darkest anguish of humanity. Another hospital was soon after founded by St. Pammachus; another of great celebrity by St. Basil, at Cæsarea. St. Basil also erected at Cæsarea what was probably the first asylum for lepers. Xenodochia, or refuges for strangers, speedily rose, especially along the paths of the pilgrims. St. Pammachus founded one at Ostia; Paula and Melania founded others at Jerusalem. The Council of Nice ordered that one should

[1] Lucian describes this in his famous picture of Peregrinus, and Julian, much later, accused the Christians of drawing men into the Church by their charities. Socrates (*Hist. Eccl.* vii. 17) tells a story of a Jew who, pretending to be a convert to Christianity, had been often baptised in different sects, and who had amassed a considerable fortune by the gifts he received on those occasions. He was at last miraculously detected by the Novatian bishop Paul. There are several instances in the *Lives of the Saints* of judgments falling on those who duped benevolent Christians.

be erected in every city. In the time of St. Chrysostom the church of Antioch supported 3,000 widows and virgins, besides strangers and sick. Legacies for the poor became common, and it was not unfrequent for men and women who desired to live a life of peculiar sanctity, and especially for priests who attained the episcopacy, as a first act to bestow their entire properties in charity. Even the early Oriental monks, who for the most part were extremely removed from the active and social virtues, supplied many noble examples of charity. St. Ephrem, in a time of pestilence, emerged from his solitude to found and superintend a hospital at Edessa. A monk named Thalasius collected blind beggars in an asylum on the banks of the Euphrates. A merchant named Apollonius founded on Mount Nitria a gratuitous dispensary for the monks. The monks often assisted by their labours provinces that were suffering from pestilence or famine. We may trace the remains of the pure socialism that marked the first phase of the Christian community in the emphatic language with which some of the Fathers proclaimed charity to be a matter not of mercy but of justice, maintaining that all property is based on usurpation, that the earth by right is common to all men, and that no man can claim a superabundant supply of its goods except as an administrator for others. A Christian, it was maintained, should devote at least one-tenth of his profits to the poor.[1]

[1] See on this subject Chastel, *Études historiques sur la Charité* (Paris, 1853); Martin Doisy, *Hist. de la Charité pendant les quatre premiers Siècles* (Paris, 1848); Champagny, *Charité chrétienne*; Tollemer, *Origines de la Charité catholique* (Paris, 1863); Ryan, *History of the Effects of Religion upon Mankind* (Dublin, 1820); and the works of Bingham and of Cave. I am also indebted, in this part of my subject, to Dean Milman's histories, Neander's *Ecclesiastical History*, and *Private Life of the Early Christians*, and to Migne's *Encyclopédie*.

The enthusiasm of charity, thus manifested in the Church, speedily attracted the attention of the Pagans. The ridicule of Lucian, and the vain efforts of Julian, to produce a rival system of charity within the limits of Paganism,[1] emphatically attested both its pre-eminence and its catholicity. During the pestilences that desolated Carthage in A.D. 326, and Alexandria in the reigns of Gallienus and of Maximian, while the Pagans fled panic-stricken from the contagion, the Christians extorted the admiration of their fellow-countrymen by the courage with which they rallied around their bishops, consoled the last hours of the sufferers, and buried the abandoned dead.[2] In the rapid increase of pauperism arising from the emancipation of numerous slaves, their charity found free scope for action, and its resources were soon taxed to the utmost by the horrors of the barbarian invasions. The conquest of Africa by Genseric, deprived Italy of the supply of corn upon which it almost wholly depended, arrested the gratuitous distribution by which the Roman poor were mainly supported, and produced all over the land the most appalling calamities.[3] The history of Italy became one monotonous tale of famine and pestilence, of starving populations and ruined cities. But everywhere

[1] See the famous epistle of Julian to Arsacius, where he declares that it is shameful that 'the Galileans should support not only their own, but also the heathen poor. Sozomen (*Hist. eccl.* v. 16), and the comments of the historian.

[2] The conduct of the Christians, on the first of these occasions, is described by Pontius, *Vit. Cypriani*, ix. 19. St. Cyprian organised their efforts. On the Alexandrian famines and pestilences, see Eusebius, *H. E.* vii. 22; ix. 8.

[3] The effects of this conquest have been well described by Sismondi, *Hist. de la Chute de l'Empire romain*, tome i. pp. 258–260. Theodoric afterwards made some efforts to re-establish the distribution, but it never regained its former proportions. The pictures of the starvation and depopulation of Italy at this time are appalling. Some fearful facts on the subject are collected by Gibbon, *Decline and Fall*, ch. xxxvi.; Chateaubriand, vime *Disc.* 2de partie.

amid this chaos of dissolution we may detect the majestic form of the Christian priest mediating between the hostile forces, straining every nerve to lighten the calamities around him. When the Imperial city was captured and plundered by the hosts of Alaric, a Christian church remained a secure sanctuary, which neither the passions nor the avarice of the Goths transgressed. When a fiercer than Alaric had marked out Rome for his prey, the Pope St. Leo, arrayed in his sacerdotal robes, confronted the victorious Hun, as the ambassador of his fellow-countrymen, and Attila, overpowered by religious awe, turned aside in his course. When, twelve years later, Rome lay at the mercy of Genseric, the same Pope interposed with the Vandal conqueror, and obtained from him a partial cessation of the massacre. The Archdeacon Pelagius interceded with similar humanity and similar success, when Rome had been captured by Totila. In Gaul, Troyes is said to have been saved from destruction by the influence of St. Lupus, and Orleans by the influence of St. Agnan. In Britain an invasion of the Picts was averted by St. Germain of Auxerrois. The relations of rulers to their subjects, and of tribunals to the poor, were modified by the same intervention. When Antioch was threatened with destruction on account of its rebellion against Theodosius, the anchorites poured forth from the neighbouring deserts to intercede with the ministers of the emperor, while the Archbishop Flavian went himself as a suppliant to Rome. St. Ambrose imposed public penance on Theodosius, on account of the massacre of Thessalonica. Synesius excommunicated for his oppressions a governor named Andronicus, and two French Councils, in the sixth century imposed the same penalty on all great men who arbitrarily ejected the poor. Special laws were found necessary to restrain the turbulent charity of some priests and monks, who impeded the course of justice, and even snatched criminals from the hands of the law.[1] St. Abraham, St. Epiphanius, and St. Basil are all said to have obtained the remission or reduction of oppressive imposts. To provide for the interests of widows and orphans was part of the official ecclesiastical duty, and a Council of Macon anathematised any ruler who brought them to trial without first apprising the bishop of the diocese. A Council of Toledo, in the fifth century, threatened with excommunication all who robbed priests, monks, or poor men, or refused to listen to their expostulations. One of the chief causes of the inordinate power acquired by the clergy was their mediatorial office, and their gigantic wealth was in a great degree due to the legacies of those who regarded them as the trustees of the poor. As time rolled on, charity assumed many forms, and every monastery became a centre from which it radiated. By the monks the nobles were overawed, the poor protected, the sick tended, travellers sheltered, prisoners ransomed, the remotest spheres of suffering explored. During the darkest period of the middle ages, monks founded a refuge for pilgrims amid the horrors of the Alpine snows. A solitary hermit often planted himself, with his little boat, by a bridgeless stream, and the charity of his life was to ferry over the traveller.[2] When the hideous disease of leprosy extended its ravages

[1] *Cod. Theod.* ix. xl. 15-16. The first of these laws was made by Theodosius, A.D. 392; the second by Honorius, A.D. 398.

[2] Cibrario, *Economica politica del Medio Evo*, lib. ii. cap. iii. The most remarkable of these saints was St. Julien l'Hospitalier, who, having under a mistake, killed his father and mother, as a penance became a ferryman of a great river, and, having embarked on a very stormy and dangerous night, at the voice of a traveller in distress, received Christ into his boat. His story is painted in a window of the thirteenth century, in Rouen Cathedral. See Langlois, *Essai historique sur la Peinture sur verre*, pp. 32–37.

over Europe, when the minds of men were filled with terror, not only by its loathsomeness and its contagion, but also by the notion that it was in a peculiar sense supernatural,[1] new hospitals and refuges overspread Europe, and monks flocked in multitudes to serve in them.[2] Sometimes, the legends say, the leper's form was in a moment transfigured, and he who came to tend the most loathsome of mankind received his reward, for he found himself in the presence of his Lord.

There is no fact of which an historian becomes more speedily or more painfully conscious than the great difference between the importance and the dramatic interest of the subjects he treats. Wars or massacres, the horrors of martyrdom or the splendours of individual prowess, are susceptible of such brilliant colouring, that with but little literary skill they can be so pourtrayed that their importance is adequately realised, and they appeal powerfully to the emotions of the reader. But this vast and unostentatious movement of charity, operating in the village hamlet and in the lonely hospital, staunching the widow's tears and following all the windings of the poor man's griefs, presents few features the imagination can grasp, and leaves no deep impression upon the mind. The greatest things are often those which are most imperfectly realised; and surely no achievements of the Christian Church are more truly great than those which it has effected in the sphere of charity. For the first time in the history of mankind, it has inspired many thousands of men and women, at the sacrifice of all worldly interests, and often

[1] The fact of leprosy being taken as the image of sin gave rise to some curious notions of its supernatural character, and to many legends of saints curing leprosy by baptism. See Maury, *Légendes pieuses du Moyen Âge*, pp. 64–65.

[2] See on these hospitals Cibrario, *Econ. politic. del Medio Evo*, lib. iii. cap. ii.

under circumstances of extreme discomfort or danger, to devote their entire lives to the single object of assuaging the sufferings of humanity. It has covered the globe with countless institutions of mercy, absolutely unknown to the whole Pagan world. It has indissolubly united, in the minds of men, the idea of supreme goodness with that of active and constant benevolence. It has placed in every parish a religious minister, who, whatever may be his other functions, has at least been officially charged with the superintendence of an organisation of charity, and who finds in this office one of the most important as well as one of the most legitimate sources of his power.

There are, however, two important qualifications to the admiration with which we regard the history of Christian charity—one relating to a particular form of suffering, and the other of a more general kind. A strong, ill-defined notion of the supernatural character of insanity had existed from the earliest times; but there were special circumstances which rendered the action of the Church peculiarly unfavourable to those who were either predisposed to or afflicted with this calamity. The reality, both of witchcraft and diabolical possession, had been distinctly recognised in the Jewish writings. The received opinions about eternal torture, and ever-present dæmons, and the continued strain upon the imagination, in dwelling upon an unseen world, were pre-eminently fitted to produce madness in those who were at all predisposed to it, and, where insanity had actually appeared, to determine the form and complexion of the hallucinations of the maniac.[1] Theology supplying

[1] Calmeil observes, 'On a souvent constaté depuis un demi-siècle que la folie est sujette à prendre la teinte des croyances religieuses, des idées philosophiques ou superstitieuses, des préjugés sociaux qui ont cours, qui sont actuellement en vogue parmi les peuples ou les nations; que cette teinte varie dans un même pays suivant le caractère des événements relatifs à la

all the images that acted most powerfully upon the imagination, most madness, for many centuries, took a theological cast. One important department of it appears chiefly in the lives of the saints. Men of lively imaginations and absolute ignorance, living apart from all their fellows, amid the horrors of a savage wilderness, practising austerities by which their physical system was thoroughly deranged, and firmly persuaded that innumerable devils were continually hovering about their cells and interfering with their devotions, speedily and very naturally became subject to constant hallucinations, which probably form the nucleus of truth in the legends of their lives. But it was impossible that insanity should confine itself to the orthodox forms of celestial visions, or of the apparitions and the defeats of devils. Very frequently it led the unhappy maniac to some delusion, which called down upon him the speedy sentence of the Church. Sometimes he imagined he was himself identified with the objects of his devotion. Thus, in the year 1300, a beautiful English girl appeared at Milan, who imagined herself to be the Holy Ghost, incarnate for the redemption of women, and who accordingly was put to death.[1] In the year 1359, a Spaniard declared himself to be the brother of the archangel Michael, and to be destined for the place in heaven which Satan had lost; and he added that he was accustomed every day both to mount into heaven and descend into hell, that the end

politique extérieure, le caractère des événements civiles, la nature des productions littéraires, des représentations théâtrales, suivant la tournure, la direction, le genre d'élan qu'y prennent l'industrie, les arts et les sciences.' *De la Folie*, tome i. pp. 122-123.

[1] 'Venit de Anglia virgo decora valde, pariterque facunda, dicens, Spiritum Sanctum incarnatum in redemptionem mulierum, et baptisavit mulieres in nomine Patris, Filii et sui. Quæ mortua ducta fuit in Mediolanum, ibi et cremata.'—*Annales Dominicanorum Colmariensium* (in the 'Rerum.' Germanic. Scriptores).

of the world was at hand, and that it was reserved for him to enter into single combat with Antichrist. The poor lunatic fell into the hands of the Archbishop of Toledo, and was burnt alive.[1] In other cases the hallucination took the form of an irregular inspiration. On this charge, Joan of Arc, and another girl who had been fired by her example, and had endeavoured, apparently under a genuine hallucination, to follow her career,[2] were burnt alive. A famous Spanish physician and scholar, named Torralba, who lived in the sixteenth century, and who imagined that he had an attendant angel continually about him, escaped with public penance and confession;[3] but a professor of theology in Lima, who laboured under the same delusion, and added to it some wild notions about his spiritual dignities, was less fortunate. He was burnt by the Inquisition of Peru.[4] Most commonly, however, the theological notions about witchcraft either produced madness or determined its form, and, through the influence of the clergy of the different sections of the Christian Church, many thousands of unhappy women, who, from their age, their loneliness, and their infirmity, were most deserving of pity, were devoted to the hatred of mankind, and, having been tortured with horrible and ingenious cruelty, were at last burnt alive.

The existence, however, of some forms of natural mad-

[1] Martin Goncalez, du diocèse de Cuenca, disoit qu'il étoit frère de l'archange S. Michel, la première vérité et l'échelle du ciel; que c'étoit pour lui que Dieu réservoit la place que Lucifer avoit perdue; que tous les jours il s'élevoit au plus haut de l'Empirée et descendoit ensuite au plus profond des enfers; qu'à la fin du monde, qui étoit proche, il iroit au devant de l'Antichrist et qu'il le terrasseroit, ayant à sa main la croix de Jésus-Christ et sa couronne d'épines. L'archevêque de Tolède, n'ayant pu convertir ce fanatique obstiné, ni l'empêcher de dogmatiser, l'avoit enfin livré au bras séculier.'—Touron, *Hist. des Hommes illustres de l'ordre de St. Dominique*, Paris, 1745 (*Vie d'Eyméricus*), tome ii. p. 635.

[2] Calmeil, *De la Folie*, tome i. p. 134.

[3] Ibid. tome i. pp. 242-247.

[4] Ibid. tome i. p. 247.

ness was generally admitted; but the measures for the relief of the unhappy victims were very few, and very ill judged. Among the ancients, they were brought to the temples, and subjected to imposing ceremonies, which were believed supernaturally to relieve them, and which probably had a favourable influence through their action upon the imagination. The great Greek physicians had devoted considerable attention to this malady, and some of their precepts anticipated modern discoveries; but no lunatic asylum appears to have existed in antiquity.[1] In the first period of the hermit life, when many anchorites became insane through their penances, a refuge is said to have been opened for them at Jerusalem.[2] This appears, however, to be a solitary instance, arising from the exigencies of a single class, and no lunatic asylum existed in Christian Europe till the fifteenth century. The Mahommedans, in this form of charity, preceded the Christians. A writer of the seventh century notices the existence of several of these institutions at Fez, and mentions that the patients were restrained by chains.[3] The asylum of Cairo is said to have been founded in A.D. 1304,[4] and it is probable that the care of the insane was a general form of charity in Mahommedan countries. Among the Christians it first appeared in quarters contiguous to the Mahommedans; but there is, I think, no real evidence that it was derived from Mahommedan example. The Knights of Malta were famous as the one order who admitted lunatics into their hospitals; but no Christian asylum expressly for their benefit existed till 1409. The honour of instituting this form of charity in Christendom belongs to Spain. A monk named Juan Gila-

[1] See Esquirol, *Maladies mentales.*

[2] Gibbon, *Decline and Fall*, ch. xxxvii.

[3] Leo Africanus, quoted by Esquirol.

[4] Desmaisons, *Asiles d'Aliénés en Espagne*, p. 53.

berto Joffre, filled with compassion at the sight of the maniacs who were hooted by crowds through the streets of Valencia, founded an asylum in that city, and his example was speedily followed in other provinces. In A.D. 1425, an asylum was erected at Saragossa. In A.D. 1436, both Seville and Valladolid followed the example, as did also Toledo, in A.D. 1483. All these institutions existed before a single lunatic asylum had been founded in any other part of Christendom.[1] Two other very honour able facts may be mentioned, establishing the pre-eminence of Spanish charity in this field. The first s, that the oldest lunatic asylum in the metropolis of Catholicism was that erected by Spaniards, in A.D. 1548.[2] The second is, that, when at the close of the last century, Pinel began his great labours in this sphere, he pronounced Spain to be the country in which lunatics were treated with most wisdom and most humanity.[3]

In most countries their condition was indeed truly deplorable. While many thousands were burnt as witches, those who were recognised as insane were compelled to endure all the horrors of the harshest imprisonment. Blows, bleeding, and chains were their usual treatment, and most horrible accounts were given of madmen who had spent decades bound in dark cells.[4] The treatment naturally aggravated their malady, and that malady in many cases rendered impossible the resignation and ultimate torpor

[1] I have taken these facts from a very interesting little work, Desmaisons, *Des Asiles d'Aliénés en Espagne; Recherches historiques et médicales* (Paris, 1859). Dr. Desmaisons conjectures that the Spaniards took their asylums from the Mahommedans; but, as it seems to me, he altogether fails to prove his point. His work, however, contains much curious information on the history of lunatic asylums.

[2] Amydemus, *Pietas Romana* (Oxford, 1687), p. 21; Desmaisons, p. 108.

[3] Pinel, *Traité médico-philosophique*, pp. 241-242.

[4] See the dreadful description in Pinel, *Traité médico-philosophique sur l'Aliénation mentale* (2nd ed.), pp. 200-202.

which alleviate the suffering of ordinary prisoners. Not until the eighteenth century was the condition of this unhappy class seriously improved. The combined progress of theological scepticism and scientific knowledge, relegated witchcraft to the world of phantoms, and the exertions of Morgagni in Italy, of Cullen in Scotland, and of Pinel in France, renovated the whole treatment of acknowledged lunatics.

The second qualification to the admiration with which we regard the history of Christian charity arises from the undoubted fact that a large proportion of charitable institutions have directly increased the poverty they were intended to relieve. The question of the utility and nature of charity is one which, since the modern discoveries of political economy, has elicited much discussion, and in many cases, I think, much exaggeration. What political economy has effected on the subject may be comprised under two heads. It has elucidated more clearly, and in greater detail than had before been done, the effect of provident self-interest in determining the welfare of societies, and it has established a broad distinction between productive and unproductive expenditure. It has shown that, where idleness is supported, idleness will become common ; that, where systematic public provision is made for old age, the parsimony of foresight will be neglected; and that therefore these forms of charity, by encouraging habits of idleness and improvidence, ultimately increase the wretchedness they were intended to alleviate. It has also shown that, while expenditure in amusements or luxury, or others of what are called unproductive forms, is undoubtedly beneficial to those who provide them, the fruit perishes in the usage, while the result of productive expenditure, such as that which is devoted to the manufacture of machines, or the improvement of the soil, or the extension of commercial enterprise, give a new impulse to the creation of wealth; that the first condition of the rapid accumulation of capital is the diversion of money from unproductive to productive channels, and that the amount of the accumulated capital is one of the two regulating influences of the wages of the labourer. From these positions some persons have inferred that charity should be condemned as a form of unproductive expenditure. But in the first place, all charities that foster habits of forethought and develope new capacities in the poorer classes, such as popular education, or the formation of savings banks, or insurance companies, or, in many cases, small and discriminating loans, or measures directed to the suppression of dissipation, are in the strictest sense productive; and the same may be said of many forms of employment, given in exceptional crises through charitable motives; and in the next place, it is only necessary to remember that the happiness of mankind, to which the accumulation of wealth should only be regarded as a means, is the real object of charity, and it will appear that many forms which are not strictly productive, in the commercial sense, are in the highest degree conducive to this end, and have no serious counteracting evil. In the alleviation of those sufferings that do not spring either from improvidence or from vice, the warmest as well as the most enlightened charity will find an ample sphere for its exertions.[1] Blindness, and other exceptional calamities, against the effects of which prudence does not and cannot provide,

[1] Malthus, who is sometimes, though most unjustly, described as an enemy to all charity, has devoted an admirable chapter (*On Population*, book iv. ch. ix.) to the 'direction of our charity;' but the fullest examination of this subject with which I am acquainted is the very interesting work of Duchâtel, *Sur la Charité*.

the miseries resulting from epidemics, from war, from famine, from the first sudden collapse of industry, produced by new inventions or changes in the channels of commerce; hospitals, which, besides other advantages, are the greatest schools of medical science, and withdraw from the crowded alley multitudes who would otherwise form centres of contagion—these, and such as these, will long tax to the utmost the generosity of the wealthy; while, even in the spheres upon which the political economist looks with the most unfavourable eye, exceptional cases will justify exceptional assistance. The charity which is pernicious is commonly not the highest but the lowest kind. The rich man, prodigal of money, which is to him of little value, but altogether incapable of devoting any personal attention to the object of his alms, often injures society by his donations; but this is rarely the case with that far nobler charity which makes men familiar with the haunts of wretchedness, and follows the object of its care through all the phases of his life. The question of the utility of charity is simply a question of ultimate consequences. Political economy has no doubt laid down some general rules of great value on the subject; but yet, the pages which Cicero devoted to it nearly two thousand years ago might have been written by the most enlightened modern economist; and it will be continually found that the Protestant lady, working in her parish, by the simple force of common sense and by a scrupulous and minute attention to the condition and character of those whom she relieves, is unconsciously illustrating with perfect accuracy the enlightened charity of Malthus.

But in order that charity should be useful, it is essential that the benefit of the sufferer should be a real object to the donor; and a very large proportion of the evils that have arisen from catholic charity may be traced to the absence of this condition. The first substitution of devotion for philanthropy, as the motive of benevolence, gave so powerful a stimulus to the affections, that it may on the whole be regarded as a benefit, though, by making compassion operate solely through a theological medium, it often produced among theologians a more than common indifference to the sufferings of all who were external to their religious community. But the new principle speedily degenerated into a belief in the expiatory nature of the gifts. A form of what may be termed selfish charity arose, which acquired at last gigantic proportions, and exercised a most pernicious influence upon Christendom. Men gave money to the poor, simply and exclusively for their own spiritual benefit, and the welfare of the sufferer was altogether foreign to their thoughts.[1]

The evil which thus arose from some forms of catholic charity, may be traced from a very early period, but it only acquired its full magnitude after some centuries. The Roman system of gratuitous distribution was, in the eyes of the political economist, about the worst that could be conceived, and the charity of the Church being, in at least a measure, discriminating, was at first a very great, though even then not an unmingled good. Labour was also not unfrequently enjoined as a duty by the Fathers, and at a later period the services of the Benedictine monks, in destroying by their example the stigma which slavery had attached to it, were very great. Still, one of the first consequences of the exuberant charity of the Church was

[1] This is very tersely expressed by a great Protestant writer: 'I give no alms to satisfy the hunger of my brother, but to fulfil and accomplish the will and command of my God.'—Sir T. Brown, *Religio Medici*, part ii. § 2. A saying almost exactly similar is, if I remember right, ascribed to St. Elizabeth of Hungary.

to multiply impostors and mendicants, and the idleness of the monks was one of the earliest complaints. Valentinian made a severe law, condemning robust beggars to perpetual slavery. As the monastic system was increased, and especially after the mendicant orders had consecrated mendicancy, the evil assumed gigantic dimensions. Many thousands of strong men, absolutely without private means, were in every country withdrawn from productive labour, and supported by charity. The notion of the meritorious nature of simple almsgiving immeasurably multiplied beggars. The stigma, which it is the highest interest of society to attach to mendicancy, it became a main object of theologians to remove. Saints wandered through the world begging money, that they might give to beggars, or depriving themselves of their garments, that they might clothe the naked, and the result of their teaching was speedily apparent. In all Catholic countries where ecclesiastical influences have been permitted to develope unmolested, the monastic organisations have proved a deadly canker, corroding the prosperity of the nation. Withdrawing multitudes from all production, encouraging a blind and pernicious almsgiving, diffusing habits of improvidence through the poorer classes, fostering an ignorant admiration for saintly poverty, and an equally ignorant antipathy to the habits and aims of an industrial civilisation, they have paralysed all energy and proved an insuperable barrier to material progress. The poverty they have relieved has been insignificant compared with the poverty they have caused. In no case was the abolition of monasteries effected in a more indefensible manner than in England; but the transfer of property that was once employed, in a great measure in charity, to the courtiers of King Henry, was ultimately a vast benefit to the English poor; for no misapplication of this property by private persons could produce as much evil as an unrestrained monasticism. The value of Catholic services in alleviating pain and sickness, and the more exceptional forms of suffering, can never be overrated. The noble heroism of her servants, who have devoted themselves to charity, has never been surpassed, and the perfection of their organisation has, I think, never been equalled; but in the sphere of simple poverty it can hardly be doubted that the Catholic Church has created more misery than it has cured.

Still, even in this field, we must not forget the benefits resulting, if not to the sufferer, at least to the donor. Charitable habits, even when formed in the first instance from selfish motives, even when so misdirected as to be positively injurious to the recipient, rarely fail to exercise a softening and purifying influence on the character. All through the darkest period of the middle ages, amid ferocity and fanaticism and brutality, we may trace the subduing influence of Catholic charity, blending strangely with every excess of violence and every outburst of persecution. It would be difficult to conceive a more frightful picture of society than is presented by the history of Gregory of Tours; but that long series of atrocious crimes, narrated with an almost appalling tranquillity, is continually interspersed with accounts of kings, queens, or prelates, who, in the midst of the disorganised society, made the relief of the poor the main object of their lives. No period of history exhibits a larger amount of cruelty, licentiousness, and fanaticism than the Crusades; but side by side with the military enthusiasm, and with the almost universal corruption, there expanded a vast movement of charity, which covered Christendom with hospitals for the relief of leprosy, and which grappled nobly, though ineffectually, with the many forms of suffering that were generated. St. Peter Nolasco, whose great labours in ransoming captive Christians I have already noticed, was an active participater in the atrocious massacre of the Albigenses.[1] Of Shane O'Neale, one of the ablest, but also one of the most ferocious Irish chieftains who ever defied the English power, it is related, amid a crowd of horrible crimes, that, 'sitting at meat, before he put one morsel into his mouth he used to slice a portion above the daily alms, and send it to some beggar at his gate, saying it was meet to serve Christ first.'[2]

The great evils produced by the encouragement of mendicants, which have always accompanied the uncontrolled development of Catholicity, have naturally given rise to much discussion and legislation. William de St. Amour denounced the mendicant orders at Paris in the thirteenth century,[3] and one of the disciples of Wycliffe, named Nicholas of Hereford, was conspicuous for his opposition to indiscriminate gifts to beggars;[4] but few measures of an extended order appear to have been taken till the Reformation.[5] In England, laws of the most savage cruelty were passed, in hopes of eradicating mendicancy. A parliament of Henry VIII., before the suppression of the monasteries, issued a law providing a system of organised

[1] See Butler's *Lives of the Saints*.

[2] Campion's *Historie of Ireland*, book ii. chap. x.

[3] Fleury, *Hist. eccl.* lib. lxxxiv. 57. It does not appear, however, that the indiscriminate charity they encouraged had any part in his invective. He wrote his *Perils of the Last Times* in the interest of the University of Paris, of which he was a Professor, and which was at war with the mendicant orders. See Milman's *Latin Christianity*, vol. vi. pp. 348–350.

[4] Henry de Knyghton, *De Eventibus Angliæ*.

[5] There was some severe legislation in England on the subject after the Black Death. Eden's *History of the Working Classes*, vol. i. p. 34. In France, too, a royal ordinance of 1350 ordered men who had been convicted of begging three times to be branded with a hot iron. Monteil, *Hist. des Français*, tome i. p. 434.

charity, and imposing on anyone who gave anything to a beggar a fine of ten times the value of his gift. A sturdy beggar was to be punished with whipping for the first offence, with whipping and the loss of the tip of his ear for the second, and with death for the third.[1] Under Edward VI., an atrocious law, which, however, was repealed in the same reign, enacted that every sturdy beggar who refused to work should be branded, and adjudged for two years as a slave to the person who gave information against him; and if he took flight during his period of servitude, for the first offence he was condemned to perpetual slavery, and for the second to death. The master was authorised to put a ring of iron round the neck of his slave, to chain him and to scourge him. Anyone might take the children of a sturdy beggar for apprentices, till the boys were twenty-four and the girls twenty.[2] Another law, made under Elizabeth, punished with death any strong man under the age of eighteen who was convicted for the third time of begging; but the penalty in this reign was afterwards reduced to a life-long service in the galleys, or to banishment, with a penalty of death to the returned convict.[3] Under the same queen the poor-law system was elaborated, and Malthus long afterwards showed that its effects in discouraging parsimony rendered it scarcely less pernicious than the monastic system that had preceded it. In many Catholic countries, severe, though less atrocious measures, were taken to grapple with the evil of mendicancy. That shrewd and sagacious pontiff, Sixtus V., who, though not the greatest man, was by far the greatest statesman who has ever sat on the papal throne, made praiseworthy efforts to check it at Rome, where ecclesiastical influence had

[1] Eden, vol. i. pp. 83–87.
[2] Ibid. pp. 101-103.
[3] Ibid. pp. 127–130.

always made it peculiarly prevalent.[1] Charles V., in 1531, issued a severe enactment against beggars in the Netherlands, but excepted from its operation mendicant friars and pilgrims.[2] Under Lewis XIV., equally severe measures were taken in France. But though the practical evil was fully felt, there was little or no philosophical investigation of its causes before the eighteenth century. Locke in England,[3] and Berkeley in Ireland,[4] briefly glanced at the subject, and in 1704 Defoe published a very remarkable tract, called, 'Giving Alms no Charity,' in which he noticed the extent to which mendicancy existed in England, though wages were higher than in any continental country.[5] A still more remarkable book, written by an author named Ricci, appeared at Modena in 1787, and excited considerable attention. The author pointed out with much force the gigantic development of mendicancy in Italy, traced it to the excessive charity of the people, and appears to have regarded as an evil all charity which sprang from religious motives, and was greater than would spring from the unaided instincts of men.[6] The freethinker Mandeville assailed charity schools,

[1] Morighini, *Institutions pieuses de Rome.*

[2] Eden, *Hist. of the Labouring Classes,* vol. i. p. 83.

[3] Locke discussed the great increase of poverty, and a bill was brought in suggesting some remedies, but did not pass. (Eden, vol. i. pp. 243–248.)

[4] In a very forcible letter addressed to the Irish Catholic clergy.

[5] This tract, which is extremely valuable for the light it throws upon the social condition of England at the time, was written in opposition to a Bill providing that the poor in the poor-houses should do wool, hemp, iron, and other works. Defoe says that wages in England were higher than anywhere on the Continent, though the amount of mendicancy was enormous. 'The reason why so many pretend to want work is, that they can live so well with the pretence of wanting work. . . . I affirm of my own knowledge, when I have wanted a man for labouring work, and offered nine shillings per week to strolling fellows at my door, they have frequently told me to my face they could get more a-begging.'

[6] *Reforma degl' Instituti pii di Modena* (published first anonymously at Modena). It has been reprinted in the library of the Italian economists.

and the whole system of endeavouring to elevate the poor,[1] and Magdalen asylums and foundling hospitals have had fierce, though I believe much mistaken, adversaries.[2] The reforms of the poor-laws, and the writings of Malthus, gave a new impulse to discussion on the subject; but with the qualifications I have stated, no new discoveries have, I conceive, thrown any just cloud upon Christian charity; and though its administration is often extremely injudicious, the principles that regulate it, in Protestant countries at least, require but little reform.

The last method by which Christianity has laboured to soften the characters of men has been by accustoming the imagination to expatiate continually upon images of tenderness and of pathos. Our imaginations, though less influential than our occupations, probably affect our moral characters more deeply than our judgments, and, in the case of the poorer classes especially, the cultivation of this part of our nature is of inestimable importance. Rooted, for the most part, during their entire lives, to a single spot, excluded by their ignorance and their circumstances from most of the varieties of interest that animate the minds of other men, condemned to constant and plodding labour, and engrossed for ever with the minute cares of an immediate and an anxious present, their whole natures would have been hopelessly contracted, were

[1] *Essay on Charity Schools.*

[2] Magdalen Asylums have been very vehemently assailed by M. Charles Comte, in his *Traité de Législation.* On the subject of Foundling Hospitals there is a whole literature. They were vehemently attacked by, I believe, Lord Brougham, in the *Edinburgh Review*, in the early part of this century. Writers of this stamp, and indeed most political economists, greatly exaggerate the forethought of men and women, especially in matters where the passions are concerned. It may be questioned whether one woman in a hundred, who plunges into a career of vice, is in the smallest degree influenced by a consideration of whether or not charitable institutions are provided for the support of aged penitents.

there no sphere in which their imaginations could expand. Religion is the one romance of the poor. It alone extends the narrow horizon of their thoughts, supplies the images of their dreams, allures them to the supersensual and the ideal. The graceful beings with which the creative fancy of Paganism peopled the universe shed a poetic glow on the peasants' toil. Every stage of agriculture was presided over by a divinity, and the world grew bright by the companionship of the gods. But it is the peculiarity of the Christian types, that while they have fascinated the imagination, they have also purified the heart. The tender, winning, and almost feminine beauty of the Christian Founder, the Virgin mother, the agonies of Gethsemane or of Calvary, the many scenes of compassion and suffering that fill the sacred writings, are the pictures which, for eighteen hundred years, have governed the imaginations of the rudest and most ignorant of mankind. Associated with the fondest recollections of childhood, with the music of the church bells, with the clustered lights and the tinsel splendour, that seem to the peasant the very ideal of majesty; painted over the altar where he received the companion of his life, around the cemetery where so many whom he had loved were laid, on the stations of the mountain, on the portal of the vineyard, on the chapel where the storm-tossed mariner fulfils his grateful vow; keeping guard over his cottage door, and looking down upon his humble bed, forms of tender beauty and gentle pathos for ever haunt the poor man's fancy, and silently win their way into the very depths of his being. More than any spoken eloquence, more than any dogmatic teaching, they transform and subdue his character, till he learns to realise the sanctity of weakness and suffering, the supreme majesty of compassion and gentleness.

Imperfect and inadequate as is the sketch I have drawn, it will be sufficient to show how great and multiform have been the influences of Christian philanthropy. The shadows that rest upon the picture I have not concealed; but when all due allowance has been made for them, enough will remain to claim our deepest admiration. The high conception that has been formed of the sanctity of human life, the protection of infancy, the elevation and final emancipation of the slave classes, the suppression of barbarous games, the creation of a vast and multifarious organisation of charity, and the education of the imagination by the Christian type, constitute together a movement of philanthropy which has never been paralleled or approached in the Pagan world. The effects of this movement in promoting happiness have been very great. Its effect in determining character has probably been still greater. In that proportion or disposition of qualities which constitutes the ideal character, the gentler and more benevolent virtues have obtained, through Christianity, the foremost place. In the first and purest period they were especially supreme, but in the third century a great ascetic movement arose, which gradually brought a new type of character into the ascendant, and diverted the enthusiasm of the Church into new channels.

Tertullian, writing in the second century, in a passage which has been very frequently quoted, contrasts the Christians of his day with the gymnosophists or hermits of India, declaring that, unlike these, the Christians did not fly from the world, but mixed with the Pagans in the forum, in the market-places, in the public baths, in the ordinary business of life.[1] But although the life of the

[1] *Apol.* ch. xlii.

hermit or the monk was unknown in the Church for more than two hundred years after its foundation, we may detect, almost from the earliest time, a tone of feeling which produces it. The central conceptions of the monastic system are the meritoriousness of complete abstinence from all sexual intercourse, and of complete renunciation of the world. The first of these notions appeared in the very earliest period, in the respect attached to the condition of virginity, which was always regarded as sacred, and especially esteemed in the clergy, though for a long time it was not imposed as an obligation. The second was shown in the numerous efforts that were made to separate the Christian community as far as possible from the society in which it existed. Nothing could be more natural than that, when the increase and afterwards the triumph of the Church had thrown the bulk of the Christians into active political or military labour, some should, as an exercise of piety, have endeavoured to imitate the separation from the world which was once the common condition of all. Besides this, a movement of asceticism had long been raging like a mental epidemic through the world. Among the Jews—whose law, from the great stress it laid upon marriage, the excellence of the rapid multiplication of population, and the hope of being the ancestor of the Messiah, was peculiarly repugnant to monastic conceptions—the Essenes had constituted a complete monastic society, abstaining from marriage and separating themselves wholly from the world. In Rome, whose practical genius was, if possible, even more opposed than that of the Jews to an inactive monasticism, and even among those philosophers who most represented its active and practical spirit, the same tendency was shown. The Cynics of the later empire recommended a complete renunciation of civic and domestic ties, and a life spent wholly in the contemplation of wisdom. The Egyptian philosophy, that soon after acquired an ascendency in Europe, anticipated still more closely the monastic ideal. On the outskirts of the Church, the many sects of Gnostics and Manicheans all held under different forms the essential evil of matter. The Docetæ, following the same notion, denied the reality of the body of Christ. The Montanists and the Novatians surpassed and stimulated the private penances of the orthodox.[1] The soil was thus thoroughly prepared for a great outburst of asceticism, whenever the first seed was sown. This was done during the Decian persecution. Paul, the hermit, who fled to the desert during that persecution, is said to have been the first of the tribe.[2] Antony, who speedily followed, greatly extended the movement, and in a few years the hermits had become a mighty nation. Persecution, which in the first instance drove great numbers as fugitives to the deserts, soon aroused a passionate religious enthusiasm that showed itself in an ardent desire for those sufferings which were believed to lead directly to heaven, and this enthusiasm, after the peace of Constantine, found its natural vent and sphere in the macerations of the desert life. The imaginations of men were fascinated by the poetic circumstances of that life which St. Jerome most eloquently embellished. Women were pre-eminent in recruiting for it. The same

[1] On these penances, see Bingham, *Antiq.* book vii. Bingham, I think, justly divides the history of asceticism into three periods. During the first, which extends from the foundation of the Church to A.D. 250, there were men and women who, with a view of spiritual perfection, abstained from marriage, relinquished amusements, accustomed themselves to severe fasts, and gave up their property to works of charity; but did this in the middle of society and without leading the life of either a hermit or a monk. During the second period, which extended from the Decian persecution, anchorites were numerous, but the custom of a common or cœnobitic life was unknown. It was originated in the time of Constantine by Pachomius.

[2] This is expressly stated by St. Jerome (*Vit. Pauli*).

spirit that had formerly led the wife of the Pagan official to entertain secret relations with the Christian priests, now led the wife of the Christian to become the active agent of the monks. While the father designed his son for the army, or for some civil post, the mother was often straining every nerve to induce him to become a hermit; the monks secretly corresponded with her, they skilfully assumed the functions of education, in order that they might influence the young; and sometimes, to evade the precautions or the anger of the father, they concealed their profession, and assumed the garb of lay pedagogues.[1] The pulpit, which had almost superseded, and immeasurably transcended in influence, the chairs of the rhetoricians, and which was filled by such men as Ambrose, Augustine, Chrysostom, Basil, and the Gregories, was continually exerted in the same cause, and the extreme luxury of the great cities produced a violent, but not unnatural, reaction of asceticism. The dignity of the monastic position, which sometimes brought men who had been simple peasants into connection with the emperors, the security it furnished to fugitive slaves and criminals, the desire of escaping from those fiscal burdens which, in the corrupt and oppressive administration of the empire, had acquired an intolerable weight, and especially the barbarian invasions, which produced every variety of panic and wretchedness, conspired with the new religious teaching in peopling the desert. A theology of asceticism was speedily formed. The examples of Elijah and Elisha, to the first of whom, by a bold flight of the imagination, some later Carmelites ascribed the origin of their order, and the more recent instance of the

[1] See on this subject some curious evidence in Neander's *Life of Chrysostom.* St. Chrysostom wrote a long work to console fathers whose sons were thus seduced to the desert.

Baptist were at once adduced. To an ordinary layman the life of the anchorite might appear in the highest degree opposed to that of the Teacher who began His mission in a marriage feast; who was continually reproached by His enemies for the readiness with which He mixed with the world, and who selected from the female sex some of His purest and most devoted followers; but the monkish theologians avoiding, for the most part, these topics, dilated chiefly on His immaculate birth, His virgin mother, His life of celibacy, His exhortation to the rich young man. The fact that St. Peter, to whom a general primacy was already ascribed, was unquestionably married, was a difficulty which was in a measure met by a tradition that he, as well as the other married apostles, abstained from intercourse with their wives after their conversion.[1] St. Paul, however, was probably unmarried, and his writings showed a decided preference for the unmarried state, which the ingenuity of theologians also discovered in some quarters where it might be least expected. Thus, St. Jerome assures us that when the clean animals entered the ark by sevens, and the unclean ones by pairs, the odd number typified the celibate, and the even the married condition. Even of the unclean animals but one pair of each kind was admitted, lest they should perpetrate the enormity of second marriage.[2] Ecclesiastical tradition sustained the tendency, and the apostle James, as he has been portrayed by Hegesippus, became a kind of ideal saint, a faithful picture of what, according to the notions of theologians, was the true type of human nobility. He 'was converted,' it was said, 'from his mother's womb.' He drank neither wine nor fermented liquors, and abstained from animal

[1] On this tradition see Champagny, *Les Antonins*, tome i. p. 193.

[2] *Ep.* cxxiii.

food. A razor never came upon his head. He never anointed with oil, or used a bath. He alone was allowed to enter the sanctuary. He never wore woollen, but linen garments. He was in the habit of entering the temple alone, and was often found upon his bended knees, and interceding for the forgiveness of the people, so that his knees became as hard as a camel's.[1]

The progress of the monastic movement, as has been truly said, 'was not less rapid or universal than that of Christianity itself.[2] Of the actual number of the anchorites, those who are acquainted with the extreme unveracity of the first historians of the movement will hesitate to speak with confidence. It is said that St. Pachomius, who early in the fourth century founded the cœnobitic mode of life, enlisted under his jurisdiction 7,000 monks;[3] that in the days of St. Jerome nearly 50,000 monks were sometimes assembled at the Easter festivals;[4] that in the desert of Nitria alone there were, in the fourth century, 5,000 monks under a single abbot;[5] that an Egyptian city named Oxyrinchus devoted itself almost exclusively to the ascetic life, and included 20,000 virgins and 10,000 monks;[6] that St. Serapion presided over 10,000 monks,[7] and that, towards the close of the fourth century, the monastic population in that country was nearly equal to the population of the cities.[8] Egypt was the parent of monachism, and it was there that it attained both its extreme development and its most austere severity; but there was very soon scarcely any Christian country in

[1] Euseb. *Eccl. Hist.* ii. 23.

[2] Gibbon, *Decline and Fall,* ch. xxxvii.; a brief but masterly sketch of the progress of the movement.

[3] Palladius, *Hist. Laus.* xxxviii.

[4] Jerome, Preface to the Rule of St. Pachomius, § 7.

[5] Cassian, *De Cœnob. Inst.* iv. 1.

[6] Rufinus, *Hist. Monach.* ch. v. Rufinus visited it himself.

[7] Palladius, *Hist. Laus.* lxxvi.

[8] Rufinus, *Hist. Mon.* vii.

which a similar movement was not ardently propagated. St. Athanasius and St. Zeno are said to have introduced it into Italy,[1] where it soon afterwards received a great stimulus from St. Jerome. St. Hilarion instituted the first monks in Palestine, and he lived to see many thousands subject to his rule, and towards the close of his life to plant monachism in Cyprus. Eustathius, Bishop of Sebastia, spread it through Armenia, Paphlagonia, and Pontus. St. Basil laboured along the wild shores of the Euxine. St. Martin of Tours founded the first monastery in Gaul, and 2,000 monks attended his funeral. Unrecorded missionaries planted the new institution in the heart of Æthiopia, amid the little islands that stud the Mediterranean, in the secluded valleys of Wales and Ireland.[2] But even more wonderful than the many thousands who thus abandoned the world, is the reverence with which they were regarded by those who, by their attainments or their character, would seem most opposed to the monastic ideal. No one had more reason than Augustine to know the danger of enforced celibacy, but St. Augustine exerted all his energies to spread monasticism through his diocese. St. Ambrose, who was by nature an acute statesman; St. Jerome and St. Basil, who were ambitious scholars; St. Chrysostom, who was pre-eminently formed to sway the refined throngs of a metropolis, all exerted their powers in favour of the life of

[1] There is a good deal of doubt and controversy about this. See a note in Mosheim's *Eccl. Hist.* (Soame's edition), vol. i. p. 354.

[2] Most of the passages remaining on the subject of the foundation of monachism are given by Thomassin, *Discipline de l'Église*, part i. livre iii. ch. xii. This work contains also much general information about monachism. A curious collection of statistics of the numbers of the monks in different localities, additional to those I have given and gleaned from the *Lives of the Saints*, may be found in Pitra (*Vie de S. Léger*, Introd. p. lix.); 2,100, or, according to another account, 3,000 monks, lived in the monastery of Banchor.

solitude, and the three last practised it themselves. St. Arsenius, who was surpassed by no one in the extravagance of his penances, had held a high office at the court of the Emperor Arcadius. Pilgrims wandered among the deserts, collecting accounts of the miracles and the austerities of the saints, which filled Christendom with admiration; and the strange biographies which were thus formed, wild and grotesque as they are, enable us to realise very vividly the general features of the anchorite life, which became the new ideal of the Christian world.[1]

There is, perhaps, no phase in the moral history of mankind, of a deeper or more painful interest than this ascetic epidemic. A hideous, sordid, and emaciated maniac, without knowledge, without patriotism, without natural affection, passing his life in a long routine of useless and atrocious self-torture, and quailing before the ghastly phantoms of his delirious brain, had become the ideal of the nations which had known the writings of Plato and Cicero and the lives of Socrates or Cato. For about two centuries, the hideous maceration of the body was regarded as the highest proof of excellence. St. Jerome declares, with a thrill of admiration, how he had seen a monk, who for thirty years had lived exclusively

[1] The three principal are the *Historia Monachorum* of Rufinus, who visited Egypt A.D. 373, about seventeen years after the death of St. Antony; the *Institutiones* of Cassian, who, having visited the Eastern monks about A.D. 394, founded vast monasteries containing, it is said, 5,000 monks, at Marseilles, and died at a great age about A.D. 448; and the *Historia Lausiaca* (so called from Lausus, Governor of Cappadocia) of Palladius, who was himself a hermit on Mount Nitria, in A.D. 388. The first and last, as well as many minor works of the same period, are given in Rosweyde's invaluable collection of the lives of the Fathers, one of the most fascinating volumes in the whole range of literature.

The hospitality of the monks was not without drawbacks. In a church on Mount Nitria three whips were hung on a palm-tree—one for chastising monks, another for chastising thieves, and a third for chastising guests. (Palladius, *Hist. Laus.* vii.)

on a small portion of barley bread and of muddy water; another, who lived in a hole and never eat more than five figs for his daily repast;[1] a third, who cut his hair only on Easter Sunday, who never washed his clothes, who never changed his tunic till it fell to pieces, who starved himself till his eyes grew dim, and his skin 'like a pumice stone,' and whose merits, shown by these austerities, Homer himself would be unable to recount.[2] For six months, it is said, St. Macarius of Alexandria slept in a marsh, and exposed his body naked to the stings of venomous flies. He was accustomed to carry about with him eighty pounds of iron. His disciple, St. Eusebius, carried one hundred and fifty pounds of iron, and lived for three years in a dried-up well. St. Sabinus would only eat corn that had become rotten by remaining for a month in water. St. Besarion spent forty days and nights in the middle of thorn-bushes, and for forty years never lay down when he slept,[3] which last penance was also during fifteen years practised by St. Pachomius.[4] Some saints, like St. Marcian, restricted themselves to one meal a day, so small that they continually suffered the pangs of hunger.[5] Of one of them it is related that his daily food was six ounces of bread and a few herbs; that he was never seen to recline on a mat or bed, or even to place his limbs easily for sleep; but that sometimes, from excess of weariness, his eyes would close at his meals, and the food would drop into his mouth.[6] Other saints, however, eat only every second

[1] *Vita Pauli.* St. Jerome adds, that some will not believe this, because they have no faith, but that all things are possible for those that believe.

[2] *Vita St. Hilarion.*

[3] See a long list of these penances in Tillemont, *Mém. pour servir à l'Hist. ecclés.* tome viii.

[4] *Vitæ Patrum* (Pachomius). He used to lean against a wall when overcome by drowsiness.

[5] *Vitæ Patrum*, ix. 3.

[6] Sozomen, vi. 29.

day;[1] while many, if we could believe the monkish historian, abstained for whole weeks from all nourishment.[2] St. Macarius of Alexandria is said during an entire week to have never lain down, or eaten anything but a few uncooked herbs on Sunday.[3] Of another famous saint, named John, it is asserted that for three whole years he stood in prayer, leaning upon a rock; that during all that time he never sat or lay down, and that his only nourishment was the Sacrament, which was brought him on Sundays.[4] Some of the hermits lived in deserted dens of wild beasts, others in dried-up wells, while others found a congenial resting-place among the tombs.[5] Some disdained all clothes, and crawled abroad like the wild beasts, covered only by their matted hair. In Mesopotamia, and part of Syria, there existed a sect known by the name of 'Grazers,' who never lived under a roof, who eat neither flesh nor bread, but who spent their time for ever on the mountain side, and eat grass like cattle.[6] The

[1] E.g. St. Antony, according to his biographer St. Athanasius.

[2] 'Il y eut dans le désert de Scété des solitaires d'une éminente perfection. . . . On prétend que pour l'ordinaire ils passoient des semaines entières sans manger, mais apparemment cela ne se faisoit que dans des occasions particulières.'—Tillemont, *Mém. pour servir à l'Hist. eccl.* tome viii. p. 580. Even this, however, was admirable!

[3] Palladius, *Hist. Laus.* cap. xx.

[4] 'Primum cum accessisset ad eremum tribus continuis annis sub cujusdam saxi rupe stans, semper oravit, ita ut nunquam omnino resederit neque acuerit. Somni autem tantum caperet, quantum stans capere potuit; cibum vero nunquam sumpserat nisi die Dominica. Presbyter enim tunc veniebat ad eum et offerebat pro eo sacrificium idque ei solum sacramentum erat et victus.'—Rufinus, *Hist. Monach.* cap. xv.

[5] Thus St. Antony used to live in a tomb, where he was beaten by the devil. (St. Athanasius, *Life of Antony.*)

[6] Βοσκοί. See on these monks Sozomen, vi. 33; Evagrius, i. 21. It is mentioned of a certain St. Marc of Athens, that having lived for thirty years naked in the desert, his body was covered with hair like that of a wild beast. (Bollandists, March 29.) St. Mary of Egypt, during part of her period of penance, lived upon grass. (*Vitæ Patrum.*)

cleanliness of the body was regarded as a pollution of the soul, and the saints who were most admired had become one hideous mass of clotted filth. St. Athanasius relates with enthusiasm how St. Antony, the patriarch of monachism, had never, in extreme old age, been guilty of washing his feet.[1] The less constant St. Pœmen fell into this habit for the first time when a very old man, and, with a glimmering of common sense, defended himself against the astonished monks by saying that he had 'learnt to kill not his body, but his passions.'[2] St. Abraham the hermit, however, who lived for fifty years after his conversion, rigidly refused from that date to wash either his face or his feet.[3] He was, it is said, a person of singular beauty, and his biographer somewhat strangely remarks, that 'his face reflected the purity of his soul.'[4] St. Ammon had never seen himself naked.[5] A famous virgin named Silvia, though she was sixty years old, and though bodily sickness was a consequence of her habits, resolutely refused, on religious principles, to wash any part of her body except her fingers.[6] St. Euphraxia joined a convent of one hundred and thirty nuns, who never washed their feet, and who shuddered at the mention of a bath.[7] An anchorite once imagined that he was mocked by an illusion of the devil, as he saw gliding before him through

[1] *Life of Antony.*

[2] 'Il ne faisoit pas aussi difficulté dans sa vieillesse de se laver quelquefois les piez. Et comme on témoignoit s'en étonner et trouver que cela ne répondoit pas à la vie austère des anciens, il se justifioit par ces paroles: Nous avons appris à tuer, non pas notre corps mais nos passions.'—Tillemont, *Mém. Hist. eccl.* tome xv. p. 148. This saint was so very virtuous, that he sometimes remained without eating for whole weeks.

[3] 'Non appropinquavit oleum corpusculo ejus. Facies vel etiam pedes a die conversionis suæ nunquam diluti sunt.'—*Vitæ Patrum*, c. xvii.

[4] 'In facie ejus puritas animi noscebatur.'—Ibid. c. xviii.

[5] Socrates, iv. 23.

[6] Heraclidis Paradisus (Rosweyde), c. xlii.

[7] 'Nulla earum pedes suos abluebat; aliquantæ vero audientes de balneo loqui, irridentes, confusionem et magnam abominationem se audire

the desert a naked creature black with filth and years of exposure, and with white hair floating to the wind. It was a once beautiful woman, St. Mary of Egypt, who had thus, during forty-seven years, been expiating her sins.[1] The occasional decadence of the monks into habits of decency was a subject of much reproach. 'Our fathers,' said the abbot Alexander, looking mournfully back to the past, 'never washed their faces, but we frequent the public baths.'[2] It was related of one monastery in the desert, that the monks suffered greatly from want of water to drink; but at the prayer of the abbot Theodosius, a copious stream was produced. But soon some monks, tempted by the abundant supply, diverged from their old austerity, and persuaded the abbot to avail himself of the stream for the construction of the bath. The bath was made. Once, and once only, did the monks enjoy their ablutions, when the stream ceased to flow. Prayers, tears, and fastings were in vain. A whole year passed. At last the abbot destroyed the bath, which was the object of the Divine displeasure, and the waters flowed afresh.[3] But of all the evidences of the loathsome excesses to

judicabant, quæ neque auditum suum hoc audire patiebantur.'—*Vit. S. Euphrax.* c. vi. (Rosweyde.)

[1] See her acts, Bollandists, April 2, and in the *Vitæ Patrum.*

[2] 'Patres nostri nunquam facies suas lavabant, nos autem lavacra publica balneaque frequentamus.'—Moschus, *Pratum Spirituale,* clxviii.

[3] *Pratum Spirituale,* lxxx.

An Irish saint, named Coemgenus, is said to have shown his devotion in a way which was directly opposite to that of the other saints I have mentioned—by his special use of cold water—but the principle in each case was the same—to mortify nature. St. Coemgenus was accustomed to pray for an hour every night in a pool of cold water, while the devil sent a horrible beast to swim round him. An angel, however, was sent to him for three purposes. 'Tribus de causis à Domino missus est angelus ibi ad S. Coemgenum. Prima ut a diversis suis gravibus laboribus levius viveret paulisper; secunda ut horridam bestiam sancto infestam repelleret; tertia, *ut frigiditatem aquæ calefaceret.*'—Bollandists, June 3. The editors say these acts are of doubtful authenticity.

which this spirit was carried, the life of St. Simeon Stylites is probably the most remarkable. It would be difficult to conceive a more horrible or disgusting picture than is given of the penances by which that saint commenced his ascetic career. He had bound a rope around him so that it became imbedded in his flesh, which putrefied around it. 'A horrible stench, intolerable to the bystanders, exhaled from his body, and worms dropped from him whenever he moved, and they filled his bed.' Sometimes he left the monastery and slept in a dry well, inhabited, it is said, by dæmons. He built successively three pillars, the last being sixty feet high, and scarcely two cubits in circumference, and on this pillar, during thirty years, he remained exposed to every change of climate, ceaselessly and rapidly bending his body in prayer almost to the level of his feet. A spectator attempted to number these rapid motions, but desisted from weariness when he had counted 1,244. For a whole year, we are told, St. Simeon stood upon one leg, the other being covered with hideous ulcers, while his biographer was commissioned to stand by his side, to pick up the worms that fell from his body, and to replace them in the sores, the saint saying to the worm, 'Eat what God has given you.' From every quarter pilgrims of every degree thronged to do him homage. A crowd of prelates followed him to the grave. A brilliant star is said to have shone miraculously over his pillar; the general voice of mankind pronounced him to be the highest model of a Christian saint, and several other anchorites imitated or emulated his penances.[1]

There is, if I mistake not, no department of literature the importance of which is more inadequately realised

[1] See his Life by his disciple Antony, in the *Vitæ Patrum*, Evagrius, i. 13-14. Theodoret, *Philotheus*, cap. xxvi.

than the lives of the saints. Even where they have no direct historical value, they have a moral value of the very highest order. They may not tell us with accuracy what men did at particular epochs, but they display with the utmost vividness what they thought and felt, their measure of probability, and their ideal of excellence. Decrees of councils, elaborate treatises of theologians, creeds, liturgies, and canons, are all but the husks of religious history. They reveal what was professed and argued before the world, but not that which was realised in the imagination or enshrined in the heart. The history of art, which in its ruder day reflected with delicate fidelity the fleeting images of an anthropomorphic age, is in this respect invaluable; but still more important is that vast Christian mythology, which grew up spontaneously from the intellectual condition of the time, included all its dearest hopes, wishes, ideals, and imaginings, and constituted, during many centuries, the popular literature of Christendom. In the case of the saints of the deserts, there can be no question that the picture—which is drawn chiefly by eye-witnesses—however grotesque may be some of its details, is in its leading features historically true. It is true that self-torture was for some centuries regarded as the chief measure of human excellence, that tens of thousands of the most devoted men fled to the desert to reduce themselves by maceration nearly to the condition of the brute, and that this odious superstition had acquired an almost absolute ascendency in the ethics of the age. The examples of asceticism I have cited are but a few out of many hundreds, and volumes might be written, and have been written, detailing them. Till the reform of St. Benedict, the ideal was on the whole unchanged. The Western monks, from the conditions of their climate, were constitutionally incapable of rivalling the abstinence of the Egyptian anchorites, but their conception of supreme excellence was much the same, and they laboured to compensate for their inferiority in penances by claiming some superiority in miracles. From the time of St. Pachomius, the cœnobitic life was adopted by most monks; but the Eastern monasteries, with the important exception of a vow of obedience, differed little from a collection of hermitages. They were in the deserts; the monks commonly lived in separate cells; they kept silence at their repasts; they rivalled one another in the extravagance of their penances. A few feeble efforts were indeed made by St. Jerome and others to moderate austerities which frequently led to insanity and suicide, to check the turbulence of certain wandering monks, who were accustomed to defy the ecclesiastical authorities, and especially to suppress monastic mendicancy, which had appeared prominently among some heretical sects. The orthodox monks commonly employed themselves in weaving mats of palm-leaves; but, living in the deserts, with no wants, they speedily sank into a listless apathy; and those who were most admired were those who, like Simeon Stylites and the hermit John, of whom I have already spoken, were most exclusively devoted to their superstition. Diversities of individual character were, however, vividly displayed. Many anchorites, without knowledge, passions, or imagination, having fled from servile toil to the calm of the wilderness, passed the long hours in sleep or in a mechanical routine of prayer, and their inert and languid existences, prolonged to the extreme of old age, closed at last by a tranquil and almost animal death. Others made their cells by the clear fountains and clustering palm-trees of some oasis in the desert, and a blooming garden arose beneath their toil. The numerous monks who followed

St. Serapion devoted themselves largely to agriculture, and sent shiploads of corn for the benefit of the poor.[1] Of one old hermit it is related, that such was the cheerfulness of his mind, that every sorrow was dispelled by his presence, and the weary and the heartbroken were consoled by a few words from his lips.[2] More commonly, however, the hermit's cell was the scene of perpetual mournings. Tears and sobs, and frantic strugglings with imaginary dæmons, and paroxysms of religious despair, were the texture of his life, and the dread of spiritual enemies, and of that death which his superstition had rendered so terrible, embittered every hour of his existence.[3] The solace of intellectual occupations was rarely resorted to. 'The duty,' said St. Jerome, 'of a monk is not to teach, but to weep.'[4] A cultivated and disciplined mind was the least subject to those hallucinations, which were regarded as the highest evidence of Divine favour,[5] and although in an age when

[1] Palladius, *Hist. Laus.* lxxvi. [2] Rufinus, *Hist. Monach.* xxxiii.

[3] We have a striking illustration of this in St. Arsenius. His eyelashes are said to have fallen off through continual weeping, and he had always, when at work, to put a cloth on his breast to receive his tears. As he felt his death approaching, his terror rose to the point of agony. The monks who were about him said, '"Quid fles, pater? numquid et tu times?" Ille respondit, "In veritate timeo et iste timor qui nunc mecum est, semper in me fuit, ex quo factus sum monachus."'—*Verba Seniorum*, Prol. § 163. It was said of St. Abraham that no day passed after his conversion without his shedding tears. (*Vit. Patrum.*) St. John the dwarf once saw a monk laughing immoderately at dinner, and was so horrified that he at once began to cry. (Tillemont, *Mém. de l'Hist. ecclés.* tome x. p. 430.) St. Basil (*Regulæ,* interrog. xvii.) gives a remarkable disquisition on the wickedness of laughing, and he observes that this was the one bodily affection which Christ does not seem to have known. Mr. Buckle has collected a series of passages to precisely the same effect from the writings of the Scotch divines. (*Hist. of Civilisation,* vol. ii. pp. 385–386.)

[4] 'Monachus autem non doctoris habet sed plangentis officium.'—*Contr. Vigilant.* xv.

[5] As Tillemont puts it: 'Il se trouva très-peu de saints en qui Dieu ait joint les talens extérieurs de l'éloquence et de la science avec la grâce de

the passion for asceticism was general, many scholars became ascetics, the great majority of the early monks appear to have been men who were not only absolutely ignorant themselves, but who also looked upon learning with positive disfavour. St. Antony, the true founder of monachism, refused when a boy to learn letters, because it would bring him into too great intercourse with other boys.[1] At a time when St. Jerome had suffered himself to feel a deep admiration for the genius of Cicero, he was, as he himself tells us, borne in the night before the tribunal of Christ, accused of being rather a Ciceronian than a Christian, and severely flagellated by the angels.[2] This saint, however, afterwards modified his opinions about the Pagan writings, and he was compelled to defend himself at length against his more jealous brethren, who accused him of defiling his writings with quotations from Pagan authors, and of employing some monks in copying Cicero, and of explaining Virgil to some children at Bethlehem.[3] Of one monk it is related, that being especially famous as a linguist, he made it his penance to remain perfectly silent for thirty years.[4] Of another, that having discovered a few books in the cell of a brother

la prophétie et des miracles. Ce sont des dons que sa Providence a presque toujours séparéz.'—*Mém. Hist. ecclés.* tome iv. p. 315.

[1] St. Athanasius, *Vit. Anton.*

[2] *Ep.* xxii. He says his shoulders were bruised when he awoke.

[3] *Ep.* lxx.; *Adv. Rufinum*, lib. i. ch. xxx. He there speaks of his vision as a mere dream, not binding. He elsewhere (*Ep.* cxxv.) speaks very sensibly of the advantage of hermits occupying themselves, and says he learnt Hebrew to keep away unholy thoughts.

[4] Sozomen, vi. 28; Rufinus, *Hist. Monach.* ch. vi. Socrates tells rather a touching story of one of these illiterate saints, named Pambos. Being unable to read, he came to some one to be taught a psalm. Having learnt the single verse, 'I said I will take heed to my ways, that I offend not with my tongue,' he went away, saying that was enough if it were practically acquired. When asked six months, and again many years after, why he did not come to learn another verse, he answered that he had never been able truly to master this. (*H. E.* iv. 23.)

hermit, he reproached the student with having thus defrauded of their property the widow and the orphan;[1] of others, that their only books were copies of the New Testament, which they sold to relieve the poor.[2]

With such men, living such a life, visions and miracles were necessarily habitual. All the elements of hallucination were there. Ignorant and superstitious, believing as a matter of religious conviction that countless dæmons filled the air, attributing every fluctuation of his own temperament, and every exceptional phenomenon in surrounding nature to spiritual agency; delirious, too, from solitude and long-continued austerities, the hermit soon mistook for palpable realities the phantoms of his brain. In the ghastly gloom of the sepulchre, where, amid mouldering corpses, he took up his abode; in the long hours of the night of penance, when the desert wind sobbed around his lonely cell, and the cries of wild beasts were borne upon his ear, visible forms of lust or terror appeared to haunt him, and strange dramas were enacted by those who were contending for his soul. An imagination strained to the utmost limit, acting upon a frame attenuated and diseased by macerations, produced bewildering psychological phenomena, paroxysms of conflicting passions, sudden alternations of joy and anguish, which he regarded as manifestly supernatural. Sometimes, in the very ecstasy of his devotion, the memory of old scenes would crowd upon his mind. The shady groves and soft voluptuous gardens of his native city would arise, and, kneeling alone upon the burning sand, he seemed to see around him the fair groups of dancing-girls, on whose warm, undulating limbs and wanton smiles his youthful eyes had too fondly dwelt. Sometimes his temptation sprang from remem-

[1] Tillemont, x. p. 61.

[2] Ibid. viii. 490; Socrates, *H. E.* iv. 23.

bered sounds. The sweet, licentious songs of other days came floating on his ear, and his heart was thrilled with the passions of the past. And then the scene would change. As his lips were murmuring the psalter, his imagination, fired perhaps by the music of some martial psalm, depicted the crowded amphitheatre. The throng, and passion, and mingled cries of eager thousands were present to his mind, and the fierce joy of the gladiators passed through the tumult of his dream.[1] The simplest incident came at last to suggest diabolical influence. An old hermit, weary and fainting upon his journey, once thought how refreshing would be a draught of the honey of wild bees of the desert. At that moment his eye fell upon a rock on which they had built a hive. He passed on with a shudder and an exorcism, for he believed it to be a temptation of the devil.[2] But most terrible of all were the struggles of young and ardent men, through whose veins the hot blood of passion continually flowed, physically incapable of a life of celibacy, and with all that proneness to hallucination which a southern sun engenders, who were borne on the wave of enthusiasm to the desert life. In the arms of Syrian or African brides, whose soft eyes answered love with love, they might have sunk to rest, but in the lonely wilderness no peace could ever visit their souls. The lives of the saints paint with an

[1] I have combined in this passage incidents from three distinct lives. St. Jerome, in a very famous and very beautiful passage of his letter to Eustochium (*Ep.* xxii.), describes the manner in which the forms of dancing-girls appeared to surround him as he knelt upon the desert sands. St. Mary of Egypt (*Vitæ Patrum*, ch. xix.) was especially tortured by the recollection of the songs she had sung when young, which continually haunted her mind. St. Hilarion (see his *Life* by St. Jerome) thought he saw a gladiatorial show while he was repeating the psalms. The manner in which the different visions faded into one another like dissolving views is repeatedly described in the biographies.

[2] Rufinus, *Hist. Monach.* ch. xi. This saint was St. Helenus.

appalling vividness the agonies of their struggle. Multiplying with frantic energy the macerations of the body, beating their breasts with anguish, the tears for ever streaming from their eyes, imagining themselves continually haunted by ever-changing forms of deadly beauty, which acquired a greater vividness from the very passion with which they resisted them, their struggles not unfrequently ended in insanity and in suicide. It is related that when St. Pachomius and St. Palæmon were conversing together in the desert, a young monk, with his countenance distracted with madness, rushed into their presence, and, with a voice broken with convulsive sobs, poured out his tale of sorrows. A woman, he said, had entered his cell, had seduced him by her artifices, and then vanished miraculously in the air, leaving him half dead upon the ground;—and then with a wild shriek the monk broke away from the saintly listeners. Impelled, as they imagined, by an evil spirit, he rushed across the desert, till he arrived at the next village, and there, leaping into the open furnace of the public baths, he perished in the flames.[1] Strange stories were told among the monks of revulsions of passion even in the most advanced. Of one monk especially, who had long been regarded as a pattern of asceticism, but who had suffered himself to fall into that self-complacency which was very common among the anchorites, it was told that one evening a fainting woman appeared at the door of his cell, and implored him to give her shelter, and not permit her to be devoured by the wild beasts. In an evil hour he yielded to her prayer. With all the aspect of profound reverence she won his regards, and at last ventured to lay her hand upon him. But that touch convulsed his frame. Passions

[1] Life of St. Pachomius (*Vit. Patrum*), cap. ix.

long slumbering and forgotten rushed with an impetuous fury through his veins. In a paroxysm of fierce love, he sought to clasp the woman to his heart, but she vanished from his sight, and a chorus of dæmons, with peals of laughter, exulted over his fall. The sequel of the story, as it is told by the monkish writer, is, I think, of a very high order of artistic merit. The fallen hermit did not seek, as might have been expected, by penance and prayers to renew his purity. That moment of passion and of shame had revealed in him a new nature, and severed him irrevocably from the hopes and feelings of the ascetic life. The fair form that had arisen upon his dream, though he knew it to be a deception luring him to destruction, still governed his heart. He fled from the desert, plunged anew into the world, avoided all intercourse with the monks, and followed the light of that ideal beauty even into the jaws of hell.[1]

Anecdotes of this kind, circulated among the monks, contributed to heighten the feelings of terror with which they regarded all communication with the other sex. But to avoid such communication was sometimes very difficult. Few things are more striking in the early historians of the movement we are considering, than the manner in which narratives of the deepest tragical interest alternate with extremely whimsical accounts of the profound admiration with which the female devotees

[1] Rufinus, *Hist. Monach.* cap. i. This story was told to Rufinus by St. John the hermit. The same saint described his own visions very graphically. 'Denique etiam me frequenter dæmones noctibus seduxerunt, et neque orare neque requiescere permiserunt, phantasias quasdam per noctem totam sensibus meis et cogitationes suggerentes. Mane vero velut cum quadam illusione prosternebant se ante me dicentes, Indulge nobis, abbas, quia laborem tibi incussimus tota nocte.'—Ibid. St. Benedict in the desert is said to have been tortured by the recollection of a beautiful girl he had once seen, and only regained his composure by rolling in thorns. (St. Greg. *Dial.* ii. 2.)

regarded the most austere anchorites, and the unwearied perseverance with which they endeavoured to force themselves upon their notice. Some women seem in this respect to have been peculiarly fortunate. St. Melania, who devoted a great portion of her fortune to the monks, accompanied by the historian Rufinus, made near the end of the fourth century a long pilgrimage through the Syrian and Egyptian hermitages.[1] But with many of the hermits it was a rule never to look upon the face of any woman, and the number of years they had escaped this contamination was commonly stated as a conspicuous proof of their excellence. St. Basil would only speak to a woman under extreme necessity.[2] St. John of Lycopolis had not seen a woman for forty-eight years.[3] A tribune was sent by his wife on a pilgrimage to St. John the hermit to implore him to allow her to visit him, her desire being so intense that she would probably, in the opinion of her husband, die if it was ungratified. At last the hermit told his suppliant that he would that night visit his wife when she was in bed in her house. The tribune brought this strange message to his wife, who that night saw the hermit in a dream.[4] A young Roman girl made a pilgrimage from Italy to Alexandria, to look upon the face, and obtain the prayers of St. Arsenius, into whose presence she forced herself. Quailing beneath his rebuffs, she flung herself at his feet, imploring him with tears to grant her only request—to remember her, and to pray for her. 'Remember you,' cried the indignant

[1] She lived also for some time in a convent at Jerusalem which she had founded. Melania (who was one of St. Jerome's friends) was a lady of rank and fortune, who devoted her property to the monks. See her journey in Rosweyde, lib. ii.

[2] See his life in Tillemont.

[3] Ibid. x. p. 14. A certain Didymus lived entirely alone till his death, which took place when he was ninety. (Socrates, *H. E.* iv. 23.)

[4] Rufinus, *Hist. Monachorum*, cap. i.

saint, 'It shall be the prayer of my life that I may forget you.' The poor girl sought consolation from the Archbishop of Alexandria, who comforted her by assuring her that though she belonged to the sex by which dæmons commonly tempt saints, he doubted not the hermit would pray for her soul, though he would try to forget her face.[1] Sometimes this female enthusiasm took another and a more subtle form, and on more than one occasion women were known to attire themselves as men, and to pass their lives undisturbed as anchorites. Among others, St. Pelagia, who had been the most beautiful, and one of the most dangerously seductive actresses of Antioch, having been somewhat strangely converted, was appointed by the bishops to live in penance with an elderly virgin of irreproachable piety; but impelled, we are told, by her desire for a more austere life, she fled from her companion, assumed a male attire, took refuge among the monks on the Mount of Olives, and, with something of the skill of her old profession, supported her feigned character so consistently, that she acquired great renown, and it was only (it is said) after her death that the saints discovered who had been living among them.[2]

[1] *Verba Seniorum*, § 65.

[2] Pelagia was very pretty, and, according to her own account, 'her sins were heavier than the sand.' The people of Antioch, who were very fond of her, called her Marguerita, or the pearl. 'Il arriva un jour que divers évesques, appelez par celui d'Antioche pour quelques affaires, estant ensemble à la porte de l'église de S.-Julien, Pélagie passa devant eux dans tout l'éclat des pompes du diable, n'ayant pas seulement une coeffe sur sa teste ni un mouchoir sur ses épaules, ce qu'on remarque comme le comble de son impudence. Tous les évesques baissèrent les yeux en gémissant pour ne pas voir ce dangereux objet de péché, hors Nonne, très-saint évesque d'Héliople, qui la regarda avec une attention qui fit peine aux autres.' However, this bishop immediately began crying a great deal, and reassured his brethren, and a sermon which he preached led to the conversion of the actress. (Tillemont, *Mém. d'Hist. ecclés.* tome xii. pp. 378–380.) See, too, on women, 'under pretence of religion,' attiring themselves as men, Sozomen, iii. 14.)

The foregoing anecdotes and observations will, I hope, have given a sufficiently clear idea of the general nature of the monastic life in its earliest phase, and also of the writings it produced. We may now proceed to examine the ways in which this mode of life affected both the ideal type and the realised condition of Christian morals. And in the first place, it is manifest that the proportion of virtues was altered. If an impartial person were to glance over the ethics of the New Testament, and were asked what was the central and distinctive virtue to which the sacred writers most continually referred, he would doubtless answer, that it was that which is described as love, charity, or philanthropy. If he were to apply a similar scrutiny to the writings of the fourth and fifth centuries, he would answer that the cardinal virtue of the religious type was not love, but chastity. And this chastity, which was regarded as the ideal state, was not the purity of an undefiled marriage. It was the absolute suppression of the whole sensual side of our nature. The chief form of virtue, the central conception of the saintly life, was a perpetual struggle against all unchaste impulses, by men who altogether refused the compromise of marriage. From this fact, if I mistake not, some interesting and important consequences may be deduced.

In the first place, religion gradually assumed a very sombre hue. The business of the saint was to eradicate a natural appetite, to attain a condition which was emphatically abnormal. The depravity of human nature, and especially the essential evil of the body, were felt with a degree of intensity that could never have been attained by moralists who were occupied mainly with transient or exceptional vices, such as envy, anger, or cruelty. And in addition to the extreme inveteracy of the appetite which it was desired to eradicate, it should be remembered that a somewhat luxurious and indulgent life, even when that indulgence is not itself distinctly evil, even when it has a tendency to mollify the character, has naturally the effect of strengthening the animal passions, and is therefore directly opposed to the ascetic ideal. The consequence of this was first of all a very deep sense of the habitual and innate depravity of human nature, and in the next place, a very strong association of the idea of pleasure with that of vice. All this was the necessary consequence of the supreme value placed upon virginity. The tone of calm and joyousness that characterises Greek philosophy, the almost complete absence of all sense of struggle and innate sin that it displays, is probably in a very large degree to be ascribed to the fact that, in the department of morals we are considering, Greek moralists made no serious efforts to improve our nature, and Greek public opinion acquiesced, without scandal, in an almost boundless indulgence of illicit pleasures.

But while the great prominence at this time given to the conflicts of the ascetic life threw a dark shade upon the popular estimate of human nature, it contributed, I think, very largely to sustain and deepen that strong conviction of the freedom of the human will which the Catholic Church has always so strenuously upheld; for there is, probably, no other form of moral conflict in which men are so habitually and so keenly sensible of that distinction between our will and our desires, upon the reality of which all moral freedom ultimately depends. It had also, I imagine, another result, which it is difficult to describe with the same precision. What may be called a strong animal nature—a nature, that is, in which the passions are in vigorous, and at the same time healthy action, is that in which we should most naturally expect to find several moral qualities. Good humour, frankness, generosity, active courage, sanguine energy, buoyancy of temper, are the usual and appropriate accompaniments of a vigorous animal temperament, and they are much more rarely found either in natures that are essentially feeble and effeminate, or in natures which have been artificially emasculated by penances, distorted from their original tendency, and habitually held under severe control. The ideal type of Catholicism being, on account of the supreme value placed upon virginity, of the latter kind, the qualities I have mentioned have always ranked very low in the Catholic conceptions of excellence, and the steady tendency of Protestant and industrial civilisation has been to elevate them.

I do not know whether the reader will regard these speculations—which I advance with some diffidence—as far-fetched and fanciful. Our knowledge of the physical antecedents of different moral qualities is so scanty, that it is difficult to speak on these matters with much confidence; but few persons, I think, can have failed to observe that the physical temperaments I have described, differ not simply in the one great fact of the intensity of the animal passions, but also in the aptitude of each to produce a distinct moral type, or, in other words, in the harmony of each with several qualities, both good and evil. A doctrine, therefore, which connects one of these two temperaments indissolubly with the moral ideal, affects the appreciation of a large number of moral qualities. But whatever may be thought of the moral results springing from the physical temperament which asceticism produced, there can be little controversy as to the effects springing from the condition of life which it enjoined. Severance from the interests and affections of all around him, was the chief object of the anchorite, and the first consequence of the prominence of asceticism was a profound discredit thrown upon the domestic virtues.

The extent to which this discredit was carried, the intense hardness of heart and ingratitude manifested by the saints towards those who were bound to them by the closest of earthly ties, is known to few who have not studied the original literature on the subject. These things are commonly thrown into the shade by those modern sentimentalists who delight in idealising the devotees of the past. To break by his ingratitude the heart of the mother who had borne him, to persuade the wife who adored him that it was her duty to separate from him for ever, to abandon his children, uncared for and beggars, to the mercies of the world, was regarded by the true hermit as the most acceptable offering he could make to his God. His business was to save his own soul. The serenity of his devotion would be impaired by the discharge of the simplest duties to his family. Evagrius, when a hermit in the desert, received, after a long interval, letters from his father and mother. He could not bear that the equable tenor of his thoughts should be disturbed by the recollection of those who loved him, so he cast the letters unread into the fire.[1] A man named Mutius, accompanied by his only child, a little boy of eight years old, once abandoned his possessions and demanded admission in a monastery. The monks received him, but they proceeded to discipline his heart. 'He had already forgotten that he was rich; he must next be taught to forget that

[1] Tillemont, tome x. pp. 376–377. Apart from family affections, there are some curious instances recorded of the anxiety of the saints to avoid distractions. One monk used to cover his face when he went into his garden, lest the sight of the trees should disturb his mind. (*Verb. Seniorum.*) St. Arsenius could not bear the rustling of the reeds (Ibid.); and a saint named Boniface struck dead a man who went about with an ape and a cymbal, because he had (apparently quite unintentionally) disturbed him at his prayers. (St. Greg. *Dial.* i. 9.)

he was a father.'[1] His little child was separated from him, clothed in dirty rags, subjected to every form of gross and wanton hardship, beaten, spurned, and ill treated. Day after day the father was compelled to look upon his boy wasting away with sorrow, his once happy countenance for ever stained with tears, distorted by sobs of anguish. But yet, says the admiring biographer, 'though he saw this day by day, such was his love for Christ, and for the virtue of obedience, that the father's heart was rigid and unmoved.' 'He thought little of the tears of his child. He was anxious only for his own humility and perfection in virtue.'[2] At last the abbot told him to take his child and throw it into the river. He proceeded, without a murmur or apparent pang, to obey, and it was only at the last moment that the monks interposed, and on the very brink of the river saved the child. Mutius afterwards rose to a high position among the ascetics, and was justly regarded as having displayed in great perfection the temper of a saint.[3] An inhabitant of Thebes once came to the abbot Sisoes, and asked to be made a monk. The abbot asked if he had anyone belonging to him. He answered, 'A son.' 'Take your son,' rejoined the old man, 'and throw him into the river, and then you may become a monk.' The father hastened to fulfil the command, and the deed was almost consummated when a messenger sent by Sisoes revoked the order.[4]

Sometimes the same lesson was taught under the form of a miracle. A man had once deserted his three children

[1] 'Quemadmodum se jam divitem non esse sciebat, ita etiam patrem se esse nesciret.'—Cassian, *De Cœnobiorum Institutis*, iv. 27.

[2] 'Cumque taliter infans sub oculis ejus per dies singulos ageretur, pro amore nihilominus Christi et obedientiæ virtute, rigida semper atque immobilia patris viscera permanserunt. . . . parum cogitans de lacrymis ejus, sed de propria humilitate ac perfectione sollicitus.'—Ibid.

[3] Ibid.

[4] Bollandists, July 6; *Verba Seniorum*, xiv.

to become a monk. Three years after, he determined to bring them into the monastery, but, on returning to his home, found that the two eldest had died during his absence. He came to his abbot, bearing in his arms his youngest child, who was still little more than an infant. The abbot turned to him, and said, 'Do you love this child?' The father answered, 'Yes.' Again the abbot said, 'Do you love it dearly?' The father answered as before. 'Then take the child,' said the abbot, 'and throw it into the fire upon yonder hearth.' The father did as he was commanded, and the child remained unharmed amid the flames.[1] But it was especially in their dealings with their female relations that this aspect of the monastic character was vividly displayed. In this case the motive was not simply to mortify family affections—it was also to guard against the possible danger resulting from the presence of a woman. The fine flower of that saintly purity might have been disturbed by the sight of a mother's or a sister's face. The ideal of one age appears sometimes too grotesque for the caricature of another; and it is curious to observe how pale and weak is the picture which Molière drew of the affected prudery of Tartuffe,[2] when compared with the narratives that are gravely propounded in the lives of the saints. When the abbot Sisoes had become a very old, feeble, and decrepit man, his disciples exhorted

[1] *Verba Seniorum*, xiv.

[2] TARTUFFE (*tirant un mouchoir de sa poche*).

'Ah, mon Dieu, je vous prie,
Avant que de parler, prenez-moi ce mouchoir.

DORINE.

Comment!

TARTUFFE.

Couvrez ce sein que je ne saurois voir;
Par de pareils objets des âmes sont blessées,
Et cela fait venir de coupables pensées.'

*Tartuffe*, Acte iii. scène 2.

him to leave the desert for an inhabited country. Sisoes seemed to yield; but he stipulated as a necessary condition, that in his new abode he should never be compelled to encounter the peril and perturbation of looking on a woman's face. To such a nature of course the desert alone was suitable, and the old man was suffered to die in peace.[1] A monk was once travelling with his mother —in itself a most unusual circumstance—and, having arrived at a bridgeless stream, it became necessary for him to carry her across. To her surprise, he began carefully wrapping up his hands in cloths; and upon her asking the reason, he explained that he was alarmed lest he should be unfortunate enough to touch her, and thereby disturb the equilibrium of his nature.[2] The sister of St. John of Calama loved him dearly, and earnestly implored him that she might look upon his face once more before she died. On his persistent refusal, she at last declared that she would make a pilgrimage to him in the desert. The alarmed and perplexed saint at last wrote to her, promising to visit her if she would engage to relinquish her design. He went to her in disguise, received a cup of water from her hands, and came away without being discovered. She wrote to him, reproaching him with not having fulfilled his promise. He answered her, that he had indeed visited her, that 'by the mercy of Jesus Christ he had not been recognised,' and that she must never see him again.[3] The mother of St. Theodorus came armed with letters from the bishops to see her son, but he implored his abbot, St. Pachomius, to permit him to

[1] Bollandists, July 6.

[2] *Verba Seniorum*, iv. The poor woman, being startled and perplexed at the proceedings of her son, said, 'Quid sic operuisti manus tuas, fili? Ille autem dixit: Quia corpus mulieris ignis est, et ex eo ipso quo te contingebam veniebat mihi commemoratio aliarum feminarum in animo.'

[3] Tillemont, *Mém. de l'Hist. ecclés.* tome x. pp. 444–445.

decline the interview; and, finding all her efforts in vain, the poor woman retired into a convent, together with her daughter, who had made a similar expedition with similar results.[1] The mother of St. Marcus persuaded his abbot to command the saint to go out to her. Placed in a dilemma between the sin of disobedience and the perils of seeing his mother, St. Marcus extricated himself by an ingenious device. He went to his mother with his face disguised and his eyes shut. The mother did not recognise her son. The son did not see his mother.[2] The sister of St. Pior in like manner induced the abbot of that saint to command him to admit her to his presence. The command was obeyed, but St. Pior resolutely kept his eyes shut during the interview.[3] St. Pœmen and his six brothers had all deserted their mother to cultivate the perfections of an ascetic life. But ingratitude can seldom quench the love of a mother's heart, and the old woman, now bent by infirmities, went alone into the Egyptian desert to see once more the children she had so dearly loved. She caught sight of them as they were about leaving their cell for the church, but they immediately ran back into the cell, and before her tottering steps could reach it, one of her sons rushed forward and flung the door to in her face. She remained outside weeping bitterly. St. Pœmen then, coming to the door, but without opening it, said, 'Why do you, who are already stricken with age, pour forth such cries and lamentations?' But she, recognising the voice of her son, answered, 'It is because I long to see you, my sons. What harm could it do you that I should see you? Am I not your mother? did I not give you suck? I am now an old and wrinkled woman, and my heart is troubled at

[1] *Vit. S. Pachomius*, ch. xxxi.; *Verba Seniorum*.

[2] *Verba Seniorum*, xiv.

[3] Palladius, *Hist. Laus.* cap. lxxxvii.

the sound of your voices.'[1] The saintly brothers, however, refused to open their door. They told their mother that she would see them after death; and the biographer says she at last went away contented with the prospect. St. Simeon Stylites, in this as in other respects, stands in the first line. He had been passionately loved by his parents, and, if we may believe his eulogist and biographer, he began his saintly career by breaking the heart of his father, who died of grief at his flight. His mother, however, lingered on. Twenty-seven years after his disappearance, at a period when his austerities had made him famous, she heard for the first time where he was, and hastened to visit him. But all her labour was in vain. No woman was admitted within the precincts of his dwelling, and he refused to permit her even to look upon his face. Her entreaties and tears were mingled with words of bitter and eloquent reproach.[2]

[1] Bollandists, June 6. I avail myself again of the version of Tillemont. 'Lorsque S. Pemen demeuroit en Égypte avec ses frères, leur mère, qui avoit un extrême désir de les voir, venoit souvent au lieu où ils estoient, sans pouvoir jamais avoir cette satisfaction. Une fois enfin elle prit si bien son temps qu'elle les rencontra qui alloient à l'église, mais dès qu'ils la virent ils s'en retournèrent en haste dans leur cellule et fermèrent la porte sur eux. Elle les suivit, et trouvant la porte, elle les appeloit avec des larmes et des cris capables de les toucher de compassion. . . . Pemen s'y leva et s'y en alla, et l'entendant pleurer il luy dit, tenant toujours la porte fermée, "Pourquoi vous lassez-vous inutilement à pleurer et crier? N'êtes-vous pas déjà assez abattue par la vieillesse?" Elle reconnut la voix de Pemen, et s'efforçant encore davantage, elle s'écria, "Hé, mes enfans, c'est que je voudrois bien vous voir: et quel mal y a-t-il que je vous voie? Ne suis-je pas votre mère, et ne vous ai-je pas nourri du lait de mes mammelles? Je suis déjà toute pleine de rides, et lorsque je vous ay entendu, l'extrême envie que j'ay de vous voir m'a tellement émue que je suis presque tombée en défaillance."'—*Mémoires de l'Hist. ecclés.* tome xv. pp. 157–158.

[2] The original is much more eloquent than my translation. 'Fili, quare hoc fecisti? Pro utero quo te portavi, satiasti me luctu, pro lactatione qua te lactavi dedisti mihi lacrymas, pro osculo quo te osculata sum, dedisti mihi amaras cordis angustias; pro dolore et labore quem passa sum, imposuisti mihi sævissimas plagas.'—*Vita Simeonis* (in Rosweyde).

'My son,' she is represented as having said, 'Why have you done this? I bore you in my womb, and you have wrung my soul with grief. I gave you milk from my breast, you have filled my eyes with tears. For the kisses I gave you, you have given me the anguish of a broken heart; for all that I have done and suffered for you, you have repaid me by the most bitter wrongs.' At last the saint sent a message to tell her that she would soon see him. Three days and three nights she had wept and entreated in vain, and now, exhausted with grief and age and privation, she sank feebly to the ground and breathed her last sigh before that inhospitable door. Then for the first time the saint, accompanied by his followers, came out. He shed some pious tears over the corpse of his murdered mother, and offered up a prayer consigning her soul to heaven. Perhaps it was but fancy, perhaps life was not yet wholly extinct, perhaps the story is but the invention of the biographer; but a faint motion—which appears to have been regarded as miraculous—is said to have passed over her prostrate form. Simeon once more commended her soul to heaven, and then, amid the admiring murmurs of his disciples, the saintly matricide returned to his devotions.

The glaring mendacity that characterises the lives of the Catholic saints, probably to a greater extent than any other important branch of existing literature, makes it not unreasonable to hope that many of the foregoing anecdotes represent much less events that actually took place than ideal pictures generated by the enthusiasm of the chroniclers. They are not, however, on that account the less significant of the moral conceptions which the ascetic period had created. The ablest men in the Christian community vied with one another in inculcating as the highest form of duty the abandonment of social ties and the mortification of domestic affections. A few faint restrictions were indeed occasionally made. Much—on which I shall hereafter touch—was written on the liberty of husbands and wives deserting one another; and something was written on the cases of children forsaking or abandoning their parents. At first, those who, when children, were devoted to the monasteries by their parents, without their own consent, were permitted, when of mature age, to return to the world; and this liberty was taken from them for the first time by the fourth Council of Toledo, in A.D. 633.[1] The Council of Gangra condemned the heretic Eustathius for teaching that children might through religious motives forsake their parents, and St. Basil wrote in the same strain;[2] but cases of this kind of rebellion against parental authority were continually recounted with admiration in the lives of the saints, applauded by some of the leading Fathers, and virtually sanctioned by a law of Justinian, which prohibited parents either from restraining their children from entering monasteries, or disinheriting them if they had done so without their consent.[3] St. Chrysostom relates with enthusiasm the case of a young man who had been designed by his father for the army, and who was lured away into a monastery.[4] The eloquence of St. Ambrose is said to have been so seductive, that mothers were accustomed to shut up their daughters to guard them against his fascinations.[5] The position of affectionate parents was at this time extremely painful. The touching language is still preserved, in which the mother of St. Chrysostom—who had a distinguished part in the conversion of her son—implored him, if he thought it his duty to fly to the desert life, at least to postpone the act till she had died.[6]

[1] Bingham, *Antiquities*, book vii. ch. iii. [2] Ibid. [3] Ibid.
[4] Milman's *Early Christianity* (ed. 1867), vol. iii. p. 122.
[5] Ibid. vol. iii. p. 153. [6] Ibid. vol. iii. p. 120.

St. Ambrose devoted a chapter to proving that, while those are worthy of commendation who entered the monasteries with the approbation, those are still more worthy of praise who do so against the wishes, of their parents; and he proceeded to show how small were the penalties the latter could inflict when compared with the blessings asceticism could bestow.[1] Even before the law of Justinian, the invectives of the clergy were directed against those who endeavoured to prevent their children flying to the desert. St. Chrysostom explained to them that they would certainly be damned.[2] St. Ambrose showed, that even in this world they might not be unpunished. A girl, he tells us, had resolved to enter into a convent, and as her relations were expostulating with her on her intention, one of those present tried to move her by the memory of her dead father, asking whether, if he were still alive, he would have suffered her to remain unmarried. 'Perhaps,' she calmly answered, 'it was for this very purpose he died, that he should not throw any obstacle in my way.' Her words were more than an answer, they were an oracle. The indiscreet questioner almost immediately died, and the relations, shocked by the manifest providence, desisted from their opposition, and even implored the young saint to accomplish her design.[3] St. Jerome tells with rapturous enthusiasm of a little girl, named Asella, who, when only twelve years old, devoted herself to this religious life, refused to look on the face of any man, and whose knees, by constant prayer, became at last like those of a camel.[4] A famous widow, named Paula, upon the death of her husband, deserted her family, listened with 'dry eyes' to her children, who were imploring her to stay, fled to the society of the monks at Jerusalem,

[1] *De Virginibus*, i. 11. [2] Milman's *Early Christianity*, vol. iii. p. 121.
[3] *De Virginibus*, i. 11. [4] *Epist.* xxiv.

made it her desire that 'she might die a beggar, and leave not one piece of money to her son,' and having dissipated the whole of her fortune in charities, bequeathed to her children only the embarrassment of her debts.[1] It was carefully inculcated that all money given or bequeathed to the poor, or to the monks, produced spiritual benefit to the donors or testators, but that no spiritual benefit sprang from money bestowed upon relations; and the more pious minds recoiled from disposing of their property in a manner that would not redound to the advantage of their souls. Sometimes parents made it a dying request of their children that they would preserve none of their property, but would bestow it all among the poor.[2] It was one of the most honourable incidents of the life of St. Augustine, that he, like Aurelius, Bishop of Carthage, refused to receive legacies or donations which unjustly spoliated the relatives of the benefactor.[3] Usually, however, to outrage the affections of the nearest and dearest relations was not only regarded as innocent, but proposed as the highest virtue. 'A young man,' it was acutely said, 'who has learnt to despise a mother's grief, will easily bear any other labour that is imposed

[1] St. Jerome describes the scene at her departure with admiring eloquence. 'Descendit ad portum fratre, cognatis, affinibus et quod majus est liberis prosequentibus, et clementissimam matrem pietate vincere cupientibus. Jam carbasa tendebantur, et remorum ductu navis in altum protrahebatur. Parvus Toxotius supplices manus tendebat in littore, Ruffina jam nubilis ut suas expectaret nuptias tacens fletibus obsecrabat. Et tamen illa siccos tendebat ad cælum oculos, pietatem in filios pietate in Deum superans. Nesciebat se matrem ut Christi probaret ancillam.'—*Ep.* cviii. In another place he says of her, 'Testis est Jesus, ne unum quidem nummum ab ea filiæ derelictum, sed, ut ante jam dixi, derelictum magnum æs alienum.'—Ibid. And again, 'Vis, lector, ejus breviter scire virtutes? Omnes suos pauperes, pauperior ipsa dimisit.'—Ibid.

[2] See Chastel, *Études historiques sur la Charité*, p. 231. The parents of St. Gregory Nazianzen had made this request, which was faithfully observed.

[3] Chastel, p. 232.

upon him.'[1] St. Jerome, when exhorting Heliodorus to desert his family and become a hermit, expatiated with a fond minuteness on every form of natural affection he desired him to violate. 'Though your little nephew twine his arms around your neck; though your mother, with dishevelled hair and tearing her robe asunder, point to the breast with which she suckled you; though your father fall down on the threshold before you, pass on over your father's body. Fly with tearless eyes to the banner of the cross. In this matter cruelty is the only piety. . . . Your widowed sister may throw her gentle arms around you. . . . Your father may implore you to wait but a short time to bury those near to you, who will soon be no more; your weeping mother may recall your childish days, and may point to her shrunken breast and to her wrinkled brow. Those around you may tell you that all the household rests upon you. Such chains as these, the love of God and the fear of hell can easily break. You say that Scripture orders you to obey your parents, but he who loves them more than Christ loses his soul. The enemy brandishes a sword to slay me. Shall I think of a mother's tears?'[2]

The sentiment manifested in these cases continued to be displayed in the later ages. Thus, St. Gregory the Great assures us that a certain young boy, though he had enrolled himself as a monk, was unable to repress his love for his parents, and one night stole out secretly to visit them. But the judgment of God soon marked the enormity of the offence. On coming back to the monastery, he died that very day, and when he was

[1] See a characteristic passage from the *Life of St. Fulgentius,* quoted by Dean Milman. 'Facile potest juvenis tolerare quemcunque imposuerit laborem qui poterit maternum jam despicere dolorem.'—*Hist. of Latin Christianity,* vol. ii. p. 82.

[2] *Ep.* xiv. (*Ad Heliodorum*).

buried, the earth refused to receive so heinous a criminal. His body was repeatedly thrown up from the grave, and it was only suffered to rest in peace when St. Benedict had laid the Sacrament upon its breast.[1] One nun revealed, it is said, after death, that she had been condemned for three days to the fires of purgatory, because she had loved her mother too much.[2] Of another saint it is recorded, that his benevolence was such that he was never known to be hard or inhuman to anyone except his relations.[3] St. Romuald, the founder of the Camaldolites, counted his father among his spiritual children, and on one occasion punished him by flagellation.[4] The first nun, whom St. Francis of Assisi enrolled, was a beautiful girl of Assisi, named Clara Scifi, with whom he had for some time carried on a clandestine correspondence, and whose flight from her father's home he both counselled and planned.[5] As the first enthusiasm of asceticism died away, what was lost in influence by the father was gained by the priest. The confessional made this personage the confidant in the most delicate secrets of domestic life. The supremacy of authority, of sympathy, and sometimes even of affection, passed away beyond the domestic circle, and by establishing an absolute authority over the most secret thoughts and feelings of nervous and credulous women, the priests laid the foundation of the empire of the world.

The picture I have drawn of the inroads made in the first period of asceticism upon the domestic affections, tells, I think, its own story, and I shall only add a very

[1] St. Greg. *Dial.* ii. 24.

[2] Bollandists, May 3 (vol. vii. p. 561).

[3] 'Hospitibus omni loco ac tempore liberalissimus fuit. . . . Solis consanguineis durus erat et inhumanus, tamquam ignotos illos respiciens.'—Bollandists, May 29.

[4] See Helyot, *Dict. des Ordres religieux*, art. 'Camaldules.'

[5] See the charming sketch in the *Life of St. Francis*, by Hase.

few words of comment. That it is necessary for many men who are pursuing a truly heroic course to break loose from the trammels which those about them would cast over their actions or their opinions, and that this severance often constitutes at once one of the noblest and one of the most painful incidents in their career, are unquestionable truths; but the examples of such occasional and exceptional sacrifices, endured rather than relinquish some great unselfish end, cannot be compared with the conduct of those who regarded the mortification of domestic love as in itself a form of virtue, and whose ends were mainly or exclusively selfish. The sufferings endured by the ascetic who fled from his relations were often, no doubt, very great. Many anecdotes remain to show that warm and affectionate hearts sometimes beat under the cold exterior of the monk,[1] and St. Jerome, in one of his letters, remarked, with much complacency and congratulation, that the very bitterest pang of captivity is simply this irrevocable separation which the superstition he preached induced multitudes to inflict upon themselves. But if, putting aside the intrinsic excellence of an act, we attempt to estimate the nobility of the agent, we must consider not only the cost of what he did, but also the motive which induced him to do it. It is this last consideration which renders it impossible for us to place the heroism of the ascetic on the same level with that of the great patriots of Greece or Rome. A man may be as

[1] The legend of St. Scholastica, the sister of St. Benedict, has been often quoted. He had visited her, and was about to leave in the evening, when she implored him to stay. He refused, and she then prayed to God, who sent so violent a tempest that the saint was unable to depart. (St. Greg. *Dial.* ii. 33.) Cassian speaks of a monk who thought it his duty never to see his mother, but who laboured for a whole year to pay off a debt she had incurred. (Cœnob. *Inst.* v. 38.) St. Jerome mentions the strong natural affection of Paula, though she considered it a virtue to mortify it. (*Ep.* cviii.)

truly selfish about the next world as about this. Where an overpowering dread of future torments, or an intense realisation of future happiness, is the leading motive of action, the theological virtue of faith may be present, but the ennobling quality of disinterestedness is assuredly absent. In our day, when pictures of rewards and punishments beyond the grave act but feebly upon the imagination, a religious motive is commonly an unselfish motive; but it has not always been so, and it was undoubtedly not so in the first period of asceticism. The terrors of a future judgment drove the monk into the desert, and the whole tenor of the ascetic life, while isolating him from human sympathies, fostered an intense, though it may be termed a religious selfishness.

The effect of the mortification of the domestic affections upon the general character was probably very pernicious. The family circle is the appointed sphere not only for the performance of manifest duties, but also for the cultivation of the affections; and the extreme ferocity which so often characterised the ascetic was the natural consequence of the discipline he imposed upon himself. Severed from all other ties, the monks clung with a desperate tenacity to their opinions and to their Church, and hated those who dissented from them with all the intensity of men whose whole lives were concentrated on a single subject, whose ignorance and bigotry prevented them from conceiving the possibility of any good thing in opposition to themselves, and who had made it a main object of their discipline to eradicate all natural sympathies and affections. We may reasonably attribute to the fierce biographer the words of burning hatred of all heretics which St. Athanasius puts in the mouth of the dying patriarch of the hermits;[1] but ecclesiastical history, and especially the

[1] *Life of Antony*. See, too, the sentiments of St. Pachomius, *Vit.* cap.

writings of the later Pagans, abundantly prove that the sentiment was a general one. To the Christian bishops it is mainly due that the wide and general, though not perfect recognition of religious liberty in the Roman legislation was replaced by laws of the most minute and stringent intolerance. To the monks, acting as the executive of an omnipresent, intolerant, and aggressive clergy, is due an administrative change, perhaps even more important than the legislative change that had preceded it. The system of conniving at, neglecting, or despising forms of worship that were formally prohibited, which had been so largely practised by the sceptical Pagans, and under the lax police system of the empire, and which is so important a fact in the history of the rise of Christianity, was absolutely destroyed. Wandering in bands through the country, the monks were accustomed to burn the temples, to break the idols, to overthrow the altars, to engage in fierce conflicts with the peasants, who often defended with desperate courage the shrines of their gods. It would be impossible to conceive men more fitted for the task. Their fierce fanaticism, their persuasion that every idol was tenanted by a literal dæmon, and their belief that death incurred in this iconoclastic crusade was a form of martyrdom, made them careless of all consequences to themselves, while the reverence that attached to their profession rendered it scarcely possible for the civil power to arrest them. Men who had learnt to look with indifference on the tears of a broken-hearted mother, and whose ideal was indissolubly connected with the degradation of the body, were but little likely to be moved either by the pathos of old associations, and of reverent, though mistaken worship, or by the grandeur of the Serapeum, or the noble statues of Phidias and Praxiteles. Sometimes the civil power ordered the reconstruction of Jewish synagogues or heretical churches which had been illegally destroyed ; but the doctrine was early maintained, that such a reconstruction was a deadly sin. Under Julian some Christians suffered martyrdom sooner than be parties to it; and St. Ambrose from the pulpit of Milan, and Simeon Stylites from his desert pillar, united in denouncing Theodosius, who had been guilty of issuing this command.

Another very important moral result to which asceticism largely contributed, was the depression and sometimes almost the extinction of the civic virtues. A candid examination will show that the Christian civilisations have been as inferior to the Pagan ones in civic and intellectual virtues as they have been superior to them in the virtues of humanity and of chastity. We have already seen that one remarkable feature of the intellectual movement that preceded Christianity was the gradual decadence of patriotism. In the early days both of Greece and Rome, the first duty enforced was that of a man to his country. This was the rudimentary or cardinal virtue of the moral type. It gave the tone to the whole system of ethics, and different moral qualities were valued chiefly in proportion to their tendency to form illustrious citizens. The destruction of this spirit in the Roman Empire was due, as we have seen, to two causes—one of them being political and the other intellectual. The political cause was the amalgamation of the different nations in one great despotism, which gave indeed an ample field for personal and intellectual freedom, but extinguished the sentiment of nationality and closed almost every sphere of political activity. The intellectual cause, which was by no means unconnected with the political one, was the growing ascendency of Oriental philosophies, which dethroned the active stoicism of the early empire, and placed its ideal of excellence in contemplative virtues and in elaborate purifications. By this decline of the patriotic sentiment the progress of the new faith was greatly aided. In all matters of religion the opinions of men are governed much more by their sympathies than by their judgments, and it rarely or never happens that a religion which is opposed to a strong national sentiment, as Christianity was in Judea, as Catholicism and Episcopalian Protestantism have been in Scotland, and as Anglicanism is even now in Ireland, can win the acceptance of the people.

The relations of Christianity to the sentiment of patriotism were from the first very unfortunate. While the Christians were, from obvious reasons, completely separated from the national spirit of Judea, they found themselves equally at variance with the lingering remnants of Roman patriotism. Rome was to them the power of Antichrist, and its overthrow the necessary prelude to the millennial reign. They formed an illegal organisation, directly opposed to the genius of the empire, anticipating its speedy destruction, looking back with something more than despondency to the fate of the heroes who had adorned its past, and refusing resolutely to participate in those national spectacles which were the symbols and the expressions of patriotic feeling. Though scrupulously averse to all rebellion, they rarely concealed their sentiments, and the whole tendency of their teaching was to withdraw men as far as possible both from the functions and the enthusiasm of public life. It was at once their confession and their boast, that no interests were more indifferent to them than those of their country.[1] They regarded the lawfulness of taking arms as very questionable, and all those proud and aspiring qualities

[1] 'Nec ulla res aliena magis quam publica.'—Tertullian, *Apol.* ch. xxxviii.

that constitute the distinctive beauty of the soldier's character as emphatically unchristian. Their home and their interests were in another world, and, provided only they were unmolested in their worship, they avowed with frankness, long after the empire had become Christian, that it was a matter of indifference to them under what rule they lived.[1] Asceticism, drawing all the enthusiasm of Christendom to the desert life, and elevating as an ideal the extreme and absolute abnegation of all patriotism,[2] formed the culmination of the movement, and was undoubtedly one cause of the downfall of the Roman Empire.

There are, probably, few subjects on which popular judgments are commonly more erroneous than upon the relations between positive religions and moral enthusiasm.

[1] 'Quid interest sub cujus imperio vivat homo moriturus, si illi qui imperant, ad impia et iniqua non cogant.'—St. Aug. *De Civ. Dei*, v. 17.

[2] 'Monachum in patria sua perfectum esse non posse, perfectum autem esse nolle delinquere est.'—Hieron. *Ep.* xiv. Dean Milman well says of a later period, 'According to the monastic view of Christianity, the total abandonment of the world, with all its ties and duties, as well as its treasures, its enjoyments, and objects of ambition, advanced rather than diminished the hopes of salvation. Why should they fight for a perishing world, from which it was better to be estranged? . . . It is singular, indeed, that while we have seen the Eastern monks turned into fierce undisciplined soldiers, perilling their own lives and shedding the blood of others without remorse, in assertion of some shadowy shade of orthodox expression, hardly anywhere do we find them asserting their liberties or their religion with intrepid resistance. Hatred of heresy was a more stirring motive than the dread or the danger of Islamism. After the first defeats the Christian mind was still further prostrated by the common notion that the invasion was a just and heaven-commissioned visitation; . . . resistance a vain, almost an impious struggle to avert inevitable punishment.'—Milman's *Latin Christianity*, vol. ii. p. 206. Compare Massillon's famous *Discours au Régiment de Catinat*:—'Ce qu'il y a ici de plus déplorable, c'est que dans une vie rude et pénible, dans des emplois dont les devoirs passent quelquefois la rigueur des cloîtres les plus austères, vous souffrez toujours en vain pour l'autre vie. . . . Dix ans de services ont plus usé votre corps qu'une vie entière de pénitence . . . un seul jour de ces souffrances, consacré au Seigneur, vous aurait peut-être valu un bonheur éternel.'

Religions have, no doubt, a most real power of evoking a latent energy which, without their existence, would never have been called into action; but their influence is on the whole probably more attractive than creative. They supply the channel in which moral enthusiasm flows, the banner under which it is enlisted, the mould in which it is cast, the ideal to which it tends. The first idea the phrase 'a very good man' would have suggested to an early Roman, would probably have been that of great and distinguished patriotism, and the passion and interest of such a man in his country's cause were in direct proportion to his moral elevation. Ascetic Christianity decisively diverted moral enthusiasm into another channel, and the civic virtues, in consequence, necessarily declined. The extinction of all public spirit, the base treachery and corruption pervading every department of the Government, the cowardice of the army, the despicable frivolity of character that led the people of Treves, when fresh from their burning city, to call for theatres and circuses, and the people of Roman Carthage to plunge wildly into the excitement of the chariot races, on the very day when their city succumbed beneath the Vandal;[1] all these things coexisted with extraordinary displays of ascetic and of missionary devotion. The genius and the virtue that might have defended the empire were engaged in fierce disputes about the Pelagian controversy, at the very time when Attila was encircling Rome with his armies,[2] and there was no subtlety of theological metaphysics which did not kindle a deeper interest in the Christian leaders than

[1] See a very striking passage in Salvian, *De Gubern. Div.* lib. vi.

[2] Chateaubriand very truly says, 'qu'Orose et saint Augustin étoient plus occupés du schisme de Pélage que de la désolation de l'Afrique et des Gaules.'—*Études histor.* vi^me^ discours, 2^de^ partie. The remark might certainly be extended much further.

the throes of their expiring country. The moral enthusiasm that in other days would have fired the armies of Rome with an invincible valour, impelled thousands to abandon their country and their homes, and consume the weary hours in a long routine of useless and horrible macerations. When the Goths had captured Rome, St. Augustine, as we have seen, pointed with a just pride to the Christian Church, which remained an unviolated sanctuary during the horrors of the sack, as a proof that a new spirit of sanctity and of reverence had descended upon the world. The Pagan, in his turn, pointed to what he deemed a not less significant fact—the golden statues of Valour and of Fortune were melted down to pay the ransom to the conquerors.[1] Many of the Christians contemplated with an indifference that almost amounted to complacency what they regarded as the predicted ruin of the city of the fallen gods.[2] When the Vandals swept over Africa, the Donatists, maddened by the persecution of the orthodox, received them with open arms, and contributed their share to that deadly blow.[3] The immortal pass of Thermopylæ was surrendered without a struggle to the Goths. A Pagan writer accused the monks of having betrayed it.[4] It is more probable that they had absorbed or diverted the heroism that in other days would have defended it. The conquest, at a later date, of Egypt by the Mahommedans, was in a great measure due to an invitation from the persecuted Monophysites.[5] Subsequent religious wars have again and again exhibited the

[1] Zosimus, *Hist.* v. 41. This was on the first occasion when Rome was menaced by Alaric.

[2] See Merivale's *Conversion of the Northern Nations*, pp. 207–210.

[3] See Sismondi, *Hist. de la Chute de l'Empire romain*, tome i. p. 230.

[4] Eunapius. There is no other authority for the story of the treachery, which is not believed by Gibbon.

[5] Sismondi, *Hist. de la Chute de l'Empire romain*, tome ii. pp. 52–54; Milman, *Hist. of Latin Christianity*, vol. ii. p. 213. The Monophysites were

same phenomenon. The treachery of a religionist to his country no longer argued an absence of all moral feeling. It had become compatible with the deepest religious enthusiasm, and with all the courage of a martyr.

It is somewhat difficult to form a just estimate of how far the attitude assumed by the Church to the barbarian invaders has on the whole proved beneficial to mankind. The empire, as we have seen, had already been, both morally and politically, in a condition of manifest decline; its fall, though it might have been retarded, could scarcely have been averted, and the new religion, even in its most superstitious form, while it did much to displace, did also much to elicit moral enthusiasm. It is impossible to deny that the Christian priesthood contributed very materially, both by their charity and by their arbitration, to mitigate the calamities that accompanied the dissolution of the empire;[1] and it is equally impossible to doubt that their political attitude greatly increased their power for good. Standing between the conflicting forces, almost indifferent to the issue, and notoriously exempt from the passions of the combat, they obtained with the conqueror, and used for the benefit of the conquered, a degree of influence they would never have possessed, had they been regarded as Roman patriots. Their attitude, however, marked a complete, and, as it has proved, a permanent change in

greatly afflicted because, after the conquest, the Mahommedans tolerated the orthodox, who believed that two concurring wills existed in Christ, as well as themselves, who believed that Christ had only one will. In Gaul, the orthodox clergy favoured the invasions of the Franks, who alone, of the barbarous conquerors of Gaul, were Catholics, and St. Aprunculus was obliged to fly, the Burgundians desiring to kill him on account of his suspected connivance with the invaders. (Greg. *Tur.* ii. 23.)

[1] Dean Milman says of the Church, 'If treacherous to the interests of the Roman Empire, it was true to those of mankind.'—*Hist. of Christianity*, vol. iii. p. 48. So Gibbon, 'If the decline of the Roman Empire was hastened by the conversion of Constantine, the victorious religion broke the violence of the fall and mollified the ferocious temper of the conquerors.'—Ch. xxxviii.

the position assigned to patriotism in the moral scale. It has occasionally happened, in later times, that Churches have found it for their interest to appeal to this sentiment in their conflict with opposing creeds, or that patriots have found the objects of churchmen in harmony with their own; and in these cases a fusion of theological and patriotic feeling has taken place, in which each has intensified the other. Such has been the effect of the conflict between the Spaniards and the Moors, between the Poles and the Russians, between the Scotch Puritans and the English Episcopalians, between the Irish Catholics and the English Protestants. But patriotism itself, as a duty, has never found any place in Christian ethics, and a strong theological feeling has usually been directly hostile to its growth. Ecclesiastics have no doubt taken a very large share in political affairs, but this has been in most cases solely with the object of wresting them into conformity with ecclesiastical designs; and no other body of men have so uniformly sacrificed the interests of their country to the interests of their class. For the repugnance between the theological and the patriotic spirit, three reasons may, I think, be assigned. The first is that tendency of strong religious feeling to divert the mind from all terrestrial cares and passions, of which the ascetic life was the extreme expression, but which has always, under different forms, been manifested in the Church. The second arises from the fact that each form of theological opinion embodies itself in a visible and organised church, with a government, interest, and policy of its own, and a frontier often intersecting rather than following national boundaries; and these churches attract to themselves the attachment and devotion that would naturally be bestowed upon our country and its rulers. The third reason is, that the saintly and the heroic characters, which represent the ideals of religion and of patriotism, are generically different; for although they have no doubt many common elements of virtue, the distinctive excellence of each is derived from a proportion or disposition of qualities altogether different from that of the other.[1]

Before dismissing this very important revolution in moral history, I may add two remarks. In the first place, we may observe that the relation of the two great schools of morals to active and political life has been completely changed. Among the ancients, the Stoics, who regarded virtue and vice as generically different from all other things, participated actively in public life, and made this participation one of the first of duties, while the Epicureans, who resolved virtue into utility, and esteemed happiness its supreme motive, abstained from public life, and taught their disciples to neglect it. Asceticism followed the stoical school in teaching that virtue and happiness are generically different things; but it was at the same time eminently unfavourable to civic virtue. On the other hand, that great industrial movement which has arisen since the abolition of slavery, and which has always been essentially utilitarian in its spirit, has been one of the most active and influential elements of political progress. This change, though, as far as I know, entirely

[1] Observe with what a fine perception St. Augustine notices the essentially unchristian character of the moral dispositions to which the greatness of Rome was due. He quotes the sentence of Sallust: 'Civitas, incredibile memoratu est, adeptâ libertate quantum brevi creverit, tanta cupido gloriæ incesserat;' and adds, 'Ista ergo laudis aviditas et cupido gloriæ multa illa miranda fecit, laudabilia scilicet atque gloriosa secundum hominum existimationem . . . causa honoris, laudis et gloriæ consuluerunt patriæ, in qua ipsam gloriam requirebant, salutemque ejus saluti suæ præponere non dubitaverunt, pro isto uno vitio, id est, amore laudis, pecuniæ cupiditatem et multa alia vitia comprimentes. . . . Quid aliud amarent quam gloriam, qua volebant etiam post mortem tanquam vivere in ore laudantium?'—*De Civ. Dei*, v. 12-13.

unnoticed by historians, constitutes, I believe, one of the great landmarks of moral history.

The second observation I would make relates to the estimate we form of the value of patriotic actions. However much an historian may desire to extend his researches to the private and domestic virtues of a people, civic virtues are always those which must appear most prominently in his pages. History is concerned only with large bodies of men. The systems of philosophy or religion, which produce splendid results on the great theatre of public life, are fully and easily appreciated, and readers and writers are both liable to give them very undue advantages over those systems which do not favour civic virtues, but exercise their beneficial influence in the more obscure fields of individual self-culture, domestic morals, or private charity. If valued by the self-sacrifice they imply, or by their effects upon human happiness, these last rank very high, but they scarcely appear in history, and they therefore seldom obtain their due weight in historical comparisons. Christianity has, I think, suffered peculiarly from this cause. Its moral action has always been much more powerful upon individuals than upon societies, and the spheres in which its superiority over other religions is most incontestable, are precisely those which history is least capable of realising.

In attempting to estimate the moral condition of the Roman and Byzantine Empires during the Christian period, and before the old civilisation had been dissolved by the barbarian or Mohammedan invasions, we must continually bear this last consideration in mind. We must remember, too, that Christianity had acquired the ascendency among nations which were already deeply tainted by the inveterate vices of a corrupt and decaying civilisation, and also that many of the censors from whose pages we are obliged to form our estimate of the age were men who judged human frailties with all the fastidiousness of ascetics, and who expressed their judgments with all the declamatory exaggeration of the pulpit. Modern critics will probably not lay much stress upon the relapse of the Christians into the ordinary dress and usages of the luxurious society about them, upon the ridicule thrown by Christians on those who still adhered to the primitive austerity of the sect, or upon the fact that multitudes who were once mere nominal Pagans had become mere nominal Christians. We find, too, a frequent disposition on the part of moralists to single out some new form of luxury, or some trivial custom which they regarded as indecorous, for the most extravagant denunciation, and to magnify its importance in a manner which in a later age it is difficult even to understand. Examples of this kind may be found both in Pagan and in Christian writings, and they form an extremely curious page in the history of morals. Thus Juvenal exhausts his vocabulary of invective in denouncing the atrocious criminality of a certain noble, who in the very year of his consulship did not hesitate—not, it is true, by day, but at least in the sight of the moon and of the stars—with his own hand to drive his own chariot along the public road.[1] Pliny assures us that the most monstrous of all criminals was the man who first devised the luxurious custom of wearing golden rings.[2] Apuleius was compelled to defend

[1] 'Præter majorum cineres atque ossa, volucri
Carpento rapitur pinguis Damasippus et ipse,
Ipse rotam stringit multo sufflamine consul;
Nocte quidem; sed luna videt, sed sidera testes
Intendunt oculos. Finitum tempus honoris
Quum fuerit, clara Damasippus luce flagellum
Sumet.'—Juvenal, *Sat.* viii. 146.

[2] 'Pessimum vitæ scelus fecit, qui id [aurum] primus induit digitis. . . .

himself for having eulogised tooth-powder, and he did so, among other ways, by arguing that nature has justified this form of propriety, for crocodiles were known periodically to leave the waters of the Nile, and to lie with open jaws upon the banks, while a certain bird proceeds with its beak to clean their teeth.[1] If we were to measure the degree of criminality of the different customs of the time by the vehemence of the patristic denunciations, we might almost conclude that the most atrocious offence of their day was the custom of wearing false hair, or dyeing natural hair. Clement of Alexandria questioned whether the validity of certain ecclesiastical ceremonies might not be affected by wigs; for he asked, when the priest is placing his hand on the head of the person who kneels before him, if that hand is resting upon false hair, who is it he is really blessing? Tertullian shuddered at the thought that Christians might have the hair of those who were in hell upon their heads, and he found in the tiers of false hair that were in use a distinct rebellion against the assertion that no one can add to his stature, and in the custom of dyeing the hair, a contravention of the declaration that man cannot make one hair white or black. Centuries rolled away. The Roman Empire tottered to its fall, and floods of vice and sorrow overspread the world; but still the denunciations of the Fathers were unabated. St. Ambrose, St. Jerome, and St. Gregory Nazianzen continued with uncompromising vehemence the war against false hair, which Tertullian and Clement of Alexandria had began.[2]

quisquis primus instituit cunctanter id fecit, lævisque manibus, latentibusque induit.'—Plin. *Hist. Nat.* xxxiii. 4.

[1] See a curious passage in his *Apologia.* It should be said that we have only his own account of the charges brought against him.

[2] The history of false hair has been written with much learning by M. Guerle in his *Éloge des Perruques.*

But although the vehemence of the Fathers on such trivial matters might appear at first sight to imply the existence of a society in which grave corruption was rare, such a conclusion would be totally untrue. The pictures of the Roman society by Ammianus Marcellinus, of the society of Marseilles, by Salvian, of the society of Asia Minor and of Constantinople, by Chrysostom, as well as the whole tenor of history, and innumerable incidental notices in the writers of the time, exhibit, after every legitimate allowance has been made, a condition of depravity, and especially of degradation, which few societies have surpassed.[1] The corruption had reached classes and institutions that appeared the most holy. The Agapæ, or love feasts, which formed one of the most touching symbols of Christian unity, had become scenes of drunkenness and of riot. Denounced by the Fathers, condemned by the Council of Laodicea in the fourth century, and afterwards by the Council of Carthage, they lingered as a scandal and an offence till they were finally suppressed by the Council of Trullo, at the end of the seventh century.[2] The commemoration of the martyrs soon degenerated into scandalous dissipation. Fairs were held on the occasion, gross breaches of chastity were frequent, and the annual festival was suppressed on account of the immorality it produced.[3] The ambiguous position of the clergy with reference to marriage already led to grave disorder. In the time of St. Cyprian, before the outbreak of the Decian persecution, it had been common to find

[1] The fullest view of this age is given in a very learned little work by Peter Erasmus Müller (1797), *De Genio Ævi Theodosiani.* Montfaucon has also devoted two essays to the moral condition of the Eastern world, one of which is given in Jortin's *Remarks on Ecclesiastical History.*

[2] See on these abuses Mosheim, *Eccl. Hist.* (Soame's ed.), vol. i. p. 463; Cave's *Primitive Christianity*, part i. ch. xi.

[3] Cave's *Primitive Christianity*, part i. ch. vii.

clergy professing celibacy, but keeping, under various pretexts, their mistresses in their houses;[1] and, after Constantine, the complaints on this subject became loud and general.[2] Virgins and monks often lived together in the same house, and with a curious audacity of hypocrisy, which is very frequently noticed, they professed to have so overcome the passions of their nature that they shared in chastity the same bed.[3] Rich widows were surrounded by swarms of clerical sycophants, who addressed them in tender diminutives, studied and consulted their every foible, and, under the guise of piety, lay in wait for their gifts or bequests.[4] The evil attained such a point, that a law was made under Valentinian, depriving the Christian priests and monks of that power of receiving legacies which was

[1] *Ep.* lxi.

[2] Evagrius describes with much admiration how certain monks of Palestine, by 'a life wholly excellent and divine,' had so overcome their passions that they were accustomed to bathe with women; for neither sight nor touch, nor a woman's embrace, could make them relapse into their natural condition. Among men they desired to be men, and among women, women.' (*H. E.* i. 21.)

[3] These 'Muliers Subintroductæ,' as they were called, are continually noticed by Cyprian, Jerome, and Chrysostom. See Müller, *De Genio Evi Theodosiani*, and also the *Codex Theod.* xvi. tit. ii. lex 44, with the Comments. Dr. Todd, in his learned *Life of St. Patrick* (p. 91), quotes (I shall not venture to do so) from the *Lives of the Irish Saints* an extremely curious legend of a kind of contest of sanctity between St. Scuthinus and St. Brendan, in which it was clearly proved that the former had mastered the passions of the flesh more completely than the latter. An enthusiast named Robert d'Arbrisselles is said in the twelfth century to have revived the old custom. (Jortin's *Remarks*, A.D. 1106.)

[4] St. Jerome gives (*Ep.* lii.) an extremely curious picture of these clerical flatteries, and several examples of the terms of endearment they were accustomed to employ. The tone of flattery which St. Jerome himself, though doubtless with the purest motives, employs in his copious correspondence with his female admirers, is to a modern layman peculiarly repulsive, and sometimes verges upon blasphemy. In his letter to Eustochium, whose daughter as a nun had become the 'bride of Christ,' he calls the mother 'Socrus Dei,' the mother-in-law of God. See, too, the extravagant flatteries of Chrysostom in his correspondence with Olympias.

possessed by every other class of the community; and St. Jerome has mournfully acknowledged that the prohibition was necessary.[1] Great multitudes entered the Church to avoid municipal offices;[2] the deserts were crowded with men whose sole object was to escape from honest labour, and even soldiers used to desert their colours for the monasteries.[3] Noble ladies, pretending a desire to live a life of continence, abandoned their husbands to live with low-born lovers.[4] Palestine, which soon became the centre of pilgrimages, had become, in the time of St. Gregory of Nyssa, a hotbed of debauchery.[5] The evil reputation of pilgrimages long continued; and in the eighth century we find St. Boniface writing to the Archbishop of Canterbury, imploring the English bishops to take some measures to restrain or regulate the pilgrimages of their fellow-countrywomen; for there were few towns in central Europe, on the way to Rome, where English ladies, who started as pilgrims, were not living in open prostitution.[6] The luxury and ambition of the higher prelates,

[1] 'Pudet dicere sacerdotes idolorum, mimi et aurigæ et scorta hæreditates capiunt; solis clericis et monachis hoc lege prohibetur, et prohibetur non a persecutoribus, sed a principibus Christianis. Nec de lege conqueror sed doleo cur meruerimus hanc legem.'—*Ep.* lii.

[2] See Milman's *Hist. of Early Christianity*, vol. ii. p. 314.

[3] This was one cause of the disputes between St. Gregory the Great and the Emperor Eustace. St. Chrysostom frequently notices the opposition of the military and the monastic spirits.

[4] Hieron. *Ep.* cxxviii.

[5] St. Greg. Nyss. *Ad eund. Hieros.* Some Catholic writers have attempted to throw doubt upon the genuineness of this epistle, but, Dean Milman thinks, with no sufficient reason. Its account of Jerusalem is to some extent corroborated by St. Jerome. (*Ad Paulinum, Ep.* xxix.)

[6] 'Præterea non taceo charitati vestræ, quia omnibus servis Dei qui hic vel in Scriptura vel in timore Dei probatissimi esse videntur, displicet quod bonum et honestas et pudicitia vestræ ecclesiæ illuditur; et aliquod levamentum turpitudinis esset, si prohiberet synodus et principes vestri mulieribus et velatis feminis illud iter et frequentiam, quam ad Romanam civitatem veniendo et redeundo faciunt, quia magna ex parte pereunt, paucis remeantibus integris. Perpaucæ enim sunt civitates in Longobardia vel

and the passion for amusements of the inferior priests,[1] were bitterly acknowledged. St. Jerome complained that the banquets of many bishops eclipsed in splendour those of the provincial governors, and the intrigues by which they obtained offices, and the fierce partisanship of their supporters, appear in every page of ecclesiastical history.

In the lay world, perhaps the chief characteristic was extreme childishness. The moral enthusiasm was greater than it had been in most periods of Paganism, but, being drawn away to the desert, it had little influence upon society. The simple fact that the quarrels between the factions of the chariot races for a long period eclipsed all political, intellectual, and even religious differences, filled the streets again and again with bloodshed, and more than once determined great revolutions in the State, is sufficient to show the extent of the decadence. Patriotism and courage had almost disappeared, and notwithstanding the rise of a Belisarius or a Narses, the level of public men was extremely depressed. The luxury of the court, the servility of the courtiers, and the prevailing splendour of dress and of ornament, had attained an extravagant height. The world grew accustomed to a dangerous alternation of extreme asceticism and gross vice, and sometimes, as in the case of Antioch,[2] it was the most vicious and luxurious cities that produced the most numerous anchorites. There existed a combination of vice and superstition which is eminently prejudicial to the nobility, though not equally detrimental to the happiness of man. Public opinion was so low, that very many forms of vice attracted little condemnation and punishment, while un-

in Francia aut in Gallia in qua non sit adultera vel meretrix generis Anglorum, quod scandalum est et turpitudo totius ecclesiæ vestræ.'—(A.D. 745) *Ep.* lxiii.

[1] See Milman's *Latin Christianity*, vol. ii. p. 8.

[2] Tillemont, *Hist. eccl.* tome xi. p. 547.

doubted belief in the absolving efficacy of superstitious rites calmed the imagination and allayed the terrors of conscience. There was more falsehood and treachery than under the Cæsars, but there was much less cruelty, violence, and shamelessness. There was also less public spirit, less independence of character, less intellectual freedom.

In some respects, however, Christianity had already effected a great improvement. The gladiatorial games had disappeared from the West, and had not been introduced into Constantinople. The vast schools of prostitution which had grown up under the name of temples of Venus were suppressed. Religion, however deformed and debased, was at least no longer a seedplot of depravity, and under the influence of Christianity the effrontery of vice had in a great measure disappeared. The gross and extravagant indecency of representation, of which we have still examples in the paintings on the walls and the signs on many of the portals of Pompeii; the banquets of rich patricians, served by naked girls; the hideous excesses of unnatural lust, in which some of the Pagan emperors had indulged with so much publicity, were no longer tolerated. Although sensuality was very general, it was less obtrusive, and unnatural and eccentric forms had become rare. The presence of a great Church, which, amid much superstition and fanaticism, still taught a pure morality, and enforced it by the strongest motives, was everywhere felt—controlling, strengthening, or overawing. The ecclesiastics were a great body in the State. The cause of virtue was strongly organised: it drew to itself the best men, determined the course of vacillating but amiable natures, and placed some restraint upon the vicious. A bad man might be insensible to the moral beauties of religion, but he was still haunted by the recollection of its threatenings. If he emancipated himself from its influence in health and prosperity, its power returned in periods of sickness or danger, or on the eve of the commission of some great crime. If he had nerved himself against all its terrors, he was at least checked and governed at every turn by the public opinion which it had created. That total absence of all restraint, all decency, and all fear and remorse, which had been evinced by some of the monsters of crime who occupied the Pagan throne, and which proves most strikingly the decay of the Pagan religion, was no longer possible. The virtue of the best Pagans was perhaps of as high an order as that of the best Christians, though it was of a somewhat different type, but the vice of the worst Pagans certainly far exceeded that of the worst Christians. The pulpit had become a powerful centre of attraction, and charities of many kinds were actively developed.

The moral effects of the first great outburst of asceticism, as far as we have as yet traced them, appear almost unmingled evils. In addition to the essentially distorted ideal of perfection it produced, the simple withdrawal from active life of that moral enthusiasm which is the leaven of society was extremely pernicious, and there can be little doubt that to this cause we must in a great degree attribute the conspicuous failure of the Church, for some centuries, to effect any more considerable amelioration in the moral condition of Europe. There were, however, some distinctive excellencies springing even from the first phase of asceticism, which, although they do not, as I conceive, suffice to counterbalance these evils, may justly qualify our censure.

The first condition of all really great moral excellence is a spirit of genuine self-sacrifice and self-renunciation. The habits of compromise, moderation, reciprocal self-restraint, gentleness, courtesy, and refinement, which are appropriate to luxurious or utilitarian civilisations, are very favourable to the development of many secondary virtues; but there is in human nature a capacity for a higher and more heroic reach of excellence, which demands very different spheres for its display, accustoms men to far nobler aims, and exercises a far greater attractive influence upon mankind. Imperfect and distorted as was the ideal of the anchorite; deeply, too, as it was perverted by the admixture of a spiritual selfishness, still the example of many thousands, who, in obedience to what they believed to be right, voluntarily gave up everything that men hold dear, cast to the winds every compromise with enjoyment, and made extreme self-abnegation the very principle of their lives, was not wholly lost upon the world. At a time when increasing riches had profoundly tainted the Church, they taught men 'to love labour more than rest, and ignominy more than glory, and to give more than to receive.'[1] At a time when the passion for ecclesiastical dignities had become the scandal of the empire, they systematically abstained from them, teaching, in their quaint but energetic language, that 'there are two classes a monk should especially avoid—bishops and women.'[2] The very eccentricities of their lives, their uncouth forms, their horrible penances, won the admiration of rude men, and the superstitious reverence thus excited gradually passed to the charity and the self-denial which formed the higher elements of the monastic character. Multitudes of barbarians were converted to Christianity at the sight of St. Simeon Stylites.

[1] This was enjoined in the rule of St. Paphnutius. See Tillemont, tome x. p. 45.

[2] 'Omnimodis monachum fugere debere mulieres et episcopos.'—Cassian, *De Cœnob. Inst.* xi. 17.

The hermit, too, was speedily idealised by the popular imagination. The more repulsive features of his life and appearance were forgotten. He was thought of only as an old man with long white beard and gentle aspect, weaving his mats beneath the palm-trees, while dæmons vainly tried to distract him by their stratagems, and the wild beasts grew tame in his presence, and every disease and every sorrow vanished at his word. The imagination of Christendom, fascinated by this ideal, made it the centre of countless legends, usually very childish, and occasionally, as we have seen, worse than childish, yet full of beautiful touches of human nature, and often conveying admirable moral lessons.[1] Nursery tales, which first determine the course of the infant imagination, play no inconsiderable part in the history of humanity. In the fable of Psyche—that bright tale of passionate love with which the Greek mother lulled her child to rest—Pagan antiquity has bequeathed us a single specimen of transcendent beauty, and the lives of the saints of the desert often exhibit an imagination different indeed in kind, but scarcely less brilliant in its display. St. Antony, we are told, was thinking one night that he was the best man in the desert, when it was revealed to him that there was another hermit far holier than himself. In the morning he started across the desert to visit this unknown saint. He met first of all a centaur, and afterwards a little man

[1] We also find now and then, though I think very rarely, intellectual flashes of some brilliancy. Two of them strike me as especially noteworthy. St. Arsenius refused to separate young criminals from communion, though he had no hesitation about old men; for he had observed that young men speedily get accustomed and indifferent to the state of excommunication, while old men feel continually, and acutely, the separation. (Socrates, iv. 23.) St. Apollonius explained the Egyptian idolatry with the most intelligent rationalism. The ox, he thought, was in the first instance worshipped for its domestic uses; the Nile, because it was the chief cause of the fertility of the soil, &c. (Rufinus, *Hist. Mon.* cap. vii.)

with horns and goat's feet, who said that he was a faun; and these, having pointed out the way, he arrived at last at his destination. St. Paul the hermit, at whose cell he stopped, was one hundred and thirteen years old, and, having been living for a very long period in absolute solitude, he at first refused to admit the visitor, but at last consented, embraced him, and began, with a very pardonable curiosity, to question him minutely about the world he had left; 'whether there was much new building in the towns, what empire ruled the world, whether there were any idolaters remaining?' The colloquy was interrupted by a crow, which came with a loaf of bread, and St. Paul, observing that during the last sixty years his daily allowance had been only half a loaf, declared that this was a proof that he had done right in admitting Antony. The hermits returned thanks, and sat down together by the margin of a glassy stream. But now a difficulty arose. Neither could bring himself to break the loaf before the other. St. Paul alleged that St. Antony, being his guest, should take the precedence; but St. Antony, who was only ninety years old, dwelt upon the greater age of St. Paul. So scrupulously polite were these old men, that they passed the entire afternoon disputing on this weighty question, till at last, when the evening was drawing in, a happy thought struck them, and, each holding one end of the loaf, they pulled together. To abridge the story, St. Paul soon died, and his companion, being a weak old man, was unable to bury him, when two lions came from the desert and dug the grave with their paws, deposited the body in it, raised a loud howl of lamentation, and then knelt down submissively before St. Antony, to beg a blessing. The authority for this history is no less a person than St. Jerome, who relates it as literally true, and intersperses his narrative with severe reflections on all who might question his accuracy.

The historian Palladius assures us that he heard from the lips of St. Macarius of Alexandria an account of a pilgrimage which that saint had made, under the impulse of curiosity, to visit the enchanted garden of Jannes and Jambres, tenanted by dæmons. For nine days Macarius traversed the desert, directing his course by the stars, and, from time to time, fixing reeds in the ground, as landmarks for his return; but this precaution proved useless, for the devils tore up the reeds, and placed them during the night by the head of the sleeping saint. As he drew near the garden, seventy dæmons of various forms came forth to meet him, and reproached him for disturbing them in their home. St. Macarius promised simply to walk round and inspect the wonders of the garden, and then depart without doing it any injury. He fulfilled his promise, and a journey of twenty days brought him again to his cell.[1] Other legends are, however, of a less fantastic nature; and many of them display, though sometimes in very whimsical forms, a spirit of courtesy which seems to foreshadow the later chivalry, and some of them contain striking protests against the very superstitions that were most prevalent. When St. Macarius was sick, a bunch of grapes was once given to him, but his charity impelled him to give them to another hermit, who in his turn refused to keep them, and at last, having made the circuit of the entire desert, they were returned to the saint.[2] The same saint, whose usual beverage was putrid water, never failed to drink wine when set before him by the hermits he visited, atoning privately for this relaxation, which he thought the laws of courtesy required, by abstaining from water

[1] Palladius, *Hist. Laus.* cap. xix.

[2] Rufinus, *Hist. Monach.* cap. xxix.

for as many days as he had drunk glasses of wine.[1] One of his disciples once meeting an idolatrous priest running in great haste across the desert, holding a great stick in his hand, cried out in a loud voice, 'Where are you going, dæmon?' The priest, naturally indignant, beat the Christian severely, and was proceeding on his way, when he met St. Macarius, who accosted him so courteously and so tenderly, that the Pagan's heart was touched, he became a convert, and his first act of charity was to tend the Christian whom he had beaten.[2] St. Avitus being on a visit to St. Marcian, this latter saint placed before him some bread, which Avitus refused to eat, saying that it was his custom never to touch food till after sunset. St. Marcian professing his own inability to defer his repast, implored his guest for once to break this custom, and being refused, exclaimed, 'Alas! I am filled with anguish that you have come here to see a wise man and a saint, and you see only a glutton.' St. Avitus was grieved, and said, 'he would rather even eat flesh than hear such words,' and he sat down as desired. St. Marcian then confessed that his own custom was the same as that of his brother saint; 'but,' he added, 'we know that charity is better than fasting; for charity is enjoined by the Divine law, but fasting is left in our own power and will.'[3] St. Epiphanius having invited St. Hilarius to his cell, placed before him a dish of fowl. 'Pardon me, father,' said St. Hilarius, 'but since I have become a monk I have never eaten flesh.' 'And I,' said St. Epiphanius, 'since I have become a monk have never suffered the sun to go down upon my wrath.' 'Your rule,' rejoined the other, 'is more excellent than mine.'[4] While a rich lady was courteously

[1] Tillemont, *Hist. eccl.* tome viii. pp. 583–584.

[2] Ibid. p. 589.

[3] Theodoret, *Philoth.* cap. iii.

[4] *Verba Seniorum.*

fulfilling the duties of hospitality to a monk, her child, whom she had for this purpose left, fell into a well. It lay unharmed upon the surface of the water, and afterwards told its mother that it had seen the arms of the saint sustaining it below.[1] At a time when it was the custom to look upon the marriage state with profound contempt, it was revealed to St. Macarius of Egypt, that two married women in a neighbouring city were more holy than he was. The saint immediately visited them, and asked their mode of life, but they utterly repudiated the notion of their sanctity. 'Holy father,' they said, 'suffer us to tell you frankly the truth. Even this very night we did not shrink from sleeping with our husbands, and what good works, then, can you expect from us?' The saint, however, persisted in his inquiries, and they then told him their stories. 'We are,' they said, 'in no way related, but we married two brothers. We have lived together for fifteen years, without one licentious or angry word. We have entreated our husbands to let us leave them, to join the societies of holy virgins, but they refused to permit us, and we then promised before Heaven that no worldly word should sully our lips.' 'Of a truth,' cried St. Macarius, 'I see that God regards not whether one is virgin or married, whether one is in a monastery or in the world. He considers only the disposition of the heart, and gives the Spirit to all who desire to serve Him, whatever their condition may be.'[2]

I have multiplied these illustrations to an extent that must, I fear, have already somewhat taxed the patience of my readers; but the fact that, during a long period of history, these saintly legends formed the ideals guiding the imagination and reflecting the moral sentiment of

[1] Theodoret, *Philoth.* cap. ii.

[2] Tillemont, tome viii. pp. 594–595.

the Christian world, gives them an importance far beyond their intrinsic value. Before dismissing the saints of the desert, there is one other class of legends to which I desire to advert. I mean those which describe the connection between saints and the animal world. These legends are, I think, worthy of special notice in moral history, as representing probably the first, and at the same time one of the most striking efforts ever made in Christendom to inculcate a feeling of kindness and pity towards the brute creation. In Pagan antiquity, considerable steps had been made to raise this form of humanity to a recognised branch of ethics. The way had been prepared by numerous anecdotes growing for the most part out of simple ignorance of natural history, which all tended to diminish the chasm between men and animals, by representing the latter as possessing to a very high degree both moral and rational qualities. Elephants, it was believed, were endowed not only with reason and benevolence, but also with reverential feelings. They worshipped the sun and moon, and in the forests of Mauritania were accustomed to assemble every new moon, at a certain river, to perform religious rites.[1] The hippopotamus taught men the medicinal value of bleeding, being accustomed, when affected by plethory, to bleed itself with a thorn, and afterwards close the wound with slime.[2] Pelicans committed suicide to feed their young, and bees, when they had broken the laws of their sovereign.[3] A temple was erected at Sestos to commemorate the affection of an eagle which loved a young girl, and

[1] Pliny, *Hist. Nat.* viii. 1. Many anecdotes of elephants are collected (viii. 1–12). See, too, Dion Cassius, xxxix. 38.

[2] Pliny, viii. 40.

[3] Donne's *Biathanatos*, p. 22. This habit of bees is mentioned by St. Ambrose. The pelican, as is well known, afterwards became an emblem of Christ.

upon her death cast itself in despair into the flames by which her body was consumed.[1] Numerous anecdotes are related of faithful dogs which refused to surviv their masters, and one of these had, it was said, been transformed into the dog-star.[2] The dolphin, especially, became the subject of many beautiful legends, and its affection for its young, for music, and above all for little children, excited the admiration not only of the populace, but of the most distinguished naturalists.[3] Many philosophers also ascribed to animals a rational soul, like that of man. According to the Pythagoreans, human souls transmigrate after death into animals. According to the Stoics and others, the souls of men and animals were alike parts of the all-pervading Divine Spirit that animates the world.[4]

We may even find traces from an early period of a certain measure of legislative protection for animals. By a very natural process, the ox, as a principal agent in agriculture, and therefore a kind of symbol of civilisation, was in many different countries regarded with a peculiar reverence. The sanctity attached to it in Egypt is well known. That tenderness to animals, which is one of the most beautiful features in the Old Testament writings, shows itself, among other ways, in the command not to muzzle the ox that treadeth out the corn, or to yoke together the ox and the ass.[5] Among the early Romans,

[1] Plin. *Hist. Nat.* x. 6.

[2] A long list of legends about dogs is given by Legendre, in the very curious chapter on animals, in his *Traité de l'Opinion*, tome i. pp. 308–327.

[3] Pliny tells some extremely pretty stories of this kind (*Hist. Nat.* ix. 8-9). See, too, Aulus Gellius, xvi. 19. The dolphin, on account of its love for its young, became a common symbol of Christ among the early Christians.

[4] A very full account of the opinions, both of ancient and modern philosophers, concerning the souls of animals, is given by Bayle, *Dict.* arts. 'Pereira E,' 'Rorarius K.'

[5] The Jewish law did not confine its care to oxen. The reader will re-

the same feeling was carried so far, that for a long time it was actually a capital offence to slaughter an ox, that animal being pronounced, in a special sense, the fellow-labourer of man.[1] A similar law is said to have in early times existed in Greece.[2] The beautiful passage in which the Psalmist describes how the sparrow could find a shelter and a home in the altar of the temple, was as applicable to Greece as to Jerusalem. The sentiment of Xenocrates who, when a bird pursued by a hawk took refuge in his breast, caressed and finally released it, saying to his disciples, that a good man should never give up a suppliant,[3] was believed to be shared by the gods, and it was regarded as an act of impiety to disturb the birds who had built their nests beneath the porticoes of the temple.[4] A case is related of a child who was even put to death on account of an act of aggravated cruelty to birds.[5]

member the touching provision, 'Thou shalt not seethe a kid in his mother's milk' (Deut. xiv. 21); and the law forbidding men to take a parent bird that was sitting on its young or on its eggs. (Deut. xxii. 6-7.)

1 'Cujus tanta fuit apud antiquos veneratio, ut tam capital esset bovem necuisse quam civem.'—Columella, lib. vi. in proœm. 'Hic socius hominum in rustico opere et Cereris minister. Ab hoc antiqui manus ita abstinere voluerunt ut capite sanxerint si quis occidisset.'—Varro, *De Re Rustic.* lib. ii. cap. v.

2 See Legendre, tome ii. p. 338. The sword with which the priest sacrificed the ox was afterwards pronounced accursed. (Ælian, *Hist. Var.* lib. viii. cap. iii.)

3 Diog. Laërt. *Xenocrates.*

4 There is a story told in some classical writer, of an ambassador who was sent by his fellow-countrymen to consult the oracle of Apollo about a suppliant who had taken refuge in the city, and was demanded with menace by the enemies. The oracle, being bribed, enjoined the surrender. The ambassador on leaving, with seeming carelessness, disturbed the sparrows under the portico of the temple, when the voice from behind the altar denounced his impiety for disturbing the guests of the gods. The ambassador replied with an obvious and withering retort. Ælian says (*Hist. Var.*) that the Athenians condemned to death a boy for killing a sparrow that had taken refuge in the temple of Æsculapius.

5 Quintillian, *Inst.* v. 9.

The general tendency of nations, as they advance from a rude and warlike to a refined and peaceful condition, from the stage in which the realising powers are faint and dull, to those in which they are sensitive and vivid, is undoubtedly to become more gentle and humane in their actions; but this, like all other general tendencies in history, may be counteracted or modified by many special circumstances. The law I have mentioned about oxen was obviously one of those that belong to a very early stage of progress, when legislators are labouring to form agricultural habits among a warlike and nomadic people.[1] The games in which the slaughter of animals bore so large a part, having been introduced but a little before the extinction of the republic, did very much to arrest or retard the natural progress of humane sentiments. In ancient Greece, besides the bull-fights of Thessaly, the combats of quails and cocks[2] were favourite amusements, and were much encouraged by the legis-

[1] In the same way we find several chapters in the *Zendavesta* about the criminality of injuring dogs; which is explained by the great importance of shepherds' dogs to a pastoral people.

[2] On the origin of Greek cock-fighting, see Ælian, *Hist. Var.* ii. 28. Many particulars about it are given by Athenæus. Chrysippus maintained that cock-fighting was the final cause of cocks, these birds being made by Providence in order to inspire us by the example of their courage. (Plutarch, *De Repug. Stoic.*) The Greeks do not, however, appear to have known 'cock-throwing,' the favourite English game of throwing a stick called a 'cock-stick' at cocks. It was a very ancient and very popular amusement, and was practised especially on Shrove Tuesday, and by school-boys. Sir Thomas More had been famous for his skill in it. (Strutt's *Sports and Pastimes*, p. 283.) Three origins of it have been given:—1st, that in the Danish wars the Saxons failed to surprise a certain city, in consequence of the crowing of cocks, and had in consequence a great hatred of that bird; 2nd, that the cocks (*galli*) were special representatives of Frenchmen, with whom the English were constantly at war; and 3rd, that they were connected with the denial of St. Peter. As Sir Charles Sedley said:—

'Mayst thou be punished for St. Peter's crime,
And on Shrove Tuesday perish in thy prime.'

Knight's *Old England*, vol. ii. p. 126.

lators, as furnishing examples of valour to the soldiers. The colossal dimensions of the Roman games, the circumstances that favoured them, and the overwhelming interest they speedily excited, I have described in a former chapter. We have seen, however, that notwithstanding the gladiatorial shows, the standard of humanity towards men was considerably raised during the empire. It is also well worthy of notice, that notwithstanding the passion for the combats of wild beasts, Roman literature and the later literature of the nations subject to Rome abound in delicate touches displaying in a very high degree a sensitiveness to the feelings of the animal world. This tender interest in animal life is one of the most distinctive features of the poetry of Virgil. Lucretius, who rarely struck the chords of pathos, had at a still earlier period drawn a very beautiful picture of the sorrows of the bereaved cow, whose calf had been sacrificed upon the altar.[1] Plutarch mentions, incidentally, that he could never bring himself to sell, in its old age, the ox which had served him faithfully in the time of its strength.[2] Ovid expressed a similar sentiment with an almost equal emphasis.[3] Juvenal speaks of a Roman lady with her eyes filled with tears on account of the death of a sparrow.[4] Apollonius of Tyana, on the ground

[1] *De Natura Rerum*, lib. ii.

[2] *Life of Marc. Cato.*

[3] 'Quid meruere boves, animal sine fraude dolisque,
Innocuum, simplex, natum tolerare labores?
Immemor est demum nec frugum munere dignus,
Qui potuit curvi dempto modo pondere aratri
Ruricolam mactare suum.'—*Metamorph.* xv. 120–124.

[4] 'Cujus
Turbavit nitidos extinctus passer ocellos.'
Juvenal, *Sat.* vi. 7–8.

There is a little poem in Catullus (iii.) to console his mistress upon the death of her favourite sparrow; and Martial more than once alludes to the pets of the Roman ladies.

of humanity, refused, even when invited by a king, to participate in the chase.[1] Arrian, the friend of Epictetus, in his book upon coursing, anticipated the beautiful picture which Addison has drawn of the huntsman refusing to sacrifice the life of the captured hare which had given him so much pleasure in its flight.[2]

These touches of feeling, slight as they may appear, indicate, I think, a vein of sentiment such as we should scarcely have expected to find coexisting with the gigantic slaughter of the amphitheatre. The progress, however, was not simply one of sentiment—it was also shown in distinct and definite teaching. Pythagoras and Empedocles were quoted as the founders of this branch of ethics. The moral duty of kindness to animals was in the first instance based upon a dogmatic assertion of the transmigration of souls, and the doctrine that animals are within the circle of human duty, being thus laid down, subsidiary considerations of humanity were alleged. The rapid growth of the Pythagorean school, in the latter days of the empire, made these considerations familiar to the people.[3] Porphyry elaborately advocated, and even

Compare the charming description of the Prioress, in Chaucer:—

'She was so charitable and so pitous,
She wolde wepe if that she saw a mous
Caughte in a trappe, if it were ded or bledde.
Of smale houndes had she that she fedde
With rosted flesh and milke and wastel brede,
But sore wept she if on of them were dede,
Or if men smote it with a yerde smert:
And all was conscience and tendre herte.'

*Prologue to the 'Canterbury Tales.'*

[1] Philost. *Apol.* i. 38.

[2] See the curious chapter in his Κυνηγετικός, xvi. and compare it with No. 116 in the *Spectator.*

[3] In his *De Abstinentia Carnis.* The controversy between Origen and Celsus furnishes us with a very curious illustration of the extravagancies into which some Pagans of the third century fell about animals. Celsus objected to the Christian doctrine about the position of men in the universe;

Seneca for a time practised, abstinence from flesh But the most remarkable figure in this movement is unquestionably Plutarch. Casting aside the dogma of transmigration, or at least speaking of it only as a doubtful conjecture, he places the duty of kindness to animals on the broad ground of the affections, and he urges that duty with an emphasis and a detail to which no adequate parallel can, I believe, be found in the Christian writings for at least seventeen hundred years. He condemns absolutely the games of the amphitheatres, dwells with great force upon the effect of such spectacles in hardening the character, enumerates in detail, and denounces with unqualified energy, the refined cruelties which gastronomic fancies had produced, and asserts in the strongest language that every man has duties to the animal world as truly as to his fellow-men.[1]

If we now pass to the Christian Church, we shall find that little or no progress was at first made in this sphere. Among the Manicheans, it is true, the mixture of Oriental notions was shown in an absolute prohibition of animal food, and abstinence from this food was also frequently practised upon totally different grounds by the orthodox. One or two of the Fathers have also mentioned with approbation the humane councils of the Pythagoreans.[2] But, on the other hand, the doctrine of transmigration was emphatically repudiated by the Catholics; the human race was isolated, by the scheme of re-

that many of the animals were at least the equals of men both in reason and in religious feeling and knowledge. (Orig. *Cont. Cels.* lib. iv.)

[1] These views are chiefly defended in his two tracts on eating flesh. Plutarch has also recurred to the subject, incidentally, in several other works; especially in a very beautiful passage in his *Life of Marcus Cato.*

[2] See, for example, a striking passage in Clem. Alex. *Strom.* lib. ii. St. Clement imagines Pythagoras had borrowed his sentiments on this subject from Moses.

demption, more than ever from all other races; and in the range and circle of duties inculcated by the early Fathers those to animals had no place. This is indeed the one form of humanity which appears more prominently in the Old Testament than in the New. The many beautiful traces of it in the former, which indicate a sentiment,[1] even where they do not very strictly define a duty, gave way before an ardent philanthropy which regarded human interests as the one end, and the relations of man to his Creator as the one question of life, and dismissed somewhat contemptuously, as an idle sentimentalism, notions of duty to animals.[2] A refined and subtle sympathy with animal feeling is indeed rarely found among those who are engaged very actively in the affairs of life, and it was not without a meaning or a reason that Shakspeare placed that exquisitely pathetic analysis of the sufferings of the wounded stag, which is perhaps its most perfect poetical expression, in the midst of the morbid dreamings of the diseased and melancholy Jacques.

But while what are called the rights of animals had no place in the ethics of the Church, a feeling of sympathy with the irrational creation was in some degree inculcated indirectly by the incidents of the hagiology. It was very natural that the hermit, living in the lonely deserts of the East, or in the vast forests of Europe, should come into

[1] There is, I believe, no record of any wild beast combats existing among the Jews, and the rabbinical writers have been remarkable for the great emphasis with which they inculcated the duty of kindness to animals. See some passages from them, cited in Wollaston, *Religion of Nature,* § ii. § 1, note. Maimonides believed in a future life for animals, to recompense them for their sufferings here. (Bayle, *Dict.* art. 'Rorarius D.') There is a curious collection of the opinions of different writers on this last point in a little book called the *Rights of Animals,* by William Drummond (London, 1838), pp. 197-205.

[2] Thus St. Paul (1 Cor. ix. 9) turned aside the precept, 'Thou shalt not muzzle the mouth of the ox that treadeth out the corn,' from its natural meaning, with the contemptuous question, 'Doth God take care for oxen?'

an intimate connection with the animal world, and it was no less natural that the popular imagination, when depicting the hermit life, should make this connection the centre of many picturesque and sometimes touching legends. The birds, it was said, stooped in their flight at the old man's call; the lion and the hyena crouched submissively at his feet; his heart, which was closed to all human interests, expanded freely at the sight of some suffering animal; and something of his own sanctity descended to the companions of his solitude and the objects of his miracles. The wild beasts attended St. Theon when he walked abroad, and the saint rewarded them by giving them drink out of his well. An Egyptian hermit had made a beautiful garden in the desert, and used to sit beneath the palm-trees while a lion eat fruit from his hand. When St. Pœmen was shivering in a winter night, a lion crouched beside him, and became his covering. Lions buried St. Paul the hermit and St. Mary of Egypt. They appear in the legends of St. Jerome, St. Gerasimus, St. John the Silent, St. Simeon, and many others. When an old and feeble monk, named Zosimas, was on his journey to Cæsarea, with an ass which bore his possessions, a lion seized and devoured the ass, but, at the command of the saint, the lion itself carried the burden to the city gates. St. Helenus called a wild ass from its herd to bear his burden through the wilderness. The same saint, as well as St. Pachomius, crossed the Nile on the back of a crocodile, as St. Scuthinus did the Irish Channel on a sea monster. Stags continually accompanied saints upon their journeys, bore their burdens, ploughed their fields, revealed their relics. The hunted stag was especially the theme of many picturesque legends. A Pagan, named Branchion, was once pursuing an exhausted stag, when it took refuge in a cavern, whose threshold no inducement could persuade the hounds to cross. The astonished hunter entered, and found himself in presence of an old hermit, who at once protected the fugitive and converted the pursuer. In the legends of St. Eustachius and St. Hubert, Christ is represented as having assumed the form of a hunted stag, which turned upon its pursuer, with a crucifix glittering on its brow, and, addressing him with a human voice, converted him to Christianity. In the full frenzy of a chase, hounds and stags stopped and knelt down together to venerate the relics of St. Fingar. On the festival of St. Regulus, the wild stags assembled at the tomb of the saint, as the ravens used to do at that of St. Apollinar of Ravenna. St. Erasmus was the special protector of oxen, and they knelt down voluntarily before his shrine. St. Anthony was the protector of hogs, who were usually introduced into his pictures. St. Bridget kept pigs, and a wild boar came from the forest to subject itself to her rule. A horse foreshadowed by its lamentations the death of St. Columba. The three companions of St. Colman were a cock, a mouse, and a fly. The cock announced the hour of devotion, the mouse bit the ear of the drowsy saint till he got up, and if in the course of his studies he was afflicted by any wandering thoughts, or called away to other business, the fly alighted on the line where he had left off, and kept the place. Legends, not without a certain whimsical beauty, described the moral qualities existing in animals. A hermit was accustomed to share his supper with a wolf, which, one evening entering the cell before the return of the master, stole a loaf of bread. Struck with remorse, it was a week before it ventured again to visit the cell, and when it did so, its head hung down, and its whole demeanour manifested the most profound contrition. The hermit 'stroked with a gentle hand its bowed down head,' and gave it a double portion as a token of forgiveness. A lioness knelt down with lamentations before another saint, and then led him to its cub, which was blind, but which received its sight at the prayer of the saint. Next day the lioness returned, bearing the skin of a wild beast as a mark of its gratitude. Nearly the same thing happened to St. Macarius of Alexandria; a hyena knocked at his door, brought its young, which was blind, and which the saint restored to sight, and repaid the obligation soon afterwards, by bringing a fleece of wool. 'O hyena!' said the saint, 'how did you obtain this fleece? you must have stolen and eaten a sheep.' Full of shame, the hyena hung its head down, but persisted in offering its gift, which, however, the holy man refused to receive till the hyena 'had sworn' to cease for the future to rob. The hyena bowed its head in token of its acceptance of the oath, and St. Macarius afterwards gave the fleece to St. Melania. Other legends simply speak of the sympathy between saints and the irrational world. The birds came at the call of St. Cuthbert, and a dead bird was resuscitated by his prayer. When St. Aengussius, in felling wood, had cut his hand, the birds gathered round, and with loud cries lamented his misfortune. A little bird, struck down and mortally wounded by a hawk, fell at the feet of St. Kieranus, who shed tears as he looked upon its torn breast, and offered up a prayer, upon which the bird was instantly healed.[1]

[1] I have taken these illustrations from the collection of hermit literature in Rosweyde, from different volumes of the Bollandists, from the *Dialogues* of Sulpicius Severus, and from what is perhaps the most interesting of all collections of saintly legends, Colgan's *Acta Sanctorum Hiberniæ.* M. Alfred Maury, in his most valuable work, *Légendes pieuses du Moyen Âge,* has examined minutely the part played by animals in symbolising virtues and vices, and has shown the way in which the same incidents were

Many hundreds, I should perhaps hardly exaggerate were I to say many thousands of legends, of this kind exist in the lives of the saints. Suggested in the first instance by that desert life which was at once the earliest phase of monachism and one of the earliest sources of Christian mythology, strengthened by the symbolism which represented different virtues and vices under the forms of animals, and by the reminiscences of the rites and the superstitions of Paganism, the connection between men and animals became the key-note of an infinite variety of fantastic tales. In our eyes they may appear extravagantly puerile, yet it will scarcely, I hope, be necessary to apologise for introducing them into what purports to be a grave work, when it is remembered that for many centuries they were universally accepted by mankind, and were so interwoven with all local traditions, and with all the associations of education, that they at once determined and reflected the inmost feelings of the heart. Their tendency to create a certain feeling of sympathy towards animals is manifest, and this is probably the utmost the Catholic Church has done in that direction.[1] A very few authentic instances may, indeed, be cited of saints whose natural gentleness of disposition was displayed in kindness to the animal world. Of St. James of Venice—an obscure saint of the thirteenth century—it is told that he was accustomed to buy and release the birds with which Italian boys used to play by attaching

repeated, with slight variations, in different legends. M. de Montalembert has devoted what is probably the most beautiful chapter of his *Moines d'Occident* ('Les Moines et la Nature') to the relations of monks and the animal world; but the numerous legends he cites are all, with one or two exceptions, different from those I have given.

[1] Chateaubriand speaks, however (*Études historiques*, étude vi[me], partie 1[re]), of an old Gallic law, forbidding to throw a stone at an ox attached to the plough, or to make its yoke too tight.

them to strings, saying that 'he pitied the little birds of the Lord,' and that his 'tender charity recoiled from all cruelty, even to the most diminutive of animals.'[1] St. Francis of Assisi was a more conspicuous example of the same spirit. 'If I could only be presented to the emperor,' he used to say, 'I would pray him, for the love of God, and of me, to issue an edict prohibiting anyone from catching or imprisoning my sisters the larks, and ordering that all who have oxen or asses should at Christmas feed them particularly well.' A crowd of legends turning upon this theme were related of him. A wolf, near Gubbio, being adjured by him, promised to abstain from eating sheep, placed its paw in the hand of the saint, to ratify the promise, and was afterwards fed from house to house by the inhabitants of the city. A crowd of birds, on another occasion, came to hear the saint preach, as fish did to hear St. Anthony of Padua. A falcon awoke him at his hour of prayer. A grasshopper encouraged him by her melody to sing praises to God. The noisy swallows kept silence when he began to teach.[2]

On the whole, however, Catholicism has done very little to inculcate humanity to animals. The fatal vice of theologians, who have always looked upon others solely through the medium of their own special dogmatic views, has been an obstacle to all advance in this direction. The animal world, being altogether external to the scheme of

[1] Bollandists, May 31. Leonardo da Vinci is said to have had the same fondness for buying and releasing caged birds, and (to go back a long way) Pythagoras to have purchased one day, near Metapontus, from some fishermen all the fish in their net, that he might have the pleasure of releasing them. (Apuleius, *Apologia.*)

[2] See these legends collected by Hase (*St. Francis. Assisi*). It is said of Cardinal Bellarmine, that he used to allow vermin to bite him, saying, 'We shall have heaven to reward us for our sufferings, but these poor creatures have nothing but the enjoyment of this present life.' (Bayle, *Dict. philos.* art. 'Bellarmine.')

redemption, was regarded as beyond the range of duty, and the notion of our having any kind of obligation to them has never been inculcated—has never, I believe, been even admitted by Catholic theologians. In the popular legends, and in the recorded traits of individual amiability, it is curious to observe how constantly those who have sought to inculcate kindness to animals have done so by endeavouring to associate them with something distinctively Christian. The legends I have noticed glorified them as the companions of the saints. The stag was honoured as especially commissioned to reveal the relics of saints, and as the deadly enemy of the serpent. In the feast of asses, that animal was led with veneration into the churches, and a rude hymn proclaimed its dignity, because it had borne Christ in His flight to Egypt, and on His entry into Jerusalem. St. Francis always treated lambs with a peculiar tenderness, as being symbols of his Master. Luther grew sad and thoughtful at a hare hunt, for it seemed to him to represent the pursuit of souls by the devil. Many popular legends exist, associating some bird or animal with some incident in the evangelical narrative, and securing for them, in consequence, an unmolested life. But such influences have never extended far. There are two distinct objects which may be considered by moralists in this sphere. They may regard the character of the men, or they may regard the sufferings of the animals. The amount of callousness or of conscious cruelty displayed or elicited by amusements or practices that inflict sufferings on animals, bears no kind of proportion to the intensity of that suffering. Could we follow with adequate realisation the pangs of the wounded birds that are struck down in our sports, or of the timid hare in the long course of its flight, we should probably conclude that they were not really less than those caused by the Spanish bull-fight, or by the English pastimes of the last century. But the excitement of the chase refracts the imagination; the diminutive size of the victim, and the undemonstrative character of its suffering, withdraw it from our sight, and these sports do not, in consequence, exercise that prejudicial influence upon character which they would exercise if the sufferings of the animals were vividly realised, and were at the same time accepted as an element of the enjoyment. That class of amusements of which the ancient combats of wild beasts form the type, have no doubt nearly disappeared from Christendom, and it is possible that the softening power of Christian teaching may have had some indirect influence in abolishing them; but a candid judgment will confess that it has been very little. During the periods, and in the countries, in which theological influence was supreme, they were unchallenged.[1] They disappeared[2] at last, because a luxurious and industrial civilisation involved a refinement of manners; because a fastidious taste recoiled with a sensation of disgust from pleasures that an uncultivated taste would keenly relish; because the drama, at once reflecting and accelerating the change, gave a new form to popular amusements, and because, in consequence of this

[1] I have noticed, in my *History of Rationalism*, that although some Popes did undoubtedly try to suppress Spanish bull-fights, this was solely on account of the destruction of human life they caused. Full details on this subject will be found in Concina, *De Spectaculis* (Romæ, 1752). Bayle says, 'Il n'y a point de casuiste qui croie qu'on pèche en faisant combattre des taureaux contre des dogues,' &c. (*Dict. philos.* 'Rorarius, C.')

[2] On the ancient amusements of England the reader may consult Seymour's *Survey of London* (1734), vol. i. pp. 227–235; Strutt's *Sports and Pastimes of the English People.* Cock-fighting was a favourite children's amusement in England as early as the twelfth century. (Hampson's *Medii Ævi Kalendarii*, vol. i. p. 160. It was, with foot-ball and several other amusements, for a time suppressed by Edward III., on the ground that they were diverting the people from archery, which was necessary to the military greatness of England.

revolution, the old practices being left to the dregs of society, they became the occasions of scandalous disorders.[1] In Protestant countries the clergy have, on the

[1] The decline of these amusements in England began with the great development of the theatre under Elizabeth. An order of the Privy Council, in July 1591, prohibits the exhibition of plays on Thursday, because on Thursdays bear-baiting and suchlike pastimes had been usually practised, and an injunction to the same effect was sent to the Lord Mayor, wherein it was stated that, 'in divers places the players do use to recite their plays, to the great hurt and destruction of the game of bear-baiting and like pastimes, which are maintained for Her Majesty's pleasure.'—Nichols, *Progresses of Queen Elizabeth* (ed. 1823), vol. i. p. 438. The reader will remember the picture in *Kenilworth* of the Duke of Sussex petitioning Elizabeth against Shakespeare, on the ground of his plays distracting men from bear-baiting. Elizabeth (see Nichols) was extremely fond of bear-baiting. James I. especially delighted in cock-fighting, and in 1610 was present at a great fight between a lion and a bear. (Home, *Every Day Book*, vol. i. pp. 255–299). The theatres, however, rapidly multiplied, and a writer who lived about 1629 said, 'that no less than seventeen playhouses had been built in or about London within threescore years.' (Seymour's *Survey*, vol. i. p. 229.) The Rebellion suppressed all public amusements, and when they were re-established after the Restoration, it was found that the tastes of the better classes no longer sympathised with the bear-garden. Pepys' (*Diary*, August 14, 1666) speaks of bull-baiting as 'a very rude and nasty pleasure,' and says he had not been in the bear-garden for many years. Evelyn (*Diary*, June 16, 1670), having been present at these shows, describes them as 'butcherly sports, or rather barbarous cruelties,' and says he had not visited them before for twenty years. A paper in the *Spectator* (No. 141, written in 1711) talks of those who 'seek their diversion at the bear-garden, . . . where reason and good manners have no right to disturb them.' In 1751, however, Lord Kames was able to say, 'The bear-garden, which is one of the chief entertainments of the English, is held in abhorrence by the French and other polite nations.'—*Essay on Morals* (1st ed.), p. 7; and he warmly defends (p. 30) the English taste. During the latter half of the last century there was constant controversy on the subject (which may be traced in the pages of the *Annual Register*), and several forgotten clergymen published sermons upon it, and the frequent riots resulting from the fact that the bear-gardens had become the resort of the worst classes assisted the movement. The London magistrates took measures to suppress cock-throwing in 1769 (Hampson's *Med. Æv. Kalend.* p. 160); but bull-baiting continued far into the present century. Windham and Canning strongly defended it; Dr. Parr is said to have been fond of it (Southey's *Commonplace Book*, vol. iv. p. 585); and as late as 1824, Sir Robert (then Mr.) Peel argued strongly against its prohibition. (*Parliamentary Debates*, vol. x. pp. 132–133, 491–495.)

whole, sustained this movement. In Catholic countries it has been much more faithfully represented by the school of Voltaire and Beccaria. In treating, however, amusements which derived their zest from a display of the natural ferocious instincts of animals, and which suggest the alternative between death endured in the frenzy of combat and that endured in the remote slaughter-house, a judicious moralist may reasonably question whether they have, in any appreciable degree, added to the sum of animal misery, and will dwell less upon the suffering inflicted upon the animal than upon the injurious influence the spectacle may sometimes exercise on the character of the spectator. But there are forms of cruelty which must be regarded in a different light. The horrors of vivisection, often so wantonly, so needlessly practised,[1] the prolonged and atrocious tortures, sometimes inflicted in

[1] Bacon, in an account of the deficiencies of medicine, recommends vivisection in terms that seem to imply that it was not practised in his time. 'As for the passages and pores, it is true which was anciently noted, that the more subtle of them appear not in anatomies, because they are shut and latent in dead bodies, though they be open and manifest in live; which being supposed, though the inhumanity of *anatomia vivorum* was by Celsus justly reproved, yet, in regard of the great use of this observation, the enquiry needed not by him so slightly to have been relinquished altogether, or referred to the casual practices of surgery; but might have been well diverted upon the dissection of beasts alive, which, notwithstanding the dissimilitude of their parts, may sufficiently satisfy this enquiry.'—*Advancement of Learning*, x. 4. Harvey speaks of vivisections as having contributed to lead him to the discovery of the circulation of blood. (Acland's *Harveian Oration* (1865), p. 55.) Bayle, describing the treatment of animals by men, says, 'Nous fouillons dans leurs entrailles pendant leur vie afin de satisfaire notre curiosité.'—*Dict. philos.* art. 'Rorarius, C.' Public opinion in England was very strongly directed to the subject in the present century, by the atrocious cruelties perpetrated by Majendie at his lectures. See a most frightful account of them in a speech by Mr. Martin (an eccentric Irish member, who was generally ridiculed during his life, and has been almost forgotten since his death, but to whose untiring exertions the legislative protection of animals in England is due).—*Parliament. Hist.* vol. xii. p. 652. Mandeville, in his day, was a very strong advocate of kindness to animals.—*Commentary on Fable of the Bees.*

order to procure some gastronomic delicacy, are so far removed from the public gaze, that they exercise little influence on the character of men. Yet no humane man can reflect upon them without a shudder. To bring these things within the range of ethics, to create the notion of duties towards the animal world, has, so far as Christian countries are concerned, been one of the peculiar merits of the last century, and, for the most part, of Protestant nations. However fully we may recognise the humane spirit, transmitted to the world in the form of legends, from the saints of the desert, it must not be forgotten that the inculcation of humanity to animals on a wide scale is mainly the work of a recent and a secular age; that the Mohammedans and the Brahmins have in this sphere considerably surpassed the Christians, and that Spain and Southern Italy, in which Catholicism has most deeply planted its roots, are even now, probably beyond all other countries in Europe, those in which inhumanity to animals is most wanton and most unrebuked.

The influence the first form of monachism has exercised upon the world, as far as it has been beneficial, has been chiefly through the imagination, which has been fascinated by its legends. In the great periods of theological controversy, the Eastern monks had furnished some leading theologians, but in general, in Oriental lands, the hermit life predominated, and extreme maceration was the chief merit of the saint. But in the West monachism assumed very different forms, and exercised far higher functions. At first the Oriental saints were the ideals of Western monks. The Eastern St. Athanasius had been the founder of Italian monachism. St. Martin of Tours excluded labour from the discipline of his monks, and he and they, like the Eastern saints, were accustomed to wander abroad, destroying the idols of the temples.[1] But three great causes conspired to direct the monastic spirit in the West into practical channels. Conditions of race and climate have ever impelled the inhabitants of these lands to active life, and have at the same time rendered them constitutionally incapable of enduring the austerities or enjoying the hallucinations of the sedentary Oriental. There arose, too, in the sixth century, a great legislator, whose form may be dimly traced through a cloud of fantastic legends, and the order of St. Benedict, with that of St. Columba and some others, founded on substantially the same principle, soon ramified through the greater part of Europe, tempered the wild excesses of useless penances, and, making labour an essential part of the monastic system, directed the movement to the purposes of general civilisation. In the last place, the barbarian invasions, and the dissolution of the Western Empire, distorting the whole system of government and almost resolving society into its primitive elements, naturally threw upon the monastic corporations social, political, and intellectual functions of the deepest importance.

It has been observed that the capture of Rome by Alaric, involving as it did the destruction of the grandest religious monuments of Paganism, in fact established in that city the supreme authority of Christianity.[2] A similar remark may be extended to the general downfall of the Western civilisation. In that civilisation Christianity had indeed been legally enthroned; but the philosophies and traditions of Paganism, and the ingrained habits of an ancient, and at the same time an effete society, continually paralysed its energies. What Europe would have been without the barbarian invasions, we may partly divine

[1] See his life by Sulpicius Severus.

[2] Milman.

from the history of the Lower Empire, which represented, in fact, the old Roman civilisation prolonged and Christianised. The barbarian conquests, breaking up the old organisation, provided the Church with a virgin soil, and made it, for a long period, the supreme and indeed sole centre of civilisation.

It would be difficult to exaggerate the skill and courage displayed by the ecclesiastics in this most trying period. We have already seen the noble daring with which they interfered between the conqueror and the vanquished, and the unwearied charity with which they sought to alleviate the unparalleled sufferings of Italy, when the colonial supplies of corn were cut off, and when the fairest plains were desolated by the barbarians. Still more wonderful is the rapid conversion of the barbarian tribes. Unfortunately this, which is one of the most important, is also one of the most obscure pages in the history of the Church. Of whole tribes or nations it may be truly said that we are absolutely ignorant of the cause of their change. The Goths had already been converted by Ulphilas, before the downfall of the empire, and the conversion of the Germans and of several northern nations was long posterior to it; but the great work of Christianising the barbarian world was accomplished almost in the hour when that world became supreme. Rude tribes, accustomed in their own lands to pay absolute obedience to their priests, found themselves in a foreign country, confronted by a priesthood far more civilised and imposing than that which they had left, by gorgeous ceremonies, well fitted to entice, and by threats of coming judgment, well fitted to scare their imaginations. Disconnected from all their old associations, they bowed before the majesty of civilisation, and the Latin religion, like the Latin language, though with many adulterations, reigned over the new society. The doctrine of exclusive salvation, and the doctrine of dæmons, had an admirable missionary power. The first produced an ardour of proselytising which the polytheist could never rival, while the Pagan, who was easily led to recognise the Christian God, was menaced with eternal fire if he did not take the further step of breaking off from his old divinities. The second dispensed the convert from the perhaps impossible task of disbelieving his former religion, for it was only necessary for him to degrade it, attributing its prodigies to infernal beings. The priests, in addition to their noble devotion, carried into their missionary efforts the most masterly judgment. The barbarian tribes usually followed without enquiry the religion of their sovereign, and it was to the conversion of the king, and still more to the conversion of the queen, that the Christians devoted all their energies. Clotilda, the wife of Clovis, Bertha, the wife of Ethelbert, and Theodolinda, the wife of Lothaire, were the chief instruments in converting their husbands and their nations. Nothing that could affect the imagination was neglected. It is related of Clotilda, that she was careful to attract her husband by the rich draperies of the ecclesiastical ceremonies.[1] In another case, the first work of proselytising was confided to an artist, who painted before the terrified Pagans the last judgment and the torments of hell.[2] But especially the belief, which was sincerely held, and sedulously inculcated, that temporal success followed in the train of Christianity, and that every pestilence, famine, or military disaster was the penalty of idolatry, heresy, sacrilege, or vice, assisted the movement. The

[1] Greg. Turon. ii. 29.

[2] This was the first step towards the conversion of the Bulgarians.—Milman's *Latin Christianity*, vol. iii. p. 249.

theory was so wide, that it met every variety of fortune, and being taught with consummate skill, to barbarians who were totally destitute of all critical power, and strongly predisposed to accept it, it proved extremely efficacious, and hope, fear, gratitude, and remorse drew multitudes into the Church. The transition was softened by the substitution of Christian ceremonies and saints for the festivals and the divinities of the Pagans.[1] Besides the professed missionaries, the Christian captives zealously diffused their faith among their Pagan masters. When the chieftain had been converted, and the army had followed his profession, an elaborate monastic and ecclesiastical organisation grew up to consolidate the conquest, and repressive laws soon crushed all opposition to the faith.

In these ways the victory of Christianity over the barbarian world was achieved. But that victory, though very great, was less decisive than might appear. A religion which professed to be Christianity, and which contained many of the ingredients of pure Christianity, had risen into the ascendant, but it had undergone a profound modification through the struggle. Religions, as well as worshippers, had been baptised. The festivals, images, and names of saints had been substituted for those of the idols, and the habits of thought and feeling of the ancient faith reappeared in new forms and a new language. The tendency to a material, idolatrous, and polytheistic faith, which had long been encouraged by the monks, and which the heretics Jovinian, Vigilantius, and Aerius had vainly resisted, was fatally strengthened by the infusion of a barbarian element into the Church, by the general depression of intellect in Europe, and by the many accommodations that were made to facilitate con-

[1] A remarkable collection of instances of this kind is given by Ozanam, *Civilisation in the Fifth Century* (Eng. trans.), vol. i. pp. 124–127.

version. Though apparently defeated and crushed, the old gods still retained, under a new faith, no small part of their influence over the world.

To this tendency the leaders of the Church made in general no resistance, though in another form they were deeply persuaded of the vitality of the old gods. Many curious and picturesque legends attest the popular belief that the old Roman and the old barbarian divinities, in their capacity of dæmons, were still waging an unrelenting war against the triumphant faith. A great Pope of the sixth century relates how a Jew, being once benighted on his journey, and finding no other shelter for the night, lay down to rest in an abandoned temple of Apollo. Shuddering at the loneliness of the building, and fearing the dæmons who were said to haunt it, he determined, though not a Christian, to protect himself by the sign of the cross, which he had often heard possessed a mighty power against spirits. To that sign he owed his safety. For at midnight the temple was filled with dark and threatening forms. The god Apollo was holding his court at his deserted shrine, and his attendant dæmons were recounting the temptations they had devised against the Christians.[1] A newly married Roman, when one day playing ball, took off his wedding-ring, which he found an impediment in the game, and he gaily put it on the finger of a statue of Venus, which was standing near. When he returned, the marble finger had bent so that it was impossible to withdraw the ring, and that night the goddess appeared to him in a dream, and told him that she was

[1] St. Gregory, *Dial.* iii. 7. The particular temptation the Jew heard discussed was that of the bishop of the diocese, who, under the instigation of one of the dæmons, was rapidly falling in love with a nun, and had proceeded so far as jocosely to stroke her on the back. The Jew, having related the vision to the bishop, the latter reformed his manners, the Jew became a Christian, and the temple was turned into a church.

now his wedded wife, and that she would abide with him for ever.[1] When the Irish missionary St. Gall was fishing one night upon a Swiss lake, near which he had planted a monastery, he heard strange voices sweeping over the lonely deep. The Spirit of the Water and the Spirit of the Mountains were consulting together how they could expel the intruder who had disturbed their ancient reign.[2]

The details of the rapid propagation of Western monachism have been amply treated by many historians, and the causes of its success are sufficiently manifest. Some of the reasons I have assigned for the first spread of asceticism continued to operate, while others of a still more powerful kind had arisen. The rapid decomposition of the entire Roman Empire by continuous invasions of barbarians rendered the existence of an inviolable asylum and centre of peaceful labour a matter of transcendent importance, and the monastery as organised by St. Benedict soon combined the most heterogeneous elements of attraction. It was at once eminently aristocratic and intensely democratic. The power and princely position of the abbot was coveted, and usually obtained, by members of the most illustrious families, while emancipated serfs or peasants, who had lost their all in the invasions, or were harassed by savage nobles, or had fled from military service, or desired to lead a more secure and easy life, found in the monastery an unfailing refuge. The institution exercised all the influence of great wealth, expended for the most part with great charity, while the monk himself was invested with the aureole of a sacred poverty. To ardent and philanthropic natures, the profession opened boundless vistas of missionary, charitable,

[1] This is mentioned by one of the English historians—I think by Mathew of Westminster.

[2] See Milman's *Hist. of Latin Christianity*, vol. ii. p. 293.

and civilising activity. To the superstitious it was the plain road to heaven. To the ambitious it was the portal to bishoprics, and, after the monk St. Gregory, not unfrequently to the Popedom. To the studious it offered the only opportunity then existing in the world of seeing many books and passing a life of study. To the timid and the retiring it afforded the most secure, and probably the least laborious, life a poor peasant could hope to find. Vast as were the multitudes that thronged the monasteries, the means for their support were never wanting. The belief that gifts or legacies to a monastery opened the doors of heaven, was in a superstitious age sufficient to secure for the community an almost boundless wealth, which was still further increased by the skill and perseverance with which the monks tilled the waste lands, by the exemption of their domains from all taxation, and by the tranquillity which in the most turbulent ages they usually enjoyed. In France, the Low Countries, and Germany they were pre-eminently agriculturists. Gigantic forests were felled, inhospitable marshes reclaimed, barren plains cultivated by their hands. The monastery often became the nucleus of a city. It was the centre of civilisation and industry, the symbol of moral power in an age of turbulence and war.

It must be observed, however, that the beneficial influence of the monastic system was necessarily transitional, and the subsequent corruption the normal and inevitable result of its constitution. Vast societies living in enforced celibacy, exercising an unbounded influence, and possessing enormous wealth, must necessarily have become hotbeds of corruption when the enthusiasm that had created them expired. The services they rendered as the centres of agriculture, the refuge of travellers, the sanctuaries in war, the counterpoise of the baronial castle, were no longer required when the convulsions of invasion had ceased, and when civil society was definitely organised. And a similar observation may be extended even to their moral type. Thus, while it is undoubtedly true that the Benedictine monks, by making labour an essential element of their discipline, did very much to efface the stigma which slavery had affixed upon it, it is also true that when industry had passed out of its initial stage, the monastic theories of the sanctity of poverty, and the evil of wealth, were its most deadly opponents. The dogmatic condemnation by theologians of loans at interest, which are the basis of industrial enterprise, was the expression of a far deeper antagonism of tendencies and ideals.

In one important respect, the transition from the eremite to the monastic life involved not only a change of circumstances, but also a change of character. The habit of obedience, and the virtue of humility, assumed a position which they had never previously occupied. The conditions of the hermit life contributed to develope to a very high degree a spirit of independence and spiritual pride, which was still further increased by a curious habit that existed in the Church of regarding each eminent hermit as the special model or professor of some particular virtue, and making pilgrimages to him, in order to study this aspect of his character.[1] These pilgrimages, combined with the usually solitary and self-sufficing life of the hermit, and also with the habit of measuring progress almost entirely by the suppression of a physical appetite, which it is quite possible wholly to destroy, very naturally produced an extreme arrogance.[2] But in

[1] Cassian. *Cœnob. Instit.* v. 4. See, too, some striking instances of this in the life of St. Antony.

[2] This spiritual pride is well noticed by Neander, *Ecclesiastical History* (Bohn's ed.), vol. iii. pp. 321-323. It appears in many traits scattered through the lives of their saints. I have already cited the instances of St.

the highly organised and disciplined monasteries of the West, passive obedience and humility were the very first things that were inculcated. The monastery, beyond all other institutions, was the school for their exercise; and as the monk represented the highest moral ideal of the age, obedience and humility acquired a new value in the minds of men. Nearly all the feudal and other organisations that arose out of the chaos that followed the destruction of the Roman Empire were intimately related to the Church, not simply because the Church supplied in itself an admirable model of an organised body, but also because it had done much to educate men in habits of obedience. The special value of this education depended upon the peculiar circumstances of the time. The ancient civilisations, and especially that of Rome, had been by no means deficient in those habits, but it was in the midst of the dissolution of an old society, and of the ascendency of barbarians, who exaggerated to the highest degree their personal independence, that the Church proposed to the reverence of mankind a life of passive obedience as the highest ideal of virtue.

The habit of obedience was no new thing in the world, but the disposition of humility was pre-eminently and almost exclusively a Christian virtue; and there has probably never been any sphere in which it has been so largely and so successfully inculcated as in the monastery. The

Antony and St. Macarius, and the visions telling them they were not the best of living people; and also the case of the hermit, who was deceived by a devil in the form of a woman, because he had been exalted by pride. Another hermit, being very holy, received pure white bread every day from heaven, but, being extravagantly elated, the bread got worse and worse till it became perfectly black. (Tillemont, tome x. pp. 27–28.) A certain Isidore affirmed that he had not been conscious of sin, even in thought, for forty years. (Socrates, iv. 23.) It was a saying of St. Antony, that a solitary man in the desert is free from three wars—of sight, speech, and hearing; he has to combat only fornication. (*Apothegmata Patrum.*)

whole penitential discipline, the entire mode or tenor of the monastic life, was designed to tame every sentiment of pride, and to give humility a foremost place in the hierarchy of virtues. We have here one great source of the mollifying influence of Catholicism. The gentler virtues —benevolence and amiability—may, and in an advanced civilisation often do, subsist in natures that are completely devoid of genuine humility; but on the other hand, it is scarcely possible for a nature to be pervaded by a deep sentiment of humility without this sentiment exercising a softening influence over the whole character. To transform a fierce warlike nature into a character of a gentler type, the first essential is to awaken this feeling. In the monasteries, the extinction of social and domestic feelings, the narrow corporate spirit, and, still more, the atrocious opinions that were prevalent concerning the guilt of heresy, produced in many minds an extreme and most active ferocity; but the practice of charity, and the ideal of humility, never failed to exercise some softening influence upon Christendom.

But, however advantageous the temporary pre-eminence of this moral type may have been, it was obviously unsuited for a later stage of civilisation. Political liberty is almost impossible where the monastic system is supreme, not merely because the monasteries divert the energies of the nation from civic to ecclesiastical channels, but also because the monastic ideal is the very apotheosis of servitude. Catholicism has been admirably fitted at once to mitigate and to perpetuate despotism. When men have learnt to reverence a life of passive, unreasoning obedience as the highest type of perfection, the enthusiasm and passion of freedom necessarily decline. In this repect there is an analogy between the monastic and the military spirit, both of which promote and glorify passive obedience, and therefore prepare the minds of men for despotic rule; but on the whole, the monastic spirit is probably more hostile to freedom than the military spirit, for the obedience of the monk is based upon humility, while the obedience of the soldier coexists with pride. Now, a considerable measure of pride, or self-assertion, is an invariable characteristic of free communities.

The ascendency which the monastic system gave to the virtue of humility has not continued. This virtue is indeed the crowning grace and beauty of the most perfect characters of the saintly type; but experience has shown that among common men humility is more apt to degenerate into servility than pride into arrogance; and modern moralists have appealed more successfully to the sense of dignity than to the opposite feeling. Two of the most important steps of later moral history have consisted of the creation of a sentiment of pride as the parent and the guardian of many virtues. The first of these encroachments on the monastic spirit was chivalry, which called into being a proud and jealous military honour that has never since been extinguished. The second was the creation of that feeling of self-respect which is one of the most remarkable characteristics that distinguish Protestant from most Catholic populations, and which has proved among the former an invaluable moral agent, forming frank and independent natures, and checking every servile habit and all mean and degrading vice.[1] The peculiar

[1] 'Pride, under such training [that of modern rationalistic philosophy], instead of running to waste, is turned to account. It gets a new name; it is called self-respect. . . . It is directed into the channel of industry, rugality, honesty, and obedience, and it becomes the very staple of the religion and morality held in honour in a day like our own. It becomes the safeguard of chastity, the guarantee of veracity, in high and low; it is the very household god of the Protestant, inspiring neatness and decency in the servant-girl, propriety of carriage and refined manners in her mistress, upright-

vigour with which it has been developed in Protestant countries may be attributed to the suppression of monastic institutions and habits; to the stigma Protestantism has attached to mendicancy, which Catholicism has usually glorified and encouraged; and lastly, to the action of free political institutions, which have taken deepest root where the principles of the Reformation have been accepted.

The relation of the monasteries to the intellectual virtues, which we have next to examine, opens out a wide field of discussion; and in order to appreciate it, it will be necessary to revert briefly to a somewhat earlier stage of ecclesiastical history. And in the first place, it may be observed, that the phrase intellectual virtue, which is often used in a metaphorical sense, is susceptible of a strictly literal interpretation. If a sincere and active desire for truth be a moral duty, the discipline and the dispositions that are plainly involved in every honest search fall rigidly within the range of ethics. To love truth sincerely means to pursue it with an earnest, conscientious, unflagging zeal. It means to be prepared to follow the light of evidence even to the most unwelcome conclusions; to labour earnestly to emancipate the mind from early prejudices; to resist the current of the desires, and the refracting influence of the passions; to proportion on all occasions conviction to evidence, and to be ready, if need be, to

ness, manliness, and generosity in the head of the family. . . . It is the stimulating principle of providence, on the one hand, and of free expenditure on the other; of an honourable ambition and of elegant enjoyment.'—Newman, *On University Education*, Discourse ix. In the same lecture (which is, perhaps, the most beautiful of the many beautiful productions of its illustrious author), Dr. Newman describes, with admirable eloquence, the manner in which modesty has supplanted humility in the modern type of excellence. It is scarcely necessary to say that the lecturer strongly disapproves of the movement he describes.

exchange the calm of assurance for all the suffering of a perplexed and disturbed mind. To do this is very difficult and very painful; but it is clearly involved in the notion of earnest love of truth. If, then, any system stigmatises as criminal the state of doubt, denounces the examination of some one class of arguments or facts, seeks to introduce the bias of the affections into the enquiries of the reason, or regards the honest conclusion of an upright investigator as involving moral guilt, that system is subversive of intellectual honesty.

Among the ancients, although the methods of enquiry were often very faulty, and generalisations very hasty, a respect for the honest search after truth was widely diffused.[1] There were, as we have already seen, instances in which certain religious practices which were regarded as attestations of loyalty, or as necessary to propitiate the gods in favour of the State, were enforced by law; there were even a few instances of philosophies, which were believed to lead directly to immoral results or social convulsions, being suppressed; but as a general rule, speculation was untrammelled, the notion of there being any necessary guilt in erroneous opinion was unknown, and the boldest enquirers were regarded with honour and admiration. The religious theory of Paganism had in this respect some influence. Polytheism, with many faults, had three great merits. It was eminently poetical, eminently patriotic, and eminently tolerant. The conception of a vast hierarchy of beings more glorious than, but not wholly unlike, men, presiding over all the developments of nature, and filling the universe with their deeds, supplied the chief nutriment of the Greek imagination. The national

[1] Thus, 'indagatio veri' was reckoned among the leading virtues, and the high place given to σοφία and 'prudentia' in ethical writings, preserved the notion of the moral duties connected with the discipline of the intellect.

religions, interweaving religious ceremonies and associations with all civic life, concentrated and intensified the sentiment of patriotism, and the notion of many distinct groups of gods led men to tolerate many forms of worship and great variety of creeds. In that colossal amalgam of nations of which Rome became the metropolis, intellectual liberty still further advanced; the vast variety of philosophies and beliefs expatiated unmolested; the search for truth was regarded as an important element of virtue, and the relentless and most sceptical criticism which Socrates had applied in turn to all the fundamental propositions of popular belief remained as an example to his successors.

We have already seen that one leading cause of the rapid progress of the Church was, that its teachers enforced their distinctive tenets as absolutely essential to salvation, and thus assailed at a great advantage the supporters of all other creeds which did not claim this exclusive authority. We have seen, too, that in an age of great and growing credulity they had been conspicuous for their assertion of the duty of absolute, unqualified, and unquestioning belief. The notion of the guilt, both of error and of doubt, grew rapidly, and, being soon regarded as a fundamental tenet, it determined the whole course and policy of the Church.

And here, I think, it will not be unadvisable to pause for a moment, and endeavour to ascertain what misconceived truth lay at the root of this fatal tenet. Considered abstractedly and by the light of nature, it is as unmeaning to speak of the immorality of an intellectual mistake as it would be to talk of the colour of a sound. If a man has sincerely persuaded himself that it is possible for parallel lines to meet, or for two straight lines to enclose a space, we pronounce his judgment to be absurd; but it is free from all tincture of immorality. And if, instead of failing to appreciate a demonstrable truth, his error consisted in a false estimate of the conflicting arguments of an historical problem, this mistake—assuming always that the enquiry was an upright one—is still simply external to the sphere of morals. It is possible that his conclusion, by weakening some barrier against vice, may produce vicious consequences, like those which might ensue from some ill-advised modification of the police force; but it in no degree follows from this that the judgment is in itself criminal. If a student applies himself with the same dispositions to Roman and Jewish histories, the mistakes he may make in the latter are no more immoral than those which he may make in the former.

There are, however, two cases in which an intellectual error may be justly said to involve, or at least to represent, guilt. In the first place, error very frequently springs from the partial or complete absence of that mental disposition which is implied in a real love of truth. Hypocrites, or men who through interested motives profess opinions which they do not really believe, are probably rarer than is usually supposed; but it would be difficult to over-estimate the number of those whose genuine convictions are due to the unresisted bias of their interests. By the term interests, I mean not only material well-being, but also all those mental luxuries, all those grooves or channels for thought, which it is easy and pleasing to follow, and painful and difficult to abandon. Such are the love of ease, the love of certainty, the love of system, the bias of the passions, the associations of the imagination, as well as the coarser influences of social position, domestic happiness, professional interest, party feeling, or ambition. In most men, the love of truth is so languid, and their reluctance to encounter mental suffering is so great, that they yield their judgments without an effort to the current, withdraw their minds from all opinions or arguments opposed to their own, and thus speedily convince themselves of the truth of what they wish to believe. He who really loves truth, is bound at least to endeavour to resist these distorting influences, and in so far as his opinions are the result of his not having done so, in so far they represent a moral failing.

In the next place, it must be observed that every moral disposition brings with it an intellectual bias which exercises a great and often a controlling and decisive influence even upon the most earnest enquirer. If we know the character or disposition of a man, we can usually predict with tolerable accuracy many of his opinions. We can tell to what side of politics, to what canons of taste, to what theory of morals he will naturally incline. Stern, heroic, and haughty natures tend to systems in which these qualities occupy the foremost position in the moral type, while gentle natures will as naturally lean towards systems in which the amiable virtues are supreme. Impelled by a species of moral gravitation, the enquirer will glide insensibly to the system which is congruous to his disposition, and intellectual difficulties will seldom arrest him. He can have observed human nature with but little fruit who has not remarked how constant is this connection, and how very rarely men change fundamentally the principles they had deliberately adopted on religious, moral, or even political questions, without the change being preceded, accompanied, or very speedily followed, by a serious modification of character. So, too, a vicious and depraved nature, or a nature which is hard, narrow, and unsympathetic, will tend, much less by calculation or indolence than by natural affinity, to low and degrading views of human nature. Those who have never felt the higher emotions will scarcely appreciate them. The materials with which the intellect builds are often derived from the heart, and a moral disease is therefore not unfrequently at the root of an erroneous judgment.

Of these two truths the first cannot, I think, be said to have had any influence in the formation of the theological notion of the guilt of error. An elaborate process of mental discipline, with a view to strengthening the critical powers of the mind, is utterly remote from the spirit of theology; and this is one of the great reasons why the growth of an inductive and scientific spirit is invariably hostile to theological interests. To raise the requisite standard of proof, to inculcate hardness and slowness of belief, is the first task of the inductive reasoner. He looks with great favour upon the condition of a suspended judgment; he encourages men rather to prolong than to abridge it; he regards the tendency of the human mind to rapid and premature generalisations as one of its most fatal vices; he desires especially that that which is believed should not be so cherished that the mind should be indisposed to admit doubt, or, on the appearance of new arguments, to revise with impartiality its conclusions. Nearly all the greatest intellectual achievements of the last three centuries have been preceded and prepared by the growth of scepticism. The historic scepticism which Vico, Beaufort, Pouilly, and Voltaire in the last century, and Niebuhr and Lewes in the present century, applied to ancient history, lies at the root of all the great modern efforts to reconstruct the history of mankind. The splendid discoveries of physical science would have been impossible but for the scientific scepticism of the school of Bacon, which dissipated the old theories of the universe, and led men to demand a severity of proof altogether unknown to the ancients. The philosophic scepticism of Hume and Kant has given the greatest modern impulse to metaphysics and ethics. Exactly in proportion, therefore, as men are educated in the inductive school, they are alienated from those theological systems which represent a condition of doubt as sinful, seek to govern the reason by the interests and the affections, and make it a main object to destroy the impartiality of the judgment.

But although it is difficult to look upon Catholicism in any other light than as the most deadly enemy of the scientific spirit, it has always cordially recognised the most important truth, that character in a very great measure determines opinions. To cultivate the moral type that is most congenial to the opinions it desires to recommend, has always been its effort, and the conviction that a deviation from that type has often been the predisposing cause of intellectual heresy, had doubtless a large share in the first persuasion of the guilt of error. But priestly and other influences soon conspired to enlarge this doctrine. A crowd of speculative, historical, and administrative propositions were asserted as essential to salvation, and all who rejected them were wholly external to the bond of Christian sympathy.

If, indeed, we put aside the pure teaching of the Christian founders, and consider the actual history of the Church since Constantine, we shall find no justification for the popular theory, that beneath its influence the narrow spirit of patriotism faded into a wide and cosmopolitan philanthropy. A real though somewhat languid feeling of universal brotherhood had already been created in the world by the universality of the Roman Empire. In the new faith the range of genuine sympathy was strictly limited by the creed. According to the popular belief, all who differed from the teaching of the orthodox lived under the hatred of the Almighty, and were destined after death for an eternity of anguish. Very naturally, therefore, they were wholly alienated from the true believers, and no moral or intellectual excellence could atone for their crime in propagating error. The eighty or ninety sects[1] into which Christianity speedily divided, hated one another with an intensity that extorted the wonder of Julian and the ridicule of the Pagans of Alexandria, and the fierce riots and persecutions that hatred produced appear in every page of ecclesiastical history. There is, indeed, something at once grotesque and ghastly in the spectacle. The Donatists, having separated from the orthodox simply on the question of the validity of the consecration of a certain bishop, declared that all who adopted the orthodox view must be damned, refused to perform their rites in the orthodox churches which they had seized, till they had burnt the altar and scraped the wood, beat multitudes to death with clubs, blinded others by anointing their eyes with lime, filled Africa, during nearly two centuries, with war and desolation, and contributed largely to its final ruin.[2] The childish and almost unintelligible quarrels between the Homoiousians and the Homoousians, between those who maintained that the nature of Christ was like that of the Father and those who maintained that it was the same, filled the world with riot and hatred. The Catholics tell how an Arian emperor caused eighty orthodox priests to be drowned on a single occasion;[3] how three thousand persons perished in the riots that convulsed Constantinople when the Arian bishop Macedonius superseded the Athanasian Paul;[4] how George of

1 St. Augustine reckoned eighty-eight sects as existing in his time.

2 See a full account of these persecutions in Tillemont, *Mém. d'Histoire ecclés.* tome vi.

3 Socrates, *H. E.*, iv. 16. This anecdote is much doubted by modern historians.

4 Milman's *Hist. of Christianity* (ed. 1867), vol. ii. p. 422.

Cappadocia, the Arian bishop of Alexandria, caused the widows of the Athanasian party to be scourged on the soles of their feet, the holy virgins to be stripped naked, to be flogged with the prickly branches of palm-trees, or to be slowly scorched over fires till they abjured their creed.[1] The triumph of the Catholics in Egypt was accompanied (if we may believe the solemn assertions of eighty Arian bishops) by every variety of plunder, murder, sacrilege, and outrage,[2] and Arius himself was probably poisoned by Catholic hands.[3] The followers of St. Cyril of Alexandria, who were chiefly monks, filled their city with riot and bloodshed, wounded the prefect Orestes, dragged the pure and gifted Hypatia into one of their churches, murdered her, tore the flesh from her bones with sharp shells, and, having stripped her body naked, flung the mangled remains into the flames.[4] In Ephesus, during the contest between St. Cyril and the Nestorians, the cathedral itself was the theatre of a fierce and bloody conflict.[5] Constantinople, on the occasion of the deposition of St. Chrysostom, was for several days in a condition of absolute anarchy.[6] After the Council of Chalcedon, Jerusalem and Alexandria were again convulsed, and the bishop of the latter city was murdered in his baptistery.[7] About fifty years later, when the Monophysite controversy was at its height, the palace of the

[1] St. Athanasius, *Historical Treatises* (Library of the Fathers), pp. 192, 284.

[2] Milman, *Hist. of Christianity*, ii. pp. 436–437.

[3] The death of Arius, as is well known, took place suddenly (his bowels, it is said, coming out) when just about to make his triumphal entry into the Cathedral of Constantinople. The death never seems to have been regarded as natural, but it was a matter of controversy whether it was a miracle or a murder.

[4] Socrates, *H. E.*, vii. 13–15.

[5] Milman, *Hist. of Latin Christianity*, vol. i. pp. 214–215.

[6] Milman, *Hist. of Christianity*, vol. iii. p. 145.

[7] Milman, *Latin Christianity*, vol. i. pp. 290–291.

emperor at Constantinople was blockaded, the churches were besieged, and the streets commanded by furious bands of contending monks.[1] Repressed for a time, the riots broke out two years after with an increased ferocity, and almost every leading city of the East was filled by the monks with bloodshed and with riots.[2] St. Augustine himself is accused of having excited every kind of popular persecution against the Semi-Pelagians.[3] The Councils, animated by an almost frantic hatred, urged on by their anathemas the rival sects.[4] In the 'Robber Council' of Ephesus, Flavianus, the Bishop of Constantinople, was kicked and beaten by the Bishop of Alexandria, or at least by his followers, and a few days later died from the effect of the blows.[5] In the contested election that

[1] Milman, *Hist. of Latin Christianity*, vol. i. pp. 310-311.

[2] Ibid. vol. i. pp. 314-318. Dean Milman thus sums up the history: 'Monks in Alexandria, monks in Antioch, monks in Jerusalem, monks in Constantinople, decide peremptorily on orthodoxy and heterodoxy. The bishops themselves cower before them. Macedonius in Constantinople, Flavianus in Antioch, Elias in Jerusalem, condemn themselves and abdicate, or are driven from their sees. Persecution is universal—persecution by every means of violence and cruelty; the only question is, in whose hands is the power to persecute. . . . Bloodshed, murder, treachery, assassination, even during the public worship of God—these are the frightful means by which each party strives to maintain its opinions and to defeat its adversary.'

[3] See a striking passage from Julianus of Eclana, cited by Milman, *Hist. of Latin Christianity*, vol. i. p. 164.

[4] 'Nowhere is Christianity less attractive than in the Councils of the church. . . . Intrigue, injustice, violence, decisions on authority alone, and that the authority of a turbulent majority . . . detract from the reverence and impugn the judgments of at least the later Councils. The close is almost invariably a terrible anathema, in which it is impossible not to discern the tones of human hatred, of arrogant triumph, of rejoicing at the damnation imprecated against the humiliated adversary.'—Ibid. vol. i. p. 202.

[5] See the account of this scene in Gibbon, *Decline and Fall*, ch. xlvii.; Milman, *Latin Christianity*, vol. i. p. 263. There is a conflict of authorities as to whether the Bishop of Alexandria himself kicked his adversary, or, to speak more correctly, the act which is charged against him by some

issued in the election of St. Damasus as Pope of Rome, though no theological question appears to have been at issue, the riots were so fierce, that one hundred and thirty-seven corpses were found in one of the churches.[1] The precedent of the Jewish persecutions of idolatry having been adduced by St. Cyprian, in the third century, in favour of excommunication,[2] was urged by Optatus, in the reign of Constantine, in favour of persecuting the Donatists;[3] in the next reign we find a large body of Christians presenting to the emperor a petition, based upon this precedent, imploring him to destroy by force the Pagan worship.[4] About fifteen years later, the whole Christian Church was prepared, on the same grounds, to support the persecuting policy of St. Ambrose,[5] the contending sects having found, in the duty of crushing religious liberty, the solitary tenet on which they were agreed. The most unaggressive and unobtrusive forms of Paganism were persecuted with the same ferocity.[6] To offer a sacrifice was to commit a capital offence; to hang up a simple chaplet was to incur the forfeiture of an estate. The noblest works of Asiatic architecture and of Greek sculpture perished by the same iconoclasm that shattered the humble temple at which the peasant loved to pray, or the household gods which consecrated his home. There were no varieties of belief

contemporary writers is not charged against him by others. The violence was certainly done by his followers and in his presence.

[1] Ammianus Marcellinus, xxvii. 3.

[2] Cyprian, *Ep.* lxi.

[3] Milman, *Hist. of Christianity,* vol. ii. p. 306.

[4] Ibid. iii. 10.

[5] 'By this time the Old Testament language and sentiment with regard to idolatry were completely incorporated with the Christian feeling; and when Ambrose enforced on a Christian emperor the sacred duty of intolerance against opinions and practices which scarcely a century before had been the established religion of the empire, his zeal was supported by almost the unanimous applause of the Christian world.'—Milman's *Hist. of Christianity,* vol. iii. p. 150.

[6] See the Theodosian laws of Paganism.

too minute for the new intolerance to embitter. The question of the proper time of celebrating Easter was believed to involve the issue of salvation or damnation;[1] and when, long after, in the fourteenth century, the question of the nature of the light at the transfiguration was discussed at Constantinople, those who refused to admit that that light was uncreated, were deprived of the honours of Christian burial.[2]

Together with these legislative and ecclesiastical measures, a literature arose surpassing in its mendacious ferocity any other the world had known. The polemical writers habitually painted as dæmons those who diverged from the orthodox belief, gloated with a vindictive piety over the sufferings of the heretic upon earth, as upon a Divine punishment, and sometimes, with an almost superhuman malice, passing in imagination beyond the threshold of the grave, exulted in no ambiguous terms on the tortures which they believed to be reserved for him for ever. A few men, such as Synesius, Basil, or Salvian, might still find some excellence in Pagans or heretics, but their candour was altogether exceptional; and he who will compare the beautiful pictures the Greek poets gave of their Trojan adversaries, or the Roman historians of the enemies of their country, with those which ecclesiastical writers, for many centuries, almost invariably gave of all who were opposed to their Church,

1 This appears from the whole history of the controversy; but the prevailing feeling is, I think, expressed with peculiar vividness in the following passage—'Eadmer says (following the words of Bede) in Colman's times there was a sharp controversy about the observing of Easter, and other rules of life for churchmen; therefore, this question deservedly excited the minds and feeling of many people, fearing lest, perhaps, after having received the name of Christians, they should run, or had run in vain.'—King's *Hist. of the Church of Ireland*, book ii. ch. vi.

2 Gibbon, chap. lxiii.

may easily estimate the extent to which cosmopolitan sympathy had retrograded.

At the period, however, when the Western monasteries began to discharge their intellectual functions, the supremacy of Catholicism was nearly established, and polemical ardour had begun to wane. The literary zeal of the Church took other forms, but all were deeply tinged by the monastic spirit. It is difficult or impossible to conceive what would have been the intellectual future of the world had Catholicism never arisen—what principles or impulses would have guided the course of the human mind, or what new institutions would have been created for its culture. Under the influence of Catholicism, the monastery became the one sphere of intellectual labour, and it continued during many centuries to occupy that position. Without entering into anything resembling a literary history, which would be foreign to the objects of the present work, I shall endeavour briefly to estimate the manner in which it discharged its functions.

The first idea that is naturally suggested by the mention of the intellectual services of monasteries is the conservation of the writings of the Pagans. I have already observed, that among the early Christians there was a marked difference on the subject of their writings. The school which was represented by Tertullian regarded them with abhorrence, while the Platonists, who were represented by Justin Martyr, Clement of Alexandria, and Origen, not merely recognised with great cordiality their beauties, but even imagined that they could detect in them both the traces of an original Divine inspiration, and plagiarisms from the Jewish writings. While avoiding, for the most part, these extremes, St. Augustine, the great organiser of Western Christianity, treats the Pagan writings with appreciative respect. He had himself ascribed his first conversion from a course of vice to the 'Hortensius' of Cicero, and his works are full of discriminating, and often very beautiful applications, of the old Roman literature. The attempt of Julian to prevent the Christians from teaching the classics, and the extreme resentment which that attempt elicited, show how highly the Christian leaders of that period valued this form of education; and it was naturally the more cherished on account of the contest. The influence of Neoplatonism, the baptism of multitudes of nominal Christians after Constantine, and the decline of zeal which necessarily accompanied prosperity, had all in different ways the same tendency. In Synesius we have the curious phenomenon of a bishop who, not content with proclaiming himself the admiring friend of the Pagan Hypatia, openly declared his complete disbelief in the resurrection of the body, and his firm adhesion to the Platonic doctrine of the pre-existence of souls.[1] Had the ecclesiastical theory prevailed which gave such latitude even to the leaders of the Church, the course of Christianity would have been very different. A reactionary spirit, however, arose at Rome. The doctrine of exclusive salvation supplied its intellectual basis; the political and organising genius of the Roman ecclesiastics impelled them to reduce belief into a rigid form; the genius of St. Gregory guided the movement,[2] and a series of

[1] An interesting sketch of this very interesting prelate has, lately been written by M. Druon, *Étude sur la Vie et les Œuvres de Synésius* (Paris, 1859).

[2] Tradition has pronounced Gregory the Great to have been the destroyer of the Palatine library, and to have been especially zealous in burning the writings of Livy, because they described the achievements of the Pagan gods. For these charges, however (which I am sorry to find repeated by so eminent a writer as Dr. Draper), there is no real evidence, for they are not found in any writer earlier than the twelfth century. (See Bayle, *Dict.* art. Greg.) The extreme contempt of Gregory for Pagan literature is,

historical events, of which the ecclesiastical and political separation of the Western empire from the speculative Greeks, and the invasion and conversion of the barbarians, were the most important, definitely established the ascendency of the Catholic type. In the convulsions that followed the barbarian invasions, intellectual energy of a secular kind almost absolutely ceased. A parting gleam issued, indeed, in the sixth century, from the Court of Theodoric, at Ravenna, which was adorned by the genius of Boëthius, and the talent of Cassiodorus and Symmachus; but after this time, for a long period, literature consisted almost exclusively of sermons and lives of saints, which were composed in the monasteries.[1] Gregory of Tours was succeeded as an annalist by the still feebler Fredegarius, and there was then a long and absolute blank. A few outlying countries showed some faint animation. St. Leander and St. Isidore planted at Seville a school, which flourished in the seventh century, and the distant monasteries of Ireland continued somewhat later to be the

however, sufficiently manifested in his famous and very curious letter to Desiderius, Bishop of Vienne, rebuking him for having taught certain persons Pagan literature, and thus mingling 'the praises of Jupiter with the praises of Christ;' doing what would be impious even for a religious layman, 'polluting the mind with the blasphemous praises of the wicked.' Some curious evidence of the feelings of the Christians of the fourth, fifth, and sixth centuries, about Pagan literature, is given in Guinguené, *Hist. littéraire de l'Italie*, tome i. p. 29–31, and some legends of a later period are candidly related by one of the most enthusiastic English advocates of the Middle Ages. (Maitland, *Dark Ages.*)

[1] Probably the best account of the intellectual history of these times is still to be found in the admirable introductory chapters with which the Benedictines prefaced each century of their *Hist. littéraire de la France.* The Benedictines think (with Hallam) that the eighth century was, on the whole, the darkest on the continent, though England attained its lowest point somewhat later. Of the great protectors of learning Theodoric was unable to write (see Guinguené, tome i. p. 31), and Charlemagne (Eginhard) only began to learn when advanced in life, and was never quite able to master the accomplishment. Alfred, however, was distinguished in literature.

receptacles of learning; but the rest of Europe sank into an almost absolute torpor, till the rationalism of Abelard, and the events that followed the crusade, began the revival of learning. The principal service which Catholicism rendered during this period to Pagan literature was probably the perpetuation of Latin as a sacred language. The complete absence of all curiosity about that literature is shown by the fact that Greek was suffered to become almost absolutely extinct, though there was no time when the Western nations had not some relations with the Greek empire, or when pilgrimages to the Holy Land altogether ceased. The study of the Latin classics was for the most part positively discouraged. The writers, it was believed, were burning in hell; the monks were too inflated with their imaginary knowledge to regard with any respect a Pagan writer, and periodical panics about the approaching termination of the world continually checked any desire for secular learning.[1] There existed a custom among some monks, when they were under the discipline of silence, and desired to ask for Virgil or Horace, or any other Gentile work, to indicate their wish by scratching their ears like a dog, to which animal it was thought the Pagans might be reasonably compared.[2] The monasteries

[1] The belief that the world was just about to end was, as is well known, very general among the early Christians, and greatly affected their lives. It appears in the New Testament, and very clearly in the epistle ascribed to Barnabas in the first century. The persecutions of the second and third centuries revived it, and both Tertullian and Cyprian (*in Demetrianum*) strongly assert it. With the triumph of Christianity the apprehension for a time subsided; but it reappeared with great force when the dissolution of the empire was manifestly impending, when it was accomplished, and in the prolonged anarchy and suffering that ensued. Gregory of Tours, writing in the latter part of the sixth century, speaks of it as very prevalent (*Prologue to the First Book*); and St. Gregory the Great, about the same time, constantly expresses it. The panic that filled Europe at the end of the tenth century has been often described.

[2] Maitland's *Dark Ages*, p. 403.

contained, it is said, during some time, the only libraries in Europe, and were therefore the sole receptacles of the Pagan manuscripts; but we cannot infer from this, that if the monasteries had not existed, similar libraries would not have been called into being in their place. To the occasional industry of the monks, in copying the works of antiquity, we must oppose the industry they displayed, though chiefly at a somewhat later period, in scraping the ancient parchments, in order that, having obliterated the writing of the Pagans, they might cover them with their own legends.[1]

There are some aspects, however, in which the monastic period of literature appears eminently beautiful. The fretfulness and impatience and extreme tension of modern literary life, the many anxieties that paralyse, and the feverish craving for applause that perverts, so many noble intellects, were then unknown. Severed from all the cares of active life, in the deep calm of the monastery, where the turmoil of the outer world could never come, the monkish scholar pursued his studies in a spirit which has now almost faded from the world. No doubt had ever disturbed his mind. To him the problem of the universe seemed solved. Expatiating for ever with unfaltering faith upon the unseen world, he had learnt to live for it alone. His hopes were not fixed upon human greatness or fame, but upon the pardon of his sins, and the rewards of a happier world. A crowd of quaint and often beautiful legends illustrate the deep union that subsisted between literature and religion. It is related of

[1] This passion for scraping MSS. became common, according to Montfaucon, after the twelfth century. (Maitland, p. 40.) According to Hallam, however (*Middle Ages*, ch. ix. part i.), it must have begun earlier, being chiefly caused by the cessation or great diminution of the import of Egyptian papyrus, which was a consequence of the capture of Alexandria by the Saracens, early in the seventh century.

Cædmon, the first great poet of the Anglo-Saxons, that he found in the secular life no vent for his hidden genius. When the warriors assembled at their banquets, sang in turn the praises of war or beauty, as the instrument passed to him, he rose and went out with a sad heart, for he alone was unable to weave his thoughts in verse. Wearied and desponding he lay down to rest, when a figure appeared to him in his dream and commanded him to sing the Creation of the World. A transport of religious fervour thrilled his brain, his imprisoned intellect was unlocked, and he soon became the foremost poet of his land.[1] A Spanish boy having long tried in vain to master his task, and driven to despair by the severity of his teacher, ran away from his father's home. Tired with wandering, and full of anxious thoughts, he sat down to rest by the margin of a well, when his eye was caught by the deep furrow in the stone. He asked a girl who was drawing water to explain it, and she told him that it had been worn by the constant attrition of the rope. The poor boy, who was already full of remorse for what he had done, recognised in the reply a Divine intimation. 'If,' he thought, 'by daily use the soft rope could thus penetrate the hard stone, surely a long perseverance could overcome the dullness of my brain. He returned to his father's house; he laboured with redoubled earnestness, and he lived to be the great St. Isidore of Spain.[2] A monk who had led a vicious life was saved, it is said, from hell, because it was found that his sins, though very numerous, were just outnumbered by the letters of a ponderous and devout book he had written.[3] The Holy

[1] Bede, *H. E.* iv. 24.

[2] Mariana *De Rebus Hispaniæ,* vi. 7. Mariana says the stone was in his time preserved as a relic.

[3] Odericus Vitalis, quoted by Maitland (*Dark Ages*, pp. 268–269). The monk was restored to life that he might have an opportunity of reformation.

Spirit, in the shape of a dove, had been seen to inspire St. Gregory; and the writings of St. Thomas Aquinas and of several other theologians, had been expressly applauded by Christ or by his saints. When, twenty years after death, the tomb of a certain monkish writer was opened, it was found that, although the remainder of the body had crumbled into dust, the hand that had held the pen remained flexible and undecayed.[1] A young and nameless scholar was once buried near a convent at Bonn. The night after his funeral, a nun whose cell overlooked the cemetery was awakened by a brilliant light that filled the room. She started up, imagining that the day had dawned, but on looking out she found that it was still night, though a dazzling splendour was around. A female form of matchless loveliness was bending over the scholar's grave. The effluence of her beauty filled the air with light, and she clasped to her heart a snow-white dove that rose to meet her from the tomb. It was the Mother of God come to receive the soul of the martyred scholar; 'for scholars too,' adds the old chronicler, 'are martyrs if they live in purity and labour with courage.'[2]

But legends of this kind, though not without a very real beauty, must not blind us to the fact that the period of Catholic ascendency was on the whole one of the most deplorable in the history of the human mind. The energies of Christendom were diverted from all useful and progressive studies, and were wholly expended on theological disquisitions. A crowd of superstitions, attri-

The escape was a narrow one, for there was only one letter against which no sin could be adduced—a remarkable instance of the advantages of a diffuse style.

[1] Digby, *Mores Catholici*, book x. p. 246. Mathew of Westminster tells of a certain king who was very charitable, and whose right hand (which had assuaged many sorrows) remained undecayed after death (A.D. 644).

[2] See Hauréau, *Hist. de la Philosophie scolastique*, tome i. pp. 24–25.

buted to infallible wisdom, barred the path of knowledge, and the charge of magic, or the charge of heresy, crushed every bold enquiry in the sphere of physical nature or of opinions. Above all, the conditions of true enquiry had been cursed by the Church. A blind unquestioning credulity was inculcated as the first of duties, and the habit of doubt, the impartiality of a suspended judgment, the desire to hear both sides of a disputed question, and to emancipate the judgment from unreasoning prejudice, were all in consequence condemned. The belief in the guilt of error and doubt became universal, and that belief may be confidently pronounced to be the most pernicious superstition that has ever been accredited among mankind. Mistaken facts are rectified by enquiry. Mistaken methods of research, though far more inveterate, are gradually altered; but the spirit that shrinks from enquiry as sinful, and deems a state of doubt a state of guilt, is the most enduring disease that can afflict the mind of man. Not till the education of Europe passed from the monasteries to the universities, not till Mahommedan science, and classical freethought, and industrial independence broke the sceptre of the Church, did the intellectual revival of Europe begin.

I am aware that so strong a statement of the intellectual darkness of the middle ages is likely to encounter opposition from many quarters. The blindness which the philosophers of the eighteenth century manifested to their better side has produced a reaction which has led many to an opposite, and, I believe, far more erroneous extreme. Some have become eulogists of the period through love of its distinctive theological doctrines, and others through archæological enthusiasm, while a very pretentious and dogmatic, but I think sometimes superficial, school of writers who loudly boast themselves the regenerators of history, and treat with supreme contempt all the varieties of theological opinion, are accustomed, partly through a very shallow historical optimism which scarcely admits the possibility of retrogression, and partly through sympathy with the despotic character of Catholicism, to extol the mediæval society in the most extravagant terms. Without entering into a lengthy examination of this subject, I may be permitted to indicate shortly two or three fallacies which are continually displayed in their appreciations.

It is an undoubted truth that, for a considerable period, almost all the knowledge of Europe was included in the monasteries, and from this it is continually inferred that, had these institutions not existed, knowledge would have been absolutely extinguished. But such a conclusion I conceive to be altogether untrue. During the period of the Pagan empire, intellectual life had been diffused over a vast portion of the globe. Egypt and Asia Minor had become great centres of civilisation. Greece was still a land of learning. Spain, Gaul, and even Britain [1] were full of libraries and teachers. The schools of Narbonne, Arles, Bordeaux, Toulouse, Lyons, Marseilles, Poitiers, and Trêves were already famous. The Christian emperor Gratian, in A.D. 376, carried out in Gaul a system similar to that which had already, under the Antonines, been pursued in Italy, ordaining that teachers should be supported by the State in every leading city.[2] To suppose that Latin literature, having been so widely diffused, could have totally perished, or that all interest in it could have permanently ceased, even under the extremely unfavourable circumstances that followed the downfall of

[1] On the progress of Roman civilisation in Britain, see Tacitus, *Agricola*, xxi.

[2] See the Benedictine *Hist. littér. de la France*, tome i. part ii. p. 9.

the Roman Empire and the Mahommedan invasions, is, I conceive, absurd. If Catholicism had never existed, the human mind would have sought other spheres for its development, and at least a part of the treasures of antiquity would have been preserved in other ways. The monasteries, as corporations of peaceful men protected from the incursions of the barbarians, became very naturally the reservoirs to which the streams of literature flowed; but much of what they are represented as creating, they had in reality only attracted. The inviolable sanctity which they secured rendered them invaluable receptacles of ancient learning in a period of anarchy and perpetual war, and the industry of the monks in transcribing probably more than counterbalanced their industry in effacing the classical writings. The ecclesiastical unity of Christendom was also of extreme importance in rendering possible a general interchange of ideas. Whether these services outweighed the intellectual evils resulting from the complete diversion of the human mind from all secular learning, and from the persistent inculcation, as a matter of duty, of that habit of abject credulity which it is the first task of the intellectual reformer to eradicate, may be reasonably doubted.

It is not unfrequent, again, to hear the preceding fallacy stated in a somewhat different form. We are reminded that almost all the men of genius during several centuries were great theologians, and we are asked to conceive the more than Egyptian darkness that would have prevailed had the Catholic theology which produced them not existed. This judgment resembles that of the prisoner in a famous passage of Cicero, who, having spent his entire life in a dark dungeon, and knowing the light of day only from a single ray which passed through a fissure in the wall, inferred that if the wall were removed, as the fissure would no longer exist, all light would be excluded. Mediæval Catholicism discouraged and suppressed in every way secular studies, while it conferred a monopoly of wealth and honour and power upon the distinguished theologian. Very naturally, therefore, it attracted into the path of theology the genius that would have existed without it, but would have been displayed in other forms.

It is not to be inferred, however, from this, that mediæval Catholicism had not, in the sphere of intellect, any real creative power. A great moral or religious enthusiasm always evokes a certain amount of genius that would not otherwise have existed, or at least been displayed, and the monasteries were peculiarly fitted to develope certain casts of mind, which in no other sphere could have so perfectly expanded. The great writings of St. Thomas Aquinas[1] and his followers, and, in more modern times, the massive and conscientious erudition of the Benedictines, will always make certain periods of the monastic history venerable to the scholar. But, when we remember that during many centuries nearly every one possessing any literary taste or talents became a monk, when we recollect that these monks were familiar with the language, and might easily have been familiar with the noble literature of ancient Rome, and when we also consider the mode of their life, which would seem, from its absence of care, and from the very monotony of its routine, peculiarly calculated to impel them to study, we can hardly fail to wonder how very little of any real

[1] A biographer of St. Thomas Aquinas modestly observes: 'L'opinion généralement répandue parmi les théologiens c'est que la *Somme de Théologie* de St.-Thomas est non-seulement son chef-d'œuvre mais aussi celui de l'esprit humain' (! !).—Carle, *Hist. de St.-Thomas d'Aquin*, p. 140.

value they added, for so long a period, to the knowledge of mankind. It is indeed a remarkable fact, that even in the ages when the Catholic ascendency was most perfect, the greatest achievements were either opposed to, or simply external to, ecclesiastical influence. Roger Bacon having been a monk, is frequently spoken of as a creature of Catholic teaching. But there never was a more striking instance of the force of a great genius in resisting the tendencies of his age. At a time when physical science was continually neglected, discouraged, or condemned, at a time when all the great prizes of the world were open to men who pursued a very different course, Bacon applied himself with transcendent genius to the study of nature. Fourteen years of his life were spent in prison, and when he died, his name was blasted as a magician. The mediæval laboratories were chiefly due to the pursuit of alchemy, or to Mohammedan encouragement. The inventions of the mariner's compass, of gunpowder, and of rag paper were all, indeed, of extreme importance; but they were great inventions only from their effects, and in no degree from the genius they implied. They were all unconnected with the prevailing intellectual tendencies or teachings, and might have equally appeared in any age and under any religion. The monasteries cultivated formal logic to great perfection. They produced many patient and laborious, though, for the most part, wholly uncritical scholars, and many philosophers who, having assumed their premises with unfaltering faith, reasoned from them with admirable subtlety; but they taught men to regard the sacrifice of secular learning as a noble thing; they impressed upon them a theory of the habitual government of the universe, which is absolutely untrue, and they diffused, wherever their influence extended, habits of credulity and intolerance that are the most deadly poisons to the human mind.

It is, again, very frequently observed among the more philosophic eulogists of the mediæval period, that although the Catholic Church is a trammel and an obstacle to the progress of civilised nations, although it would be scarcely possible to exaggerate the misery her persecuting spirit caused, when the human mind had outstripped her teaching; yet there was a time when she was greatly in advance of the age, and the complete and absolute ascendency she then exercised was intellectually eminently beneficial. That there is much truth in this view, I have myself repeatedly maintained. But when men proceed to isolate the former period, and to make it the theme of unqualified eulogy, they fall, I think, into a grave error. The evils that sprang from the later period of Catholic ascendency were not an accident or a perversion, but a normal and necessary consequence of the previous despotism. The principles which were imposed on the mediæval world, and which were the conditions of so much of its distinctive excellence, were of such a nature that they claimed to be final, and could not possibly be discarded without a struggle and a convulsion. We must estimate the influence of these principles considered as a whole, and during the entire period of their operation. There are some poisons which, before they kill men, allay pain and diffuse a soothing sensation through the frame. We may recognise the hour of enjoyment they procure, but we must not separate it from the price at which it was purchased.

The extremely unfavourable influence the Catholic Church long exercised upon intellectual development had important moral consequences. Although moral progress does not necessarily depend upon intellectual progress, it is materially affected by it, intellectual activity being the most important element in the growth of that great and complex organism which we call civilisation. The mediæval credulity had also a more direct moral influence in producing that indifference to truth, which is the most repulsive feature of so many Catholic writings. The very large part that must be assigned to deliberate forgeries in the early apologetic literature of the Church we have already seen, and no impartial reader can, I think, investigate the innumerable grotesque and lying legends that were deliberately palmed upon mankind as undoubted facts, during the whole course of the middle ages, can follow the histories of the false decretals, and the discussions that were connected with them, or can observe the complete and absolute incapacity the polemical historians of Catholicism so frequently display, of conceiving any good thing in the ranks of their opponents, and their systematic suppression of whatever can tell against their cause, without acknowledging how serious and how inveterate has been the evil. There have, no doubt, been many noble individual exceptions. Yet it is, I believe, difficult to exaggerate the extent to which this moral defect exists in most of the ancient and very much of the modern literature of Catholicism. It is this which makes it so unspeakably repulsive to all independent and impartial thinkers, and has led a great German historian[1] to declare, with much bitterness, that the phrase Christian veracity deserves to rank with the phrase Punic faith. But this absolute indifference to truth whenever falsehood could subserve the interests of the Church, is perfectly explicable, and was found in multitudes, who, in other respects, exhibited the noblest virtue. An age which has ceased to value impartiality of

[1] Herder.

judgment will soon cease to value accuracy of statement, and when credulity is inculcated as a virtue, falsehood will not long be stigmatised as a vice. When, too, men are firmly convinced that salvation can only be found within their Church, and that their Church can absolve from all guilt, they will speedily conclude that nothing can possibly be wrong which is beneficial to it. They exchange the love of truth for what they call the love of the truth. They regard morals as derived from and subordinate to theology, and they regulate all their statements, not by the standard of veracity, but by the interests of their creed.

Another important moral consequence of the monastic system was the great importance that was given to the pecuniary compensations for crime. It had been at first one of the broad distinctions between Paganism and Christianity, that while the rites of the former were for the most part unconnected with moral dispositions, Christianity made purity of heart an essential element of all its worship. Among the Pagans a few faint efforts had, it is true, been made in this direction. An old precept or law, which is referred to by Cicero, and which was strongly reiterated by Apollonius of Tyana, and the Pythagoreans, declared that 'no impious man should dare to appease the anger of the divinities by his gifts'[1] and oracles are said to have more than once proclaimed that the hecatombs of noble oxen with gilded horns that were offered up ostentatiously by the rich, were less pleasing to the gods than the wreaths of flowers and the modest and reverential worship of the poor.[2] In general, however, in the Pagan world, the service of the temple had

[1] 'Impius ne audeto placare donis iram Deorum.'—Cicero, *De Leg.* ii. 9. See, too, Philost. in Apoll. Tyan. i. 11.

[2] There are three or four instances of this related by Porphyry, *Abstin. Carnis*, lib. ii.

little or no connection with morals, and the change which Christianity effected in this respect was one of its most important benefits to mankind. It was natural, however, and perhaps inevitable, that in the course of time, and under the action of very various causes, the old Pagan sentiment should revive, and even with an increased intensity. In no respect had the Christians been more nobly distinguished than by their charity. It was not surprising that the fathers, while exerting all their eloquence to stimulate this charity—especially during the calamities that accompanied the dissolution of the empire—should have dilated in extremely strong terms upon the spiritual benefits the donor would receive for his gift. It is also not surprising that this selfish calculation should gradually, and among hard and ignorant men, have absorbed all other motives. A curious legend, which is related by a writer of the seventh century, illustrates the kind of feeling that had arisen. The Christian bishop Synesius succeeded in converting a Pagan named Evagrius, who for a long time, however, felt doubts about the passage, 'He who giveth to the poor lendeth to the Lord.' On his conversion, and in obedience to this verse, he gave Synesius three hundred pieces of gold to be distributed among the poor; but he exacted from the bishop, as being the representative of Christ, a promissory note, engaging that he should be repaid in the future world. When, many years later, Evagrius was on his deathbed, he commanded his sons, when they buried him, to place the note in his hand, and to do so without informing Synesius. His dying injunction was observed, and three days afterwards he appeared to Synesius in a dream, told him that the debt had been paid, and ordered him to go to the tomb, where he would find a written receipt. Synesius did as he was commanded, and the grave being opened, the promissory note was found in the hand of the dead man, with an endorsement declaring that the debt had been paid by Christ. The note, it is said, was long after preserved as a relic in the church of Cyrene.[1]

The kind of feeling which this legend displays was soon turned with tenfold force into the channel of monastic life. A law of Constantine accorded, and several later laws enlarged, the power of bequests to ecclesiastics. Ecclesiastical property was at the same time exonerated from the public burdens, and this measure not only directly assisted its increase, but had also an important indirect influence; for, when taxation was heavy, many laymen ceded the ownership of their estates to the monasteries, with a secret condition that they should as vassals receive the revenues unburdened by taxation, and subject only to a slight payment to the monks as to their feudal lords.[2] The monks were regarded as the trustees of the poor, and also as themselves typical poor, and all the promises that applied to those who gave to the poor, applied, it was said, to the benefactors of the monasteries. The monastic chapel also contained the relics of saints or sacred images of miraculous power, and throngs of worshippers were attracted by the miracles, and desired to place themselves under the protection, of the saint. It is no exaggeration to say, that to give money to the priests was for several centuries

[1] Moschus, *Pratum Spirituale* (Rosweyde), cap. cxcv. M. Wallon quotes from the *Life of St.-Jean l'Aumônier* an even stranger event which happened to St. Peter Telonearius. 'Pour repousser les importunités des pauvres, il leur jetait des pierres. Un jour, n'en trouvant pas sous la main, il leur jeta un pain à la tête. Il tomba malade et eut une vision. Ses mérites étaient comptés; d'un côté étaient tous ses crimes, de l'autre ce pain jeté comme une insulte aux pauvres et accepté comme une aumône par Jésus-Christ.'—*Hist. de l'Esclavage*, tome iii. p. 397.

I may mention here that the ancient Gauls were said to have been accustomed to lend money on the condition of its being repaid by the lender in the next life. (Val. Maximus, lib. ii. cap. vi. § 10.)

[2] Muratori, *Antich. Italiane*, diss. lxvii.

the first article of the moral code. Political minds may have felt the importance of aggrandising a pacific and industrious class in the centre of a disorganised society, and family affection may have predisposed many in favour of institutions which contained at least one member of most families; but in the overwhelming majority of cases the motive was simple superstition. In seasons of sickness, of danger, of sorrow, or of remorse, whenever the fear or the conscience of the worshipper was awakened, he hastened to purchase with money the favour of a saint. Above all, in the hour of death, when the terrors of the future world loomed darkly upon his mind, he saw in a gift or legacy to the monks a sure means of effacing the most monstrous crimes, and securing his ultimate happiness. A rich man was soon scarcely deemed a Christian, if he did not leave a portion of his property to the Church, and the charters of innumerable monasteries in every part of Europe attest the vast tracts of land that were ceded by will to the monks 'for the benefit of the soul' of the testator.[1]

It has been observed by a great historian, that we may trace three distinct phases in the history of the Church. In the first period religion was a question of morals; in the second period, which culminated in the fifth century, it had become a question of orthodoxy; in the third period, which dates from the seventh century, it was a question of munificence to monasteries.[2] The despotism

[1] See on the causes of the wealth of the monasteries, two admirable dissertations by Muratori, *Antich. Italiane*, lxvii. lxviii.; Hallam's *Middle Ages*, ch. vii. part i.

[2] 'Lors de l'établissement du christianisme la religion avoit essentiellement consisté dans l'enseignement moral; elle avoit exercé les cœurs et les âmes par la recherche de ce qui étoit vraiment beau, vraiment honnête. Au cinquième siècle on l'avoit surtout attachée à l'orthodoxie, au septième on l'avoit réduite à la bienfaisance envers les couvens.'—Sismondi, *Hist. des Français*, tome ii. p. 50.

of Catholicism, and the ignorance that followed the barbarian invasions, had repressed the struggles of heresy, and in the period of almost absolute darkness that continued from the sixth to the twelfth century, the theological ideal of unquestioning faith and of perfect unanimity was all but realised in the West. All the energy that in previous ages had been expended in combating heresy was now expended in acquiring wealth. The people compounded for the most atrocious crimes by gifts to shrines of those saints whose intercession was supposed to be unfailing. The monks, partly by the natural cessation of their old enthusiasm, partly by the absence of any hostile criticism of their acts, and partly too by the very wealth they had acquired, sank into gross and general immorality. The great majority of them had probably at no time been either saints actuated by a strong religious motive, nor yet diseased and desponding minds seeking a refuge from the world; they had been simply peasants, of no extraordinary devotion or sensitiveness, who preferred an ensured subsistence, with no care, little labour, a much higher social position than they could otherwise acquire, and the certainty, as they believed, of going to heaven, to the laborious and precarious existence of the serf, relieved, indeed, by the privilege of marriage, but exposed to military service, to extreme hardships, and to constant oppression. Very naturally, when they could do so with impunity, they broke their vows of chastity. Very naturally, too, they availed themselves to the full of the condition of affairs, to draw as much wealth as possible into their community.[1] The belief in the approaching end

[1] Mr. Hallam, speaking of the legends of the miracles of saints, says: 'It must not be supposed that these absurdities were produced as well as nourished by ignorance. In most cases they were the work of deliberate imposture. Every cathedral or monastery had its tutelar saint, and every saint his legend, fabricated in order to enrich the churches under his pro-

of the world, especially at the close of the tenth century, the crusades, which gave rise to a profitable traffic in the form of a pecuniary commutation of vows, and the black death, which produced a paroxysm of religious fanaticism, stimulated the movement. In the monkish chronicles, the merits of sovereigns are almost exclusively judged by their bounty to the Church, and in some cases this is the sole part of their policy which has been preserved.[1]

There were, no doubt, a few redeeming points in this dark period. The Irish monks are said to have been honourably distinguished for their reluctance to accept the lavish donations of their admirers,[2] and some missionary monasteries of a high order of excellence were scattered through Europe. A few legends, too, may perhaps be cited censuring the facility with which money acquired by crime was accepted as an atonement for crime.[3] But these cases were very rare, and the religious

tection, by exaggerating his virtues, his miracles, and consequently his power of serving those who paid liberally for his patronage.'—*Middle Ages*, ch. ix. part i. I do not think this passage makes sufficient allowance for the unconscious formation of many saintly myths, but no impartial person doubts its substantial truth.

[1] Sismondi, *Hist. des Français*, tome ii. pp. 54, 62–63.

[2] Milman's *Hist. of Latin Christianity*, vol. ii. p. 257.

[3] Durandus, a French bishop of the thirteenth century, tells how, 'when a certain bishop was consecrating a church built out of the fruits of usury and pillage, he saw behind the altar the devil in a pontifical vestment, standing in the bishop's throne, who said unto the bishop, "Cease from consecrating the church; for it pertaineth to my jurisdiction, since it is built from the fruits of usuries and robberies." Then the bishop and the clergy having fled thence in fear, immediately the devil destroyed that church with a great noise.'—*Rationale Divinorum*, i. 6 (translated for the Camden Society).

A certain St. Launomar is said to have refused a gift for his monastery from a rapacious noble, because he was sure it was derived from pillage. (Montalembert's *Moines d'Occident*, tome ii. pp. 350–351.) When prostitutes were converted in the early Church, it was a rule that the money of which they had become possessed should never be applied to ecclesiastical purposes, but should be distributed among the poor.

history of several centuries is little more than a history of the rapacity of priests and of the credulity of laymen. In England, the perpetual demands of the Pope excited a fierce resentment; and we may trace with remarkable clearness, in every page of Mathew Paris, the alienation of sympathy arising from this cause, which prepared and foreshadowed the final rupture of England from the Church. Ireland, on the other hand, had been given over by two Popes to the English invader, on the condition of the payment of Peter's pence. The outrageous and notorious immorality of the monasteries, during the century before the Reformation, was chiefly due to their great wealth, and that immorality, as the writings of Erasmus and Ulric Von Hutten show, gave a powerful impulse to the new movement, while the abuses of the indulgences were the immediate cause of the revolt of Luther. But these things arrived only after many centuries of successful fraud. The religious terrorism that was unscrupulously employed had done its work, and the chief riches of Christendom had passed into the coffers of the Church.

The part which was played by the Catholic doctrine of future torture was indeed probably greater in the monastic phase of the Church than it had been even in the great work of converting the Pagans. Although two or three amiable theologians had made faint and altogether abortive attempts to question the eternity of punishment; although there had been some slight difference of opinion concerning the future of some Pagan philosophers who had lived before the introduction of Christianity, and also upon the question whether infants who died unbaptised were simply deprived of all joy, or were actually subjected to never-ending agony, there was no question as to the main features of the Catholic doctrine. According to the patristic theologians, it was part of the gospel revelation that the misery and suffering the human race endures upon earth is but a feeble image of that which awaits it in the future world; that the entire human race beyond the Church, as well as a very large proportion of those who are within its pale, are doomed to an eternity of agony in a literal and undying fire. The monastic legends took up this doctrine, which in itself is sufficiently revolting, and they developed it with an appalling vividness and minuteness. St. Macarius, it is said, when walking one day through the desert, saw a skull upon the ground. He struck it with his staff and it began to speak. It told him that it was the skull of a Pagan priest who had lived before the introduction of Christianity into the world, and who had accordingly been doomed to hell. As high as the heaven is above the earth, so high does the fire of hell mount in waves above the souls that are plunged into it. The damned souls were pressed together back to back, and the lost priest made it his single entreaty to the saint, that he would pray that they might be turned face to face, for he believed that the sight of a brother's face might afford him some faint consolation in the eternity of agony that was before him.[1] The story is well known of how St. Gregory, seeing on a bas-relief a representation of the goodness of Trajan to a poor widow, pitied the Pagan emperor, whom he knew to be in hell, and he prayed that he might be released. He was told that his prayer was altogether unprecedented; but at last, on his promising that he would never make such a prayer again, it was partially granted. Trajan was not withdrawn from hell, but he was freed from the torments which the remainder of the Pagan world endured.[2]

[1] *Verba Seniorum*, Prol. § 172.

[2] This vision is not related by St. Gregory himself, and some Catholics

An entire literature of visions describing the torments of hell, was soon produced by the industry of the monks. The apocryphal Gospel of Nicodemus, which purported to describe the descent of Christ into the lower world, contributed to foster it, and St. Gregory the Great has related many visions in a more famous work, which professed to be compiled with scrupulous veracity from the most authentic sources,[1] and of which it may be confidently averred, that it scarcely contains a single page which is not tainted with grotesque and deliberate falsehood. Men, it was said, passed into a trance or temporary death, and were then carried for a time to hell. Among others, a certain man named Stephen, from whose lips the saint declares that he had heard the tale, had died by mistake. When his soul was borne to the gates of hell, the Judge declared that it was another Stephen who was wanted; the disembodied spirit, after inspecting hell, was restored to its former body, and the next day it was known that another Stephen had died.[2] Volcanoes were the portals of hell, and a hermit had seen the soul of the Arian emperor Theodoric, as St. Eucherius afterwards did the soul of Charles Martel, carried down that in the Island of Lipari.[3] The craters in Sicily, it was remarked, were continually agitated and continually increasing, and this, as St. Gregory observes, was probably due to the

are perplexed about it, on account of the vision of another saint, who afterwards asked whether Trajan was saved, and received for answer, 'I wish men to rest in ignorance of this subject, that the Catholics may become stronger. For this emperor, though he had great virtues, was an unbaptised infidel.' The whole subject of the vision of St. Gregory is discussed by Champagny, *Les Antonins,* tome i. pp. 372–373. This devout writer says, 'Cette légende fut acceptée par tout le moyen-âge, *indulgent pour les païens illustres* et tout disposé à les supposer chrétiens et sauvés.'

[1] See the solemn asseveration of the care which he took in going only to the most credible and authorised sources for his materials, in the Preface to the First Book of *Dialogues.*

[2] *Dial.* iv. 36.

[3] *Dial.* iv. 30.

impending ruin of the world, when the great press of lost souls would render it necessary to enlarge the approaches to their prisons.[1]

But the glimpses of hell that are furnished in the 'Dialogues' of St. Gregory appear meagre and unimaginative, compared with those of some later monks. A long series of monastic visions, of which that of St. Fursey, in the seventh century, was one of the first, and which followed in rapid succession, till that of Tundale, in the twelfth century, professed to describe with the most detailed accuracy the condition of the lost.[2] It is impossible to conceive more ghastly, grotesque, and material conceptions of the future world than they evince, or more hideous calumnies against that Being who was supposed to inflict upon His creatures such unspeakable misery. The devil was represented bound by red-hot chains, on a burning gridiron in the centre of hell. The screams of his never-ending agony made its rafters to resound; but his hands were free, and with these he seized the lost souls, crushed them like grapes against his teeth, and then drew them by his breath down the fiery cavern of his throat. Dæmons with hooks of red-hot iron plunged souls alternately into fire and ice. Some of the lost were hung up by their tongues, other were sawn asunder,

[1] *Dial.* iv. 35.

[2] The fullest collection of these visions with which I am acquainted, is that made for the Philobiblon Society (vol. ix.), by M. Delepierre, called *L'Enfer décrit par ceux qui l'ont vu*, of which I have largely availed myself. See, too, Wright's *Purgatory of St. Patrick*, and an interesting collection of visions given by Mr. Longfellow, in his translation of Dante. In an older work, Rusca *De Inferno*, there is, I believe, a complete collection of these visions, but it has not come in my way. The Irish saints were, I am sorry to say, prominent in producing this branch of literature. St. Fursey, whose vision is one of the earliest, and Tondale, or Tundale, whose vision is one of the most detailed, were both Irish. The English historians contain several of these visions. Bede relates two or three—William of Malmesbury that of Charles the Fat; Mathew Paris three visions of purgatory.

others gnawed by serpents, others beaten together on an anvil and welded into a single mass, others boiled and then strained through a cloth, others twined in the embraces of dæmons whose limbs were of flame. The fire of earth, it was said, was but a picture of that of hell. The latter was so immeasurably more intense, that it alone could be called real. Sulphur was mixed with it, partly to increase its heat, and partly, too, in order that an insufferable stench might be added to the misery of the lost, while, unlike other flames, it emitted, according to some visions, no light, that the horror of darkness might be added to the horror of pain. A narrow bridge spanned the abyss, and from it the souls of sinners were plunged into the darkness that was below.[1]

Such catalogues of horrors, though they now awake in an educated man a sentiment of mingled disgust, weariness, and contempt, were able for many centuries to create a degree of panic and of misery we can scarcely realise. With the exception of the heretic Pelagius, whose noble genius, anticipating the discoveries of modern science, had repudiated the theological notion of death having been introduced into the world on account of the act of Adam, it was universally held among Christians, that all the forms of suffering and dissolution that are manifested on earth were penal inflictions. The destruction of the world was generally believed to be at hand. The minds of men were filled with the images of the approaching catastrophe, and innumerable legends of visible dæmons were industriously circulated. It was the custom then, as it is the custom now, for Catholic

[1] The narrow bridge over hell (in some visions covered with spikes), which is a conspicuous feature in the Mohammedan pictures of the future world, appears very often in Catholic visions. See Greg. Tur. iv. 33; St. Greg. *Dial.* iv. 36; and the vision of Tundale, in Delepierre.

priests to stain the imaginations of young children by ghastly pictures of future misery, to imprint upon the virgin mind atrocious images which they hoped, not unreasonably, might prove indelible.[1] In hours of weakness and of sickness their overwrought fancy seemed to see hideous beings hovering around, and hell itself yawning to receive its victim. St. Gregory describes how a monk, who though apparently a man of exemplary and even saintly piety, had been accustomed secretly to eat meat, saw on his deathbed a fearful dragon twining its tail round his body, and with open jaws sucking his breath;[2] and how a little boy of five years old, who had learnt from his

[1] Few Englishmen, I imagine, are aware of the infamous publications written with this object, that are circulated by the Catholic priests among the poor. I have before me a tract 'for children and young persons,' called *The Sight of Hell*, by the Rev. J. Furniss, C.S.S.R., published, 'permissu superiorum,' by Duffy (Dublin and London). It is a detailed description of the dungeons of hell, and a few sentences may serve as a sample. 'See! on the middle of that red-hot floor stands a girl; she looks about sixteen years old. Her feet are bare. She has neither shoes nor stockings. . . . Listen! she speaks. She says, I have been standing on this red-hot floor for years. Day and night my only standing-place has been this red-hot floor. . . . Look at my burnt and bleeding feet. Let me go off this burning floor for one moment, only for one single short moment. . . . The fourth dungeon is the boiling kettle . . . in the middle of it there is a boy. . . . His eyes are burning like two burning coals. Two long flames come out of his ears. . . . Sometimes he opens his mouth, and blazing fire rolls out. But listen! there is a sound like a kettle boiling. . . . The blood is boiling in the scalded veins of that boy. The brain is boiling and bubbling in his head. The marrow is boiling in his bones. . . . The fifth dungeon is the red-hot oven. . . . The little child is in this red-hot oven. Hear how it screams to come out. See how it turns and twists itself about in the fire. It beats its head against the roof of the oven. It stamps its little feet on the floor. . . . God was very good to this child. Very likely God saw it would get worse and worse, and would never repent, and so it would have to be punished much more in hell. So God in his mercy called it out of the world in its early childhood.' If the reader desires to follow this subject further, he may glance over a companion tract by the same reverend gentleman, called *A Terrible Judgment on a Little Child*; and also a book on *Hell*, translated from the Italian of Pinamonti, and with illustrations depicting the various tortures.

[2] St. Greg. *Dial.* iv. 38.

father to repeat blasphemous words, saw, as he lay dying, exulting dæmons who were waiting to carry him to hell.[1] To the jaundiced eye of the theologian, all nature seemed stricken and forlorn, and its brightness and beauty suggested no ideas but those of deception and of sin. The redbreast, according to one popular legend, was commissioned by the Deity to carry a drop of water to the souls of unbaptised infants in hell, and its breast was singed in piercing the flames.[2] In the calm, still hour of evening, when the peasant boy asked why the sinking sun, as it dipped beneath the horizon, flushed with such a glorious red, he was answered, in the words of an old Saxon catechism, because it is then looking into hell.[3]

It is related in the vision of Tundale, that as he gazed upon the burning plains of hell, and listened to the screams of ceaseless and hopeless agony that were wrung from the sufferers, the cry broke from his lips, 'Alas, Lord, what truth is there in what I have so often heard—the earth is filled with the mercy of God?'[4] It is indeed one of the most curious things in moral history, to observe how men who were sincerely indignant with Pagan writers for attributing to their divinities the frailties of an occasional jealousy or an occasional sensuality, for

[1] Ibid. iv. 18.

[2] Alger's *History of the Doctrine of a Future Life* (New York, 1866), p. 414. The ignis fatuus was sometimes supposed to be the soul of an unbaptised child. There is, I believe, another Catholic legend about the redbreast, of a very different kind—that its breast was stained with blood when it was trying to pull out the thorns from the crown of Christ.

[3] Wright's *Purgatory of St. Patrick*, p. 26. M. Delepierre quotes a curious theory of Father Hardouin (who is chiefly known for his suggestion that the classics were composed by the mediæval monks) that the rotation of the earth is caused by the lost souls trying to escape from the fire that is at the centre of the globe, climbing, in consequence, on the inner crust of the earth, which is the wall of hell, and thus making the whole revolve, as the squirrel by climbing turns its cage! (*L'Enfer décrit par ceux qui l'ont vu*, p. 151.)

[4] Delepierre, p. 70.

representing them, in a word, like men of mingled characters and passions, have nevertheless unscrupulously attributed to their own Divinity a degree of cruelty which may be confidently said to transcend the utmost barbarity of which human nature is capable. Neither Nero nor Phalaris could have looked complacently for ever on millions enduring the torture of fire—most of them because of a crime which was committed, not by themselves, but by their ancestors, or because they had adopted some mistaken conclusion on intricate questions of history or metaphysics.[1] To those who do not regard such teaching as true, it must appear without exception the most odious in the religious history of the world, subversive of the very foundations of morals, and well fitted to transform the man who at once realised it, and

[1] Thus Jeremy Taylor, in two singularly unrhetorical and unimpassioned chapters, deliberately enumerates the most atrocious acts of cruelty in human history, and says that they are surpassed by the tortures inflicted by the Deity. A few instances will suffice. Certain persons 'put rings of iron stuck fast with sharp points of needles, about their arms and feet, in such a manner as the prisoners could not move without wounding themselves; then they compassed them about with fire, to the end that, standing still, they might be burnt alive, and if they stirred the sharp points pierced their flesh. . . . What, then, shall be the torment of the damned where they shall burn eternally without dying, and without the possibility of removing? . . Alexander, the son of Hyrcanus, caused eight hundred to be crucified, and whilst they were yet alive caused their wives and children to be murdered before their eyes, that so they might not die once, but many deaths. This rigour shall not be wanting in hell. . . . Mezentius tied a living body to the dead until the putrefied exhalations of the dead had killed the living. . . . What is this in respect of hell, when each body of the damned is more loathsome and unsavoury than a million of dead dogs? . . . Bonaventure says, if one of the damned were brought into this world it were sufficient to infect the whole earth. . . . We are amazed to think of the inhumanity of Phalaris, who roasted men alive in his brazen bull. That was a joy in respect of that fire of hell. . . . The torment . . . comprises as many torments as the body of man has joints, sinews, arteries, &c., being caused by that penetrating and real fire, of which this temporal fire is but a painted fire. . . . What comparison will there be between burning for an hundred years' space, and to be burning without interruption as long as God is God?'—*Contemplations on the State of Man*, book ii. ch. 6–7.

who accepted it with pleasure, into a monster of barbarity. Of the writers of the mediæval period, certainly one of the two or three most eminent was Peter Lombard, whose 'Sentences,' though now, I believe, but little read, were for a long time the basis of all theological literature in Europe. More than four thousand theologians are said to have written commentaries upon them[1]—among others, Albert the Great, St. Bonaventura, and St. Thomas Aquinas. Nor is the work unworthy of its former reputation. Calm, clear, logical, subtle, and concise, the author professes to expound the whole system of Catholic theology and ethics, and to reveal the interdependence of their various parts. Having explained the position and the duties, he proceeds to examine the prospects, of man. He maintains that until the day of judgment the inhabitants of heaven and hell will continually see one another; but that, in the succeeding eternity, the inhabitants of heaven alone will see those of the opposite world; and he concludes his great work by this most impressive passage. 'In the last place, we must enquire whether the sight of the punishment of the condemned will impair the glory of the blest, or whether it will augment their beatitude. Concerning this, Gregory says the sight of the punishment of the lost will not obscure the beatitude of the just; for when it is accompanied by no compassion it can be no diminution of happiness. And although their own joys might suffice to the just, yet to their greater glory they will see the pains of the evil, which by grace they have escaped. . . . The elect will go forth, not indeed locally, but by intelligence and by a clear vision, to behold the torture of the impious, and as they see them they will not grieve. Their minds will be sated

[1] Perrone, *Historiæ Theologiæ cum Philosophia comparata Synopsis,* p. 29. Peter Lombard's work was published in A.D. 1160.

with joy as they gaze on the unspeakable anguish of the impious, returning thanks for their own freedom. Thus Esaias, describing the torments of the impious, and the joy of the righteous in witnessing it, says, 'The elect in truth will go out and will see the corpses of men who have prevaricated against Him; their worm will not die, and they will be to the satiety of vision to all flesh, that is, to the elect. The just man will rejoice when he shall see the vengeance.'[1]

This passion for visions of heaven and hell was, in fact, a natural continuation of the passion for dogmatic definition, which had raged during the fifth century. It was natural that men, whose curiosity had left no conceivable question of theology undefined, should have endeavoured to describe with corresponding precision the condition of the dead. Much, however, was due to the hallucinations of solitary and ascetic life, and much more to deliberate imposture. It is impossible for men to continue long in a condition of extreme panic, and superstition speedily discovers remedies to allay the fears it had created. If a malicious dæmon was hovering around the believer, and if the jaws of hell were opening to

[1] 'Postremo quæritur, An pœna reproborum visa decoloret gloriam beatorum? an eorum beatitudini proficiat? De hoc ita Gregorius ait, Apud animum justorum non obfuscat beatitudinem aspecta pœna reproborum; quia ubi jam compassio miseriæ non erit, minuere beatorum lætitiam non valebit. Et licet justis sua gaudia sufficiant, ad majorem gloriam vident pœnas malorum quas per gratiam evaserunt. . . . Egredientur ergo electi, non loco, sed intelligentia vel visione manifesta ad videndum impiorum cruciatus; quos videntes non dolore afficientur sed lætitia satiabuntur, agentes gratias de sua liberatione visa impiorum ineffabili calamitate. Unde Esaias impiorum tormenta describens et ex eorum visione lætitiam bonorum exprimens, ait, Egredientur electi scilicet et videbunt cadavera virorum qui prævaricati sunt in me. Vermis eorum non morietur et ignis non extinguetur, et erunt usque ad satietatem visionis omni carni, id est electis. Lætabitur justus cum viderit vindictam.'—Peter Lombard, *Senten.* lib. iv. finis. These amiable views have often been expressed both by Catholic and by Puritan divines. See Alger's *Doctrine of a Future Life*, p. 541.

receive him, he was defended, on the other hand, by countless angels; a lavish gift to a Church or monastery could always enlist a saint in his behalf, and priestly power could protect him against the dangers which priestly sagacity had revealed. When the angels were weighing the good and evil deeds of a dead man, the latter were found by far to preponderate; but a priest of St. Lawrence came in, and turned the scale by throwing down among the former a heavy gold chalice, which the deceased had given to the altar.[1] Dagobert was snatched from the very arms of dæmons by St. Denis, St. Maurice, and St. Martin.[2] Charlemagne was saved, because the monasteries he had built outweighed his evil deeds.[3] Others, who died in mortal sin, were raised from the dead at the desire of their patron saint, to expiate their guilt. To amass relics, to acquire the patronage of saints, to endow monasteries, to build churches, became the chief part of religion, and the more the terrors of the unseen world were unfolded, the more men sought tranquillity by the consolations of superstition.[4]

The extent to which the custom of materialising religion was carried, can only be adequately realised by those who have examined the mediæval literature itself. That which strikes a student in perusing this literature, is not so much the existence of these superstitions, as

[1] *Legenda Aurea.* There is a curious fresco representing this transaction, on the portal of the church of St. Lorenzo, near Rome.

[2] Aimoni, *De Gestis Francorum Hist.* iv. 34.

[3] Turpin's *Chronicle,* ch. 32. In the vision of Watlin, however (A.D. 824) Charlemagne was seen tortured in purgatory on account of his excessive love of women. (Delepierre, *L'Enfer décrit par ceux qui l'ont vu,* pp. 27–28.)

[4] As the Abbé Mably observes: 'On croyoit en quelque sorte dans ces siècles grossiers que l'avarice étoit le premier attribut de Dieu, et que les saints faisoient un commerce de leur crédit et de leur protection. De-là les richesses immenses données aux églises par des hommes dont les mœurs déshonoroient la religion.'—*Observations sur l'Hist. de France,* i. 4.

their extraordinary multiplication, the many thousands of grotesque miracles wrought by saints, monasteries, or relics, that were deliberately asserted and universally believed. Christianity had assumed a form that was quite as polytheistic and quite as idolatrous as the ancient Paganism. The low level of intellectual cultivation, the religious feelings of half-converted barbarians, the interests of the clergy, the great social importance of the monasteries, and perhaps also the custom of compounding for nearly all crimes by pecuniary fines, which was so general in the penal system of the barbarian tribes, combined in their different ways, with the panic created by the fear of hell, in driving men in the same direction, and the wealth and power of the clergy rose to a point that enabled them to overshadow all other classes. They had found, as has been well said, in another world, the standing-point of Archimedes from which they could move this. No other system had ever appeared so admirably fitted to endure for ever. The Church had crushed or silenced every opponent in Christendom. It had an absolute control over education in all its branches and in all its stages. It had absorbed all the speculative knowledge and art of Europe. It possessed or commanded wealth, rank, and military power. It had so directed its teaching, that everything which terrified or distressed mankind drove men speedily into its arms, and it had covered Europe with a vast network of institutions, admirably adapted to extend and perpetuate its power. In addition to all this, it had guarded with consummate skill all the approaches to its citadel. Every doubt was branded as a sin, and a long course of doubt must necessarily have preceded the rejection of its tenets. All the avenues of enquiry were painted with images of appalling suffering, and of malicious dæmons. No sooner did the worshipper begin to question any article of faith, or to lose his confidence in the virtue of the ceremonies of his Church, than he was threatened with a doom that no human heroism could brave, that no imagination could contemplate undismayed.

Of all the suffering that was undergone by those brave men who in ages of ignorance and superstition dared to break loose from the trammels of their Church, and who laid the foundation of the liberty we now enjoy, it is this which was probably the most poignant, and which is the least realised. Our imaginations can reproduce with much vividness gigantic massacres like those of the Albigenses or of St. Bartholomew. We can conceive, too, the tortures of the rack and of the boots, the dungeon, the scaffold, and the slow fire. We can estimate, though less perfectly, the anguish which the bold enquirer must have undergone from the desertion of those he most dearly loved, from the hatred of mankind, from the malignant calumnies that were heaped upon his name. But in the chamber of his own soul, in the hours of his solitary meditation, he must have found elements of a suffering that was still more acute. Taught from his earliest childhood to regard the abandonment of his hereditary opinions as the most deadly of crimes, and to ascribe it to the instigation of deceiving dæmons, persuaded that if he died in a condition of doubt he must pass into a state of everlasting torture, his imagination saturated with images of the most hideous and appalling anguish, he found himself alone in the world, struggling with his difficulties and his doubts. There existed no rival sect in which he could take refuge, and where, in the professed agreement of many minds, he could forget the anathemas of the Church. Physical science, that has disproved the theological theories which attribute death to human sin, and suffering to Divine vengeance, and all natural phenomena to isolated acts of Divine intervention—historical criticism, which has dispelled so many imposing fabrics of belief, traced so many elaborate superstitions to the normal action of the undisciplined imagination, and explained and defined the successive phases of religious progress, were both unknown. Every comet that blazed in the sky, every pestilence that swept over the land, appeared a confirmation of the dark threats of the theologian. A spirit of blind and abject credulity, inculcated as the first of duties, and exhibited on all subjects and in all forms, pervaded the atmosphere he breathed. Who can estimate aright the obstacles against which a sincere enquirer in such an age must have struggled? Who can conceive the secret anguish he must have endured in the long months or years during which rival arguments gained an alternate sway over his judgment, while all doubt was still regarded as damnable? And even when his mind was convinced, his imagination would still often revert to his old belief. Our thoughts in after years flow spontaneously, and even unconsciously, in the channels that are formed in youth. In moments when the controlling judgment has relaxed its grasp, old intellectual habits reassume their sway, and images painted on the imagination will live, when the intellectual propositions on which they rested have been wholly abandoned. In hours of weakness, of sickness, and of drowsiness, in the feverish and anxious moments that are known to all, when the mind floats passively upon the stream, the phantoms which reason had exorcised must have often reappeared, and the bitterness of an ancient tyranny must have entered into his soul.

It is one of the greatest of the many services that were rendered to mankind by the Troubadours, that they cast such a flood of ridicule upon the visions of hell, by which the monks had been accustomed to terrify mankind, that they completely discredited and almost suppressed them.[1] Whether, however, the Catholic mind, if unassisted by the literature of Paganism and by the independent thinkers who grew up under the shelter of Mahommedanism, could have ever unwound the chains that had bound it, may well be questioned. The growth of towns, which multiplied secular interests and feelings, the revival of learning, the depression of the ecclesiastical classes that followed the crusades, and at last, the dislocation of Christendom by the Reformation, gradually impaired the ecclesiastical doctrine, which ceased to be realised before it ceased to be believed. There was, however, another doctrine which exercised a still greater influence in augmenting the riches of the clergy, and in making donations to the Church the chief part of religion. I allude, of course, to the doctrine of purgatory.

A distinguished modern apologist for the middle ages has made this doctrine the object of his special and very characteristic eulogy, because, as he says, by providing a finite punishment graduated to every variety of guilt, and adapted for those who, without being sufficiently virtuous to pass at once into heaven, did not appear sufficiently vicious to pass into hell, it formed an indispensable corrective to the extreme terrorism of the doctrine of eternal punishment.[2] This is one of those theories which, though exceedingly popular with a large and influential class of the writers of our day, must appear, I think, almost grotesque to those who have examined the actual operation of the doctrine during the middle ages.

[1] Many curious examples of the way in which the Troubadours burlesqued the monkish visions of hell are given by Delepierre, p. 144.—Wright's *Purgatory of St. Patrick*, pp. 47–52.

[2] Comte, *Philosophie positive*, tome v. p. 269.

According to the practical teaching of the Church, the expiatory powers at the disposal of its clergy were so great, that those who died believing its doctrines, and fortified in their last hours by its rites, had no cause whatever to dread the terrors of hell. On the other hand, those who died external to the Church had no prospect of entering into purgatory. This latter was designed altogether for true believers; it was chiefly preached at a time when no one was in the least disposed to question the powers of the Church to absolve any crime, however heinous, or to free the worst men from hell, and it was assuredly never regarded in the light of a consolation. Indeed, the popular pictures of purgatory were so terrific that it may be almost doubted whether the imagination could ever fully realise, though the reason could easily recognise the difference between this state and that of the lost. The fire of purgatory, according to the most eminent theologians, was like the fire of hell—a literal fire, prolonged, it was sometimes said, for ages. The declamations of the pulpit described the sufferings of the saved souls in purgatory as incalculably greater than were endured by the most wretched mortals upon earth.[1] The rude artists of mediævalism exhausted their

[1] 'Saint-Bernard, dans son sermon *De obitu Humberti*, affirme que tous les tourments de cette vie sont joies si on les compare à une seconde des peines du purgatoire. "Imaginez-vous donc, délicates dames," dit le père Valladier (1613) dans son sermon du 3me dimanche de l'Avent, "d'estre au travers de vos chenets, sur vostre petit feu pour une centaine d'ans : ce n'est rien au respect d'un moment de purgatoire. Mais si vous vistes jamais tirer quelqu'un à quatre chevaux, quelqu'un brusler à petit feu, enrager de faim ou de soif, une heure de purgatoire est pire que tout cela." '—Meray, *Les libres Prêcheurs* (Paris, 1860), pp. 130–131 (an extremely curious and suggestive book). I now take up the first contemporary book of popular Catholic devotion on this subject, which is at hand, and read, 'Compared with the pains of purgatory, then all those wounds and dark prisons, all those wild beasts, hooks of iron, red-hot plates, &c., which the holy martyrs suffered, are nothing.' 'They (souls in purgatory) are in a real, though miraculous

efforts in depicting the writhings of the dead in the flames that encircled them. Innumerable visions detailed with a ghastly minuteness the various kinds of torture they underwent,[1] and the monk, who described what he professed to have seen, usually ended by the characteristic moral, that could men only realise those sufferings, they would shrink from no sacrifice to rescue their friends from such a state. A special place, it was said, was reserved in purgatory for those who had been slow in paying their tithes.[2] St. Gregory tells a curious story of a man who was, in other respects, of admirable virtue; but who, in a contested election for the popedom, supported the wrong candidate, and without, as it would appear, in any degree refusing to obey the successful candidate when elected, continued secretly of opinion that the choice was an unwise one. He was accordingly placed for some time after death in boiling water.[3] Whatever may be thought of its other aspects, it is impossible to avoid recognising in this teaching a masterly

manner, tortured by fire, which is of the same kind (says Bellarmine) as our element fire.' 'The Angelic Doctor affirms "that the fire which torments the damned is like the fire which purges the elect."' 'What agony will not those holy souls suffer when tied and bound with the most tormenting chains of a living fire like to that of hell? and we, while able to make them free and happy, shall we stand like uninterested spectators?' 'St. Austin is of opinion that the pains of a soul in purgatory during the time required to open and shut one's eye, is more severe than what St. Lawrence suffered on the gridiron;' and much more to the same effect. (*Purgatory opened to the Piety of the Faithful.* Richardson, London.)

[1] See Delepierre, Wright, and Alger.

[2] This appears from the vision of Thurcill. (Wright's *Purgatory*, p. 42.) Brompton (*Chronicon*) tells of an English landlord who had refused to pay tithes. St. Augustine, having vainly reasoned with him, at last convinced him by a miracle. Before celebrating mass he ordered all excommunicated persons to leave the church, whereupon a corpse got out of a grave and walked away. The corpse, on being questioned, said it was the body of an ancient Briton who refused to pay tithes, and had in consequence been excommunicated and damned.

[3] Greg. *Dial.* iv. 40.

skill in the adaptation of means to ends, which almost rises to artistic beauty. A system which deputed its minister to go to the unhappy widow in the first dark hour of her anguish and her desolation, to tell her that he who was dearer to her than all the world besides was now burning in a fire, and that he could only be relieved by a gift of money to the priests, was assuredly of its own kind not without an extraordinary merit.

If we attempt to realise the moral condition of the society of Western Europe in the period that elapsed between the downfall of the Roman empire and Charlemagne, during which the religious transformations I have noticed chiefly arose, we shall be met by some formidable difficulties. In the first place, our materials are very scanty. From the year A.D. 642, when the meagre chronicle of Fredigarius closes, to the biography of Charlemagne by Eginhard, a century later, there is almost a complete blank in trustworthy history, and we are reduced to a few scanty and very doubtful notices in the chronicles of monasteries, the lives of saints, and the decrees of Councils. All secular literature had almost disappeared, and the thought of posterity seems to have vanished from the world.[1] Of the first half of the seventh century, however, and of the two centuries that preceded it, we have much information from Gregory of Tours, and Fredigarius, whose tedious and repulsive pages illustrate with considerable clearness the conflict of races and the dislocation of governments that for centuries existed. In Italy, the traditions and habits of the old empire had in some degree reasserted their sway, but in Gaul the

[1] As Sismondi says, 'Pendant quatre-vingts ans, tout au moins, il n'y eut pas un Franc qui songeât à transmettre à la postérité la mémoire des événements contemporains, et pendant le même espace de temps il n'y eut pas un personnage puissant qui ne bâtit des temples pour la postérité la plus reculée.'—*Hist. des Français*, tome ii. p. 46.

Church subsisted in the midst of barbarians, whose native vigour had never been emasculated by civilisation and refined by knowledge. The picture which Gregory of Tours gives us is that of a society which was almost absolutely anarchical. The mind is fatigued by the monotonous account of acts of violence and of fraud springing from no fixed policy, tending to no end, leaving no lasting impress upon the world.[1] The two queens Frédégonde and Brunehaut rise conspicuous above other figures for their fierce and undaunted ambition, for the fascination they exercised over the minds of multitudes, and for the number and atrocity of their crimes. All classes seem to have been almost equally tainted with vice. We read of a bishop named Cautinus, who had to be carried, when intoxicated, by four men from the table;[2] who, upon the refusal of one of his priests to surrender some private property, deliberately ordered that priest to be buried alive, and who, when the victim, escaping by a happy chance from the sepulchre in which

[1] Gibbon says of the period during which the Merovingian dynasty reigned, that 'it would be difficult to find anywhere more vice or less virtue.' Hallam reproduces this observation, and adds, 'The facts of these times are of little other importance than as they impress on the mind a thorough notion of the extreme wickedness of almost every person concerned in them, and consequently of the state to which society was reduced.'—*Hist. of the Middle Ages*, ch. i. Dean Milman is equally unfavourable and emphatic in his judgment. 'It is difficult to conceive a more dark and odious state of society than that of France under her Merovingian kings, the descendants of Clovis, as described by Gregory of Tours. In the conflict of barbarism with Roman Christianity, barbarism has introduced into Christianity all its ferocity with none of its generosity and magnanimity; its energy shows itself in atrocity of cruelty, and even of sensuality. Christianity has given to barbarism hardly more than its superstition and its hatred of heretics and unbelievers. Throughout, assassinations, parricides, and fratricides intermingle with adulteries and rapes.'—*History of Latin Christianity*, vol. i. p. 365.

[2] Greg. Tur. iv. 12. Gregory mentions (v. 41) another bishop who used to become so intoxicated as to be unable to stand, and St. Boniface, after

he had been immured, revealed the crime, received no greater punishment than a censure.[1] The worst sovereigns found flatterers or agents in ecclesiastics. Frédégonde deputed two clerks to murder Childebert,[2] and another clerk to murder Brunehaut;[3] she caused a bishop of Rouen to be assassinated at the altar—a bishop and an archdeacon being her accomplices;[4] and she found in another bishop, named Ægidius, one of her most devoted instruments and friends.[5] The pope, St. Gregory the Great, was an ardent flatterer of Brunehaut.[6] Gundebald having murdered his three brothers, was consoled by St. Avitus, the Bishop of Vienne, who, without intimating the slightest disapprobation of the act, assured him that by removing his rivals he had been a providential agent in preserving the happiness of his people.[7] The bishoprics were filled by men of nctorious debauchery, or by grasping misers.[8] The priests sometimes celebrated the sacred mysteries 'gorged with food and dull with wine.'[9] They had already begun to carry arms, and

describing the extreme sensuality of the clergy of his time, adds, that there are some bishops 'qui licet dicant se fornicarios vel adulteros non esse, sed sunt ebriosi et injuriosi,' &c.—*Ep.* xlix.

1 Greg. Tur. iv. 12.

2 Id. viii. 29. She gave them knives with hollow grooves, filled with poison, in the blades.

3 Greg. Tur. vii. 20.

4 Id. viii. 31–41.

5 Id. v. 19.

6 See his very curious correspondence with her.—*Ep.* vi. 5, 50, 59; ix. 11, 117; xi. 62–63.

7 Avitus, *Ep.* v. He adds, 'Minuebat regni felicitas numerum regalium personarum.'

8 See the emphatic testimony of St. Boniface in the eighth century. 'Modo autem maxima ex parte per civitates episcopales sedes traditæ sunt laicis cupidis ad possidendum, vel adulteratis clericis, scortatoribus et publicanis sæculariter ad perfruendum.'—*Epist.* xlix. 'ad Zachariam.' The whole epistle contains an appalling picture of the clerical vices of the times.

9 More than one Council made decrees about this. See the *Vie de St. Léger*, by Dom Pitra, pp. 172–177.

Gregory tells of two bishops of the fifth century who had killed many enemies with their own hands.[1] There was scarcely a reign that was not marked by some atrocious domestic tragedy. There were few sovereigns who were not guilty of at least one deliberate murder. Never, perhaps, was the infliction of mutilation, and prolonged and agonising forms of death, more common. We read, among other atrocities, of a bishop being driven to a distant place of exile upon a bed of thorns;[2] of a king burning together his rebellious son, his daughter-in-law, and their daughters;[3] of a queen condemning a daughter she had had by a former marriage to be drowned, lest her beauty should excite the passions of her husband;[4] of another queen endeavouring to strangle her daughter with her own hands;[5] of an abbot, with the assistance of one of his clerks, driving a poor man by force out of his house, that he might commit adultery with his wife, and being murdered, together with his partner, in the act;[6] of a prince who made it an habitual amusement to torture his slaves with fire, and who buried two of them alive, because they had married without his permission;[7] of a bishop's wife, who besides other crimes, was accustomed to mutilate men and to torture women, by applying red-hot irons to the most sensitive parts of their bodies;[8] of

[1] Greg. Tur. iv. 43. St. Boniface, at a much later period (A.D. 742), talks of bishops 'Qui pugnant in exercitu armati et effundunt propria manu sanguinem hominum.'—*Ep.* xlix.

[2] Greg. Tur. iv. 26.

[3] Id. iv. 20.

[4] Id. iii. 26.

[5] Id. ix. 34.

[6] Greg. Tur. viii. 19. Gregory says this story should warn clergymen not to meddle with the wives of other people, but 'content themselves with those that they may possess without crime.' The abbot had previously tried to seduce the husband within the precincts of the monastery, that he might murder him.

[7] Greg. Tur. v. 3.

[8] Id. viii. 39. She was guilty of many other crimes, which the historian says 'it is better to pass in silence.' The bishop himself had been

great numbers who were deprived of their ears and noses, tortured through several days, and at last burnt alive or broken slowly on the wheel. Brunehaut, at the close of her long and in some respects great, though guilty career, fell into the hands of Clotaire, and the old queen, having been subjected for three days to various kinds of torture, was led out on a camel for the derision of the army, and at last bound to the tail of a furious horse, and dashed to pieces in its course.[1]

And yet this age was, in a certain sense, eminently religious. All literature had become sacred. Heresy of every kind was rapidly expiring. The priests and monks had acquired enormous power, and their wealth was inordinately increasing.[2] Several sovereigns voluntarily abandoned their thrones for the monastic life.[3] The seventh century, which, together with the eighth, forms the darkest period of the dark ages, is famous in the hagiology, as having produced more saints than any other century, except that of the martyrs.[4]

guilty of outrageous and violent tyranny. The marriage of ecclesiastics appears at this time to have been common in Gaul, though the best men commonly deserted their wives when they were ordained. Another bishop's wife (iv. 36) was notorious for her tyrannies.

[1] Fredigarius, xlii. The historian describes Clotaire as a perfect paragon of Christian graces.

[2] 'Au sixième siècle on compte 214 établissements religieux des Pyrénées à la Loire et des bouches du Rhône aux Vosges.'—Ozanam, *Études germaniques*, tome ii. p. 93. In the two following centuries the ecclesiastical wealth was enormously increased.

[3] Mathew of Westminster (A.D. 757) speaks of no less than eight Saxon kings having done this.

[4] 'Le septième siècle est celui peut-être qui a donné le plus de saints au calendrier.'—Sismondi, *Hist. de France*, tome ii. p. 50. 'Le plus beau titre du septième siècle à une réhabilitation c'est le nombre considérable de saints qu'il a produits. . . . Aucun siècle n'a été ainsi glorifié sauf l'âge des martyrs dont Dieu s'est réservé de compter le nombre. Chaque année fournit sa moisson, chaque jour a sa gerbe. . . . Si donc il plaît à Dieu et au Christ de répandre à pleines mains sur un siècle les splendeurs des saints, qu'importe que l'histoire et la gloire humaine en tiennent peu compte?'—

The manner in which events were regarded by historians was also exceedingly characteristic. Our principal authority, Gregory of Tours, was a bishop of great eminence, and a man of the most genuine piety, and of very strong affections.[1] He describes his work as a record 'of the virtues of saints, and the disasters of nations,'[2] and the student who turns to his pages from those of the Pagan historians, is not more struck by the extreme prominence he gives to ecclesiastical events, than by the uniform manner in which he views all secular events in their religious aspect, as governed and directed by a special Providence. Yet, in questions where the difference between orthodoxy and heterodoxy are concerned, his ethics sometimes exhibit the most singular distortion. Of this, probably the most impressive example is the manner in which he has described the career of Clovis, the great representative of orthodoxy.[3] Having recounted the circumstances of his conversion, Gregory proceeds to tell us, with undisguised admiration, how that chieftain, as the first-fruits of his doctrine, professed to be grieved at seeing that part of Gaul was held by an Arian sovereign; how he accordingly resolved to invade and appropriate that territory; how with admirable piety, he commanded his soldiers to abstain from all devastations when traversing the territory of St. Martin, and how several miracles attested the Divine approbation of the expedition. The war—which is the first of the long series of professedly religious wars that have been undertaken by Christians—was fully successful, and Clovis proceeded to direct his ambition to new fields. In his

Pitra, *Vie de St. Léger*, Introd. p. x.-xi. This learned and very credulous writer (who is now a cardinal) afterwards says that we have the record of more than eight hundred saints of the seventh century. (Introd. p. lxxx.)

[1] See, e.g. the very touching passage about the death of his children, v. 35.

[2] Lib. ii. Prologue.

[3] Greg. Tur. ii. 27-43.

expedition against the Arians, he had found a faithful ally in his relative Sighebert, the old and infirm king of the Ripuarian Franks. He now proceeded artfully to suggest to the son of Sighebert the advantages he would obtain if his father were dead. The hint was taken. Sighebert was murdered, and Clovis sent ambassadors to the parricide, professing a warm friendship, but with secret orders on the first opportunity to kill him. This being done, and the kingdom being left entirely without a head, Clovis proceeded to Cologne, the capital of Sighebert; he assembled the people, professed with much solemnity his horror of the tragedies that had taken place, and his complete innocence of all connection with them;[1] but suggested, that as they were now without a ruler, they should place themselves under his protection. The proposition was received with acclamation. The warriors elected him as their king, and thus, says the episcopal historian, 'Clovis received the treasures and dominions of Sighebert, and added them to his own. Every day God caused his enemies to fall beneath his hand, and enlarged his kingdom, because he walked with a right heart before the Lord, and did the things that were pleasing in his sight.'[2] His ambition was, however, still unsated. He proceeded, in a succession of expeditions, to unite the whole of Gaul under his sceptre, invading, defeating, capturing, and slaying the lawful sovereigns, who were for the most part his own relations. Having secured himself against dangers from without, by killing all his relations, with the exception of his wife and children, he

[1] He observes how impossible it was that he could be guilty of shedding the blood of a relation: 'Sed in his ego nequaquam conscius sum. Nec enim possum sanguinem parentum meorum effundere.'—Greg. Tur. ii. 40.

[2] 'Prosternebat enim quotidie Deus hostes ejus sub manu ipsius, et augebat regnum ejus eo quod ambularet recto corde coram eo, et faceret quæ placita erant in oculis ejus.'—Greg. Tur. ii. 40.

is reported to have lamented before his courtiers his isolation, declaring that he had no relations remaining in the world to assist him in his adversity; but this speech, Gregory assures us, was a stratagem; for the king desired to discover whether any possible pretender to the throne had escaped his knowledge and his sword. Soon after, he died full of years and honours, and was buried in a cathedral which he had built.

Having recounted all these things with unmoved composure, Gregory of Tours requests his reader to permit him to pause, to draw the moral of the history. It is the admirable manner in which Providence guides all things for the benefit of those whose opinions concerning the Trinity are strictly orthodox. Having briefly referred to Abraham, Jacob, Moses, Aaron, and David, all of whom are said to have intimated the correct doctrine on this subject, and all of whom were exceedingly prosperous, he passes to more modern times. 'Arius, the impious founder of the impious sect, his entrails having fallen out, passed into the flames of hell; but Hilary, the blessed defender of the undivided Trinity, though exiled on that account, found his country in Paradise. The King Clovis, who confessed the Trinity, and by its assistance crushed the heretics, extended his dominions through all Gaul. Alaric, who denied the Trinity, was deprived of his kingdom and his subjects, and, what was far worse, was punished in the future world.'[1]

It would be easy to cite other, though perhaps not quite such striking instances, of the degree in which the moral judgments of this unhappy age were distorted by

[1] Lib. iii. Prologue. St. Avitus enumerates in glowing terms the Christian virtues of Clovis (*Ep.* xli.), but as this was in a letter addressed to the king himself, the eulogy may easily be explained.

superstition.[1] Questions of orthodoxy, or questions of fasting, appeared to the popular mind immeasurably more important than what we should now call the fundamental principles of right and wrong. A law of Charlemagne, and also a law of the Saxons, condemned to death any one who eat meat in Lent,[2] unless the priest was satisfied that it was a matter of absolute necessity. The moral enthusiasm of the age chiefly drove men to abandon their civic or domestic duties, to immure themselves in monasteries, and to waste their strength by prolonged and extravagant maceration.[3] Yet, in the midst of all this superstition, there can be no question that in some respects the religious agencies were operating for good. The monastic bodies that everywhere arose, formed secure asylums for the multitudes who had been persecuted by their enemies, constituted an invaluable counterpoise to the rude military forces of the time, familiarised the imagination of men with religious types, that could hardly fail in some degree to soften the character, and led the

[1] Thus Hallam says, 'There are continual proofs of immorality in the monkish historians. In the history of Rumsey Abbey, one of our best documents for Anglo-Saxon times, we have an anecdote of a bishop who made a Danish nobleman drunk, that he might cheat him out of an estate, which is told with much approbation. Walter de Hemingford records, with excessive delight, the well-known story of the Jews who were persuaded by the captain of their vessel to walk on the sands at low water till the rising tide drowned them.'—Hallam's *Middle Ages* (12th ed.), iii. p. 306.

[2] Canciani, *Leges Barbarorum*, vol. iii. p. 64. Canciani notices, that among the Poles the teeth of the offending persons were pulled out. The following passage, from Bodin, is, I think, very remarkable :—'Les loix et canons veulent qu'on pardonne aux hérétiques repentis (combien que les magistrats en quelques lieux par cy-devant, y ont eu tel esgard, que celui qui avoit mangé de la chair au Vendredy estoit bruslé tout vif, comme il fut faict en la ville d'Angers l'an mil cinq cens trente-neuf, s'il ne s'en repentoit : et jaçoit qu'il se repentist si estoit-il pendu par compassion).'—*Démonomanie des Sorciers*, p. 216.

[3] A long list of examples of extreme maceration from lives of the saints of the seventh or eighth century is given by Pitra, *Vie de St.-Léger*, Introd. pp. cv.–cvii.

way in most forms of peaceful labour. When men, filled with admiration at the reports of the sanctity, and the miracles of some illustrious saint, made pilgrimages to behold him, and found him attired in the rude garb of a peasant, with thick shoes, and with a scythe on his shoulder, superintending the labours of the farmers,[1] or sitting in a small attic mending lamps,[2] whatever other benefit they might derive from the interview, they could scarcely fail to return with an increased sense of the dignity of labour. It was probably at this time as much for the benefit of the world as of the Church, that the ecclesiastical sanctuaries and estates should remain inviolate, and the numerous legends of Divine punishment having overtaken those who transgressed them,[3] attest the zeal with which the clergy sought to establish that inviolability. The great sanctity that was attached to holidays was also an important boon to the servile classes. The celebration of the first day of the week, in commemoration of the resurrection, and as a period of religious exercises, dates from the earliest age of the Church. The Christian festival was carefully distinguished from the Jewish Sabbath, with which it never appears to have been confounded till the close of the sixteenth century; but some Jewish converts who considered the Jewish law to be still in force observed both days. In general, however, the Christian festival alone was observed, and the Jewish Sabbatical obligation, as St. Paul most explicitly

[1] This was related of St. Equitius.—Greg. *Dialog.* i. 4.

[2] Ibid. i. 5. This saint was named Constantius.

[3] A vast number of miracles of this kind are recorded. See, e.g., Greg. Tur. *De Miraculis*, i. 61–66; *Hist.* iv. 49. Perhaps the most singular instance of the violation of the sanctity of the church was that by the nuns of a convent founded by St. Radegunda. They, having broken into rebellion, four bishops, with their attendant clergy, went to compose the dispute, and having failed, they excommunicated the rebels, whereupon the nuns almost beat them to death in the church.—Greg. Tur. ix. 41.

affirms, no longer rested upon the Christians. The grounds of the observance of Sunday were the manifest propriety and expediency of devoting a certain portion of time to devout exercises, the tradition which traced the sanctification of Sunday to apostolical times, and the right of the Church to appoint certain seasons to be kept holy by its members. When Christianity acquired an ascendency in the empire, its policy on this subject was manifested in one of the laws of Constantine, which, without making any direct reference to religious motives, ordered that, 'on the day of the sun,' no servile work should be performed except agriculture, which, being dependent on the weather, could not, it was thought, be reasonably postponed. Theodosius took a step further, and suppressed the public spectacles on that day. During the centuries that immediately followed the dissolution of the Roman empire, the clergy devoted themselves with great and praiseworthy zeal to the suppression of labour both on Sundays and on the other leading Church holidays. More than one law was made, forbidding all Sunday labour, and this prohibition was reiterated by Charlemagne in his Capitularies.[1] Several Councils made decrees on the subject,[2] and several legends were circulated, of men who had been struck miraculously with disease or death, for having been guilty of this sin.[3] Although the moral side of religion was greatly degraded or forgotten, there was, as I have already intimated, one

[1] See Canciani, *Leges Barbarorum*, vol. iii. pp. 19, 151.

[2] Much information about these measures is given by Dr. Hessey, in his *Bampton Lectures on Sunday*. See, especially, lect. 3. See, too, Moehler, *Le Christianisme et l'Esclavage*, pp. 186-187.

[3] Gregory of Tours enumerates some instances of this in his extravagant book *De Miraculis*, ii. 11; iv. 57; v. 7. One of these cases, however, was for having worked on the day of St. John the Baptist. Some other miracles of the same nature, taken, I believe, from English sources, are given in Hessey's *Sunday* (3rd edition), p. 321.

important exception. Charity was so interwoven with the superstitious parts of ecclesiastical teaching, that it continued to grow and flourish in the darkest period. Of the acts of Queen Bathilda, it is said we know nothing except her donations to the monasteries, and the charity with which she purchased slaves and captives, and released them or converted them into monks.[1] St. Germanus, the Bishop of Paris, near the close of the sixth century, was especially famous for his zeal in ransoming captives.[2] While many of the bishops were men of gross and scandalous vice, there were always some who laboured assiduously in the old episcopal vocation of protecting the oppressed, interceding for the captives, and opening their sanctuaries to the fugitives. The fame acquired by St. Germanus was so great, that prisoners are said to have called upon him to assist them, in the interval between his death and his burial; and the body of the saint becoming miraculously heavy, it was found impossible to carry it to the grave till the captives had been released.[3] In the midst of the complete eclipse of all secular learning, in the midst of a reign of ignorance, imposture, and credulity which cannot be paralleled in history, there grew up a vast legendary literature, clustering around the form of the ascetic, and the lives of the saints among very

[1] Compare Pitra, *Vie de St.-Léger*, p. 137. Sismondi, *Hist. des Français*, tome ii. p. 62–63.

[2] See a remarkable passage from his life, cited by Guizot, *Hist. de la Civilisation en France*, xvii[me] leçon. The English historians contain several instances of the activity of charity in the darkest period. Alfred and Edward the Confessor were conspicuous for it. Ethelwolf is said to have provided 'for the good of his soul,' that, till the day of judgment, one poor man in ten should be provided with meat, drink, and clothing. (Asser's *Life of Alfred.*) There was a popular legend of a poor man who, having in vain asked alms of some sailors, all the bread in their vessel was turned into stone. (Roger of Wendover, A.D. 606.) See, too, another legend of charity in Mathew of Westminster, A.D. 611.

[3] Greg. Tur. *Hist.* v. 8.

much that is grotesque, childish, and even immoral, contain some fragments of the purest and most touching religious poetry.[1]

But the chief title of the period we are considering, to the indulgence of posterity, was its great missionary labours. The stream of missionaries which had at first flowed from Palestine and Italy began to flow from the West. The Irish monasteries furnished the earliest, and probably the most numerous, labourers in the field. A great portion of the north of England was converted by the Irish monks of Lindisfarne. The fame of St. Columbanus in Gaul, in Germany, and in Italy, for a time even balanced that of St. Benedict himself, and the school he founded at Luxeuil became the great seminary for mediæval missionaries, while the monastery he planted at Bobbio continued to the present century. The Irish missionary, St. Gall, gave his name to a portion of Switzerland he had converted, and a crowd of other Irish missionaries penetrated to the remotest forests of Germany. The movement which began with St. Columba in the middle of the sixth century, was communicated to England and Gaul about a century later. Early in the eighth century it found a great leader in the Anglo-Saxon St. Boniface, who spread Christianity far and wide through Germany, and at once excited and disciplined an ardent enthusiasm, which appears to have attracted all that was morally best in the Church. During about three centuries, and while Europe had sunk into the most extreme moral, intellectual, and political degradation, a constant stream of missionaries poured forth from the monasteries, who spread the knowledge of the Cross and the seeds of

[1] M. Guizot has given several specimens of this, (*Hist. de la Civilis.* xvii$^{me}$ leçon.)

a future civilisation through every land, from Lombardy to Sweden.[1]

On the whole, however, it would be difficult to exaggerate the superstition and the vice of the period between the dissolution of the Empire and the reign of Charlemagne. But in the midst of the chaos the elements of a new society may be detected, and we may already observe in embryo the movement which ultimately issued in the crusades, the feudal system, and chivalry. It is exclusively with the moral aspect of this movement that the present work is concerned, and I shall endeavour, in the remainder of this chapter, to describe and explain its incipient stages. It consisted of two parts—a fusion of Christianity with the military spirit, and an increasing reverence for secular rank.

It had been an ancient maxim of the Greeks, that no more acceptable gifts can be offered in the temples of the gods than the trophies won from an enemy in battle.[2] Of this military religion Christianity had been at first the extreme negation. I have already had occasion to observe that it had been one of its earliest rules that no arms should be introduced within the church, and that soldiers returning even from the most righteous war should not be admitted to communion until after a period of penance and purification. A powerful party, which counted among its leaders Clement of Alexandria, Tertullian, Origen, Lactantius, and Basil, maintained that

[1] This portion of mediæval history has lately been well traced by Mr. Maclear, in his *History of Christian Missions in the Middle Ages* (1863). See, too, Montalembert's *Moines d'Occident*; Ozanam's *Études germaniques*. The original materials are to be found in Bede, and in the *Lives of the Saints*—especially that of St. Columba, by Adamnan. On the French missionaries, see the Benedictine *Hist. lit. de la France*, tome iv. p. 5; and on the English missionaries, Sharon Turner's *Hist. of England*, book x. ch. ii.

[2] Dion Chrysostom, *Or.* ii. (*De Regno*).

all warfare was unlawful for those who had been converted, and this opinion had its martyr in the celebrated Maximilianus, who suffered death under Diocletian solely because, having been enrolled as a soldier, he declared that he was a Christian, and that therefore he could not fight. The extent to which this doctrine was disseminated, has been suggested with much plausibility as one of the causes of the Diocletian persecution.[1] It was the subject of one of the reproaches of Celsus, and Origen, in reply, frankly accepted the accusation that Christianity was incompatible with military service, though he maintained that the prayers of the Christians were more efficacious than the swords of the legions.[2] At the same time, there can be no question that many Christians, from a very early date, did enlist in the army, and that they were not cut off from the Church. The legend of the thundering legion, under Marcus Aurelius, whatever we may think of the pretended miracle, attested the fact, which is expressly asserted by Tertullian.[3] The first fury of the Diocletian persecution fell upon Christian soldiers, and by the time of Constantine the army appears to have become, in a great degree, Christian. A Council of Arles, under Constantine, condemned soldiers who, through religious motives, deserted their colours; and St. Augustine threw his great influence into the same scale. But even where the calling was seldom regarded as sinful, it was strongly discouraged. The ideal or type of supreme excellence conceived by the imagination of the Pagan world, and to which all their purest moral enthusiasm naturally aspired, was the patriot and soldier. The ideal of the Catholic legends was the ascetic, whose

[1] Gibbon, ch. xvi.

[2] Origen, *Cels.* lib. viii.

[3] 'Navigamus et nos vobiscum et militamus.'—Tert. *Apol.* xlii. See too Grotius *De Jure*, i. cap. ii.

first duty was to abandon all secular feelings and ties. In most family circles the conflict between the two principles appeared, and in the moral atmosphere of the fourth and fifth centuries it was almost certain that every young man who was animated by any pure or genuine enthusiasm would turn from the army to the monks. St. Martin, St. Ferreol, St. Tarrachus, and St. Victricius, were among those who through religious motives abandoned the army.[1] When Ulphilas translated the Bible into Gothic, he is said to have excepted the four books of Kings, through fear that they might encourage the martial disposition of the barbarians.[2]

The first influence that contributed to bring the military profession into friendly connection with religion was the received doctrine concerning the Providential government of affairs. It was generally taught that all national catastrophes were penal inflictions, resulting, for the most part, from the vices or the religious errors of the leading men, and that temporal prosperity was the reward of orthodoxy and virtue. A great battle, on the issue of which the fortunes of a people or of a monarch depended, was therefore supposed to be the special occasion of Providential interposition, and the hope of obtaining military success became one of the most frequent motives of conversion. The conversion of Constantine was professedly, and the conversion of Clovis was perhaps really, due to the persuasion that the Divine interposition had in a critical moment given them the victory; and I have already noticed how large a part must be assigned to this

[1] See an admirable dissertation on the opinions of the early Christians about military service, in Le Blant, *Inscriptions chrétiennes de la Gaule*, tome i. pp. 81–87. The subject is frequently referred to by Barbeyrac, *Morale des Pères*, and Grotius *De Jure*, lib. i. cap. ii.

[2] Philostorgius, ii. 5.

order of ideas in facilitating the progress of Christianity among the barbarians. When a cross was said to have appeared miraculously to Constantine, with an inscription announcing the victory of the Milvian bridge; when the same holy sign, adorned with the sacred monogram, was carried in the forefront of the Roman armies; when the nails of the cross, which Helena had brought from Jerusalem, were converted by the emperor into a helmet, and into bits for his warhorse, it was evident that a great change was passing over the once pacific spirit of the Church.[1]

Many circumstances conspired to accelerate it. Northern tribes, who had been taught that the gates of the Walhalla were ever open to the warrior who presented himself stained with the blood of his vanquished enemies, were converted to Christianity; but they carried their old feelings into their new creed. The conflict of many races, and the paralysis of all government that followed the fall of the empire, made force everywhere dominant, and petty wars incessant. The military obligations attached to the 'benefices' which the sovereigns gave to their leading chiefs, connected the idea of military service with that of rank, and rendered it doubly honourable in the eyes of men. Many bishops and abbots, partly from the turbulence of their times and characters, and partly, at a later period, from their position as great feudal lords, were accustomed to lead their followers in battle; and this custom, though prohibited by Charlemagne, may be traced to so late a period as the battle of Agincourt.[2]

[1] See some excellent remarks on this change, in Milman's *History of Christianity*, vol. ii. pp. 287–288.

[2] Mably, *Observations sur l'Histoire de France*, i. 6; Hallam's *Middle Ages*, ch. ii. part ii.

The stigma which Christianity had attached to war was thus gradually effaced. At the same time, the Church remained, on the whole, a pacific influence. War was rather condoned than consecrated, and, whatever might be the case with a few isolated prelates, the Church did nothing to increase or encourage it. The transition from the almost Quaker tenets of the primitive Church to the essentially military Christianity of the Crusades was chiefly due to another cause—to the terrors and to the example of Mahommedanism.

This great religion, which so long rivalled the influence of Christianity, had indeed spread the deepest and most justifiable panic through Christendom. Without any of those aids to the imagination which pictures and images can furnish, without any elaborate sacerdotal organisation, preaching the purest Monotheism among ignorant and barbarous men, and inculcating, on the whole, an extremely high and noble system of morals, it spread with a rapidity and it acquired a hold over the minds of its votaries, which it is probable that no other religion has altogether equalled. It borrowed from Christianity that doctrine of salvation by belief, which is perhaps the most powerful impulse that can be applied to the characters of masses of men, and it elaborated so minutely the charms of its sensual heaven, and the terrors of its material hell, as to cause the alternative to appeal with unrivalled force to the gross imaginations of the people. It possessed a book which, however inferior to that of the opposing religion, has nevertheless been the consolation and the support of millions in many ages. It taught a fatalism which in its first age nerved its adherents with a matchless military courage, and which, though in later days, it has often paralysed their active energies, has also rarely failed to support them under the pressure of inevitable calamity. But, above all, it discovered the great, though fatal secret of uniting indissolubly the passion of the soldier with the passion of the devotee. Making the conquest of the infidel the first of duties, and proposing heaven as the certain reward of the valiant soldier, it created a blended enthusiasm that soon overpowered the divided counsels and the voluptuous governments of the East, and within a century of the death of Mahomet, his followers had almost extirpated Christianity from its original home, founded great monarchies in Asia and Africa, planted a noble, though transient and exotic civilisation in Spain, menaced the capital of the Eastern empire, and, but for the issue of a single battle, they would probably have extended their sceptre over the energetic and progressive races of Central Europe. The wave was broken by Charles Martel, at the battle of Poictiers, and it is now useless to speculate what might have been the consequences had Mahommedanism unfurled its triumphant banner among those Teutonic tribes who have so often changed their creed, and on whom the course of civilisation has so largely depended. But one great change was in fact achieved. The spirit of Mahommedanism slowly passed into Christianity, and transformed it into its image. The spectacle of an essentially military religion fascinated men who were at once very warlike and very superstitious. The panic that had palsied Europe was after a long interval succeeded by a fierce reaction of resentment. Pride and religion conspired to urge the Christian warriors against those who had so often defeated the armies and wasted the territory of Christendom, who had shorn the empire of the Cross of many of its fairest provinces, and profaned that holy city which was venerated not only for its past associations, but also for the spiritual blessings it could still bestow upon the pilgrim. The papal indulgences proved not less efficacious in stimulating the military spirit than the promises of Mahomet, and for about two centuries every pulpit in Christendom proclaimed the duty of war with the unbeliever, and represented the battle field as the sure path to heaven. The religious orders which arose united the character of the priest with that of the warrior, and when, at the hour of sunset, the soldier knelt down to pray before his cross, that cross was the handle of his sword.

It would be impossible to conceive any more complete transformation than Christianity had thus undergone, and it is melancholy to contrast with its aspects during the crusades the impression it had once most justly made upon the world, as the spirit of gentleness and of peace encountering the spirit of violence and war. Among the many curious habits of the Pagan Irish, one of the most significant was that of perpendicular burial. With a feeling something like that which induced Vespasian to declare that a Roman emperor should die standing, the Pagan warriors shrank from the notion of being prostrate even in death, and they appear to have regarded this martial burial as a special symbol of Paganism. An old Irish manuscript tells how, when Christianity had been introduced into Ireland, a king of Ulster on his death-bed charged his son never to become a Christian, but to be buried standing upright like a man in battle, with his face for ever turned to the south, defying the men of Leinster.[1] As late as the sixteenth century, it is said that in some parts of Ireland children were baptised by immersion; but the right arms of the males were carefully

[1] Wakeman's *Archæologia Hibernica*, p. 21. However, Giraldus Cambrensis observes that the Irish saints were peculiarly vindictive, and St. Columba and St. Comgall are said to have been leaders in a sanguinary conflict about a church near Coleraine. See Reeves' edition of Adamnan's *Life of St. Columba*, pp. lxxvii. 253.

held above the water, in order that, not having been dipped in the sacred stream, they might strike the more deadly blow.[1]

It had been boldly predicted by some of the early Christians, that the conversion of the world would lead to a cessation of all war. In looking back, with our present experience, we are driven to the melancholy conclusion that not only has ecclesiastical influence had no appreciable effect in diminishing the number of wars, but that it has actually and very seriously increased it. We may look in vain for any period since Constantine, in which the clergy, as a body, exerted themselves to repress the military spirit, or to prevent or abridge a particular war, with an energy or a success the least comparable to what they displayed during several centuries in stimulating the fanaticism of the crusaders, in producing the atrocious massacre of the Albigenses, in embittering the religious wars that followed the Reformation. Private wars were, no doubt, in some degree repressed by their influence; for the institution of the 'Truce of God' was for a time of much value, and when, towards the close of the middle ages, the custom of duels arose, it was strenuously condemned by the clergy; but we shall probably not place any great value on their exertions in this field, when we remember that duels were almost or altogether unknown to the Pagan world; that, having arisen in a period of great superstition, the anathemas of the Church were almost impotent to discourage them; and that in our own century they are rapidly disappearing before the simple censure of an industrial society. It is possible—though it would, I imagine, be difficult to prove it—that the mediatorial office, so often exercised by bishops, may sometimes have

Campion's *Historie of Ireland* (1571), book i. ch. vi.

prevented wars; and it is certain that during the periods of the religious wars, so much military spirit existed in Europe, that it must necessarily have found a vent, and under no circumstances could the period have been one of perfect peace. But when all these qualifications have been fully admitted, the broad fact will remain, that, with the exception of Mahommedanism, no other religion has done so much to produce war as was done by the religious teachers of Christendom during several centuries. The military fanaticism they evoked by the indulgences of the popes, by the ceaseless exhortations of the pulpit, by the religious importance that was attached to the relics at Jerusalem, and by the extreme antipathy they fostered towards all who differed from their theology, has scarcely ever been equalled in its intensity, and it has caused the effusion of oceans of blood, and has been productive of incalculable misery to the world. Religious fanaticism was a main cause of the earlier wars, and an important ingredient in the later ones. The peace principles, that were so common before Constantine, have found scarcely any echo except from Erasmus, the Quakers, and the Anabaptists;[1] and although some very important pacific agencies have arisen out of the industrial progress of modern times, these have been, for the most part, wholly unconnected with, and have in some cases been directly opposed to, theological interests.

But although theological influences cannot reasonably be said to have diminished the number of wars, they have had a very real and beneficial effect in diminishing their

[1] It seems curious to find in so calm and unfanatical a writer as Justus Lipsius the following passage: 'Jam et invasio quædam legitima videtur etiam sine injuria, ut in barbaros et moribus aut *religione* prorsum a nobis abhorrentes.'—*Politicorum sive Civilis Doctrinæ libri* (Paris. 1594), lib. iv. ch. ii. cap. iv.

atrocity, by improving the condition of the vanquished. On few subjects have the moral opinions of different ages exhibited so marked a variation as in their judgments of what punishment may justly be imposed on a conquered enemy, and these variations have often been cited as an argument against those who believe in the existence of natural moral perceptions. To those, however, who accept that doctrine, with the limitations that have been stated in the first chapter, they can cause no perplexity. In the first dawning of the human intelligence (as I have said) the notion of duty, as distinguished from that of interest, appears, and the mind, in reviewing the various emotions by which it is influenced, recognises the unselfish and benevolent motives as essentially and generically superior to the selfish and the cruel. But it is the general condition of society alone that determines the standard of benevolence—the classes towards which every good man will exercise it. At first, the range of duty is the family, the tribe, the state, the confederation. Within these limits every man feels himself under moral obligations to those about him; but he regards the outer world as we regard wild animals, as beings upon whom he may justifiably prey. Hence, we may explain the curious fact that the terms brigand or corsair conveyed in the early stages of society no notion of moral guilt.[1] Such

[1] 'Con l' occasione di queste cose Plutarco nel *Teseo* dice che gli eroi si recavano a grande onore e si reputavano in pregio d' armi con l' esser chiamati ladroni; siccome a' tempi barbari ritornati quello di Corsale era titolo riputato di signoria; d' intorno a' quali tempi venuto Solone, si dice aver permesso nelle sue leggi le società per cagion di prede; tanto Solone ben intese questa nostra compiuta Umanità, nella quale costoro non godono del diritto natural delle genti! Ma quel che fa più maraviglia è che Platone ed Aristotile posero il ladroneccio fralle spezie della caccia e con tali e tanti filosofi d' una gente umanissima convengono con la loro barbarie i Germani antichi; appo i quali al referire di Cesare i ladronecci non solo non eran infami, ma si tenevano tra gli esercizi della virtù siccome tra quelli che per costume non appli-

men were looked upon simply as we look upon huntsmen, and if they displayed courage and skill in their pursuit, they were deemed fit subjects for admiration. Even in the writings of the most enlightened philosophers of Greece, war with barbarians is represented as a form of chase, and the simple desire of obtaining the barbarians as slaves was considered a sufficient reason for invading them. The right of the conqueror to kill his captives was generally recognised, nor was it at first restricted by any considerations of age or sex. Several instances are recorded of Greek and other cities being deliberately destroyed by Greeks or by Romans, and the entire populations ruthlessly massacred.[1] The whole career of the early republic of Rome, though much idealised and transfigured by later historians, was probably governed by these principles.[2] The normal fate of the captive, which, among barbarians, had been death, was, in civilised antiquity, slavery; but many thousands were condemned to the gladiatorial shows, and the vanquished general was commonly slain in the Mamertine prison, while his conqueror ascended in triumph to the Capitol.

cando ad arte alcuna così fuggivano l' ozio.'—Vico, *Scienza Nuova*, ii. 6. See too Whewell's *Elements of Morality*, book vi. ch. ii.

[1] The ancient right of war is fully discussed by Grotius *De Jure*, lib. iii. See, especially, the horrible catalogue of tragedies in cap. 4. The military feeling that regards capture as disgraceful, had probably some, though only a very subordinate influence, in producing cruelty to the prisoners.

[2] Le jour ou Athènes décréta que tous les Mityléniens, sans distinction de sexe ni d'âge, seraient exterminés, elle ne croyait pas dépasser son droit; quand le lendemain elle revint sur son décret et se contenta de mettre à mort mille citoyens et de confisquer toutes les terres, elle se crut humaine et indulgente. Après la prise de Platée les hommes furent égorgés, les femmes vendues, et personne n'accusa les vainqueurs d'avoir violé le droit. . . . C'est en vertu de ce droit de la guerre que Rome a étendu la solitude autour d'elle; du territoire où les Volsques avaient vingt-trois cités elle a fait les marais pontins; les cinquante-trois villes du Latium ont disparu; dans le Samnium on put longtemps reconnaître les lieux où les armées romaines avaient passé, moins aux vestiges de leurs camps qu'à la solitude qui régnait aux environs.'—Fustel de Coulanges, *La Cité antique*, pp. 263-264.

A few traces of a more humane spirit may, it is true, be discovered. Plato had advocated the liberation of all Greek prisoners upon payment of a fixed ransom,[1] and the Spartan general, Callicratidas, had nobly acted upon this principle;[2] but his example never appears to have been generally followed. In Rome, the notion of international obligation was very strongly felt. No war was considered just which had not been officially declared; and even in the case of wars with barbarians, the Roman historians often discuss the sufficiency or insufficiency of the motives of the wars, with a conscientious severity a modern historian could hardly surpass.[3] The later Greek and Latin writings occasionally contain maxims which exhibit a considerable progress in this sphere. The sole legitimate object of war, both Cicero and Sallust declared to be an assured peace. That war, according to Tacitus, ends well which ends with a pardon. Pliny refused to apply the epithet great to Cæsar, on account of the torrents of human blood he had shed. Two Roman conquerors[4] are credited with the saying, that it is better to save the life of one citizen than to destroy a thousand enemies. Marcus Aurelius mournfully assimilated the career of a conqueror to that of a simple robber. Nations or armies which voluntarily submitted to Rome were habitually treated with extreme leniency, and numerous acts of individual magnanimity are recorded. The violation of the chastity of conquered women by soldiers in a siege was denounced as a rare and atrocious

[1] Plato, *Republic*, lib. v.; Bodin, *République*, liv. i. cap. 5.

[2] Grote, *Hist. of Greece*, vol. viii. p. 224. Agesilaus was also very humane to captives.—Ibid. pp. 365–6.

[3] This appears continually in Livy, but most of all, I think, in the Gaulish historian, Florus.

[4] Scipio and Trajan.

crime.[1] The extreme atrocities of ancient war appear at last to have been practically, though not legally, restricted to two classes.[2] Cities where Roman ambassadors had been insulted, or where some special act of ill faith or cruelty was said to have taken place, were razed to the ground, and their populations massacred or delivered into slavery. Barbarian prisoners were regarded almost as wild beasts, and sent in thousands to fill the slave market or to combat in the arena.

The changes Christianity effected in the rights of war were very important, and they may, I think, be comprised under three heads. In the first place, it suppressed the gladiatorial shows, and thereby saved thousands of captives from a bloody death. In the next place, it steadily discouraged the practice of enslaving prisoners, ransomed immense multitudes with charitable contributions, and by slow and insensible gradations proceeded on its path of mercy till it became a recognised principle of international law, that no Christian prisoners should be reduced to slavery.[3] In the third place, it had a more indirect

[1] See some very remarkable passages in Grotius, *de Jure Bell.* lib. iii. cap. 4, § 19.

[2] These mitigations are fully enumerated by Ayala, *De Jure et Officiis Bellicis* (Antwerp, 1597), Grotius, *De Jure.* It is remarkable that both Ayala and Grotius base their attempts to mitigate the severity of war chiefly, Ayala almost entirely, upon the writings and examples of the Pagans. There is an interesting discussion of the limits of the right of conquerors and of the just causes of war in Cicero, *De Offic.* lib. i.

[3] In England the change seems to have immediately followed conversion. 'The evangelical precepts of peace and love,' says a very learned historian, 'did not put an end to war, they did not put an end to aggressive conquests, but they distinctly humanised the way in which war was carried on. From this time forth the never-ending wars with the Welsh cease to be wars of extermination. The heathen English had been satisfied with nothing short of the destruction and expulsion of their enemies; the Christian English thought it enough to reduce them to political subjection. . . . The Christian Welsh could now sit down as subjects of the Christian Saxon. The Welshman was acknowledged as a man and a citizen, and was put under the protection of the law.'—Freeman's *Hist. of the Norman Conquest,*

but very powerful influence, by the creation of a new warlike ideal. The ideal knight of the Crusades and of chivalry, uniting all the force and fire of the ancient warrior, with all the tenderness and humility of the Christian saint, sprang from the conjunction of the two streams of religious and of military feeling; and although this ideal, like all others, was a creation of the imagination, although it was rarely or never perfectly realised in life, yet it remained the type and model of warlike excellence, to which many generations aspired; and its softening influence may even now be largely traced in the character of the modern gentleman.

Together with the gradual fusion of the military spirit with Christianity, we may dimly descry, in the period before Charlemagne, the first stages of that consecration of secular rank which at a later period, in the forms of chivalry, the divine right of kings, and the reverence for aristocracies, played so large a part both in moral and in political history. We have already seen that the course of events in the Roman empire had been towards the continual aggrandisement of the imperial power. The representative despotism of Augustus was at last succeeded by the oriental despotism of Diocletian. The senate sank into a powerless assembly of imperial nominees, and the spirit of Roman freedom wholly perished with the extinction of Stoicism.

vol. i. pp. 33-34. Christians who assisted infidels in wars against Christians were ipso facto excommunicated, and might therefore be enslaved, but all others were free from slavery. 'Et quidem inter Christianos laudabili et antiqua consuetudine introductum est, ut capti hinc inde, utcunque justo bello, non fierent servi, sed liberi servarentur donec solvant precium redemptionis.'—Ayala, lib. i. cap. 5. 'This rule, at least,' says Grotius, '(though but a small matter) the reverence for the Christian law has enforced, which Socrates vainly sought to have established among the Greeks.' The Mahommedans also made it a rule not to enslave their co-religionists.—Grotius *de Jure*, iii. 7. § 9. Pagan and barbarian prisoners were, however, sold as slaves (especially by the Spaniards) till very recently.

It would probably be a needless refinement to seek any deeper causes for this change than may be found in the ordinary principles of human nature. Despotism is the normal and legitimate government of an early society in which knowledge has not yet developed the powers of the people; but when it is introduced into a civilised community, it is of the nature of a disease, and a disease which, unless it be checked, has a continual tendency to spread. When free nations abdicate their political functions, they gradually lose both the capacity and the desire for freedom. Political talent and ambition, having no sphere for action, steadily decay, and servile, enervating, and vicious habits proportionately increase. Nations are organic beings in a constant process of expansion or decay, and where they do not exhibit a progress of liberty they usually exhibit a progress of servitude.

It can hardly be asserted that Christianity had much influence upon this change. By accelerating in some degree the withdrawal of the virtuous energies of the people from the sphere of government which had long been in process, it prevented the great improvement of morals, which it undoubtedly effected, from appearing perceptibly in public affairs. It taught a doctrine of passive obedience, which its disciples nobly observed in the worst periods of persecution. On the other hand, the Christians emphatically repudiated the ascription of Divine honours to the sovereign, and they asserted with heroic constancy their independent worship, in defiance of the law. After the time of Constantine, however, their zeal became far less pure, and sectarian interests wholly governed their principles. Much misapplied learning has been employed in endeavouring to extract from the Fathers a consistent doctrine on the subject of the relations of subjects to their sovereigns; but every impartial observer may discover that the principle upon which they acted was exceedingly simple. When a sovereign was sufficiently orthodox in his opinions, and sufficiently zealous in patronising the Church and in persecuting the heretics, he was extolled as an angel. When his policy was opposed to the Church, he was represented as a dæmon. The estimate which Gregory of Tours has given of the character of Clovis, though far more frank, is not a more striking instance of moral perversion than the fulsome and indeed blasphemous adulation which Eusebius poured upon Constantine—a sovereign whose character was at all times of the most mingled description, and who, shortly after his conversion, put to a violent death his son, his nephew, and his wife. If we were to estimate the attitude of ecclesiastics to sovereigns by the language of Eusebius, we should suppose that they ascribed to them a direct Divine inspiration, and exalted the Imperial dignity to an extent that was before unknown.[1] But when Julian mounted the throne, the whole aspect of the Church was changed. This great and virtuous, though misguided, sovereign, whose private life was a model of purity, who carried to the throne the manners, tastes, and friendships of a philosophic life, and who proclaimed, and, with very slight exceptions, acted with the largest and most generous toleration, was an enemy of the Church, and all the vocabulary of invective was in consequence habitually lavished upon him. Ecclesiastics and laymen combined in insulting him, and when, after a brief but glorious reign of less than two years, he met an honourable death on the battle-field, neither the disaster that had befallen the Roman arms, nor the present dangers of the army, nor the heroic courage which the fallen emperor had

[1] The character of Constantine, and the estimate of it in Eusebius, are well treated by Dean Stanley, *Lectures on the Eastern Church* (Lect. vi.).

displayed, nor the majestic tranquillity of his end, nor the tears of his faithful friends, could shame the Christian community into the decency of silence. A peal of brutal merriment filled the land. In Antioch the Christians assembled in the theatres and in the churches, to celebrate with rejoicing, the death which their emperor had met in fighting against the enemies of his country.[1] A crowd of vindictive legends expressed the exultation of the Church,[2] and St. Gregory Nazianzen devoted his eloquence to immortalising it. His brother had at one time been a high official in the empire, and had fearlessly owned his Christianity under Julian; but that emperor not only did not remove him from his post, but even honoured him with his warm friendship.[3] The body of Julian had been laid but a short time in the grave, when St. Gregory delivered two fierce invectives against his memory, collected the grotesque calumnies that had been heaped upon his character, expressed a regret that his remains had not been flung after death into the common sewer, and regaled the hearers by an emphatic assertion of the tortures that were awaiting him in hell. Among the Pagans a charge of the gravest kind was brought against the Christians. It was said that Julian died by the spear, not of an enemy, but of one of his own Christian soldiers. When we remember that he was at once an emperor and a general, that he fell when bravely and confidently leading his army in the field, and in the critical moment of a battle on which the fortunes of the empire largely depended, this charge which Libanius has made, appears to involve as large an amount of base treachery as any that can be conceived. That it was a

[1] Theodoret, iii. 28.

[2] They are collected by Chateaubriand, *Études hist.* 2me disc. 2me partie.

[3] See St. Gregory's oration on *Cesairius.*

groundless calumny will now scarcely be questioned; but the manner in which it was regarded among the Christians is singularly characteristic. 'Libanius,' says one of the ecclesiastical historians, 'clearly states that the emperor fell by the hand of a Christian; and this, probably, was the truth. It is not unlikely that some of the soldiers who then served in the Roman army might have conceived the idea of acting like the ancient slayers of tyrants who exposed themselves to death in the cause of liberty, and fought in defence of their country, their families, and their friends, and whose names are held in universal admiration. Still less is he deserving of blame who, for the sake of God and of religion, performed so bold a deed.'[1]

It may be asserted, I think, without exaggeration, that the complete subordination of all other principles to their theological interests, which characterised the ecclesiastics under Julian, continued for many centuries. No language of invective was too extreme to be applied to a sovereign who opposed their interests—no language of adulation too extravagant for a sovereign who sustained them. Of all the emperors who disgraced the throne of Constantinople, the most odious and ferocious was probably Phocas. An obscure centurion, he rose by a military revolt to the supreme power, and the emperor Maurice, with his family, fell into his hands. He resolved to put the captive emperor to death; but first of all, he ordered his five children to be brought out and to be successively murdered before the eyes of their father, who bore the awful sight with a fine mixture of antique heroism and of Christian piety, murmuring, as each child fell beneath the knife of the assassin, 'Thou art just, O Lord, and righteous are Thy judgments,' and even inter-

[1] Sozomen, vi. 2.

posing at the last moment, to reveal the heroic fraud of the nurse who desired to save his youngest child by substituting for it her own. But Maurice—who had been a weak and avaricious rather than a vicious sovereign—had shown himself jealous of the influence of the Pope, had forbidden the soldiers, during the extreme danger of their country, deserting their colours to enrol themselves as monks, and had even encouraged the pretensions of the Archbishop of Constantinople to the title of Universal Bishop; and in the eyes of the Roman priests, the recollection of these crimes was sufficient to condone the most brutal of murders. In two letters, full of passages from Scripture, and replete with fulsome and blasphemous flattery, the Pope, St. Gregory the Great, wrote to congratulate Phocas and his wife upon their triumph; he called heaven and earth to rejoice over them; he placed their images to be venerated in the Lateran, and he adroitly insinuated that it was impossible that, with their well-known piety, they could fail to be very favourable to the See of Peter.[1]

The course of events in relation to the monarchical power was for some time different in the East and the West. Constantine had himself assumed more of the pomp and manner of an oriental sovereign than any preceding emperor, and the court of Constantinople was soon characterised by an extravagance of magnificence on the part of the monarch, and of adulation on the part of the subjects, which has probably never been exceeded.[2] The imperial power in the East overshadowed the eccle-

[1] *Ep.* xiii. 31–39. In the second of these letters (which is addressed to Leontia), he says: 'Rogare forsitan debui ut ecclesiam beati Petri apostoli quæ nunc usque gravibus insidiis laboravit, haberet Vestra Tranquillitas specialiter commendatam. Sed qui scio quia omnipotentem Deum diligitis, non debeo petere quod sponte ex benignitate vestræ pietatis exhibetis.'

[2] See the graphic description in Gibbon, ch. liii.

siastical, and notwithstanding their fierce outbreak during the iconoclastic controversy, and a few minor paroxysms of revolt, the priests gradually sank into that contented subservience which has usually characterised the Eastern Church. In the West, however, the Roman bishops were in a great degree independent of the sovereigns, and in some degree opposed to their interests. The transfer of the imperial power to Constantinople, by leaving the Roman bishops the chief personages in a city which long association as well as actual power rendered the foremost in the world, was one of the great causes of the extreme aggrandisement of the Papacy and the Arianism of many sovereigns; the jealousy which others exhibited of ecclesiastical encroachments, and the lukewarmness of a few in persecuting heretics, were all causes of dissension. On the severance of the empire, the Western Church came in contact with rulers of another type. The barbarian kings were little more than military chiefs, elected for the most part by the people, surrounded by little or no special sanctity, and maintaining their precarious and very restricted authority by their courage or their skill. A few feebly imitated the pomp of the Roman emperors, but their claims had no great weight upon the world. The aureole which the genius of Theodoric cast around his throne passed away upon his death, and the Arianism of that great sovereign sufficiently debarred him from the sympathies of the Church. In Gaul, under a few bold and unscrupulous men, the Merovingian dynasty emerged from a host of petty kings, and consolidated the whole country into one kingdom; but after a short period it degenerated, the kings became mere puppets in the hands of the mayors of the palace, and these latter, holding as they did an office which had become hereditary, being the chief of the great landed proprietors, and having acquired by their position a great personal ascendency over the sovereigns, became the virtual rulers of the nation.

It was out of these somewhat unpromising conditions that the mediæval doctrine of the Divine right of kings, and the general reverence for rank, that formed the essence of chivalry, were slowly evolved. Political and moral causes conspired in producing them. The chief political causes—which are well known—may be summed up in a few words.

When Leo the Isaurian attempted, in the eighth century, to repress the worship of images, the resistance which he met at Constantinople, though violent, was speedily allayed; but the Pope, assuming a far higher position than any Byzantine ecclesiastic could attain, boldly excommunicated the emperor, and led a revolt against his authority, which issued in the virtual independence of Italy. His position was at this time singularly grand. He represented a religious cause to which the great mass of the Christian world were passionately attached. He was venerated as the emancipator of Italy. He exhibited in the hour of his triumph a moderation which conciliated many enemies, and prevented the anarchy that might naturally have been expected. He presided, at the same time, over a vast monastic organisation, which ramified over all Christendom, propagated his authority among many barbarous nations, and, by its special attachment to the Papacy, as distinguished from the Episcopacy, contributed very much to transform Christianity into a spiritual despotism. One great danger, however, still menaced his power. The barbarous Lombards were continually invading his territory, and threatening the independence of Rome. The Lombard monarch, Luitprand, had quailed in the very hour of his triumph before the menace of eternal torture;

but his successor, Astolphus, was proof against every fear, and it seemed as though the Papal city must have inevitably succumbed before his arms.

In their complete military impotence, the Popes looked abroad for some foreign succour, and they naturally turned to the Franks, whose martial tastes and triumphs were universally renowned. Charles Martel, though simply a mayor of the Palace, had saved Europe from the Mahommedans, and the Pope expected that he would unsheath his sword for the defence of the Vatican. Charles, however, was deaf to all entreaties; and although he had done more than any ruler since Constantine for the Church, his attention seems to have been engrossed by the interests of his own country, and he was much alienated from the sympathies of the clergy. An ancient legend tells how a saint saw his soul carried by dæmons into hell, because he had secularised Church property, and a more modern historian[1] has ascribed his death to his having hesitated to defend the Pope. His son, Pepin, however, actuated probably in different degrees by personal ambition, a desire for military adventure, and religious zeal, listened readily to the prayer of the Pope, and a compact was entered into between the parties, which proved one of the most important events in history. Pepin agreed to secure the Pope from the danger by which he was threatened. The Pope agreed to give his religious sanction to the ambition of Pepin, who designed to depose the Merovingian dynasty, and to become in name, as he was already in fact, the sovereign of Gaul.

It is not necessary for me to recount at length the details of these negotiations, which are described by many historians. It is sufficient to say, that the compact was religiously observed. Pepin made two expeditions to

[1] Baronius.

Italy, and completely shattered the power of the Lombards, wresting from them the rich exarchate of Ravenna, which he ceded to the Pope, who still retained his nominal allegiance to the Byzantine emperor, but who became, by this donation, for the first time avowedly an independent temporal prince. On the other hand, the deposition of Childeric was peaceably effected; the last of the Merovingians was immured in a monastery, and the Carlovingian dynasty ascended the throne under the special benediction of the Pope, who performed on the occasion the ceremony of Consecration, which had not previously been in general use,[1] placed the crown with his own hands on the head of Pepin, and delivered a solemn anathema against all who should rebel against the new king or against his successors.

The extreme importance of these events was probably not fully realised by any of the parties concerned in them. It was evident, indeed, that the Pope had been freed from a pressing danger, and had acquired a great accession of temporal power, and also that a new dynasty had arisen in Gaul under circumstances that were singularly favourable and imposing. But, much more important than these facts was the permanent consecration of the royal authority that had been effected. The Pope had successfully asserted his power of deposing and elevating kings, and had thus acquired a position which influenced the whole subsequent course of European history. The monarch, if he had become in some degree subservient to the priest, had become in a great degree independent of his people; the Divine origin of his power was regarded as a dogma of religion, and a sanctity surrounded him which immeasureably aggrandised his power. The ascription by the Pagans of divinity to kings had had no appreciable

[1] Mably, ii. 1; Gibbon, ch. xlix.

effect in increasing their authority or restraining the limits of criticism or of rebellion. The ascription of a Divine right to kings, independent of the wishes of the people, has been one of the most enduring and influential of superstitions, and it has even now not wholly vanished from the world.[1]

Mere isolated political events have, however, rarely or never this profound influence, unless they have been preceded and prepared by other agencies. The first predisposing cause of the ready reception of the doctrine of the Divine character of authority, may probably be found in the prominence of the monastic system. I have already observed that this system represents in the most extreme form that exaltation of the virtues of humility and of obedience which so broadly distinguishes the Christian from the Pagan type of excellence. I have also noticed that, owing to the concurrence of many causes, it had acquired such dimensions and influence as to supply the guiding ideal of the Christian world. Controlling or monopolising all education and literature, furnishing most of the legislators and many of the statesmen of the age, attracting to themselves all moral enthusiasm and most intellectual ability, the monks soon left their impress on the character of nations. Habits of obedience and dispositions of humility were diffused abroad, revered and

[1] There are some good remarks upon the way in which, among the free Franks, the bishops taught the duty of passive obedience, in Mably, *Obs. sur l'Histoire de France,* livre i. ch. iii. Gregory of Tours, in his address to Chilperic, had said, 'If any of us, O king, transgress the boundaries of justice, thou art at hand to correct us; but if thou shouldst exceed them, who is to condemn thee? We address thee, and if it please thee thou listenest to us; but if it please thee not, who is to condemn thee save Him who has proclaimed himself Justice.'—Greg. Tur. v. 19. On the other hand, Hincmar, Archbishop of Rheims, strongly asserted the obligation of kings to observe the law, and denounced as diabolical the doctrine that they are subject to none but God. (Allen, *On the Royal Prerogative* (1849), pp. 171–172.)

idealised, and a Church which rested mainly on tradition fostered a deep sense of the sanctity of antiquity, and a natural disposition to observe traditional customs. In this manner a tone of feeling was gradually formed that assimilated with the monarchical and aristocratical institutions of feudalism, which flourished chiefly because they corresponded with the moral feelings of the time.

In the next place, a series of social and political causes were tending to abridge the personal independence for which the barbarians had been noted. The king had at first been not the sovereign of a country, but the chief of a tribe.[1] Gradually, however, with more settled habits, the sovereignty assumed a territorial character, and we may soon discover the rudiments of a territorial aristocracy. The kings gave their leading chiefs portions of conquered land or of the royal domains, under the name of benefices. By slow and perhaps insensible stages, each of which has been the subject of fierce controversy, the obligation of military service was attached to these benefices: they were made irrevocable, and ultimately hereditary. At the same time, through causes to which I have already adverted, the free peasants for the most part sank into serfs subject to the rich and protected by the power of great landowners. In this manner a hierarchy of ranks was gradually formed, of which the sovereign was the apex and the serf the basis. The complete legal organisation of this hierarchy belongs to the period of feudalism, which is not within the scope of the present volume; but the chief elements of feudalism existed before Charlemagne, and the moral results flowing

[1] The exact degree of the authority of the barbarian kings, and the different stages by which their power was increased, are matters of great controversy. The reader may consult Thierry's *Lettres sur l'Hist. de France* (let. 9); Guizot's *Hist. de la Civilisation*; Mably, *Observ. sur l'Hist. de France*; Freeman's *Hist. of the Norman Conquest*, vol. i.

from them may be already discerned. Each rank, except the very highest, was continually brought into contact with a superior, and a feeling of constant dependence and subordination was accordingly fostered. To the serf, who depended for all things upon the neighbouring noble, to the noble, who held all his dignities on the condition of frequent military service under his sovereign, the idea of secular rank became indissolubly connected with that of supreme greatness.

It will appear evident from the foregoing observations, that in the period before Charlemagne, the moral and political causes were already in action, which at a much later period produced the organisation of chivalry, an organisation which was founded on the combination and the glorification of secular rank and military prowess. But in order that the tendencies I have described should acquire their full force, it was necessary that they should be represented or illustrated in some great personage, who, by the splendour and the beauty of his career, could fascinate the imaginations of men. It is much easier to govern great masses of men through their imagination than through their reason. Moral principles rarely act powerfully upon the world, except by way of example or ideals. When the course of events has been to glorify the ascetic or monarchical or military spirit, a great saint, or sovereign, or soldier will arise, who will concentrate in one dazzling focus the blind tendencies of his time, kindle the enthusiasm and fascinate the imagination of the people. But for the prevailing tendency, the great man would not have arisen, or would not have exercised his great influence. But for the great man, whose career appealed vividly to the imagination, the prevailing tendency would never have acquired its full intensity.

This typical figure appeared in Charlemagne, whose

colossal form towers with a majestic grandeur both in history and in romance. Of all the great rulers of men, there has probably been no other who was so truly many-sided, whose influence pervaded so completely all the religious, intellectual, and political modes of thought existing in his time. Rising in one of the darkest periods of European history, this great emperor resuscitated, with a brief but dazzling splendour, the faded glories of the empire of the West, conducted, for the most part in person, numerous expeditions against the barbarous nations around him, promulgated a vast system of legislation, reformed the discipline of every order of the Church, reduced all classes of the clergy to subservience to his will, while, by legalising tithes, he greatly increased their material prosperity; contributed, in a measure, to check the intellectual decadence by founding schools and libraries, and drawing around him all the scattered learning of Europe; reformed the coinage, extended commerce, influenced religious controversies, and created great representative assemblies, which ultimately contributed largely to the organisation of feudalism. In all these spheres the traces of his vast, organising, and far-seeing genius may be detected, and the influence which he exercised over the imaginations of men is shown by the numerous legends of which he is the hero. In the preceding ages the supreme ideal had been the ascetic. When the popular imagination embodied in legends its conception of humanity in its noblest and most attractive form, it instinctively painted some hermit-saint of many penances and many miracles. In the Romances of Charlemagne and of Arthur we may trace the dawning of a new type of greatness. The hero of the imagination of Europe was no longer a hermit but a king, a warrior, a knight. The long train of influences I have reviewed, culminating in Charlemagne, had done their work. The age of the ascetics began to fade. The age of the crusades and of chivalry succeeded it.

It is curious to observe the manner in which, under the influence of the prevailing tendency, the career of Charlemagne was transfigured by the popular imagination. This great emperor had, in fact, been in no degree actuated by the spirit of a crusader; his military enterprises had been chiefly directed against the Saxons, against whom he had made not less than thirty-two expeditions. With the Mahommedans he had but little contact. It was Charles Martel, not his grandson, who, by the great battle of Poictiers, had checked their career. Charlemagne made, in person, but a single expedition against them in Spain, and that expedition was on a scale that was altogether inconsiderable, and it was disastrous in its issue. But in the Carlovingian romances, which arose at a time when the enthusiasm of the Crusades was permeating all Christendom, events were represented in a wholly different light. Charles Martel has no place among the ideal combatants of the Church. He had appeared too early, his figure was not sufficiently great to fascinate the popular imagination, and by confiscating ecclesiastical property, and refusing to assist the Pope against the Lombards, he had fallen under the ban of the clergy. Charlemagne, on the other hand, is represented as the first and greatest of the crusaders. His wars with the Saxons were scarcely noticed. His whole life was said to have been spent in heroic and triumphant combats with the followers of Mahomet.[1] Among the achievements attributed to him was an expedition to rescue Nismes and Carcassone from their grasp, which was, in fact, a dim tradition of the victories of Charles

[1] Fauriel, *Hist. de la Poésie provençale*, tome ii. p. 252.

Martel.[1] He is even said to have carried his victorious arms into the heart of Palestine, and he is the hero of what are probably the three earliest extant romances of the Crusades.[2] In fiction, as in history, his reign forms the great landmark separating the early period of the middle ages from the age of military Christianity.

On the verge of this great change I draw this history to a close. In pursuing our long and chequered course, from Augustus to Charlemagne, we have seen the rise and fall of many types of character, and of many forms of enthusiasm. We have seen the influence of universal empire expanding, and the influence of Greek civilisation intensifying, the sympathies of Europe. We have surveyed the successive progress of Stoicism, Platonism, and Egyptian philosophies, at once reflecting and guiding the moral tendencies of society. We have traced the course of progress or retrogression in many fields of social, political, and legislative life; have watched the cradle of European Christianity, examined the causes of its triumph, the difficulties it encountered, and the priceless blessings its philanthropic spirit bestowed upon mankind. We have also pursued step by step the mournful history of its corruption, its asceticism, and its intolerance, the various transformations it produced or underwent when the turbid waters of the barbarian invasions had inundated the civilisations of Europe. It remains for me, before concluding this work, to investigate one class of subjects to which I have, as yet, but briefly adverted—to examine the effects of the changes I have described upon the character and position of woman, and upon the grave moral questions concerning the relations of the sexes.

[1] Ibid. p. 258.

[2] Le Grand D'Aussy, *Fabliaux,* préf. p. xxiv. These romances were accounts of his expeditions to Spain, to Languedoc, and to Palestine.

## CHAPTER V.

### THE POSITION OF WOMEN.

In the long series of moral revolutions that have been described in the foregoing chapters, I have more than once had occasion to refer to the position that was assigned to woman in the community, and to the virtues and vices that spring directly from the relations of the sexes. I have not, however, as yet discussed these questions with a fulness at all corresponding to their historical importance, and I propose, in consequence, before concluding this volume, to devote a few pages to their examination. Of all the many questions that are treated in this work, there is none which I approach with so much hesitation, for there is probably none which it is so difficult to treat with clearness and impartiality, and at the same time without exciting any scandal or offence. The complexity of the problem, arising from the very large place which exceptional institutions or circumstances, and especially the influence of climate and race, have had on the chastity of nations, I have already noticed, and the extreme delicacy of the matters with which this branch of ethics is connected must be palpable to all. The first duty of an historian, however, is to truth, and it is absolutely impossible to present a true picture of the moral condition of different ages, and to form a true estimate of the moral effects of different religions, without adverting to the department of morals, which has exhibited most change, and has probably exercised most influence.

It is natural that, in the period when men are still perfect barbarians, when their habits of life are still nomadic, and when war and the chase, being their sole pursuits, the qualities that are required in these are their sole measure of excellence, the inferiority of women to men should be regarded as undoubted, and their position should be extremely degraded. In all those qualities which are then most prized, women are indisputably inferior. The social qualities in which they are especially fitted to excel have no sphere for their display. The ascendency of beauty is very faint, and even if it were otherwise, few traces of female beauty could survive the hardships of the savage life. Woman is looked upon simply as the slave of man, and as the minister to his passions. In the first capacity, her life is one of continual, abject, and unrequited toil. In the second capacity, she is exposed to all the violent revulsions of feeling that follow, among rude men, the gratification of the animal passions.

Even in this early stage, however, we may trace some rudiments of those moral sentiments which are destined at a later period to expand. The institution of marriage exists. The value of chastity is commonly in some degree felt, and appears in the indignation which is displayed against the adulterer. The duty of restraining the sensual passions is largely recognised in the female, though the males are only restricted by the prohibition of adultery.

The two first steps which are taken towards the elevation of woman are probably the cessation of the custom of purchasing wives, and the construction of the family on the basis of monogamy. In the first periods of civilisation, the marriage contract was arranged between the bridegroom and the father of the bride, on the condition of a sum of money being paid by the former to the latter. This sum, which is known in the laws of the barbarians as the 'mundium,'[1] was in fact a payment to the father for the cession of his daughter, who thus became the bought slave of her husband. It is one of the most remarkable features of the ancient laws of India, that they forbade this gift, on the ground that the parent should not sell his child;[2] but there can be little doubt that this sale was at one time the ordinary type of marriage. In the Jewish writings we find Jacob purchasing Leah and Rachel by the performance of certain services for their father, and this custom, which seems to have been at first general in Judea,[3] appears in the age of Homer to have been general in Greece. At an early period, however, of Greek history, the purchase-money was replaced by the dowry, or sum of money paid by the father of the bride for the use of his daughter,[4] and this, although it passed into the hands of the husband, contributed to elevate the wife, in the first place, by the dignity it gave her, and in the next place, by special laws, which both in Greece and Rome secured it to her in

[1] The ἕδνα of the Greeks.

[2] Legouvé, *Histoire morale des Femmes*, pp. 95–96.

[3] Gen. xxix. xxxiv. 12; Deut. xxii. 29; 1 Sam. xviii. 25.

[4] The history of dowries is briefly noticed by Grote, *Hist. of Greece*, vol. ii. pp. 112–113; and more fully by Lord Kames, in the admirable chapter 'On the Progress of the Female Sex,' in his *Sketches of the History of Man*, a book less read than it deserves to be. M. Legouvé has also devoted a chapter to it in his *Hist. morale des Femmes*. See, too, Legendre, *Traitê de l'Opinion*, tome ii. pp. 329–330. We find traces of the dowry, as well as of the ἕδνα, in Homer. Penelope had received a dowry from Icarus, her father. M. Michelet, in one of those fanciful books which he has recently published, maintains a view of the object of the ἕδνα which I do not remember to have seen elsewhere, and which I do not believe. He says: 'Ce prix n'est point un achat de la femme, mais une indemnité qui dédommage la famille du père pour les enfants futurs, qui ne profiteront pas à cette famille mais à celle où la femme va entrer.'—*La Femme*, p. 166.

most cases of separation.[1] The wife thus possessed a guarantee against ill-usage by her husband. She ceased to be his slave, and became in some degree a contracting party. Among the early Germans, a different and very remarkable custom existed. The bride did not bring any dowry to her husband, nor did the bridegroom give anything to the father of the bride; but he gave his gift to the bride herself, on the morning after the first night of marriage, and this, which was called the 'Morgengab,' or morning gift, was the origin of the jointure.[2]

Still more important than the foregoing was the institution of monogamy, by which, from its earliest days, the Greek civilisation proclaimed its superiority to the Asiatic civilisations that had preceded it. We may regard monogamy either in the light of our intuitive moral sentiment on the subject of chastity, or in the light of the interests of society. By the first, I understand that universal perception or conviction which I believe to be an ultimate fact in human nature, that the sensual side of our being is the lower side, and that some degree of shame may appropriately be attached to it. In its Oriental or polygamous stage, marriage is regarded almost exclusively, in its sensual aspect, as a gratification of the animal passions, while in European marriages the mutual attachment and respect of the contracting parties, the formation of a household, and the long train of domestic feelings and duties that accompany it, have all their distinguished place among

[1] In Rome, when the separation was due to the misconduct of the wife, the dowry belonged to her husband.

[2] 'Dotem non uxor marito sed uxori maritus offert.'—Tac. *Germ.* xviii. On the Morgengab, see Canciani, *Leges Barbarorum* (Venetiis, 1781), vol. i. pp. 102–104; ii. pp. 230–231. Muratori, *Antich. Ital.* diss. xx. Luitbrand enacted that no Longobard should give more than one-fourth of his substance as a Morgengab. In Gregory of Tours (ix. 20) we have an example of the gift of some cities as a Morgengab.

the motives of the contract, and the lower element has comparatively little prominence. In this way it may be intelligibly said, without any reference to utilitarian considerations, that monogamy is a higher state than polygamy. The utilitarian arguments in its defence are also extremely powerful, and may be summed up in three sentences. Nature, by making the number of males and females nearly equal, indicates it as natural. In no other form of marriage can the government of the family, which is one of the chief ends of marriage, be so happily sustained, and in no other does woman assume the position of the equal of man.

Monogamy was the general system in Greece, though there are said to have been slight and temporary deviations into the earlier system, after some great disasters, when an increase of population was ardently desired.[1] A broad line must, however, be drawn between the legendary or poetical period, as reflected in Homer and perpetuated in the tragedians, and the later historical period. It is one of the most remarkable, and to some writers one of the most perplexing facts in the moral history of Greece, that in the former and ruder period women had undoubtedly the highest place, and their type exhibited the highest perfection. Moral ideas, in a thousand forms, have been sublimated, enlarged, and changed, by advancing civilisation; but it may be fearlessly asserted that the types of female excellence which are contained in the Greek poems, while they are among the earliest, are also among the most perfect in the literature of mankind. The conjugal tenderness of Hector and Andromache; the unwearied fidelity of Penelope, awaiting through the long revolving years the return of her storm-tossed husband,

[1] See, on this point, Aul. Gellius, *Noct. Att.* xv. 20. Euripides is said to have had two wives.

who looked forward to her as to the crown of all his labours; the heroic love of Alcestis, voluntarily dying that her husband might live; the filial piety of Antigone; the majestic grandeur of the death of Polyxena; the more subdued and saintly resignation of Iphigenia, excusing with her last breath the father who had condemned her; the joyous, modest, and loving Nausicaa, whose figure shines like a perfect idyll among the tragedies of the Odyssey—all these are pictures of perennial beauty, which Rome and Christendom, chivalry and modern civilisation, have neither eclipsed nor transcended. Virgin modesty and conjugal fidelity, the graces as well as the virtues of the most perfect womanhood, have never been more exquisitely pourtrayed. The female figures stand out in the canvas almost as prominently as the male ones, and are surrounded by an almost equal reverence. The whole history of the Siege of Troy is a history of the catastrophes that followed a violation of the nuptial tie. Yet, at the same time, the position of women was in some respects a degraded one. The custom of purchase-money given to the father of the bride was general. The husbands appear to have indulged largely, and with little or no censure, in concubines.[1] Female captives of the highest rank were treated with great harshness. The inferiority of women to men was strongly asserted, and it was illustrated and defended by a very curious physiological notion, that the generative power belonged exclusively to men, women having only a very subordinate part in the production of their children.[2] The woman Pandora was said to have been the author of all human ills.

[1] Aristotle said that Homer never gives a concubine to Menelaus, in order to intimate his respect for Helen—though false. (*Athenæus*, xiii. 3.)

[2] Euripides has put this curious notion into the mouth of Apollo, in a speech in the *Eumenides*. It has, however, been very widely diffused, and may be found in Indian, Greek, Roman, and even Christian writers.

In the historical age of Greece, the legal position of women had in some respects slightly improved, but their moral condition had undergone a marked deterioration. Virtuous women lived a life of perfect seclusion. The foremost and most dazzling type of Ionic womanhood was the courtesan, and among the males, at least, the empire of passion was almost unrestricted.

The facts in moral history, which it is at once most important and most difficult to appreciate, are what may be called the facts of feeling. It is much easier to show what men did or taught than to realise the state of mind that rendered possible such actions or teaching; and in the case before us we have to deal with a condition of feeling so extremely remote from that of our own day, that the difficulty is pre-eminently great. Very sensual, and at the same time very brilliant societies, have indeed repeatedly existed, and the histories of both France and Italy afford many examples of an artistic and intellectual enthusiasm encircling those who were morally most frail; but the peculiarity of Greek sensuality is, that it grew up, for the most part, uncensured, and indeed even encouraged, under the eyes of some of the most illustrious of moralists. If we can imagine Ninon de l'Enclos at a time when the rank and splendour of Parisian society thronged her drawing-rooms, reckoning a Bossuet or a Fénelon among her followers—if we can imagine these prelates publicly advising her about the duties of her profession,

M. Legouvé, who has devoted a very curious chapter to the subject, quotes a passage from St. Thomas Aquinas, accepting it, and arguing from it, that a father should be more loved than a mother. M. Legouvé says that when the male of one animal and the female of another is crossed, the type of the female usually predominates in the offspring. See Legouvé, *Hist. morale des Femmes*, pp. 216-228; Fustel de Coulanges, *La Cité antique*, pp. 39-40; and also a curious note by Boswell, in Croker's edition of Boswell's *Life of Johnson* (1847), p. 472.

and the means of attaching the affections of her lovers, we shall have conceived a relation scarcely more strange than that which existed between Socrates and the courtesan Theodota.

In order to reconstruct, as far as possible, the modes of feeling of the Greek moralists, it will be necessary in the first place to say a few words concerning one of the most delicate, but at the same time most important, problems with which the legislator and the moralist have to deal.

It was a favourite doctrine of the Christian Fathers, that concupiscence, or the sensual passion, was 'the original sin' of human nature; and it must be owned that the progress of knowledge, which is usually extremely opposed to the ascetic theory of life, concurs with the theological view, in showing the natural force of this appetite to be far greater than the well-being of man requires. The writings of Malthus have proved what the Greek moralists appear in a considerable degree to have seen, that the normal and temperate exercise of a purely natural appetite, in the form of marriage, would produce, if universal, the utmost calamities to the world, and that, while nature seems in the most unequivocal manner to urge the human race to early marriages, the first condition of an advancing civilisation in populous countries is to restrain or diminish them. In no highly civilised society is marriage general on the first development of the passions, and the continual tendency of increasing knowledge is to render such marriages more rare. It is also an undoubted truth that, however much moralists may enforce the obligation of extra-matrimonial chastity, this obligation has never been even approximately regarded; and in all nations, ages, and religions a vast mass of irregular indulgence has appeared, which has probably contributed more than any other single cause to the misery and the degradation of man.

There are two ends which a moralist, in dealing with this question, will especially regard—the natural duty of every man doing something for the support of the child he has called into existence, and the preservation of the domestic circle unassailed and unpolluted. The family is the centre and the archetype of the State, and the happiness and goodness of society are always in a very great degree dependent upon the purity of domestic life. The essentially exclusive nature of marital affection, and the natural desire of every man to be certain of the paternity of the child he supports, render the incursions of irregular passions within the domestic circle a cause of extreme suffering. Yet it would appear as if the excessive force of these passions would render such incursions both frequent and inevitable.

Under these circumstances, there has arisen in society a figure which is certainly the most mournful, and in some respects the most awful, upon which the eye of the moralist can dwell. That unhappy being whose very name is a shame to speak; who counterfeits with a cold heart the transports of affection, and submits herself as the passive instrument of lust; who is scorned and insulted as the vilest of her sex, and doomed, for the most part, to disease and abject wretchedness and an early death, appears in every age as the perpetual symbol of the degradation and the sinfulness of man. Herself the supreme type of vice, she is ultimately the most efficient guardian of virtue. But for her, the unchallenged purity of countless happy homes would be polluted, and not a few who, in the pride of their untempted chastity, think of her with an indignant shudder, would have known the agony of remorse and of despair. On that one degraded and ignoble form are concentrated the passions that might have filled the world with shame. She remains, while creeds and civilisations rise and fall, the eternal priestess of humanity, blasted for the sins of the people.

In dealing with this unhappy being, and with all of her sex who have violated the law of chastity, the public opinion of most Christian countries pronounces a sentence of extreme severity. In the Anglo-Saxon nations especially, a single fault of this kind is sufficient, at least in the upper and middle classes, to affix an indelible brand which no time, no virtues, no penitence can wholly efface. This sentence is probably, in the first instance, simply the expression of the religious feeling on the subject, but it is also sometimes defended by powerful arguments drawn from the interests of society. It is said that the preservation of domestic purity is a matter of such transcendent importance that it is right that the most crushing penalties should be attached to an act which the imagination can easily transfigure, which legal enactments can never efficiently control, and to which the most violent passions may prompt. It is said, too, that an anathema which drives into obscurity all evidences of sensual passions is peculiarly fitted to restrict their operation; for, more than any other passions, they are dependent on the imagination, which is readily fired by the sight of evil. It is added, that the emphasis with which the vice is stigmatised produces a corresponding admiration for the opposite virtue, and that a feeling of the most delicate and scrupulous honour is thus formed among the female population, which not only preserves from gross sin, but also dignifies and ennobles the whole character.

In opposition to these views, several considerations of much weight have been urged. It is argued that, however persistently society may ignore this form of vice, it exists nevertheless, and on the most gigantic scale, and that evil rarely assumes such inveterate and perverting forms as when it is shrouded in obscurity and veiled by a hypocritical appearance of unconsciousness. The existence in England of unhappy women, sunk in the very lowest depths of vice and misery, and numbering certainly not less than fifty thousand,[1] shows sufficiently what an appalling amount of moral evil is festering uncontrolled, undiscussed, and unalleviated, under the fair surface of a decorous society. In the eyes of every physician, and indeed in the eyes of most continental writers who have adverted to the subject, no other feature of English life appears so infamous as the fact that an epidemic, which is one of the most dreadful now existing among mankind, which communicates itself from the guilty husband to the innocent wife, and even transmits its taint to her offspring, and which the experience of other nations conclusively proves may be vastly diminished, should be suffered to rage unchecked because the legislature refuses to take official cognisance of its existence, or proper sanitary measures for its repression.[2] If the terrible censure which English public opinion passes upon every instance of female frailty in some degree diminishes their number, it does not prevent them from being extremely

[1] Dr. Vintras, in a remarkable pamphlet (London, 1867) *On the Repression of Prostitution,* shows from the police statistics that the number of prostitutes *known to the police* in England and Wales, in 1864, was 49,370; and this is certainly much below the entire number. These, it will be observed, comprise only the habitual, professional prostitutes.

[2] Some measures have recently been taken in a few garrison towns. The moral sentiment of the community, it appears, would be shocked if Liverpool were treated on the same principles as Portsmouth. This very painful and revolting, but most important subject of prostitution, has been treated with great knowledge, impartiality, and ability, by Parent-Duchâtelet, in his famous work *La Prostitution dans la ville de Paris.* The third edition contains very copious supplementary accounts, furnished by different doctors in different countries.

numerous, and it immeasurably aggravates the suffering they produce. Acts which in other European countries would excite only a slight and transient emotion, spread in England, over a wide circle, all the bitterness of unmitigated anguish. Acts which naturally neither imply nor produce a total subversion of the moral feelings, and which, in other countries, are often followed by happy, virtuous, and affectionate lives, in England almost invariably lead to absolute ruin. Infanticide is greatly multiplied, and a vast proportion of those whose reputations and lives have been blasted by one momentary sin, are hurled into the abyss of habitual prostitution—a condition which, owing to the sentence of public opinion and the neglect of legislators, is in no other European country so hopelessly vicious or so irrevocable.[1]

It is added, too, that the immense multitude who are thus doomed to the extremity of life-long wretchedness are not always, perhaps not generally, of those whose dispositions seem naturally incapable of virtue. The victims of seduction are often led aside quite as much by the ardour of their affections, and by the vivacity of their intelligence, as by any vicious propensities.[2] Even in the lowest grades, the most dispassionate observers have detected remains of higher feelings, which, in a different

[1] Parent-Duchâtelet has given many statistics, showing the very large extent to which the French system of supervision deters those who were about to enter into prostitution, and reclaims those who had entered into it. He and Dr. Vintras concur in representing English prostitution as about the most degraded, and at the same time the most irrevocable.

[2] Miss Mulock, in her amiable but rather feeble book, called *A Woman's Thoughts about Women,* has some good remarks on this point (pp. 291–293), which are all the more valuable, as the authoress has not the faintest sympathy with any opinions concerning the character and position of women which are not strictly conventional. She notices the experience of Sunday School mistresses, that, of their pupils who are seduced, an extremely large proportion are 'of the very best, refined, intelligent, truthful, and affectionate.'

moral atmosphere, and under different moral husbandry, would have undoubtedly been developed.[1] The statistics of prostitution show that a great proportion of those who have fallen into it have been impelled by the most extreme poverty, in many instances verging upon starvation.[2]

These opposing considerations, which I have very briefly indicated, and which I do not propose to discuss or to estimate, will be sufficient to exhibit the magnitude of the problem. In the Greek civilisation, legislators and moralists endeavoured to meet it by the cordial recognition of two distinct orders of womanhood[3]—the wife, whose first duty was fidelity to her husband; the hetæra, or mistress, who subsisted by her fugitive attachments. The wives of the Greeks lived in almost absolute seclusion. They were usually married when very young. Their

[1] See the very singular and painful chapter in Parent-Duchâtelet, called 'Mœurs et Habitudes des Prostituées.' He observes that they are remarkable for their kindness to one another in sickness or in distress; that they are not unfrequently charitable to poor people who do not belong to their class; that when one of them has a child, it becomes the object of very general interest and affection; that most of them have lovers, to whom they are sincerely attached; that they rarely fail to show in the hospitals a very real sense of shame; and that many of them entered into their mode of life for the purpose of supporting aged parents. One anecdote is worth giving in the words of the author: 'Un médecin n'entrant jamais dans leurs salles sans ôter légèrement son chapeau, par cette seule politesse il sut tellement conquérir leur confiance qu'il leur faisait faire tout ce qu'il voulait.' This writer, I may observe, is not a romance writer or a theorist of any description. He is simply a physician who describes the results of a very large official experience.

[2] 'Parent-Duchâtelet atteste que sur trois mille créatures perdues trente-cinq seulement avaient un état qui pouvait les nourrir, et que quatorze cents avaient été précipitées dans cette horrible vie par la misère. Une d'elles, quand elle s'y résolut, n'avait pas mangé depuis trois jours.'—Legouvé, *Hist. morale des Femmes*, pp. 322-323.

[3] Concerning the position and character of Greek women the reader may obtain ample information by consulting Becker's *Charicles* (translated by Metcalfe, 1845). Rainneville, *La Femme dans l'Antiquité* (Paris, 1865); and an article 'On Female Society in Greece,' in the twenty-second volume of the *Quarterly Review*.

occupations were to weave, to spin, to embroider, to superintend the household, to care for their sick slaves. They lived in a special and retired part of the house. The more wealthy seldom went abroad, and never except when accompanied by a female slave; never attended the public spectacles; received no male visitors except in the presence of their husbands, and had not even a seat at their own tables when male guests were there. Their pre-eminent virtue was fidelity, and it is probable that this was very strictly and very generally observed. Their remarkable freedom from temptations, the public opinion which strongly discouraged any attempt to seduce them, and the ample sphere for illicit pleasures that was accorded to the other sex, all contributed to protect it. On the other hand, living as they did, almost exclusively among their female slaves, deprived of all the educating influence of male society, and having no place at those public spectacles which were the chief means of Athenian culture, their minds must necessarily have been exceedingly contracted. Thucydides doubtless expressed the prevailing sentiment of his countrymen when he said that the highest merit of woman is not to be spoken of either for good or for evil, and Phidias illustrated the same feeling when he represented the heavenly Aphrodite standing on a tortoise, typifying thereby the secluded life of a virtuous woman.[1]

In their own restricted sphere their lives were probably not unhappy. Education and custom rendered the purely domestic life that was assigned to them a second nature, and it must in most instances have reconciled them to the extra-matrimonial connections in which their husbands too frequently indulged. The prevailing manners

[1] Plutarch, *Conj. Præc.*

were very gentle. Domestic oppression is scarcely ever spoken of; the husband lived chiefly in the Public place; causes of jealousy and of dissension could seldom occur, and a feeling of warm affection, though not a feeling of equality, must doubtless have in most cases spontaneously arisen. In the writings of Xenophon we have a charming picture of a husband who had received into his arms his young wife of fifteen, absolutely ignorant of the world and of its ways. He speaks to her with extreme kindness, but in the language that would be used to a little child. Her task, he tells her, is to be like a queen bee, dwelling continually at home and superintending the work of her slaves. She must distribute to each their tasks, must economise the family income, and must take especial care that the house is strictly orderly—the shoes, the pots, and the clothes always in their places. It is also, he tells her, a part of her duty to tend her sick slaves; but here his wife interrupted him, exclaiming, 'Nay, but that will indeed be the most agreeable of my offices, if such as I treat with kindness are likely to be grateful, and to love me more than before.' With a very tender and delicate care to avoid everything resembling a reproach, the husband persuades his wife to give up the habits of wearing high-heeled boots, in order to appear tall, and of colouring her face with vermilion and white lead. He promises her that if she faithfully performs her duties he will himself be the first and most devoted of her slaves. He assured Socrates that when any domestic dispute arose he could extricate himself admirably, if he was in the right; but that, whenever he was in the wrong, he found it impossible to convince his wife that it was otherwise.[1]

[1] Xenophon, *Econ.* ii.

We have another picture of Greek married life in the writings of Plutarch, but it represents the condition of the Greek mind at a later period than that of Xenophon. In Plutarch the wife is represented not as the mere housekeeper, or as the chief slave of her husband, but as his equal and his companion. He enforces, in the strongest terms, reciprocity of obligations, and desires that the minds of women should be cultivated to the highest point.[1] His precepts of marriage, indeed, fall little if at all below any that have appeared in modern days. His letter of consolation to his wife, on the death of their child, breathes a spirit of the tenderest affection. It is recorded of him that, having had some dispute with the relations of his wife, she feared that it might impair their domestic happiness, and she accordingly persuaded her husband to accompany her on a pilgrimage to Mount Helicon, where they offered up together a sacrifice to Love, and prayed that their affection for one another might never be diminished.

In general, however, the position of the virtuous Greek woman was a very low one. She was under a perpetual tutelage: first of all to her parents, who disposed of her hand, then to her husband, and in her days of widowhood to her sons. In cases of inheritance her male relations were preferred to her. The privilege of divorce, which she possessed equally with her husband, appears to have been practically almost nugatory, on account of the shock which public declarations in the law court gave to the habits which education and public opinion had formed. She brought with her, however, a dowry, and the recognised necessity of endowing daughters was one of the causes of those frequent expositions which were perpetrated with so little blame. The Athenian law was also

[1] Plut. *Conj. Præc.* There is also an extremely beautiful picture of the character of a good wife in Aristotle. (*Economics*, book i. cap. vii.)

peculiarly careful and tender in dealing with the interests of female orphans.[1] Plato had argued that women were equal to men; but the habits of the people were totally opposed to this theory. Marriage was regarded chiefly in a civic light, as a means of producing citizens, and in Sparta it was ordered that old or infirm husbands should cede their young wives to stronger men, who could produce vigorous soldiers for the State. The Lacedemonian treatment of women, which differed in many respects from that which prevailed in the other Greek States, while it was utterly destructive of all delicacy of feeling or action, had undoubtedly the effect of producing a fierce and masculine patriotism; and many fine examples are recorded of Spartan mothers devoting their sons on the altar of their country, rejoicing over their deaths when nobly won, and infusing their own heroic spirit into the armies of the people. For the most part, however, the names of virtuous women scarcely appear in Greek history. The simple modesty which was evinced by Phocion's wife, in the period when her husband occupied the foremost position in Athens,[2] and a few instances of conjugal and filial affection, have been recorded; but in general the only women who attracted the notice of the people were the hetæræ, or courtesans.[3]

In order to understand the position which these last

[1] See Alexander's *History of Women* (London, 1783), vol. i. p. 201.

[2] Plutarch, *Phocion.*

[3] Our information concerning the Greek courtesans is chiefly derived from the thirteenth book of the *Deipnosophists* of Athenæus, from the *Letters* of Alciphron, from the *Dialogues* of Lucian on courtesans, and from the oration of Demosthenes against Neæra. See, too, Xenophon, *Memorabilia*, iii. 11; and among modern books, Becker's *Charicles.* Athenæus was an Egyptian whose exact date was unknown, but who appears to have survived Ulpian, who died in A.D. 228. He had access to, and gave extracts from, many works on this subject, which have now perished. Alciphron is believed to have lived near the time of Lucian.

assumed in Greek life, we must transport ourselves in thought into a moral latitude totally different from our own. The Greek conception of excellence was the full and perfect development of humanity in all its organs and functions, and without any tinge of asceticism. Some parts of human nature were recognised as higher than others; and to suffer any of the lower appetites to obscure the mind, restrain the will and engross the life, was acknowledged to be disgraceful; but the systematic repression of a natural appetite was totally foreign to Greek modes of thought. Legislators, moralists, and the general voice of the people, appear to have applied these principles almost unreservedly to intercourse between the sexes, and the most virtuous men habitually and openly entered into relations which would now be almost universally censured.

The experience, however, of many societies has shown that a public opinion may accord, in this respect, almost unlimited license to one sex, without showing any corresponding indulgence to the other. But in Greece, a concurrence of causes had conspired to bring a certain section of courtesans into a position they have in no other society attained. The voluptuous worship of Aphrodite gave a kind of religious sanction to their profession. Courtesans were the priestesses in her temples, and those of Corinth were believed by their prayers to have averted calamities from their city. Prostitution is said to have entered into the religious rites of Babylon, Biblis, Cyprus, and Corinth, and these, as well as Miletus, Tenedos, Lesbos, and Abydos became famous for their schools of vice, which grew up under the shadow of the temples.[1]

[1] La Mothe le Vayer says that some of the Latins derived venerari from Venerem exercere, on account of the devotions in the temple of Venus (*Letter* xc.)—a very strange derivation.

In the next place, the intense æsthetic enthusiasm that prevailed, was eminently fitted to raise the most beautiful to honour. In a land and beneath a sky where natural beauty developed to the highest point, there arose a school of matchless artists both in painting and in sculpture, and public games and contests were celebrated, in which supreme physical perfection was crowned by an assembled people. In no other period of the world's history was the admiration of beauty in all its forms so passionate or so universal. It coloured the whole moral teaching of the time, and led the chief moralists to regard virtue simply as the highest kind of supersensual beauty. It appeared in all literature, where the beauty of form and style was the first of studies. It supplied at once the inspiration and the rule of all Greek art. It led the Greek wife to pray, before all other prayers, for the beauty of her children. It surrounded the most beautiful with an aureole of admiring reverence. The courtesan was commonly the queen of beauty. She was the model of the statues of Aphrodite, that commanded the admiration of Greece. Praxiteles was acccustomed to reproduce the form of Phryne, and her statue, carved in gold, stood in the temple of Apollo at Delphi; and when she was accused of corrupting the youth of Athens, her advocate, Hyperides, procured her acquittal by suddenly unveiling her charms before the dazzled eyes of the assembled judges. Apelles was at once the painter and the lover of Laïs, and Alexander gave him, as the choicest gift, his own favourite concubine, of whom the painter had become enamoured while pourtraying her. The chief flower-painter of antiquity acquired his skill through his love of the flower-girl Glycera, whom he was accustomed to paint among her garlands. Pindar and Simonides sang the praises of courtesans, and grave philosophers made pilgrimages to visit them, and their names were known in every city.[1]

It is not surprising that, in such a state of thought and feeling, many of the more ambitious and accomplished women should have betaken themselves to this career, nor yet that they should have attained the social position which the secluded existence and the enforced ignorance of the Greek wives had left vacant. The courtesan was the one free woman of Athens, and she often availed herself of her freedom to acquire a degree of knowledge which enabled her to add to her other charms an intense intellectual fascination. Gathering around her the most brilliant artists, poets, historians, and philosophers, she flung herself unreservedly into the intellectual and æsthetic enthusiasms of her time, and soon became the centre of a literary society of matchless splendour. Aspasia, who was as famous for her genius as for her beauty, won the passionate love of Pericles. She is said to have instructed him in eloquence, and to have composed some of his most famous orations, she was continually consulted on affairs of state; and Socrates, like other philosophers, attended her assemblies. Socrates himself has owned his deep obligations to the instructions of a courtesan named Diotima. The courtesan Leontium was among the most ardent disciples of Epicurus.[2]

Another cause probably contributed indirectly to the

[1] On the connection of the courtesans with the artistic enthusiasm, see Raoul Rochette, *Cours d'Archéologie*, pp. 278–279. See, too, Athenæus, xiii. 59; Pliny, *Hist. Nat.* xxxv. 40.

[2] See the very curious little work of Ménage, *Historia Mulierum Philosopharum* (Lugduni, MDXC.); also Rainneville, *La Femme dans l'Antiquité*, p. 244. At a much later date Lucian, in one of his works, gives a most fascinating description of the beauty, accomplishments, generosity, and even modesty, of Panthea of Smyrna, the favourite mistress of Lucius Verus.

elevation of this class, to which it is extremely difficult to allude in an English book, but which it is impossible altogether to omit, even in the most cursory survey of Greek morals. Irregular female connections were looked upon as ordinary and not disgraceful incidents in the life of a good man, for the more sensual spirits, and indeed very many of the most illustrious men in Greece, sank into that lower abyss of unnatural love, which was the deepest and strangest taint of Greek civilisation. This vice, which never appears in the writings of Homer and Hesiod, doubtless arose under the influence of the public games, which, accustoming men to the contemplation of absolutely nude figures,[1] awoke an unnatural passion,[2] totally remote from all modern feelings, but which in Greece it was regarded as heroic to resist.[3] The popular religion in this, as in other cases, was made to bend to the new vice. Hebe, the cup-bearer of the gods, was replaced by Ganymede, and

[1] A single small garment, called the ζῶσμα, was at first in use; but it was discarded, first of all by the Lacedemonians, and afterwards by the other Greeks. There are three curious memoirs tracing the history of the change, by M. Burette, in the *Hist. de l'Académie royale des Inscriptions*, tome i.

[2] On the causes of paiderastia in Greece, see the remarks of Mr. Grote in the review of the *Symposium*, in his great work on Plato. The whole subject is very ably treated by M. Maury, *Hist. des Religions de la Grèce antique*, tome iii. pp. 35–39. Many facts connected with it are collected by Döllinger, in his *Jew and Gentile*, and by Chateaubriand, in his *Études historiques*. The chief original authority for this, or for all other forms of Greek sensual vice, is the thirteenth book of Athenæus, a book of very painful interest in the history of morals.

[3] Plutarch, in his *Life of Agesilaus*, gives us a vivid picture of the intense self-control manifested by that great man, in refraining from gratifying a passion he had conceived for a boy named Megabetes, which Maximus Tyrius says deserved greater praise than the heroism of Leonidas. (*Diss.* xxv.) Diogenes Laërtius, in his *Life of Zeno*, the founder of Stoicism, the most austere of all ancient sects, praises that philosopher for being but little addicted to this vice.

the worst vices of earth were transported to Olympus.[1] Artists sought to reflect the passion in their statues of the Hermaphrodite, of Bacchus, and the more effeminate Apollo; moralists were known to praise it as the bond of friendship, and it was spoken of as the inspiring enthusiasm of the heroic Theban legion of Epaminondas.[2] In general, however, it was stigmatised as unquestionably a vice, but it was treated with a levity we can now hardly conceive. We can scarcely have a better illustration of the extent to which moral ideas and feelings have changed, than the fact that the two first Greeks who were considered worthy of statues by their fellow-countrymen, are said to have been Harmodius and Aristogeiton, who were united by an impure love, and who were glorified for a political assassination.[3]

It is probable that this cause conspired with the others to dissociate the class of courtesans from the idea of supreme depravity with which they have usually been connected. The great majority, however, were sunk in this, as in all other ages, in abject degradation,[4] comparatively few attained the condition of hetæræ, and even of these, it is probable that the greater number

[1] Some examples of the ascription of this vice to the divinities are given by Clem. Alex. *Admonitio ad Gentes.* Socrates is said to have maintained that Jupiter loved Ganymede for his wisdom, as his name is derived from γάνυμαι and μῆδος, to be delighted with prudence. (Xenophon, *Banquet.*) The disaster of Cannæ was ascribed to the jealousy of Juno because a beautiful boy was introduced into the temple of Jupiter. (Lactantius, *Inst. Div.* ii. 17.)

[2] See a curious passage in Athenæus, xiii. 78. It is elaborately vindicated in a very revolting book on different kinds of love, ascribed (it is said falsely) to Lucian. Sophocles was especially noted for his propensity to it.

[3] Pliny, *Hist. Nat.* xxxiv. 9.

[4] There is ample evidence of this in Athenæus, and in the Dialogues of Lucian on the courtesans. See, too, Terence, *The Eunuch,* act v. scene 4, which is copied from the Greek. The majority of the class were not called hetæræ, but πόρναι.

exhibited the characteristics which in all ages have attached to their class. Faithlessness, extreme rapacity, and extravagant luxury, were common among them; but yet it is unquestionable that there were many exceptions. The excommunication of society did not press upon or degrade them; and though they were never regarded with the same honour as married women, it seems generally to have been believed that the wife and the courtesan had each her place and her function in the world, and her own peculiar type of excellence. The courtesan Leæna, who was a friend of Harmodius, died in torture rather than reveal the conspiracy of her friend, and the Athenians, in allusion to her name, caused the statue of a tongueless lioness to be erected to commemorate her constancy.[1] The gentle manners and disinterested affection of a courtesan named Bacchis were especially recorded, and a very touching letter paints her character, and describes the regret that followed her to the tomb.[2] In one of the most remarkable of his pictures of Greek life, Xenophon describes how Socrates, having heard of the beauty of the courtesan Theodota, went with his disciples to ascertain for himself whether the report was true; how with a quiet humour he questioned her about the sources of the luxury of her dwelling, and how he proceeded to sketch for her the qualities she should cultivate in order to attach her lovers. She ought, he tells her, to shut the door against the insolent, to watch

[1] Plutarch, *De Garrulitate*; Plin. *Hist. Nat.* xxxiv. 19. The feat of biting out their tongues rather than reveal secrets, or yield to passion, is ascribed to a suspiciously large number of persons. Ménage cites five besides Leæna. (*Hist. Mulier. Philos.* pp. 104–108.)

[2] See, upon Bacchis, several of the letters of Alciphron, especially the very touching letter (x.) on her death, describing her kindness and disinterestedness. Athenæus (xiii. 66) relates a curious anecdote illustrating these aspects of her character.

her lovers in sickness, to rejoice greatly when they succeed in anything honourable, to love tenderly those who love her. Having carried on a cheerful and perfectly unembarrassed conversation with her, with no kind of reproach on his part, either expressed or implied, and with no trace either of the timidity or effrontery of conscious guilt upon hers, the best and wisest of the Greeks left his hostess with a graceful compliment to her beauty.[1]

My task in describing this aspect of Greek life has been an eminently unpleasing one, and I should certainly not have entered upon even the baldest and most guarded disquisition on a subject so difficult, painful, and delicate, had it not been absolutely indispensable to a history of morals to give at least an outline of the progress that has been effected in this sphere. What I have written will sufficiently explain why Greece, which was fertile, probably beyond all other lands, in great men, was so remarkably barren of great women. It will show, too, that though chastity and sensuality were regarded, as among ourselves, as respectively the higher and the lower sides of our nature, the degree of license which it was thought advisable to accord to the latter was widely different from what modern public opinion would sanction. The Christian doctrine, that it is criminal to gratify a powerful and a transient physical appetite, except under the condition of a lifelong contract, was altogether unknown. Strict duties were imposed upon Greek wives. Duties were imposed at a later period, though less strictly, upon the husband. Unnatural love was stigmatised, but with a levity of censure which to a modern mind appears inexpressibly revolting. Some slight legal disqualifications rested upon the whole class of hetæræ, and, though

[1] Xenophon, *Memorab.* iii. 11.

more admired, they were less respected than women who had adopted a domestic life; but a combination of circumstances had raised them, in actual worth and in popular estimation, to an unexampled elevation, and an aversion to marriage became very general, and illicit connections were formed with the most perfect frankness and publicity.

If we now turn to the Roman civilisation, we shall find that some important advances had been made in the condition of women. The virtue of chastity may, as I have shown, be regarded with justice in two different ways. The utilitarian view, which commonly prevails in countries where a political spirit is more powerful than a religious spirit, regards marriage as the ideal state, and to promote the happiness, sanctity, and security of this state is the main object of all its precepts. The mystical view which rests upon the feeling of shame that is naturally attached to sensual indulgences, and which, as history proves, has prevailed especially where political sentiment is very low and religious sentiment very strong, regards virginity as its supreme type, and marriage as simply the most pardonable declension from ideal purity. It is, I think, a very remarkable fact, that at the head of the religious system of Rome we find two sacerdotal bodies which appear respectively to typify these ideas. The Flamens of Jupiter and the Vestal Virgins were the two most sacred orders in Rome. The ministrations of each were believed to be vitally important to the State. Each could officiate only within the walls of Rome. Each was appointed with the most imposing ceremonies. Each was honoured with the most profound reverence. But in one important respect they differed. The Vestal was the type of virginity, and her chastity was guarded by the most terrific penalties. The

Flamen, on the other hand, was the representative of Roman marriage in its strictest and purest form. He was necessarily married. His marriage was celebrated with the most solemn rites. It could only be dissolved by death. If his wife died, he was degraded from his office.[1]

Of these two orders, there can be no question that the Flamen was the most faithful expression of the Roman society. The Roman religion was essentially domestic, and it was a main object of the legislator to surround marriage with every circumstance of dignity and solemnity. Monogamy was, from the earliest times, strictly enjoined, and it was one of the great benefits that have resulted from the expansion of Roman power, that it made this type dominant in Europe. In the legends of early Rome we have ample evidence both of the high moral estimate of women, and of their prominence in Roman life. The tragedies of Lucretia and of Virginia display a delicacy of honour, a sense of the supreme excellence of unsullied purity, which no Christian nation could surpass. The legends of the Sabine women interceding between their parents and their husbands, and thus saving the infant republic, and of the mother of Coriolanus averting by her prayers the ruin impending over her country, entitled women to claim their share in the patriotic glories of Rome. Temples were even erected to commemorate their acts. A temple of Venus Calva was the record of the devotion of Roman ladies, who, in an hour of danger, cut off their long tresses to make bowstrings for the soldiers.[2] Another temple preserved to all posterity the memory of the filial piety of that Roman girl who, when her mother was condemned to be starved to death, ob-

[1] On the Flamens, see Aulus Gell. *Noct.* x. 15.

[2] Capitolinus, *Maximinus Junior.*

tained permission to visit her in prison, and was discovered feeding her from her breast.[1]

The legal position, however, of the Roman wife was for a long period extremely low. The Roman family was constituted on the principle of the absolute authority of its head, who had a power of life and death both over his wife and over his children, and who could repudiate the former at will. Neither the custom of gifts to the father of the bride, nor the custom of dowries appears to have existed in the earliest period of Roman history; but the father disposed absolutely of the hand of his daughter, and sometimes even possessed the power of breaking off marriages that had been actually contracted.[2] In the forms of marriage, however, which were usual in the earlier periods of Rome, the absolute power passed into the hands of the husband, and he had the right, in some cases, of putting her to death.[3] Law and public opinion combined in making matrimonial purity most strict. For five hundred and twenty years, it was said, there was no such thing as a divorce in Rome,[4] and even after this example, for many years the marriage tie was regarded as absolutely indissoluble.[5] Manners were so severe, that a senator was censured for indecency because he had kissed his wife in the presence of their daughter.[6] It was considered in a high degree disgraceful for a Roman mother to delegate to

[1] Pliny, *Hist. Nat.* vii. 36.

[2] This appears from the first act of the *Stichus* of Plautus. I should imagine this cannot have applied to the marriage of confarreatio. The power appears to have become quite obsolete during the empire, but the first legal act (which was rather of the nature of an exhortation than of a command) against it was issued by Antoninus Pius, and it was only definitely abolished under Diocletian. (Laboulaye, *Recherches sur la condition civile et politique des femmes*, pp. 16–17.)

[3] Aul. Gell. *Noct.* x. 23.

[4] Val. Maximus, ii. 1. § 4; Aul. Gellius, *Noct.* iv. 3.

[5] This is noticed by Plautus.

[6] Ammianus Marcellinus, xxviii. 4.

a nurse the duty of suckling her child.[1] Sumptuary laws regulated with the most minute severity all the details of domestic economy.[2] The courtesan class, though probably numerous and certainly uncontrolled, were regarded with much contempt. The disgrace of publicly professing themselves members of it was believed to be a sufficient punishment,[3] and an old law, which was probably intended to teach in symbol the duties of married life, enjoined that no such person should touch the altar of Juno.[4] It was related of a certain ædile, that he failed to obtain redress for an assault which had been made upon him, because it had occurred in a house of ill-fame, in which it was disgraceful for a Roman magistrate to be found.[5] The sanctity of female purity was believed to be attested by all nature. The most savage animals became tame before a virgin.[6] When a woman walked naked round a field, caterpillars and all loathsome insects fell dead before her.[7] It was said that drowned men floated on their backs, and drowned women on their faces; and this, in the opinion of Roman naturalists, was due to the superior purity of the latter.[8]

It was a remark of Aristotle, that the superiority of the Greeks to the barbarians was shown, amongst other things, in the fact that the Greeks did not, like other nations, regard their wives as slaves, but treated them as helpmates and companions. A Roman writer has appealed,

[1] Tacitus, *De Oratoribus*, xxviii. [2] See Aulus Gellius, *Noct.* ii. 24.

[3] 'More inter veteres recepto, qui satis pœnarum adversum impudicas in ipsa professione flagitii credebant.'—Tacitus, *Annal.* ii. 85.

[4] Aul. Gell. iv. 3. Juno was the goddess of marriage.

[5] Ibid. iv. 14.

[6] The well-known superstition about the lion, &c., becoming docile before a virgin is, I believe, as old as Roman times. St. Isidore mentions that rhinoceroses were believed to be captured by young girls being put in their way to fascinate them. (Legendre, *Traité de l'Opinion*, tome ii p. 35.)

[7] Pliny, *Hist. Nat.* xxviii. 23. [8] Ibid. vii. 18.

on the whole with greater justice, to the treatment of wives by his fellow countrymen, as a proof of the superiority of Roman to Greek civilisation. He has observed that, while the Greeks kept their wives in a special quarter in the interior of their houses, and never permitted them to sit at banquets except with their relatives, or to see any male except in the presence of a relative, no Roman ever hesitated to lead his wife with him to the feast, or to place the mother of the family at the head of his table.[1] Whether, in the period when wives were completely subject to the rule of their husbands, much domestic oppression occurred, it is now impossible to say. A temple dedicated to a goddess named Viriplaca, whose mission was to appease husbands, was worshipped by Roman women on the Palatine,[2] and a strange and improbable, if not incredible story, is related by Livy, of the discovery, during the Republic, of a vast conspiracy by Roman wives to poison their husbands.[3] On the whole, however, it is probable that the Roman matron was from the earliest period a name of honour;[4] that the beautiful sentence of a jurisconsult of the empire, who defined marriage as a lifelong fellowship of all divine and human rights,[5] expressed most faithfully the feelings of the people, and that female virtue shone in every age conspicuously in Roman biographies.[6]

[1] 'Quem enim Romanorum pudet uxorem ducere in convivium? aut cujus materfamilias non primum locum tenet ædium, atque in celebritate versatur? quod multo fit aliter in Græcia. Nam neque in convivium adhibetur, nisi propinquorum, neque sedet nisi in interiore parte ædium quæ *gynæcontis* appellatur, quo nemo accedit, nisi propinqua cognatione conjunctus.'—Corn. Nepos, præfat.

[2] Val. Max. ii. 1. § 6.

[3] Liv. viii. 18.

[4] See Val. Max. ii. 1.

[5] 'Nuptiæ sunt conjunctio maris et feminæ, et consortium omnis vitæ divini et humani juris communicatio.'—Modestinus.

[6] Livy xxxiv. 5. There is a fine collection of legends or histories of heroic women (but chiefly Greek) in Clem. Alexand. *Strom.* iv. 19.

I have already enumerated the chief causes of that complete dissolution of Roman morals which began shortly after the Punic wars, which contributed very largely to the destruction of the Republic, and which attained its climax under the Cæsars. There are few examples in history of a revolution pervading so completely every sphere of religious, domestic, social, and political life. Philosophical scepticism corroded the ancient religions. An inundation of Eastern luxury and Eastern morals submerged all the old habits of austere simplicity. The civil wars and the empire degraded the character of the people, and the exaggerated prudery of republican manners only served to make the rebound into vice the more irresistible. In the fierce outburst of ungovernable and almost frantic depravity that marked this evil period, the violations of female virtue were infamously prominent. The vast multiplication of slaves, which is in every age peculiarly fatal to moral purity; the fact that a great proportion of those slaves were chosen from the most voluptuous provinces of the empire; the games of Flora, in which races of naked courtesans were exhibited; the pantomimes, which derived their charms chiefly from the audacious indecencies of the actors; the influx of the Greek and Asiatic hetæræ who were attracted by the wealth of the metropolis; the licentious paintings which began to adorn every house; the rise of Baiæ, which rivalled the luxury and surpassed the beauty of the chief centres of Asiatic vice, combining with the intoxication of great wealth suddenly acquired, with the disruption, through many causes, of all the ancient habits and beliefs, and with the tendency to pleasure which the closing of the paths of honourable political ambition, by the imperial despotism, naturally produced, had all their part in preparing those orgies of vice which the writers of the empire reveal.

Most scholars will, I suppose, retain a vivid recollection of the new insight into the extent and wildness of human guilt which they obtained when they first opened the pages of Suetonius or Lampridius; and the sixth Satire of Juvenal paints with a fierce energy, though probably with the natural exaggeration of a satirist, the extent to which corruption had spread among the women. It was found necessary, under Tiberius, to make a special law prohibiting members of noble houses from enrolling themselves as prostitutes.[1] The extreme coarseness of the Roman disposition prevented sensuality from assuming that æsthetic character which had made it in Greece the parent of Art, and had very profoundly modified its influence, while the passion for gladiatorial shows often allied it somewhat unnaturally with cruelty. There have certainly been many periods in history when virtue was more rare than under the Cæsars; but there has probably never been a period when vice was more extravagant or uncontrolled. Young emperors especially, who were surrounded by swarms of sycophants and pandars, and who often lived in continual dread of assassination, plunged with the most reckless and feverish excitement into every variety of abnormal lust. The reticence which has always more or less characterised modern society and modern writers was unknown, and the unblushing, undisguised obscenity of the Epigrams of Martial, of the Romances of Apuleius and Petronius, and of some of the Dialogues of Lucian, reflected but too faithfully the spirit of their time.

There had arisen, too, partly through vicious causes, and partly, I suppose, through the unfavourable influence which the attraction of the public institutions exercised on

[1] Tacitus, *Annal.* ii. 85. This decree was on account of a patrician lady named Vistilia having so enrolled herself.

domestic life, a great and general indisposition towards marriage, which Augustus attempted in vain to arrest by his laws against celibacy, and by conferring many privileges on the fathers of three children.[1] A singularly curious speech is preserved, which is said to have been delivered on this subject shortly before the close of the Republic, by Metellus Numidicus, in order, if possible, to overcome this indisposition. 'If, Romans,' he said, 'we could live without wives, we should all keep free from that source of trouble; but since nature has ordained that men can neither live sufficiently agreeably with wives, nor at all without them, let us consult the perpetual endurance of our race rather than our own brief enjoyment.'[2]

In the midst of this torrent of corruption a great change was passing over the legal position of Roman women. They had at first been in a condition of absolute subjection or subordination to their relations. They arrived, during the empire, at a point of freedom and dignity which they subsequently lost, and have never altogether regained. The Romans admitted three kinds of marriage—the 'confarreatio,' which was accompanied by the most awful religious ceremonies, was practically indissoluble, and was jealously restricted to patricians; the coemptio,' which was purely civil, which derived its name

[1] Dion Cassius, liv. 16, lvi. 10.

[2] 'Si sine uxore possemus, Quirites, esse, omnes ea molestia careremus; sed quoniam ita natura tradidit, ut nec cum illis satis commode nec sine illis ullo modo vivi possit, saluti perpetuæ potius quam brevi voluptati consulendum.'—Aulus Gellius, *Noct.* i. 6. Some of the audience, we are told, thought that, in exhorting to matrimony, the speaker should have concealed its undoubted evils. It was decided, however, that it was more honourable to tell the whole truth. Stobæus (*Sententiæ*) has preserved a number of harsh and often heartless sayings about wives, that were popular among the Greeks. It was a saying of a Greek poet, that 'marriage brings only two happy days—the day when the husband first clasps his wife to his breast, and the day when he lays her in the tomb;' and in Rome it became a proverbial saying, that a wife was only good 'in thalamo vel in tumulo.'

from a symbolical sale, and which, like the preceding form, gave the husband complete authority over the person and property of his wife; and the 'usus,' which was effected by a simple declaration of a determination to cohabit. This last form of marriage became general in the empire, and it had this very important consequence, that the woman so married remained, in the eyes of the law, in the family of her father, and was under his guardianship, not under the guardianship of her husband. But the old patria potestas had become completely obsolete, and the practical effect of the general adoption of this form of marriage was the absolute legal independence of the wife. With the exception of her dowry, which passed into the hands of her husband, she held her property in her own right; she inherited her share of the wealth of her father, and she retained it altogether independently of her husband. A very considerable portion of Roman wealth thus passed into the uncontrolled possession of women. The private man of business of the wife was a favourite character in the comedians, and the tyranny exercised by rich wives over their husbands—to whom it is said they sometimes lent money at high interest—a continual theme of satirists.[1]

A complete revolution had thus passed over the constitution of the family. Instead of being constructed on the principle of autocracy, it was constructed on the principle of coequal partnership. The legal position of the wife had become one of complete independence, while her social position was one of great dignity. The more

[1] Friedländer, *Hist. des Mœurs romaines,* tome i. pp. 360-364. On the great influence exercised by Roman ladies on political affairs some remarkable passages are collected in Denis, *Hist. des Idées Morales,* tome ii. pp. 98-99. This author is particularly valuable in all that relates to the history of domestic morals. The *Asinarius* of Plautus, and some of the epigrams of Martial, throw much light upon this subject.

conservative spirits were naturally alarmed at the change, and two measures were taken to arrest it. The Oppian law was designed to restrain the luxury of women; but, in spite of the strenuous exertions of Cato, this law was speedily repealed.[1] A more important measure was the Voconian law, which restricted within certain very narrow limits the property which women might inherit; but public opinion never fully acquiesced in it, and by several legal subterfuges its operation was partially evaded.[2]

Another and a still more important consequence resulted from the changed form of marriage. Being looked upon simply as a civil contract, entered into for the happiness of the contracting parties, its continuance depended upon mutual consent. Either party might dissolve it at will, and the dissolution gave both parties a right to remarry. There can be no question that under this system the obligations of marriage were treated with extreme levity. We find Cicero repudiating his wife Terentia, because he desired a new dowry;[3] Augustus compelling the husband of Livia to repudiate her when she was already pregnant, that he might marry her himself;[4] Cato ceding his wife, with the consent of her father, to his friend Hortensius, and resuming her after his death;[5] Mæcenas continually changing his wife;[6] Sempronius Sophus repudiating his wife, because she had

[1] See the very remarkable discussion about this repeal in Livy, lib. xxxiv. cap. 1–8.

[2] Legouvé, *Hist. Morale des Femmes*, pp. 23–26. St. Augustine denounced this law as the most unjust that could be mentioned or even conceived. 'Qua lege quid iniquius dici aut cogitari possit, ignoro.'—St. Aug. *De Civ. Dei*, iii. 21—a curious illustration of the difference between the habits of thought of his time and those of the middle ages, when daughters were habitually sacrificed without a protest, by the feudal laws.

[3] Plutarch, *Cicero*.

[4] Tacit. *Ann.* i. 10.

[5] Plutarch, *Cato*; Lucan, *Pharsal.* ii.

[6] Senec. *Ep.* cxiv.

once been to the public games without his knowledge;[1] Paulus Æmilius taking the same step without assigning any reason, and defending himself by saying, 'My shoes are new and well made, but no one knows where they pinch me.'[2] Nor did women show less alacrity in repudiating their husbands. Seneca denounced this evil with especial vehemence, declaring that divorce in Rome no longer brought with it any shame, and that there were women who reckoned their years rather by their husbands than by the consuls.[3] Christians and Pagans echoed the same complaint. According to Tertullian, 'divorce is the fruit of marriage.'[4] Martial speaks of a woman who had already arrived at her tenth husband;[5] Juvenal, of a woman having eight husbands in five years.[6] But the most extraordinary recorded instance of this kind is related by St. Jerome, who assures us that there existed at Rome a wife who was married to her twenty-third husband, she herself being his twenty-first wife.[7]

These are, no doubt, extreme cases; but it is unquestionable that the stability of married life was very seriously impaired. It would be easy, however, to exaggerate the influence of legal changes in affecting it. In a purer state of public opinion a very wide latitude of divorce might probably have been allowed to both parties, without any serious consequence. The right of repudiation, which the husband had always possessed, was, as we have seen, in the Republic never or very rarely exercised. Of those who scandalised good men by the rapid recurrence of their marriages, probably most, if marriage was

[1] Val. Max. vi. 3.

[2] Plutarch, *Paul. Æmil.* It is not quite clear whether this remark was made by Paulus himself.

[3] Sen. *de Benef.* iii. 16. See, too, *Ep.* xcv. *Ad Helv.* xvi.

[4] Apol. 6.

[5] *Epig.* vi. 7.

[6] Juv. *Sat.* vi. 230.

[7] *Ep.* 2.

indissoluble, would have refrained from entering into it, and would have contented themselves with many informal connections, or, if they had married, would have gratified their love of change by simple adultery. A vast wave of corruption had flowed in upon Rome, and under any system of law it would have penetrated into domestic life. Laws prohibiting all divorce have never secured the purity of married life in ages of great corruption, nor did the latitude which was accorded in imperial Rome prevent the existence of a very large amount of female virtue.

I have observed in a former chapter, that the moral contrasts which were shown in ancient life surpass those of modern societies, in which we very rarely find clusters of heroic or illustrious men arising in nations that are in general very ignorant or very corrupt. I have endeavoured to account for this fact by showing that the moral agencies of antiquity were in general much more fitted to develope virtue than to repress vice, and that they raised noble natures to almost the highest conceivable point of excellence, while they entirely failed to coerce or to attenuate the corruption of the depraved. In the female life of Imperial Rome we find these contrasts vividly displayed. There can be no question that the moral tone of the sex was extremely low—lower, probably, than in France under the Regency, or in England under the Restoration—and it is also certain that frightful excesses of unnatural passion, of which the most corrupt of modern courts present no parallel, were perpetrated with but little concealment on the Palatine. Yet there is probably no period in which examples of conjugal heroism and fidelity appear more frequently than in this very age, in which marriage was most free and in which corruption was so general. Much simplicity of manners continued to coexist with the excesses of an almost unbridled luxury.

Augustus, we are told, used to make his daughters and grand-daughters weave and spin, and his wife and sister made most of the clothes he wore.[1] The skill of wives in domestic economy, and especially in spinning, was frequently noticed in their epitaphs.[2] Intellectual culture was much diffused among them,[3] and we meet with several noble specimens in the sex, of large and accomplished minds united with all the gracefulness of intense womanhood, and all the fidelity of the truest love. Such were Cornelia, the brilliant and devoted wife of Pompey;[4] Marcia, the friend, and Helvia, the mother of Seneca. The Northern Italian cities had in a great degree escaped the contamination of the times, and Padua was especially noted for the chastity of its women.[5] In an age of extravagant sensuality a noble lady, named Mallonia, plunged her dagger in her heart rather than yield to the embraces of Tiberius.[6] To the period when the legal bond of marriage was most relaxed must be assigned most of those noble examples of the constancy of Roman wives, which have been for so many generations household tales among mankind. Who has not read with emotion of the tenderness and heroism of Porcia, claiming her right to share in the trouble which clouded her husband's brow; how, doubting her own courage, she did not venture to ask Brutus to reveal to her his enterprise till she had secretly tried her power of endurance by piercing her thigh with a

[1] Sueton. *Aug.* Charlemagne, in like manner, made his daughters work in wool. (Eginhardus, *Vit. Kar. Mag.* xix.)

[2] Friedländer, *Mœurs romaines du règne d'Auguste à la fin des Antonins* (trad. franç.), tome i. p. 414.

[3] Much evidence of this is collected by Friedländer, tome i. pp. 387–395.

[4] Plutarch, *Pompeius.*

[5] Martial, xi. 16, mentions the reputation of the women of Padua for virtue. The younger Pliny also notices the austere and antique virtue of Brescia (Brixia).—*Ep.* i. 14.

[6] Suet. *Tiberius,* xlv.

knife; how once, and but once in his presence, her noble spirit failed, when, as she was about to separate from him for the last time, her eye chanced to fall upon a picture of the parting interview of Hector and Andromache?[1] Paulina, the wife of Seneca, opened her own veins in order to accompany her husband to the grave; when much blood had already flowed, her slaves and freedmen bound her wounds, and thus compelled her to live; but the Romans ever after observed with reverence the sacred pallor of her countenance—the memorial of her act.[2] When Pætus was condemned to die by his own hand, those who knew the love which his wife Arria bore him, and the heroic fervour of her character, predicted that she would not long survive him. Thrasea, who had married her daughter, endeavoured to dissuade her from suicide by saying, 'If I am ever called upon to perish, would you wish your daughter to die with me?' She answered, 'Yes, if she will have then lived with you as long and as happily as I with Pætus.' Her friends attempted, by carefully watching her, to secure her safety, but she dashed her head against the wall with such force that she fell upon the ground, and then, rising up, she said, 'I told you I would find a hard way to death if you refuse me an easy way.' All attempts to restrain her were then abandoned, and her death was perhaps the most majestic in antiquity. Pætus for a moment hesitated to strike the fatal blow; but his wife, taking the dagger, plunged it deeply in her own breast, and then drawing it out, gave it, all reeking as it was, to her husband, exclaiming, with her dying breath, 'My Pætus, it does not pain.'[3]

The form of the elder Arria towers grandly above her fellows, but many other Roman wives in the days of

[1] Plutarch, *Brutus.*

[2] Tacit. *Annal.* xv. 63-64.

[3] 'Pæte, non dolet.'—Plin. *Ep.* iii. 16; Martial, *Ep.* i. 14.

the early Cæsars and Domitian exhibited a very similar fidelity. Over the dark waters of the Euxine, into those unknown and inhospitable regions from which the Roman imagination recoiled with a peculiar horror, many noble ladies freely followed their husbands, and there were some wives who refused to survive them.[1] The younger Arria was the faithful companion of Thrasea during his heroic life, and when he died she was only persuaded to live that she might bring up their daughters.[2] She spent the closing days of Domitian in exile,[3] while her daughter, who was as remarkable for the gentleness as for the dignity of her character,[4] went twice into exile with her husband Helvidius, and was once banished, after his death, for defending his memory.[5] Incidental notices in historians, and a few inscriptions which have happened to survive, show us that such instances were not uncommon, and in the Roman epitaphs that remain, no feature is more remarkable than the deep and passionate expressions of conjugal love that continually occur.[6] It would be difficult to find a more touching image of that love, than the medallion which is so common on the Roman sarcophagi, in which husband and wife are represented together, each with an arm thrown fondly over the shoulder of the other, united in death as they had been in life, and meeting it with an aspect of perfect calm, because they were companions in the tomb.

[1] Tacit. *Annal.* xvi. 10–11; *Hist.* i. 3. See, too, Friedländer, tome i. p. 406.

[2] Tacit. *Ann.* xvi. 34.

[3] Pliny mentions her return after the death of the tyrant (*Ep.* iii. 11).

[4] 'Quod paucis datum est, non minus amabilis quam veneranda.'—Plin. *Ep.* vii. 19.

[5] See Plin. *Ep.* vii. 19. Dion Cassius and Tacitus relate the exiles of Helvidius, who appears to have been rather intemperate and unreasonable.

[6] Friedländer gives many and most touching examples, tome i. pp. 410–414.

In the latter days of the Pagan Empire some measures were taken to repress the profligacy that was so prevalent. Domitian enforced the old Scantinian law against unnatural love.[1] Vespasian moderated the luxury of the court; Macrinus caused those who had committed adultery to be bound together and burnt alive.[2] A practice of men and women bathing together was condemned by Hadrian, and afterwards by Alexander Severus, but was only finally suppressed by Constantine. Alexander Severus and Philip waged an energetic war against pandars.[3] The extreme excesses of this, as of most forms of vice, were probably much diminished after the accession of the Antonines; but Rome continued to be a centre of very great corruption till the combined influence of Christianity, the removal of the court to Constantinople, and the impoverishment that followed the barbarian conquests, in a measure corrected the evil.

Among the moralists, however, some important steps were taken. One of the most important was a very clear assertion of the reciprocity of that obligation to fidelity in marriage which in the early stages of society had been imposed almost exclusively upon wives.[4] The legends of Clytemnestra and of Medea reveal the feelings of fierce resentment which were sometimes produced among Greek wives by the almost unlimited indulgence that was accorded to their husbands;[5] and

[1] Suet. *Dom.* viii.

[2] Capitolinus, *Macrinus.*

[3] Lampridius, *A. Severus.*

[4] In the oration against Neæra, which is ascribed to Demosthenes, but is of doubtful genuineness, the license accorded to husbands is spoken of as a matter of course: 'We keep mistresses for our pleasure, concubines for constant attendance, and wives to bear us legitimate children, and to be our faithful housekeepers.'

[5] There is a remarkable passage on the feelings of wives, in different nations, upon this point, in Athenæus, xiii. 3. See, too, Plutarch, *Conj. Præc.*

it is told of Andromache, as the supreme instance of her love of Hector, that she cared for his illegitimate children as much as for her own.[1] In early Rome, the obligations of husbands were never, I imagine, altogether unfelt, but they were rarely or never enforced, nor were they ever regarded as bearing any kind of equality to those imposed upon the wife. The term adultery, and all the legal penalties connected with it, were restricted to the infractions by a wife of the nuptial tie. Among the many instances of magnanimity recorded of Roman wives, few are more touching than that of Tertia Æmilia, the faithful wife of Scipio. She discovered that her husband had become enamoured of one of her slaves; but she bore her pain in silence, and when he died she gave liberty to her captive, for she could not bear that she should remain in servitude whom her dear lord had loved.[2]

Aristotle had clearly asserted the duty of husbands to observe in marriage the same fidelity as they expected from their wives,[3] and at a later period both Plutarch and Seneca enforced it in the strongest and most unequivocal manner.[4] The degree to which, in theory at least, it won

[1] Euripid. *Andromache.*

[2] Valer. Max. vi. 7, § 1. Some very scandalous instances of cynicism on the part of Roman husbands are recorded. Thus, Augustus had many mistresses, 'Quæ [virgines] sibi undique etiam *ab uxore* conquirerentur.'—Sueton. *Aug.* lxxi. When the wife of Verus, the colleague of Marcus Aurelius, complained of the tastes of her husband, he answered, 'Uxor enim dignitatis nomen est, non voluptas.'—Spartian. *Verus.*

[3] Aristotle, *Econom.* i. 4–8–9.

[4] Plutarch enforces the duty at length, in his very beautiful work on marriage. In case husbands are guilty of infidelity, he recommends their wives to preserve a prudent blindness, reflecting that it is out of respect for them that they choose another woman as the companion of their intemperance. Seneca touches briefly, but unequivocally, on the subject: 'Scis improbum esse qui ab uxore pudicitiam exigit, ipse alienarum corruptor uxorum. Scis ut illi nil cum adultero, sic nihil tibi esse debere cum pellice.'—*Ep.* xciv. 'Sciet in uxorem gravissim m esse genus injuriæ, habere pellicem.'—*Ep.* xcv.

its way in Roman life is shown by its recognition as a legal maxim by Ulpian,[1] and by its appearance in a formal judgment of Antoninus Pius, who, while issuing, at the request of a husband, a condemnation for adultery against a guilty wife, appended to it this remarkable condition: 'Provided always it is established that by your life you gave her an example of fidelity. It would be unjust that a husband should exact a fidelity he does not himself keep.'[2]

Another change, which may be dimly descried in the later Pagan society, was a tendency to regard purity rather in a mystical point of view, as essentially good, than in the utilitarian point of view. This change resulted chiefly from the rise of the Neoplatonic and Pythagorean philosophies, which concurred in regarding the body, with its passions, as essentially evil, and in representing all virtue as a purification from its taint. Its most important consequence was a somewhat stricter view of pre-nuptial unchastity, which in the case of men, and when it was not excessive, and did not take the form of adultery, had previously been uncensured, or was looked upon with a disapprobation so slight as scarcely to amount to censure. The elder Cato had expressly justified it,[3] and Cicero has left us an extremely curious judgment on the subject, which shows at a glance the feelings of the people, and the vast revolution that, under the influence of Christianity, has been effected in at least the professions of mankind. 'If there be any one,' he says,

[1] 'Periniquum enim videtur esse, ut pudicitiam vir ab uxore exigat, quam ipse non exhibeat.'—*Cod. Just. Dig.* xlviii. 5-13.

[2] Quoted by St. Augustine, *De Conj. Adult.* ii. 19. Plautus, long before, had made one of his characters complain of the injustice of the laws which punished unchaste wives but not unchaste husbands; and he asks why, since every honest woman is contented with one husband, should not every honest man be contented with one wife? (*Mercator*, Act iv. scene 5.)

[3] Horace, *Sat.* i. 2.

'who thinks that young men should be altogether restrained from the love of courtesans, he is indeed very severe. I am not prepared to deny his position; but he differs not only from the license of our age, but also from the customs and allowances of our ancestors. When, indeed, was this not done? When was it blamed? When was it not allowed? When was that which is now lawful not lawful?'[1] Epictetus, who on most subjects was among the most austere of the stoics, recommends his disciples to abstain, 'as far as possible,' from prenuptial connections, and at least from those which were adulterous and unlawful, but not to blame those who were less strict.[2] The feeling of the Romans is curiously exemplified in the life of Alexander Severus, who, of all the emperors, was probably the most energetic in legislating against vice. When appointing a provincial governor, he was accustomed to provide him with horses and servants, and, if he was unmarried, with a concubine, 'because,' as the historian very gravely observes, 'it was impossible that he could exist without one.'[3]

What was written among the Pagans in opposition to

[1] 'Verum si quis est qui etiam meretriciis amoribus interdictum juventuti putet, est ille quidem valde severus; negare non possum; sed abhorret non modo ab hujus sæculi licentia, verum etiam a majorum consuetudine atque concessis. Quando enim hoc factum non est? Quando reprehensum? Quando non permissum? Quando denique fuit ut quod licet non liceret?'—Cicero, *Pro Cœlio,* cap. xx. The whole speech is well worthy of the attention of those who would understand Roman feelings on these matters; but it should be remembered that it is the speech of a lawyer defending a dissolute client.

[2] *Περὶ ἀφροδίσια, εἰς δύναμιν πρὸ γάμου καθαρευτέον. ἁπτομένῳ δέ, ὧν νομιμόν ἐστι, μεταληπτέον, μὴ μέν τοι ἐπαχθὴς γίνου τοῖς χρωμένοις, μηδὲ ἐλεγκτικός, μηδὲ πολλαχοῦ τό, Ὅτι αὐτὸς οὐ χρῇ, παράφερε.*—*Enchir.* xxxiii.

[3] 'Et si uxores non haberent, singulas concubinas, quod sine his esse non possent.'—Lampridius, *A. Severus.* We have an amusing picture of the common tone of people of the world on this matter, in the speech Apuleius puts into the mouth of the gods, remonstrating with Venus for being angry because her son formed a connection with Psyche. (*Metam.* lib. v.)

these views was not much, but it is worthy of notice, as illustrating the tendency that had arisen. Musonius Rufus distinctly and emphatically asserted that no union of the sexes other than marriage was permissible.[1] Dion Chrysostom desired prostitution to be suppressed by law. The ascetic notion of the impurity even of marriage may be faintly traced. Apollonius of Tyana lived, on this ground, a life of celibacy.[2] Zenobia refused to cohabit with her husband, except so far as was necessary for the production of an heir.[3] Hypatia is said, like many Christian saints, to have maintained the unnatural position of a virgin wife.[4] The belief in the impurity of all corporeal things, and of the duty of rising above them, was in the third century strenuously enforced.[5] Marcus Aurelius, and Julian were both admirable representatives of the best Pagan spirit of their time. Each of them lost his wife early, each was eulogised by his biographer for the virtue he manifested after her death; but there is a curious and characteristic difference in the forms which that virtue assumed. Marcus Aurelius, we are told, did not wish to bring into his house a stepmother to rule over his children, and accordingly took a concubine.[6] Julian ever after lived in perfect continence.[7]

The foregoing facts, which I have given in the most condensed form, and almost unaccompanied by criticism or by comment, will be sufficient, I hope, to exhibit the

[1] Preserved by Stobæus. See Denis, *Hist. des Idées morales dans l'Antiquité*, tome ii. pp. 134–136, 149–150.

[2] Philos. *Apol.* i. 13. When a saying of Pythagoras, 'that a man should only have commerce with his own wife,' was quoted, he said that this concerned others.

[3] Trebellius Pollio, *Zenobia.*

[4] This is asserted by an anonymous writer quoted by Suidas. See Ménage, *Hist. Mulierum Philosopharum*, p. 58.

[5] See, e.g., Plotinus, 1st Enn. vi. 6.

[6] Capitolinus, *M. Aurelius.*

[7] Amm. Marcell. xxv. 4.

state of feeling of the Romans on this subject, and also the direction in which that feeling was being modified. Those who are familiar with this order of studies will readily understand that it is impossible to mark out with precision the chronology of a moral sentiment; but there can be no question that in the latter days of the Roman Empire the perceptions of men on this subject became more subtle and more refined than they had previously been, and it is equally certain that the Oriental philosophies which had superseded stoicism, largely influenced the change. Christianity soon constituted itself the representative of the new tendency. It regarded purity as the most important of all virtues, and it strained to the utmost all the vast agencies it possessed, to enforce it. In the legislation of the first Christian emperors we find many traces of a fiery zeal. Pandars were condemned to have molten lead poured down their throats. In the case of rape, not only the ravisher, but even the injured person, if she consented to the act, was put to death.[1] A great service was done to the cause both of purity and of philanthropy, by a law which permitted actresses, on receiving baptism, to abandon their profession, which had been made a form of slavery, and was virtually a slavery to vice.[2] Certain musical girls, who were accustomed to sing or play at the banquets of the rich, and who were regarded with extreme horror by the Fathers, were suppressed, and a very stringent law forbade the revival of the class.[3]

[1] *Cod. Theod.* lib. ix. tit. 24.

[2] *Cod. Theod.* lib. xv. tit. 7.

[3] 'Fidicinam nulli liceat vel emere vel docere vel vendere, vel conviviis aut spectaculis adhibere. Nec cuiquam aut delectationis desiderio erudita feminea aut musicæ artis studio liceat habere mancipia.'—*Cod. Theod.* xv. 7, 10. This curious law was issued in A.D. 385. St. Jerome said these musicians were the chorus of the devil, and quite as dangerous as the sirens. See the comments on the law.

Side by side with the civil legislation, the penitential legislation of the Church was exerted in the same direction. Sins of unchastity probably occupy a larger place than any other in its enactments. The cases of unnatural love, and of mothers who had made their daughters courtesans, were punished by perpetual exclusion from communion, and a crowd of minor offences were severely visited. The ascetic passion increased the prominence of this branch of ethics, and the imaginations of men were soon fascinated by the pure and noble figures of the virgin martyrs of the Church, who, in the hour of martyrdom, on more than one occasion fully equalled the courage of men, while they sometimes mingled with their heroism traits of the most exquisite feminine gentleness. For the patient endurance of excruciating physical suffering, Christianity produced no more sublime figure than Blandina, the poor servant-girl who was martyred at Lyons; and it would be difficult to find in all history a more touching picture of natural purity than is contained in one simple incident of the martyrdom of St. Perpetua. It is related of that saint that she was condemned to be slaughtered by a wild bull, and as she fell half dead from its horns upon the sand of the arena, it was observed that even in that awful moment her virgin modesty was supreme, and her first instinctive movement was to draw together her dress, which had been torn in the assault.[1]

[1] Ruinart, *Act. S. Perpetuæ.* These acts are, I believe, generally regarded as authentic. There is nothing more instructive in history than to trace the same moral feelings through different ages and religions; and I am able in this case to present the reader with an illustration of their permanence, which I think somewhat remarkable. The younger Pliny gives in one of his letters a most dreadful account of the execution of Cornelia, a vestal virgin, by the order of Domitian. She was buried alive for incest; but her innocence appears to have been generally believed; and she had been condemned unheard, and in her absence. As she was being lowered into

A crowd of very curious popular legends also arose, which, though they are for the most part without much intrinsic excellence, have their importance in history, as showing the force with which the imaginations of men were turned in this direction, and the manner in which Christianity was regarded as the great enemy of the passions of the flesh. Thus, St. Jerome relates an incredible story of a young Christian being, in the Diocletian persecution, bound with ribands of silk in the midst of a lovely garden, surrounded by everything that could charm the ear and the eye, while a beautiful courtesan assailed him with her blandishments, against which he protected himself by biting out his tongue and spitting it in her face.[1] Legends are recounted of young Christian men assuming the garb and manners of libertines, that they might obtain access to maidens who had been condemned to vice, exchanging dresses with them, and thus enabling them to escape.[2] St. Agnes was said to have been stripped naked before the people, who all turned away their

the subterranean cell her dress was caught and deranged in the descent. She turned round and drew it to her, and when the executioner stretched out his hand to assist her, she started back lest he should touch her, for this, according to the received opinion, was a pollution; and even in the supreme moment of her agony her vestal purity shrank from the unholy contact. (Plin. *Ep.* iv. 11.) If we now pass back several centuries, we find Euripides attributing to Polyxena a trait precisely similar to that which was attributed to Perpetua. As she fell beneath the sword of the executioner, it was observed that her last care was that she might fall with decency.

ἡ δὲ καὶ θνήσκουσ' ὅμως
πολλὴν πρόνοιαν εἶχεν εὐσχήμως πεσεῖν,
κρύπτουσ' ἃ κρύπτειν ὄμματ' ἀρσένων χρεών.

Euripides, *Hec.* 566–68.

1 *Vita Pauli.*

2 St. Ambrose relates an instance of this, which he says occurred at Antioch (*De Virginibus*, lib. ii. cap. iv.). When the Christian youth was being led to execution, the girl whom he had saved reappeared and died with him. Eusebius tells a very similar story, but places the scene at Alexandria.

eyes except one young man, who was instantly turned blind.[1] The sister of St. Gregory of Nyssa was afflicted with a cancer in her breast, but could not bear that a surgeon should see it, and was rewarded for her modesty by a miraculous cure.[2] To the fabled zone of beauty the Christian saints opposed their zones of chastity, which extinguished the passion of the wearer, or would only meet around the pure.[3] Dæmons were said not unfrequently to have entered into the profligate. The garment of a girl who was possessed was brought to St. Pachomius, and he discovered from it that she had a lover.[4] A courtesan accused St. Gregory Thaumaturgus of having been her lover, and having refused to pay her what he had promised. He paid the required sum, but she was immediately possessed by a dæmon.[5] The efforts of the saints to reclaim courtesans from the path of vice created a large class of legends. St. Mary Magdalene, St. Mary of Egypt, St. Afra, St. Pelagia, St. Thais, and St. Theodota, in the early Church, as well as St. Marguerite of Cortona, and Clara of Rimini, in the middle ages, had been courtesans.[6] St. Vitalius was said to have been accustomed every night to visit the dens of vice in his neighbourhood, to give the inmates money to remain without sin for that

[1] See Ceillier, *Hist. des Auteurs ecclés.* tome iii. p. 523.

[2] Ibid. tome viii. pp. 204–207.

[3] Among the Irish saints St. Colman is said to have had a girdle which would only meet around the chaste, and was long preserved in Ireland as a relic (Colgan, *Acta Sanctorum Hibernic.* (Louvain, 1645), vol. i. p. 246); and St. Fursæus a girdle that extinguished lust. (Ibid. p. 292.) The girdle of St. Thomas Aquinas seems to have had some miraculous properties of this kind. (See his life in the Bollandists, Sept. 29.) Among both the Greeks and Romans it was customary for the bride to be girt with a girdle which the bridegroom unloosed in the nuptial bed, and hence 'zonam solvere' became a proverbial expression for 'pudicitiam mulieris imminuere.' (Nieupoort, *De Ritibus Romanarum*, p. 479; Alexander's *History of Women*, vol. ii. p. 300.)

[4] *Vit. St. Pachom.* (Rosweyde).

[5] See his *Life*, by Gregory of Nyssa.

[6] A little book has been written on these legends by M. Charles de

night, and to offer up prayers for their conversion.[1] It is related of St. Serapion, that as he was passing through a village in Egypt a courtesan beckoned to him. He promised at a certain hour to visit her. He kept his appointment, but declared that there was a duty which his order imposed on him. He fell down on his knees and began repeating the Psalter, concluding every psalm with a prayer for his hostess. The strangeness of the scene, and the solemnity of his tone and manner, overawed and fascinated her. Gradually her tears began to flow. She knelt beside him and began to join in his prayers. He heeded her not, but hour after hour continued in the same stern and solemn voice, without rest and without interruption, to repeat his alternate prayers and psalms, till her repentance rose to a paroxysm of terror, and as the grey morning streaks began to illumine the horizon, she fell half dead at his feet, imploring him with broken sobs to lead her anywhere where she might expiate the sins of her past.[2]

But the services rendered by the ascetics in imprinting on the minds of men a profound and enduring conviction of the importance of chastity, though extremely great, were seriously counterbalanced by their noxious influence upon marriage. Two or three beautiful descriptions of this institution have been culled out of the immense mass of the patristic writings;[3] but in general, it would be

Bussy, called *Les Courtisanes saintes*. There is said to be some doubt about St. Afra, for while her acts represent her as a reformed courtesan, St. Fortunatus, in two lines he has devoted to her, calls her a virgin. (Ozanam, *Études german.* tome ii. p. 8.)

[1] See the *Vit. Sancti Joannis Eleemosynarii* (Rosweyde).

[2] Tillemont, tome x. pp. 61–62. There is also a very picturesque legend of the manner in which St. Paphnutius converted the courtesan Thais.

[3] See especially, Tertullian, *Ad Uxorem.* It was beautifully said at a later period, that woman was not taken from the head of man, for she was not intended to be his ruler, nor from his feet, for she was not intended

difficult to conceive anything more coarse or more repulsive than the manner in which they regarded it.[1] The relation which nature has designed for the noble purpose of repairing the ravages of death, and which, as Linnæus has shown, extends even through the world of flowers, was invariably treated as a consequence of the fall of Adam, and marriage was regarded almost exclusively in its lowest aspect. The tender love which it elicits, the holy and beautiful domestic qualities that follow in its train, were almost absolutely omitted from consideration.[2] The object of the ascetic was to attract men to a life of virginity, and as a necessary consequence, marriage was treated as an inferior state. It was regarded as being necessary, indeed, and therefore justifiable, for the propagation of the species, and to free men from greater evils; but still as a condition of degradation from which all who aspired to real sanctity could fly. To 'cut down by the axe of Virginity the wood of Marriage,' was, in the energetic language of St. Jerome, the end of the saint;[3] and if he consented to praise marriage, it was merely because it produced virgins.[4] Even when the bond had been formed, the ascetic passion retained its sting. We

to be his slave, but from his side, for she was to be his companion and his comfort. (Peter Lombard, *Senten.* lib. ii. dis. 18.)

[1] The reader may find many passages on this subject in Barbeyrac, *Morale des Pères,* ii. § 7; iii. § 8; iv. § 31–35; vi. § 31; xiii. § 2–8.

[2] 'It is remarkable how rarely, if ever (I cannot call to mind an instance), in the discussions of the comparative merits of marriage and celibacy the social advantages appear to have occurred to the mind. . . . It is always argued with relation to the interests and the perfection of the individual soul; and even with regard to that, the writers seem almost unconscious of the softening and humanising effect of the natural affections, the beauty of parental tenderness and filial love.'—Milman's *Hist. of Christianity,* vol. iii. p. 196.

[3] 'Tempus breve est, et jam securis ad radices arborum posita est, quæ silvam legis et nuptiarum evangelica castitate succidat.'—*Ep.* cxxiii.

[4] 'Laudo nuptias, laudo conjugium, sed quia mihi virgines generant.'—*Ep.* xxii.

have already seen how it embittered other relations of domestic life. Into this, the holiest of all, it infused a tenfold bitterness. Whenever any strong religious fervour fell upon a husband or a wife, its first effect was to make a happy union impossible. The more religious partner immediately desired to live a life of solitary asceticism, or at least, if no ostensible separation took place, an unnatural life of separation in marriage. The immense place this order of ideas occupies in the hortatory writings of the fathers, and in the legends of the saints, must be familiar to all who have any knowledge of this department of literature. Thus—to give but a very few examples—St. Nilus, when he had already two children, was seized with a longing for the prevailing asceticism, and his wife was persuaded, after many tears, to consent to their separation.[1] St. Ammon, on the night of his marriage, proceeded to greet his bride with an harangue upon the evils of the married state, and they agreed, in consequence, at once to separate.[2] St. Melania laboured long and earnestly to induce her husband to allow her to desert his bed, before he would consent.[3] St. Abraham ran away from his wife on the night of his marriage.[4] St. Alexis, according to a somewhat later legend, took the same step, but many years after returned from Jerusalem to his father's house, in which his wife was still lamenting her desertion, begged and received a lodging as an act of charity, and lived there despised, unrecognised, and unknown till his death.[5] St. Gregory

[1] See Ceillier, *Auteurs ecclés.* xiii. p. 147. [2] Socrates, iv. 23.

[3] Palladius, *Hist. Laus.* cxix. [4] *Vit. S. Abr.* (Rosweyde), cap. i.

[5] I do not know when this legend first appeared. I know it from two sources. M. Littré mentions having found it in a French MS. of the eleventh century (Littré, *Les Barbares*, pp. 123–124); and it also forms the subject of a very curious fresco, I imagine of a somewhat earlier date, which was discovered, within the last few years, in the subterranean church

of Nyssa—who was so unfortunate as to be married—wrote a glowing eulogy of virginity, in the course of which he mournfully observed, that this privileged state could never be his. He resembled, he assures us, an ox that was ploughing a field, the fruit of which he must never enjoy; or a thirsty man, who was gazing on a stream of which he never can drink; or a poor man, whose poverty seems the more bitter as he contemplates the wealth of his neighbours; and he proceeded to descant in feeling terms upon the troubles of matrimony.[1] Nominal marriages, in which the partners agreed to shun the marriage bed, became not uncommon. The emperor Henry II., Edward the Confessor, of England, and Alphonso II. of Spain, gave examples of it. A very famous and rather picturesque history of this kind is related by Gregory of Tours. A rich young Gaul, named Injuriosus, led to his home a young bride to whom he was passionately attached. That night, she confessed to him with tears, that she had vowed to keep her virginity, and that she regretted bitterly the marriage into which her love for him had betrayed her. He told her that they should remain united, but that she should still observe her vow; and he fulfilled his promise. When, after several years, she died, her husband, in laying her in the tomb, declared with great solemnity, that he restored her to God as immaculate as he had received her; and then a smile lit up the face of the dead woman, and she said, 'Why do you tell that which no one asked you?' The husband soon afterwards died, and a wall, which had been built to separate his tomb from that of his wife, was removed by the angels.[2]

of St. Clement at Rome. An account of it is given by Father Mullooly, in his interesting little book about the Church.

[1] *De Virgin.* cap. iii.

[2] Greg. Tur. i. 42.

The extreme disorders which such teaching produced in domestic life, and also the extravagancies which grew up among some heretics, naturally alarmed the more judicious leaders of the Church, and it was ordained that married persons should not enter into an ascetic life, except by mutual consent.[1] The ascetic ideal, however, remained unchanged. To abstain from marriage, or in marriage to abstain from a perfect union, was regarded as a proof of sanctity, and marriage was viewed in its coarsest and most degraded form. The notion of its impurity took many forms, and exercised for some centuries an extremely wide influence over the Church. Thus, it was the custom during the middle ages to abstain from the marriage bed during the night after the ceremony, in honour of the sacrament.[2] It was expressly enjoined that no married persons should participate in any of the great Church festivals, if the night before they had lain together, and St. Gregory the Great tells of a young wife who was possessed by a dæmon, because she had taken part in a procession of St. Sebastian, without fulfilling this condition.[3] The extent to which the feeling on the subject was carried is shown by the famous vision of Alberic in the twelfth century, in which a special place of torture, consisting of a lake of mingled lead, pitch, and resin is represented as existing in hell for the punishment of married people who had lain together on Church festivals or fast days.[4]

Two other consequences of this way of regarding marriage were a very strong disapproval of second marriages, and a very strong desire to secure celibacy in the clergy. The first of these notions had existed, though in

[1] The regulations on this point are given at length in Bingham.

[2] Muratori, *Antich. Ital.* diss. xx.

[3] St. Greg. *Dial.* i. 10.

[4] Delepierre, *L'Enfer décrit par ceux qui l'ont vu*, pp. 44–56.

a very different form, and connected with very different motives, among the early Romans, who were accustomed, we are told, to honour with the crown of modesty those who were content with one marriage, and to regard many marriages as a sign of illegitimate intemperance.[1] This opinion appears to have chiefly grown out of a very delicate and touching feeling which had taken deep root in the Roman mind, that the affection a wife owes her husband is so profound and so pure, that it must not cease even with his death; that it should guide and consecrate all her subsequent life, and that it never can be transferred to another object. Virgil, in very beautiful lines, puts this sentiment into the mouth of Dido;[2] and several examples are recorded of Roman wives, sometimes in the prime of youth and beauty, upon the death of their husbands, devoting the remainder of their lives to retirement, and to the memory of the dead.[3] Tacitus held up the Germans as in this respect a model to his countrymen,[4] and the epithet 'univiræ' inscribed on many Roman tombs shows how this devotion was practised and valued.[5] The family of Camillus was especially honoured for the absence of second marriages among its members.[6] 'To love a wife when living,' said one of the latest of Roman poets, 'is a pleasure; to love her when dead is an act of religion.'[7] In the case of men, the propriety of abstaining from second marriages was probably not felt as strongly as in the case of women, and what feeling on the subject existed was chiefly due to another motive—affection for

1 Val. Max. ii. 1. § 3.

2 'Ille meos, primus qui me sibi junxit, amores
Abstulit; ille habeat secum, servetque sepulchro.'—*Æn.* iv. 28.

3 E.g., the wives of Lucan, Drusus, and Pompey.

4 Tacit. *German.* xix.

5 Friedländer, tome i. p. 411.

6 Hieron. *Ep.* liv.

7 'Uxorem vivam amare voluptas;
Defunctam religio.'—Statius, *Sylv.* v. in procemio.

the children, whose interests it was thought might be injured by a stepmother.[1]

The sentiment which thus recoiled from second marriages passed with a vastly increased strength into ascetic Christianity, but it was based upon altogether different grounds. The first change, we may observe, is that an affectionate remembrance of the husband has altogether vanished from the motives of the abstinence. In the next place, we may remark that these writers, in perfect conformity with the extreme coarseness of their views about the sexes, almost invariably assumed that the motive to second or third marriages must be simply the force of the animal passions. The Montanists and the Novatians absolutely condemned second marriages.[2] The orthodox pronounced them lawful, on account of the weakness of human nature, but they viewed them with the most emphatic disapproval,[3] partly because they considered them manifest signs of incontinence, and partly because they regarded them as incompatible with the doctrine of marriage being an emblem of the union of Christ with the Church. The language of the Fathers on this subject appears to a modern mind most extraordinary, and, but for their distinct and reiterated assertion that they considered these marriages permissible,[4] would appear to

[1] By one of the laws of Charondas it was ordained that those who cared so little for the happiness of their children as to place a stepmother over them, should be excluded from the councils of the State. (Diod. Sic. xii. 12.)

[2] Tertullian expounded the Montanist view in his treatise, *De Monogamia.*

[3] A full collection of the statements of the Fathers on this subject is given by Perrone, *De Matrimonio,* lib. iii. Sæc. I.; and by Natalis Alexander, *Hist. Eccles.* Sæc. II. dissert. 18.

[4] Thus, to give but a single instance, St. Jerome, who was one of their strongest opponents, says: 'Quid igitur? damnamus secunda matrimonia? Minime, sed prima laudamus. Abjicimus de ecclesia digamos? absit; sed monogamos ad continentiam provocamus. In arca Noe non solum munda sed et immunda fuerunt animalia.'—*Ep.* cxxiii.

amount to a peremptory condemnation. Thus—to give but a few samples—digamy, or second marriage, is described by Athanagoras as 'a decent adultery;'[1] 'fornication,' according to Clement of Alexandria, 'is a lapse from one marriage into many.'[2] 'The first Adam,' said St. Jerome, 'had one wife; the second Adam had no wife. They who approve of digamy hold forth a third Adam, who was twice married, whom they follow.'[3] 'Consider,' he again says, 'that she who has been twice married, though she be an old, and decrepit, and poor woman, is not deemed worthy to receive the charity of the Church. But if the bread of charity is taken from her, how much more that bread which descends from heaven!'[4] Digamists, according to Origen, 'are saved in the name of Christ, but are by no means crowned by him.'[5] 'By this text,' said St. Gregory Nazianzen, speaking of St. Paul's comparison of marriage to the union of Christ with the Church, 'second marriages seem to me to be reproved. If there are two Christs there may be two husbands or two wives. If there is but one Christ, one Head of the Church, there is but one flesh—a second is repelled. But if he forbids a second, what is to be said of third marriages? The first is law, the second is pardon and indulgence, the third is iniquity; but he who exceeds this number is manifestly bestial.'[6] The collective judgment of the ecclesiastical authorities on this subject is shown by the rigid exclusion of digamists from the priesthood, and from all claim to the charity of the Church, and by the decrees of more than one Council, which ordained that a period of penance should be imposed upon all who married a second time, before they were admitted to

[1] *In Legat.*
[2] *Strom.* lib. iii.
[3] *Contra Jovin.* i.
[4] Ibid. See, too, *Ep.* cxxiii.
[5] Hom. xvii. in Luc.
[6] *Orat.* xxxi.

communion.[1] One of the canons of the Council of Illiberis, in the beginning of the fourth century, while in general condemning baptism by laymen, permitted it in case of extreme necessity; but provided that even then it was indispensable that the officiating layman should not have been twice married.[2] Among the Greeks fourth marriages were at one time deemed absolutely unlawful, and much controversy was excited by the emperor Leo the Wise, who, having had three wives, had taken a mistress, but afterwards, in defiance of the religious feelings of his people, determined to raise her to the position of a wife.[3]

The subject of the celibacy of the clergy, in which the ecclesiastical feelings about marriage were also shown, is an extremely large one, and I shall not attempt to deal with it, except in a most cursory manner.[4] There are two facts connected with it, which every candid student must admit. The first is, that in the earliest period of the Church, the privilege of marriage was freely accorded to the clergy. The second is, that a notion of the impurity of marriage existed, and it was felt that the clergy, as pre-eminently the holy class, should have less license than laymen. The first form this feeling took

[1] See on this decree, Perrone, *De Matr.* iii. § 1, art. 1; Natalis Alexander, *Hist. Eccles.* § ii. dissert. 18. The penances are said not to imply that the second marriage was a sin, but that the moral condition that made it necessary was a bad one.

[2] Conc. Illib. can. xxxviii. Bingham thinks the feeling of the Council to have been, that if baptism was not administered by a priest, it should at all events be administered by one who might have been a priest.

[3] Perrone, *De Matrimonio*, tome iii. p. 102.

[4] This subject has recently been treated with very great learning and with admirable impartiality by an American author, Mr. Henry C. Lea, in his *History of Sacerdotal Celibacy* (Philadelphia, 1867), which is certainly one of the most valuable works that America has produced. Since the great history of Dean Milman, I know no work in English which has thrown more light on the moral condition of the middle ages, and none which is

appears to have been the strong conviction that a second marriage of a priest, or the marriage of a priest with a widow, was unlawful and criminal.[1] This belief seems to have existed from the earliest period of the Church, and was retained with great tenacity and unanimity through many centuries. In the next place, we find, from an extremely early date, an opinion prevailing first of all, that it was an act of virtue, and then that it was an act of duty, for priests after ordination to abstain from cohabiting with their wives. The Council of Nice refrained, at the advice of Paphnutius, who was himself a scrupulous celibate, from imposing this last rule as a matter of necessity;[2] but in the course of the fourth century it was a recognised principle that clerical marriages were criminal. They were celebrated, however, habitually, and usually with the greatest openness. The various attitudes assumed by the ecclesiastical authorities in dealing with this subject form an extremely curious page of the history of morals, and supply the most crushing evidence of the evils which have been produced by the system of celibacy. I can at present, however, only refer to the vast mass of evidence which has been collected on the subject, derived from the

more fitted to dispel the gross illusions concerning that period which Positive writers, and writers of a certain ecclesiastical school, have conspired to sustain.

[1] See Lea, p. 36. The command of St. Paul, that a bishop or deacon should be the husband of *one* wife (1 Tim. iii. 2–12) was believed by all ancient and by many modern commentators to be prohibitory of second marriages; and this view is somewhat confirmed by the widows who were to be honoured and supported by the Church, being only those who had but once married (1 Tim. v. 9). See Pressensé, *Hist. des trois premiers Siècles* (1[re] série), tome ii. p. 233. Among the Jews it was ordained that the high priest should not marry a widow. (Levit. xxi. 13–14.)

[2] Socrates, *H. E.* i. 11. The Council of Illiberis (can. xxxiii.) had ordained this, but both the precepts and the practice of divines varied greatly. A brilliant summary of the chief facts is given in Milman's *History of Early Christianity*, vol. iii. pp. 277–282.

writings of Catholic divines and from the decrees of Catholic Councils during the space of many centuries. It is a popular illusion, which is especially common among writers who have little direct knowledge of the middle ages, that the atrocious immorality of monasteries, in the century before the Reformation, was a new fact, and that the ages when the faith of men was undisturbed, were ages of great moral purity. In fact, it appears from the uniform testimony of the ecclesiastical writers, that the ecclesiastical immorality of the eighth and three following centuries was little if at all less outrageous than in any other period, while the Papacy, during almost the whole of the tenth century, was held by men of infamous lives. Simony was nearly universal.[1] Barbarian chieftains married at an early age, and, totally incapable of restraint, occupied the leading positions in the Church, and gross irregularities speedily became general. An Italian bishop of the tenth century epigrammatically described the morals of his time, when he declared, that if he were to enforce the canons against unchaste people administering ecclesiastical rites, no one would be left in the Church except the boys; and if he were to observe the canons against bastards, these also must be excluded.[2] The evil acquired such magnitude, that a great feudal clergy, bequeathing the ecclesiastical benefices from father to son, appeared more than once likely to arise.[3] A tax called 'Cullagium,' which was in fact a license to clergymen to keep concubines, was during several centuries systematically levied by princes.[4]

[1] See, on the state of things in the tenth and eleventh century, Lea, pp. 162–192.

[2] Ratherius, quoted by Lea, p. 151.

[3] See some curious evidence of the extent to which the practice of the hereditary transmission of ecclesiastical offices was carried, in Lea, pp. 149, 150, 266, 299, 339.

[4] Lea, pp. 271 292, 422.

Sometimes the evil, by its very extension, corrected itself. Priestly marriages were looked upon as normal events not implying any guilt, and in the eleventh century several instances are recorded in which the fact was not regarded as any impediment to the power of working miracles.[1] But this was a rare exception. From the earliest period a long succession of Councils as well as such men as St. Boniface, St. Gregory the Great, St. Peter Damiani, St. Dunstan, St. Anselm, Hildebrand, and his successors in the Popedom, denounced priestly marriage or concubinage as an atrocious crime, and the habitual life of the priests was, in theory at least, generally recognised as a life of sin.

It was not surprising that, having once broken their vows and begun to live what they deemed a life of habitual sin, the clergy should soon have sunk far below the level of the laity. We may not lay much stress on such isolated instances of depravity as that of Pope John XXIII., who was condemned for incest, among many other crimes, and for adultery;[2] or the abbot-elect of St. Augustine, at Canterbury, who in 1171 was found, on investigation, to have seventeen illegitimate children in a single village;[3] or an abbot of St. Pelayo, in Spain, who in 1130 was proved to have kept no less than seventy concubines;[4] or Henry III. Bishop of Liége, who was deposed in 1274 for having sixty-five illegitimate children;[5] but it is impossible to resist the evidence of a long chain of Councils and ecclesiastical writers, who conspire in depicting far greater evils than simple concubinage. It was observed, that when the priests actually took wives, the knowledge that these connections were illegal was peculiarly fatal to their fidelity, and bigamy

[1] Lea, pp. 186–187.
[2] Ibid. p. 358.
[3] Ibid. p. 296.
[4] Ibid. p. 322.
[5] Ibid. p. 349.

and extreme mobility of attachments were especially common among them. The writers of the middle ages are full of accounts of nunneries that were like brothels, of the vast multitude of infanticides within their walls, and of that inveterate prevalence of incest among the clergy, which rendered it necessary again and again to issue the most stringent enactments that priests should not be permitted to live with their mothers or sisters. Unnatural love, which it had been one of the great services of Christianity almost to eradicate from the world, is more than once spoken of as lingering in the monasteries; and shortly before the Reformation, complaints became loud and frequent of the employment of the confessional for the purposes of debauchery.[1] The measures taken on the subject were very numerous and severe. At first, the evil chiefly complained of was the clandestine marriage of priests, and especially their intercourse with wives they had married previous to their ordination; and several Councils issued their anathemas against priests 'who had improper relations with their wives;' and rules were made that priests should always sleep in the presence of a subordinate clerk; and that they should only meet their wives in the open air and before at least two witnesses. Men were, however, by no means unanimous in their way of regarding this matter. Synesius, when elected to a bishopric, had at first declined, boldly alleging as one of his reasons, that he had a wife whom he loved dearly, and who, he hoped, would bear him many sons, and that he did not mean to separate from her or visit her secretly as an adulterer.[2] A bishop of Laon, at a later date, who was married to a niece of St. Rémy,

[1] The reader may find the most ample evidence of these positions in Lea. See especially pp. 138, 141, 153, 155, 260, 344.

[2] Synesius, *Ep.* cv.

and who had remained with his wife till after he had a son and a daughter, quaintly expressed his penitence by naming them respectively Latro and Vulpecula.[1] St. Gregory the Great describes the virtue of a priest, who, through motives of piety, had discarded his wife. As he lay dying, she hastened to him to watch the bed which for forty years she had not been allowed to share, and bending over what seemed the inanimate form of her husband, she tried to ascertain whether any breath still remained, when the dying saint, collecting his last energies, exclaimed, 'Woman, begone; take away the straw; there is fire yet.'[2] The destruction of priestly marriage is chiefly due to Hildebrand, who pursued this object with the most untiring resolution. Finding that his appeals to the ecclesiastical authorities and to the civil rulers were insufficient, he boldly turned to the people, exhorted them, in defiance of all Church traditions, to withdraw their obedience from married priests, and kindled among them a fierce fanaticism of asceticism, which speedily produced a fierce persecution of the offending pastors. Their wives, in immense numbers, were driven forth with hatred and with scorn, and many crimes, and much intolerable suffering, followed the disruption. The priests sometimes strenuously resisted. At Cambrai, in A.D. 1077, they burnt alive as a heretic a zealot who was maintaining the doctrines of Hildebrand. In England, half a century later, they succeeded in surprising a Papal legate in the arms of a courtesan, a few hours after he had delivered a fierce denunciation of clerical unchastity.[3] But Papal

[1] Lea, p. 122. St. Augustine had named *his* illegitimate son Adeodatus, or the Gift of God, and had made him a principal interlocutor in one of his religious dialogues.

[2] *Dialog.* iv. 11.

[3] This is mentioned by Henry of Huntingdon, who was a contemporary. (Lea, p. 293.)

resolution supported by popular fanaticism won the victory. Pope Urban II. gave license to the nobles to reduce to slavery the wives of priests who obstinately refused to abandon them, and after a few more acts of severity priestly marriage became obsolete. The extent, however, of the disorders that still existed, is shown by the mournful confessions of ecclesiastical writers, by the uniform and indignant testimony of the poets and prose satirists who preceded the Reformation, by the atrocious immoralities disclosed in the monasteries at the time of their suppression, and by the significant prudence of many lay Catholics, who were accustomed to insist that their priest should take a concubine for the protection of the families of his parishioners.[1]

It is scarcely possible to conceive a more demoralising influence than a priesthood living such a life as I have described. In Protestant countries, where the marriage of the clergy is fully recognised, it has, indeed, been productive of the greatest and the most unequivocal benefits. Nowhere, it may be confidently asserted, does Christianity

[1] The first notice of this very remarkable precaution is in a canon of the Council of Palencia (in Spain) held in 1322, which anathematises laymen who compel their pastors to take concubines. (Lea, p. 324.) Sleidan mentions that it was customary in some of the Swiss cantons for the parishioners to oblige the priest to select a concubine as a necessary precaution for the protection of his female parishioners. (Ibid. p. 355.) Sarpi, in his *Hist. of the Council of Trent*, mentions (on the authority of Zuinglius) this Swiss custom. Nicolas de Clemangis, a leading member of the Council of Constance, declared that this custom had become very common, that the laity were now firmly persuaded that priests *never* lived a life of real celibacy, and that, where no proofs of concubinage were found, they always assumed the existence of more serious vice. The passage (which had been quoted by Bayle) is too remarkable to be omitted. 'Taceo de fornicationibus et adulteriis a quibus qui alieni sunt probro cæteris ac ludibrio esse solent, spadonesque aut sodomitæ appellantur; denique laici usque adeo persuasum habent nullos cælibes esse, ut in plerisque parochiis non aliter velint presbyterum tolerare nisi concubinam habeat, quo vel sic suis sit consultum uxoribus, quæ nec sic quidem usquequaque sunt extra periculum.' Nic. de Clem. *De Præsul. Simoniac.* (Lea, p. 386.)

assume a more beneficial or a more winning form, than in those gentle clerical households which stud our land, constituting, as Coleridge said, 'the one idyll of modern life,' the most perfect type of domestic peace, and the centres of civilisation in the remotest village. Notwithstanding some class narrowness and professional bigotry, notwithstanding some unworthy, but half unconscious mannerism, which is often most unjustly stigmatised as hypocrisy, it would be difficult to find in any other quarter so much happiness at once diffused and enjoyed, or so much virtue attained with so little tension or struggle. Combining with his sacred calling a warm sympathy with the intellectual, social, and political movements of his time, possessing the enlarged practical knowledge of a father of a family, and entering with a keen zest into the occupations and the amusements of his parishioners, a good clergyman will rarely obtrude his religious convictions into secular spheres, but yet will make them apparent in all. They will be revealed by a higher and deeper moral tone, by a more scrupulous purity in word and action, by an all-pervasive gentleness, which refines, and softens, and mellows, and adds as much to the charm as to the excellence of the character in which it is displayed. In visiting the sick, relieving the poor, instructing the young, and discharging a thousand delicate offices for which a woman's tact is especially needed, his wife finds a sphere of labour which is at once intensely active and intensely feminine, and her example is not less beneficial than her ministrations.

Among the Catholic priesthood, on the other hand, where the vow of celibacy is faithfully observed, a character of a different type is formed, which with very grave and deadly faults combines some of the noblest excellencies to which humanity can attain. Separated from most of the ties and affections of earth, viewing life chiefly through the distorted medium of the casuist or the confessional, and deprived of those relationships which more than any others soften and expand the character, the Catholic priests have been but too often conspicuous for their fierce and sanguinary fanaticism, and for their indifference to all interests except those of their Church; while the narrow range of their sympathies, and the intellectual servitude they have accepted, render them peculiarly unfitted for the office of educating the young, which they so persistently claim, and which, to the great misfortune of the world, they were long permitted to monopolise. But, on the other hand, no other body of men have ever exhibited a more single-minded and unworldly zeal, refracted by no personal interests, sacrificing to duty the dearest of earthly objects, and confronting with undaunted heroism every form of hardship, of suffering, and of death.

That the middle ages, even in their darkest periods, produced many good and great men of the latter type it would be unjust and absurd to deny. It can hardly, however, be questioned that the extreme frequency of illicit connections among the clergy tended during many centuries most actively to lower the moral tone of the laity, and to counteract the great services in the cause of purity which Christian teaching had undoubtedly effected. The priestly connections were rarely so fully recognised as to enable the mistress to fill a position like that which is now occupied by the wife of a clergyman, and the spectacle of the chief teachers and exemplars of morals living habitually in an intercourse which was acknowledged to be ambiguous or wrong, must have acted most injuriously upon every class of the community. Asceticism, proclaiming war upon human nature, produced a revulsion towards its extreme opposite, and even when it was observed in act it was frequently detrimental to the purity of mind. An impure chastity was fostered, which continually looked upon marriage in its coarsest light, treated the propagation of the species as its one legitimate end, and exercised a peculiarly perverting influence upon the imagination. The exuberant piety of wives who desired to live apart from their husbands often drove the latter into serious irregularities.[1] The notion of sin was introduced into the dearest of relationships,[2] and the whole subject was distorted and degraded by priestly celibates. It was one of the great benefits of Protestantism that it did much to banish these modes of thought and feeling from the world, and to restore marriage to its simplicity and its dignity. We have a gratifying illustration of the extent to which an old superstition has declined, in the fact that when Goldsmith, in his great romance, desired to depict the harmless eccentricities of his simple-minded and unworldly vicar, he represented him as maintaining that opinion concerning the sinfulness of the second marriage of a clergyman, which was for many centuries universal in the Church.

Another injurious consequence, resulting, in a great

[1] This was energetically noticed by Luther, in his famous sermon 'De Matrimonio,' and some of the Catholic preachers of an earlier period had made the same complaint. See a curious passage from a contemporary of Boccaccio, quoted by Meray, *Les Libres prêcheurs*, p. 155. 'Vast numbers of laymen separated from their wives under the influence of the ascetic enthusiasm which Hildebrand created.'—Lea, p. 254.

[2] 'Quando enim servata fide thori causa prolis conjuges conveniunt sic excusatur coitus ut culpam non habeat. Quando vero deficiente bono prolis fide tamen servata conveniunt causa incontinentiæ non sic excusatur ut non habeat culpam, sed venialem. . . . Item hoc quod conjugati victi concupiscentia utuntur invicem, ultra necessitatem liberos procreandi, ponam in his pro quibus quotidie dicimus Dimitte nobis debita nostra. . . . Unde in sententiolis Sexti Pythagorici legitur "omnis ardentior amator propriæ uxoris adulter est."'—Peter Lombard, *Sentent.* lib. iv. dist. 31.

measure, from asceticism, was a tendency to depreciate extremely the character and the position of women. In this tendency we may detect in part the influence of the earlier Jewish writings, in which it is probable that most impartial observers will detect evident traces of the common oriental depreciation of women. The custom of purchase-money to the father of the bride was admitted. Polygamy was authorised,[1] and practised by the wisest man on an enormous scale. A woman was regarded as the origin of human ills. A period of purification was appointed after the birth of every child; but, by a very significant provision, it was twice as long in the case of a female as of a male child.[2] 'The badness of men,' a Jewish writer emphatically declared, 'is better than the goodness of women.'[3] The types of female excellence exhibited in the early period of Jewish history are in general of a low order, and certainly far inferior to those of Roman history or Greek poetry; and the warmest eulogy of a woman in the Old Testament is probably that which was bestowed upon her who, with circumstances of the most aggravated treachery, had murdered the sleeping fugitive who had taken refuge under her roof.

The combined influence of the Jewish writings, and of that ascetic feeling which treated women as the chief source of temptation to man, was shown in those fierce invectives against this sex, which form so conspicuous and so grotesque a portion of the writings of the Fathers, and which contrast so curiously with the adulation bestowed upon particular members of the sex. Woman was represented as the door of hell, as the mother of all

[1] Many wives, however, were forbidden. (Deut. xvii. 17.) Polygamy is said to have ceased among the Jews after the return from the Babylonish captivity.—Whewell's *Elements of Morality*, book iv. ch. v.

[2] Levit. xii. 1–5.

[3] Ecclesiasticus, xlii. 14.

human ills. She should be ashamed at the very thought that she is a woman. She should live in continual penance, on account of the curses she has brought upon the world. She should be ashamed of her dress, for it is the memorial of her fall. She should be especially ashamed of her beauty, for it is the most potent instrument of the dæmon. Physical beauty was indeed perpetually the theme of ecclesiastical denunciations, though one singular exception seems to have been made; for it has been observed that in the middle ages the personal beauty of bishops was continually noticed upon their tombs.[1] Women were even forbidden by a provincial Council, in the sixth century, on account of their impurity, to receive the Eucharist into their naked hands.[2] Their essentially subordinate position was continually maintained.

It is probable that this teaching had its part in determining the principles of legislation concerning the sex. The Pagan laws during the empire had been continually repealing the old disabilities of women, and the legislative movement in their favour continued with unabated force from Constantine to Justinian, and appeared also in some of the early laws of the barbarians.[3] But in the whole feudal legislation women were placed in a much lower legal position than in the Pagan empire.[4] In addition to

[1] This curious fact is noticed by Le Blant, *Inscriptions chrétiennes de Gaule*, pp. xcvii–xcviii.

[2] See the decree of a Council of Auxerre (A.D. 578), can. 36.

[3] See the last two chapters of Troplong, *Influences du Christianisme sur le Droit* (a work, however, which is written much more in the spirit of an apologist than in that of an historian), and Legouvé, pp. 27–29.

[4] Even in matters not relating to property, the position of women in feudalism was a low one. 'Tout mari,' says Beaumanoir, 'peut battre sa femme quand elle ne veut pas obéir à son commandement, ou quand elle le maudit, ou quand elle le dément, pourvu que ce soit modérément et sans que mort s'ensuive,' quoted by Legouvé, p. 148. Contrast with this the saying of the elder Cato: 'A man who beats his wife or his children lays impious hands

the personal restrictions which grew necessarily out of the Catholic doctrines concerning divorce, and the subordination of the weaker sex, we find numerous and stringent enactments, which rendered it impossible for women to succeed to any considerable amount of property, and which almost reduced them to the alternative of marriage or a nunnery.[1] The complete inferiority of the sex was continually maintained by the law, and that generous public opinion which in Rome had frequently revolted against the injustice done to girls, in depriving them of the greater part of the inheritance of their fathers, totally disappeared. Wherever the canon law has been the basis of legislation, we find laws of succession sacrificing the interests of daughters and of wives,[2] and a state of public opinion which has been formed and regulated by these laws; nor was any serious attempt made to abolish them till the close of the last century. The French revolutionists, though rejecting the proposal of Sieyès and Condorcet to accord political emancipation to women, established at least an equal succession of sons and daughters, and thus initiated a great reformation of both law and opinion, which sooner or later must traverse the world.

In their efforts to raise the standard of purity, the

on that which is most holy and most sacred in the world.'—Plutarch, *Marcus Cato.*

[1] See Legouvé, pp. 29–38; Maine's *Ancient Law*, pp. 154–159.

[2] 'No society which preserves any tincture of Christian institutions is likely to restore to married women the personal liberty conferred on them by the middle Roman law: but the proprietary disabilities of married females stand on quite a different basis from their personal incapacities, and it is by keeping alive and consolidating the former that the expositors of the canon law have deeply injured civilisation. There are many vestiges of a struggle between the secular and ecclesiastical principles; but the canon law nearly everywhere prevailed.'—Maine's *Ancient Law*, p. 158. I may observe that the Russian law was early very favourable to the proprietary rights of married women. See a remarkable letter in the *Memoirs of the Princess Daschkaw* (edited by Mrs. Bradford: London, 1840), vol. ii. p. 404.

Christian teachers derived much assistance from the incursions and the conquests of the barbarians. The dissolution of vast retinues of slaves, the suspension of most public games, and the general impoverishment that followed the invasions, were all favourable to the cause of chastity ; and in respect of this virtue the various tribes of barbarians, however violent and lawless, were far superior to the more civilised community. Tacitus, in a very famous work, had long before pourtrayed in the most flattering colours the purity of the Germans. Adultery, he said, was very rare among them. The adulteress was driven from the house with shaven hair, and beaten ignominiously through the village. Neither youth, nor beauty, nor wealth could enable a woman who was known to have sinned to secure a husband. Polygamy was restricted to the princes, who looked upon a plurality of wives rather as a badge of dignity than as a gratification of the passions. Mothers invariably gave suck to their own children. Infanticide was forbidden. Widows were not allowed to remarry. The men feared captivity, much more for their wives than for themselves; they believed that a sacred and prophetic gift resided in women; they consulted them as oracles, and followed their counsels.[1]

It is generally believed, and it is not improbable, that Tacitus in this work intended to reprove the dissolute habits of his fellow countrymen, and considerably overcoloured the virtue of the barbarians. Of the substantial justice, however, of his picture we have much evidence. Salvian, who, about three centuries later, witnessed and described the manners of the barbarians who had triumphed over the empire, attested in the strongest language the contrast which their chastity presented to

[1] Germania, cap. ix. xviii.-xx.

the vice of those whom they had subdued.[1] The Scandinavian mythology abounds in legends exhibiting the clear sentiment of the heathen tribes on the subject of purity, and the awful penalties threatened in the next world against the seducers.[2] The barbarian women were accustomed to practise medicine and to interpret dreams, and they also very frequently accompanied their husbands to battle, rallied their broken forces, and even themselves took part in the fight.[3] Augustus had discovered that it was useless to keep barbarian chiefs as hostages, and that the one way of securing the fidelity of traitors was by taking their wives, for these, at least, were never sacrificed. The grandest instances of Roman female heroism scarcely surpassed some which were related of uncivilised Germans, or of semicivilised Gauls. When Marius had vanquished an army of the Teutons, their wives besought the conqueror to permit them to become the servants of the Vestal Virgins, in order that their honour, at least, might be secure in slavery. Their request was refused, and that night they all perished by their own hands.[4] A powerful noble once solicited the hand of a Gaulish lady named Camma, who, faithful to her husband, resisted all his entreaties. Resolved at any hazard to succeed, he caused her husband to be assassinated, and when she took refuge in the temple of Diana, and enrolled herself among her priestesses, he sent noble after noble to induce her to relent. After a time, he ventured himself into her presence. She feigned a willingness to yield, but told him it was first necessary to make a libation to the goddess. She appeared as a priestess before the altar,

[1] *De Gubernatione Dei.*

[2] See, for these legends, Mallet's *Northern Antiquities.*

[3] Tacitus, *Germ.* 9; *Hist.* iv. 18; Xiphilin. lxxi. 3; Amm. Marcellinus, xv. 12; Vopiscus, *Aurelius*; Florus, iii. 3.

[4] Valer. Max. vi. 1; Hieron. *Ep.* cxxiii.

bearing in her hand a cup of wine, which she had poisoned. She drank half of it herself, handed the remainder to her guilty lover, and when he had drained the cup to the dregs, burst into a fierce thanksgiving, that she had been permitted to avenge, and was soon to rejoin, her murdered husband.[1] Another and still more remarkable instance of conjugal fidelity was furnished by a Gaulish woman named Epponina. Her husband, Julius Sabinus, had rebelled against Vespasian; he was conquered, and might easily have escaped to Germany, but could not bear to abandon his young wife. He retired to a villa of his own, concealed himself in subterranean cellars that were below it, and instructed a freedman to spread the report that he had committed suicide, while, to account for the disappearance of his body, he set fire to the villa. Epponina, hearing of the suicide, for three days lay prostrate on the ground without eating. At length the freedman came to her, and told her that the suicide was feigned. She continued her lamentations by day, but visited her husband by night. She became with child, but owing, it is said, to an ointment, she succeeded in concealing her state from her friends. When the hour of parturition was at hand, she went alone into the cellar, and without any assistance or attendance was delivered of twins, whom she brought up underground. For nine years she fulfilled her task, when Sabinus was discovered, and, to the lasting disgrace of Vespasian, was executed in spite of the supplications of his wife, who made it her last request that she might be permitted to die with him.[2]

The moral purity of the barbarians was of a kind altogether different from that which the ascetic movement

[1] Plutarch, *De Mulier. Virt.*

[2] Plutarch, *Amatorius*; Xiphilin. lxvi. 16; Tacit. *Hist.* iv. 67. The name of this heroic wife is given in three different forms.

inculcated. It was concentrated exclusively upon marriage. It showed itself in a noble conjugal fidelity; but it was little fitted for a life of celibacy, and did not, as we have seen, prevent excessive disorders among the priesthood. The practice of polygamy among the barbarian kings was also for some centuries unchecked, or at least unsuppressed by Christianity. The kings Caribert and Chilperic had both many wives at the same time.[1] Clothaire married the sister of his first wife during the lifetime of the latter, who, on the intention of the king being announced, is reported to have said, 'Let my lord do what seemeth good in his sight, only let thy servant live in thy favour.'[2] Theodebert, whose general goodness of character is warmly extolled by the episcopal historian, abandoned his first wife on account of an atrocious crime which she had committed, took, during her lifetime, another, to whom he had previously been betrothed, and upon the death of this second wife, and while the first was still living, took a third, whom, however, at a later period he murdered.[3] St. Columbanus was expelled from Gaul chiefly on account of his denunciations of the polygamy of King Thierry.[4] Dagobert had three wives, as well as a multitude of concubines.[5] Charlemagne himself had at the same time two wives, and he indulged largely in concubines.[6] After this period examples of this nature became rare. The popes and the bishops exercised a strict supervision over domestic morals, and strenuously, and in most cases

[1] On the polygamy of the first, see Greg. Tur. iv. 26; on the polygamy of Chilperic, Greg. Tur. iv. 28; v. 14.

[2] Greg. Tur. iv. 3.

[3] Ibid. iii. 25–27, 36.

[4] Fredegarius, xxxvi.

[5] Ibid. lx.

[6] Eginhardus, *Vit. Kar. Mag.* xviii. Charlemagne had, according to Eginhard, four wives, but, as far as I can understand, only two at the same time.

successfully, opposed the attempts of kings and nobles to repudiate their wives.

But notwithstanding these startling facts, there can be no doubt that the general purity of the barbarians was from the first superior to that of the later Romans, and it appears in many of their laws. It has been very happily observed,[1] that the high value placed on this virtue is well illustrated by the fact that in the Salic Code, while a charge of cowardice falsely brought against a man was only punished by a fine of three solidi, a charge of unchastity falsely brought against a woman was punished by a fine of forty-five. The Teutonic sentiment was shown in a very stern legislation against adultery and rape,[2] and curiously minute precautions were sometimes taken to guard against them. A law of the Spanish Visigoths prohibited surgeons from bleeding any free woman except in the presence of her husband, her nearest relative, or at least of some properly appointed witness, and a Salic law imposed a fine of fifteen pieces of gold upon any one who improperly pressed her hand.[3]

Under the influence of Christianity, assisted by the barbarians, a vast change passed gradually over the world. The vice we are considering was probably more rare; it certainly assumed less extravagant forms, and it was screened from observation with a new modesty. The theory of morals had become clearer, and the practice was somewhat improved. The extreme grossness of literature had disappeared, and the more glaring violations of marriage were always censured and often repressed. The penitential discipline, and the exhortations of the

[1] Smyth's *Lectures on Modern History*, vol. i. pp. 61–62.

[2] Milman's *Hist. of Latin Christianity*, vol. i. p. 363; Legouvé, *Hist. morale des Femmes*, p. 57.

[3] See, on these laws, Lord Kames *On Women*; Legouvé, p. 57.

pulpit, diffused abroad an immeasurably higher sense of the importance of purity than Pagan antiquity had known. St. Gregory the Great, following in the steps of some Pagan philosophers,[1] strenuously urged upon mothers the duty of themselves suckling their children; and many minute and stringent precepts were made against extravagances of dress and manners. The religious institutions of Greece and Asia Minor, which had almost consecrated prostitution, were for ever abolished, and the courtesan sank into a lower stage of degradation.

Besides these changes, the duty of the reciprocal fidelity in marriage was enforced with a new earnestness. The contrast between the levity with which the frailty of men has in most ages been regarded, and the extreme severity with which women who have been guilty of the same offence have generally been treated, forms one of the most singular anomalies in moral history, and appears the more remarkable when we remember that the temptation usually springs from the sex which is so readily pardoned, that the sex which is visited with such crushing penalties is proverbially the most weak, and that, in the case of women, but not in the case of men, the vice is very commonly the result of the most abject misery and poverty. For this disparity of censure several reasons have been assigned. The offence can be more surely and easily detected, and therefore more certainly punished, in the case of women than of men; and as the duty of providing for his children falls upon the father, the introduction into the family of children who are not his own is a special injury to him, while illegitimate children who do not spring from adultery will probably, on account of their father having entered into no compact to support them, ultimately become criminals or paupers,

[1] Favorinus had strongly urged it. (Aul. Gell. *Noct.* xii. 1.)

and therefore a burden to society.[1] I may be added, I think, that several causes render the observance of this virtue more difficult for one sex than for the other; that its violation, when every allowance has been made for the moral degradation which is a result of the existing condition of public opinion, is naturally more profoundly prejudicial to the character of women than of men, and also that much of our feeling on these subjects is due to laws and moral systems which were formed by men, and were in the first instance intended for their own protection.

The passages in the Fathers, asserting the equality of the obligation of chastity imposed upon both sexes, are exceedingly unequivocal;[2] and although the doctrine itself had been anticipated by Seneca and Plutarch, it had probably never before, and has never since, been so fully realised as in the early Church. It cannot, however, be said that the conquest has been retained. At the present day, although the standard of morals is far higher than in Pagan Rome, it may be questioned whether the inequality of the censure which is bestowed upon the two sexes is not as great as in the days of Paganism, and that inequality is continually the cause of the most shameful and the most pitiable injustice. In one respect, indeed, a great retrogression resulted from chivalry, and long survived its decay. The character of the seducer, and especially of the passionless seducer who pursues his

[1] These are the reasons given by Malthus, *On Population*, book iii. ch. ii.

[2] St. Augustine (*De Conj. Adult.* ii. 19) maintains that adultery is even more criminal in the man than in the woman. St. Jerome has an impressive passage on the subject: 'Aliæ sunt leges Cæsarum, aliæ Christi; aliud Papianus, aliud Paulus nostri præcepit. Apud illos viris impudicitiæ fræna laxantur et solo stupro atque adulterio condemnato passim per lupanaria et ancillulas libido permittitur, quasi culpam dignitas faciat non voluntas. Apud nos quod non licet feminis æque non licet viris; et eadem servitus pari conditione censetur.'—*Ep.* lxxvii. St. Chrysostom writes in a similar strain.

career simply as a kind of sport, and under the influence of no stronger motive than vanity or a spirit of adventure, and who designates his successes in destroying the honour of women his conquests, has been glorified and idealised in the popular literature of Christendom in a manner to which we can find no parallel in antiquity. When we reflect that the object of such a man is by the coldest and most deliberate treachery to blast the lives of innocent women; when we compare the levity of his motive with the irreparable injury he inflicts; and when we remember that he can only deceive his victim by persuading her to love him, and can only ruin her by persuading her to trust him, it must be owned that it would be difficult to conceive a cruelty more wanton and more heartless, or a character combining more numerous elements of infamy and of dishonour. That such a character should for many centuries have been the popular ideal of a vast section of literature, that it should have been the continual boast of those who most plume themselves upon their honour, is assuredly one of the most mournful facts in history, and it represents a moral deflection certainly not less than was revealed in ancient Greece by the position that was assigned to the courtesan.

The fundamental truth, that the same act can never be at once venial for a man to demand, and infamous for a woman to accord, though nobly enforced by the early Christians, has not passed into the popular sentiment of Christendom. The mystical character, however, which the Church imparted to marriage has been extremely influential. Partly by raising marriage into a sacrament, and partly by representing it as, in some mysterious and not very definable sense, an image of the union of Christ with His Church, a feeling was fostered that a lifelong union of one man and one woman is, under all circumstances, the single form of intercourse between the sexes which is not illegitimate; and this conviction has acquired the force of a primal moral intuition.

There can, I think, be little doubt that, in the stringency with which it is usually laid down, it rests not upon the law of nature, but upon positive law, although unassisted nature is sufficient to lead men many steps in its direction. Considering the subject simply in the light of unaided reason, two rules comprise the whole duty of man. He must abstain from whatever injures happiness or degrades character. Under the first head, he must include the more remote as well as the immediate consequences of his act. He must consider how his partner will be affected by the union, the light in which society will view the connection, the probable position of the children to be born, the effect of these births, and also the effect of his example upon the well-being of society at large. Some of the elements of this calculation vary in different stages of society. Thus, public opinion in one age will reprobate, and therefore punish, connections which, in another age, are fully sanctioned; and the probable position of the children, as well as the effect of the births upon society, will depend greatly upon particular and national circumstances.

Under the second head is comprised the influence of this intercourse in clouding or developing the moral feelings, lowering or elevating the tone of character, exciting or allaying the aberrations of the imagination, incapacitating men for pure affections or extending their range, making the animal part of our nature more or less predominant. We know, by the intuition of our moral nature, that this predominance is always a degraded, though it is not always an unhappy condition. We also know that it is a law of our being, that powerful and beautiful affections, which had before been latent, are evoked in some particular forms of union, while other forms of union are peculiarly fitted to deaden the affections and to pervert the character.

In these considerations we have ample grounds for maintaining that the lifelong union of one man and of one woman should be the normal or dominant type of intercourse between the sexes. We can prove that it is on the whole most conducive to the happiness, and also to the moral elevation, of all parties. But beyond this point it would, I conceive, be impossible to advance, except by the assistance of a special revelation. It by no means follows that because this should be the dominant type it should be the only one, or that the interests of society demand that all connections should be forced into the same die. Connections, which were confessedly only for a few years, have always subsisted side by side with permanent marriages; and in periods when public opinion, acquiescing in their propriety, inflicts no excommunication on one or both of the partners, when these partners are not living the demoralising and degrading life which accompanies the consciousness of guilt, and when proper provision is made for the children who are born, it would be, I believe, impossible to prove by the light of simple and unassisted reason, that such connections should be invariably condemned. It is extremely important, both for the happiness and for the moral well-being of men, that lifelong unions should not be effected simply under the imperious prompting of a blind appetite. There are always multitudes who, in the period of their lives when their passions are most strong, are incapable of supporting children in their own social rank, and who would therefore injure society by marrying in it, but are nevertheless perfectly capable of securing an honourable career for their illegitimate children in the lower social sphere to which they would naturally belong. Under the conditions I have mentioned, these connections are not injurious, but beneficial to the weaker partner; they soften the differences of rank, they stimulate social habits, and they do not produce upon character the degrading effect of promiscuous intercourse, or upon society the injurious effects of imprudent marriages, one or other of which will multiply in their absence. In the immense variety of circumstances and characters, cases will always appear in which, on utilitarian grounds, they might seem advisable.

It is necessary to dwell upon such considerations as these, if we would understand the legislation of the Pagan Empire or the changes that were effected by Christianity. The legislators of the empire distinctly recognised these connections, and made it a main object to authorise, dignify, and regulate them. The unlimited licence of divorce practically included them under the name of marriage, while that name sheltered them from stigma, and prevented many of the gravest evils of unauthorised unions. The word concubine also, which in the republic had the same signification as among ourselves, represented in the empire a strictly legal union—an innovation which was chiefly due to Augustus, and was doubtless intended as part of the legislation against celibacy, and also, it may be, as a corrective of the licentious habits that were general. This union was in essentials simply a form of marriage, for he who, having a concubine, took to himself either a wife or another concubine, was legally guilty of adultery. Like the commonest form of marriage, it was consummated without any ceremony, and was dissoluble at will. Its peculiarities were that it was contracted between men of patrician rank and freedwomen, who were forbidden by law to intermarry; that the concubine, though her position was perfectly recognised and honourable, did not share the rank of her partner, that she brought no dowry, and that her children followed her rank, and were excluded from the rank and the inheritance of their father.[1]

Against these notions Christianity declared a direct and implacable warfare, which was imperfectly reflected in the civil legislation, but appeared unequivocally in the writings of the Fathers, and in most of the decrees of the Councils.[2] It taught, as a religious dogma, invariable, inflexible, and independent of all utilitarian calculations, that all forms of intercourse of the sexes, other than lifelong unions, were criminal. By teaching men to regard this doctrine as axiomatic, and therefore inflicting severe social penalties and deep degradation on transient connections, it has profoundly modified even their utilitarian aspect, and has rendered them in most countries furtive and disguised. There is probably no other branch of ethics which has been so largely determined by special

[1] See Troplong, *Influence du Christianisme sur le Droit*, pp. 239–251.

[2] We find, however, traces of toleration of the early Roman concubines in Christianity for some time. Thus, a Council of Toledo decreed, 'Si quis habens uxorem fidelis concubinam habeat non communicet. Cæterum is qui non habet uxorem et pro uxore concubinam habet a communione non repellatur, tantum ut unius mulieris, aut uxoris aut concubinæ ut ei placuerit, sit conjunctione contentus.'—1 *Can.* 17. St. Isidore said, 'Christiano non dicam plurimas sed nec duas simul habere licitum est, nisi unam tantum aut uxorem, aut certo loco uxoris, si conjux deest, concubinam.'—*Apud Gratianum*, diss. 4. Quoted by Natalis Alexander, *Hist. Eccles.* Sæc. I. diss. 29. Mr. Lea (*Hist. of Sacerdotal Celibacy*, pp. 203–205) has devoted an extremely interesting note to tracing the history of the word concubine through the middle ages. He shows that even up to the thirteenth century a concubine was not necessarily an abandoned woman. The term was applied to marriages that were real, but not officially recognised. Coleridge notices a remarkable instance of the revival of this custom in German history.—*Notes on English Divines* (ed. 1853), vol. i. p. 221.

dogmatic theology, and there is none which would be so deeply affected by its decay.

As a part of the same movement, the purely civil marriage of the later Pagan Empire was gradually replaced by religious marriages. There is a manifest propriety in invoking a divine benediction upon an act which forms so important an epoch in life, and the mingling of a religious ceremony impresses a deeper sense of the solemnity of the contract. The essentially religious and even mystical character imparted by Christianity to marriage rendered the consecration peculiarly natural, but it was only very gradually that it came to be looked upon as absolutely necessary. As I have already noticed, it was long dispensed with in the marriage of slaves; and even in the case of freemen, though generally performed, it was not made compulsory till the tenth century.[1] In addition to its primary object of sanctifying marriage, it became in time a powerful instrument in securing the authority of the priesthood, who were able to compel men to submit to the conditions they imposed in the formation of the most important contract of life, and the modern authorisation of civil marriages as well as the general diminution of the power of the Catholic priesthood over domestic life, have been among the most severe blows ecclesiastical influence has undergone.

The absolute sinfulness of divorce was at the same time strenuously maintained by the Councils, which in this, as in many other points, differed widely from the civil law. Constantine restricted it to three cases of crime on the part of the husband, and three on the part of the wife; but the habits of the people were too strong for his enactments, and after one or two changes in the law, the full

[1] Legouvé, p. 199.

latitude of divorce reappeared in the Justinian Code. The Fathers, on the other hand, though they hesitated a little about the case of a divorce which followed an act of adultery on the part of the wife,[1] had no hesitation whatever in pronouncing all other divorces to be criminal, and periods of penitential discipline were imposed upon Christians who availed themselves of the privileges of the civil law.[2] For many centuries this duality of legislation continued. The barbarian law restricted divorce by imposing severe fines on those who repudiated their wives. Charlemagne pronounced divorce to be criminal, but did not venture to make it penal, and he practised it himself. On the other hand, the Church threatened with excommunication, and in some cases actually launched its thunders against, those who were guilty of it. It was only in the twelfth century that the victory was definitely achieved, and the civil law, adopting the principle of the canon law, prohibited all divorce.[3]

I do not propose in the present work to examine how far this total prohibition has been for the happiness or the moral well-being of men. I will simply observe that, though it is now often defended, it was not originally imposed in Christian nations upon utilitarian grounds, but was based upon the sacramental character of marriage, upon the belief that it was the special symbol of the perpetual union of Christ with His Church, and upon a well-known passage in the Gospels. The stringency of

[1] See some curious passages in Troplong, pp. 222-223. The Fathers seem to have thought dissolution of marriage was not lawful on account of the adultery of the husband, but that it was not absolutely unlawful, though not commendable, for a husband whose wife had committed adultery to remarry.

[2] Some of the great charities of Fabiola were performed as penances, on account of her crime in availing herself of the legislative permission of divorce.

[3] Laboulaye, *Recherches sur la Condition civile et politique des Femmes*, pp. 152-158.

the catholic doctrine, which forbids the dissolution of marriage even in the case of adultery, has been considerably relaxed by modern legislation, and there can, I think, be little doubt that further steps will yet be taken in the same direction; but the vast change that was effected in both practice and theory since the unlimited licence of the Pagan Empire must be manifest to all.

It was essential, or at least very important, that a union which was so solemn and so irrevocable should be freely contracted. The sentiment of the Roman patriots towards the close of the republic was, that marriage should be regarded as a means of providing children for the State, and should be entered into as a matter of duty with that view, and the laws of Augustus had imposed many disqualifications on those who abstained from it. Both of these inducements to marriage passed away under the influence of Christianity. The popular inducement disappeared with the decline of civic virtues. The laws were rescinded under the influence of the ascetic enthusiasm which made men regard the state of celibacy as pre-eminently holy.

There was still one other important condition to be attained by theologians in order to realise their ideal type of marriage. It was to prevent the members of the Church from intermarrying with those whose religious opinions differed from their own. Mixed marriages, it has been truly said, may do more than almost any other influence to assuage the rancour and the asperity of sects, and they have therefore always been bitterly opposed by theologians. It must be added, however, that a considerable measure of tolerance must have been already attained before they become possible. In a union in which each partner believes and realises that the other is doomed to an eternity of misery there can be no real happiness, no sympathy, no trust; and a domestic agreement that some of the children should be educated in one religion and some in the other would be impossible when each parent believed it to be an agreement that some children should be doomed to hell.

The domestic unhappiness arising from differences of belief was probably almost or altogether unknown in the world before the introduction of Christianity; for although differences of opinion may have before existed, the same momentous consequences were not attached to them. It has been the especial bane of periods of great religious change, such as the conversion of the Roman Empire, or the Reformation, or our own day, when far more serious questions than those which agitated the sixteenth century are occupying the attention of a large proportion of thinkers and scholars, and when the deep and widening chasm between the religious opinions of most highly educated men, and of the immense majority of women, is painfully apparent. While a multitude of scientific discoveries, critical and historical researches, and educational reforms have brought thinking men face to face with religious problems of extreme importance, women have been almost absolutely excluded from their influence. Their minds are usually by nature less capable than those of men of impartiality and suspense, and the almost complete omission from female education of those studies which most discipline and strengthen the intellect, increases the difference, while at the same time it has been usually made a main object to imbue them with a passionate faith in traditional opinions, and to preserve them from all contact with opposing views. But contracted knowledge and imperfect sympathy are not the sole fruits of this education. It has always been the peculiarity of a certain kind of theological teaching, that

58

it inverts all the normal principles of judgment, and absolutely destroys intellectual diffidence. On other subjects we find, if not a respect for honest conviction, at least some sense of the amount of knowledge that is requisite to entitle men to express an opinion on grave controversies. A complete ignorance of the subject matter of a dispute restrains the confidence of dogmatism, and an ignorant person who is aware that, by much reading and thinking in spheres of which he has himself no knowledge, his educated neighbour has modified or rejected opinions which that ignorant person had been taught, will, at least, if he is a man of sense or modesty, abstain from compassionating the benighted condition of his more instructed friend. But on theological questions this has never been so. Unfaltering belief being taught as the first of duties, and all doubt being usually stigmatised as criminal or damnable, a state of mind is formed to which we find no parallel in other fields. Many men and most women, though completely ignorant of the very rudiments of biblical criticism, historical research, or scientific discoveries, though they have never read a single page, or understood a single proposition of the writings of those whom they condemn, and have absolutely no rational knowledge either of the arguments by which their faith is defended, or of those by which it has been impugned, will nevertheless adjudicate with the utmost confidence upon every polemical question, denounce, hate, pity, or pray for the conversion of all who dissent from what they have been taught, assume, as a matter beyond the faintest possibility of doubt, that the opinions they have received without enquiry must be true, and that the opinions which others have arrived at by enquiry must be false, and make it a main object of their lives to assail what they call heresy in every way in their power, except by examining the grounds on which it rests. It is probable that the great majority of voices that swell the clamour against every book which is regarded as heretical, are the voices of those who would deem it criminal even to open that book, or to enter into any real, searching, and impartial investigation of the subject to which it relates. Innumerable pulpits support this tone of thought, and represent, with a fervid rhetoric well fitted to excite the nerves and imaginations of women, the deplorable condition of all who deviate from a certain type of opinions or of emotions; a blind propagandism or a secret wretchedness penetrates into countless households, poisoning the peace of families, chilling the mutual confidence of husband and wife, adding immeasurably to the difficulties which every searcher into truth has to encounter, and diffusing far and wide intellectual timidity, disingenuousness, and hypocrisy.

These domestic divisions became very apparent in the period of the conversion of the Roman Empire, and a natural desire to guard intact the orthodoxy and zeal of the converts, and to prevent a continual discordance, stimulated the Fathers in their very vehement denunciations of all mixed marriages. We may also trace in these denunciations the outline of a very singular doctrine, which was afterwards suffered to fall into obscurity, but was revived in the last century in England in a curious and learned work of the nonjuror Dodwell.[1] The union

[1] 'A discourse concerning the obligation to marry within the true communion, following from their style (*sic*) of being called a holy seed.' This rare discourse is appended to a sermon against mixed marriages by Leslie. (London, 1702.) The reader may find something about Dodwell in Macaulay's *Hist. of England*, ch. xiv.; but Macaulay, who does not appear to have known of Dodwell's masterpiece—his dissertation *De Paucitate Martyrum*, which is one of the finest specimens of criticism of his time—and who only knew the discourse on marriages by extracts, has, I think, done a good deal of injustice to him. However, I have not read his book about organs, which is said to be very absurd.

of Christ and His Church had been represented as a marriage; and this image was not regarded as a mere metaphor or comparison, but as intimating a mysterious unity, which, though not susceptible of any very clear definition, was not on that account the less influential. Christians were the 'limbs of Christ,' and for them to join themselves in marriage with those who were not of the Christian fold was literally, it was said, a species of adultery or fornication. The intermarriage of the Israelites, the chosen seed of the ancient world, with the Gentiles, had been described in the Old Testament as an act of impurity;[1] and in the opinion of some at least of the Fathers, the Christian community occupied towards the unbelievers a position analogous to that which the Jews had occupied towards the Gentiles. St. Cyprian denounces the crime of those 'who prostitute the limbs of Christ in marriage with the Gentiles.'[2] Tertullian described the intermarriage as fornication;[3] and after the triumph of the Church, the intermarriage of Jews and Christians was made a capital offence, and was stigmatised by the law as adultery.[4] The civil law did not prohibit the orthodox from intermarrying with heretics, but many councils denounced this as criminal in the strongest terms.

The extreme sanctity attributed to virginity, the absolute condemnation of all forms of sexual connections other than marriage, and the formation and gradual realisation

[1] Dodwell relies mainly upon this fact, and especially upon Ezra's having treated these marriages as essentially null.

[2] 'Jungere cum infidelibus vinculum matrimonii, prostituere gentilibus membra Christi.'—Cyprian, *De Lapsis.*

[3] 'Hæc cum ita sint, fideles Gentilium matrimonia subeuntes stupri reos esse constat, et arcendos ab omni communicatione fraternitatis.'—Tert. *Ad Uxor.* ii. 3.

[4] See on this law, and on the many councils which condemned the marriage of orthodox with heretics, Bingham, *Antiq.* xxii. 2, §§ 1–2.

of the Christian conception of marriage as a permanent union of a man and woman of the same religious opinions, consecrated by solemn religious services, carrying with it a deep religious signification, and dissoluble only by death, were the most obvious signs of Christian influence in the sphere of ethics we are examining. Another very important result of the new religion was to raise to a far greater honour than they had previously possessed the qualities in which women peculiarly excel.

There are few more curious subjects of enquiry than the distinctive differences between the minds and characters of men and women, and the manner in which those differences have affected the ideal types of different ages, nations, philosophies, and religions. Physically, men have the indisputable superiority in strength, and women in beauty. Intellectually, a certain inferiority of the female sex can hardly be denied when we remember how almost exclusively the foremost places in every department of science, literature, and art have been occupied by men, how infinitesimally small is the number of women who have shown in any form the very highest order of genius, how many of the greatest men have achieved their greatness in defiance of the most adverse circumstances, and how completely women have failed in obtaining the first position, even in music or painting, for the cultivation of which their circumstances would appear most propitious. It is as impossible to find a female Raphael, or a female Handel, as a female Shakspeare or Newton. Women are intellectually more desultory and volatile than men, they are more occupied with particular instances than with general principles; they judge rather by intuitive perceptions than by deliberate reasoning or past experience. They are, however, usually superior to men in nimbleness and rapidity of thought, and in the gift of tact or the power of seizing speedily and faithfully the finer inflexions of feeling, and they have therefore often attained very great eminence as conversationalists, as letter-writers, as actresses, and as novelists.

Morally, the general superiority of women over men is, I think, unquestionable. If we take the somewhat coarse and inadequate criterion of police statistics, we find that, while the male and female populations are nearly the same in number, the crimes committed by men are usually rather more than five times as numerous as those committed by women;[1] and although it may be justly observed that men, as the stronger sex, and the sex upon whom the burden of supporting the family is thrown, have more temptations than women, it must be remembered, on the other hand, that extreme poverty which verges upon starvation is most common among women, whose means of livelihood are most restricted, and whose earnings are smallest and most precarious. Self-sacrifice is the most conspicuous element of a virtuous and religious character, and it is certainly far less common among men than among women, whose whole lives are usually spent in yielding to the will and consulting the pleasures of another. There are two great departments of virtue: the impulsive, or that which springs spontaneously from the emotions, and the deliberative, or that which is performed in obedience to the sense of duty; and in both of these I imagine women are superior to men. Their

[1] Many curious statistics illustrating this fact are given by M. Bonneville de Marsangy—a Portuguese writer, who is counsellor of the Imperial Court at Paris—in his *Étude sur la Moralité comparée de la Femme et de l'Homme.* (Paris, 1862.) The writer would have done better if he had not maintained, in lawyer fashion, that the statistics of crime are absolutely decisive of the question of the comparative morality of the sexes, and also, if he had not thought it due to his official position to talk in a rather grotesque strain about the regeneration and glorification of the sex in the person of the Empress Eugénie.

sensibility is greater, they are more chaste both in thought and act, more tender to the erring, more compassionate to the suffering, more affectionate to all about them. On the other hand, those who have traced the course of the wives of the poor, and of many who, though in narrow circumstances, can hardly be called poor, will probably admit that in no other class do we so often find entire lives spent in daily persistent self-denial, in the patient endurance of countless trials, in the ceaseless and deliberate sacrifice of their own enjoyments to the well-being or the prospects of others. In active courage women are inferior to men. In the courage of endurance they are commonly their superiors; but their passive courage is not so much fortitude which bears and defies, as resignation which bears and bends. In the ethics of intellect they are decidedly inferior. To repeat an expression I have already employed, women very rarely love truth, though they love passionately what they call 'the truth,' or opinions they have received from others, and hate vehemently those who differ from them. They are little capable of impartiality or of doubt; their thinking is chiefly a mode of feeling; though very generous in their acts, they are rarely generous in their opinions, and their leaning is naturally to the side of restriction. They persuade rather than convince, and value belief rather as a source of consolation than as a faithful expression of the reality of things. They are less capable than men of perceiving qualifying circumstances, of admitting the existence of elements of good in systems to which they are opposed, of distinguishing the personal character of an opponent from the opinions he maintains. Men lean most to justice, and women to mercy. Men are most addicted to intemperance and brutality, women to frivolity and jealousy. Men excel in energy, self-reliance, perseverance, and magnanimity; women in humility, gentleness, modesty, and endurance. The realising imagination which causes us to pity and to love is more sensitive in women than in men, and it is especially more capable of dwelling on the unseen. Their religious or devotional realisations are incontestably more vivid; and it is probable that, while a father is most moved by the death of a child in his presence, a mother generally feels most the death of a child in some distant land. But though more intense, the sympathies of women are commonly less wide than those of men. Their imaginations individualise more, their affections are, in consequence, concentrated rather on leaders than on causes; and if they care for a great cause, it is generally because it is represented by a great man, or conected with some one whom they love. In politics, their enthusiasm is more naturally loyalty than patriotism. In history, they are even more inclined than men to dwell exclusively upon biographical incidents or characteristics as distinguished from the march of general causes. In benevolence, they excel in charity, which alleviates individual suffering, rather than in philanthropy, which deals with large masses, and is more frequently employed in preventing than in allaying calamity.

It was a remark of Winckelmann that 'the supreme beauty of Greek art is rather male than female;' and the justice of this remark has been amply corroborated by the greater knowledge we have of late years attained of the works of the Phidian period, in which art achieved its highest perfection, and in which, at the same time, force and freedom, and masculine grandeur, were its pre-eminent characteristics. A similar observation may be made of the moral ideal of which ancient art was simply the expression. In antiquity the virtues that were most admired were almost exclusively those which are distinctively masculine. Courage, self-assertion, magnanimity, and, above all, patriotism, were the leading features of the ideal type; and chastity, modesty, and charity, the gentler and the domestic virtues, which are especially feminine, were greatly undervalued. With the single exception of conjugal fidelity, none of the virtues that were very highly prized were virtues distinctively or pre-eminently feminine. With this exception, nearly all the most illustrious women of antiquity were illustrious chiefly because they overcame the natural conditions of their sex. It is a characteristic fact that the favourite female ideal of the artists appears to have been the Amazon.[1] We may admire the Spartan mother, or the mother of the Gracchi, repressing every sign of grief when their children were sacrificed upon the altar of their country, we may wonder at the majestic courage of a Porcia or an Arria, but we extol them chiefly because, being women, they emancipated themselves from the frailty of their sex, and displayed an heroic fortitude worthy of the strongest and the bravest of men. We may bestow an equal admiration upon the noble devotion and charity of a St. Elizabeth of Hungary, or of a Mrs. Fry, but we do not admire them because they displayed these virtues, although they were women, for we feel that their virtues were of the kind which the female nature is most fitted to produce. The change from the heroic to the saintly ideal, from the ideal of Paganism to the ideal of Christianity, was a change from a type which was essentially male to one which was essentially feminine. Of all the great schools of philosophy no other reflected so faithfully the Roman conception of moral excellence as Stoicism, and the greatest

[1] See Pliny, *Hist. Nat.* xxxiv. 19.

Roman exponent of Stoicism summed up its character in a single sentence when he pronounced it to be beyond all other sects the most emphatically masculine.[1] On the other hand, an ideal type in which meekness, gentleness, patience, humility, faith, and love are the most prominent features, is not naturally male but female. A reason probably deeper than the historical ones which are commonly alleged, why sculpture has always been peculiarly Pagan and painting peculiarly Christian, may be found in the fact, that sculpture is especially suited to represent male beauty, or the beauty of strength, and painting female beauty, or the beauty of softness; and that Pagan sentiment was chiefly a glorification of the masculine qualities of strength, and courage, and conscious virtue, while Christian sentiment is chiefly a glorification of the feminine qualities of gentleness, humility, and love. The painters whom the religious feeling of Christendom have recognised as the most faithful exponents of Christian sentiment have always been those who infused a large measure of feminine beauty even into their male characters; and we never, or scarcely ever, find that the same artist has been conspicuously successful in delineating both Christian and Pagan types. Michael Angelo, whose genius loved to expatiate on the sublimity of strength and defiance, failed signally in his representations of the Christian ideal; and Perugino was equally unsuccessful when he sought to pourtray the features of the heroes of antiquity.[2] The position that was gradually assigned to

[1] 'Tantum inter Stoicos, Serene, et ceteros sapientiam professos interesse, quantum inter fœminas et mares non immerito dixerim.'—*De Const. Sapientis*, cap. i.

[2] This is well illustrated, on the one side, by the most repulsive representations of Christ, by Michael Angelo, in the great fresco in the Sistine Chapel (so inferior to the Christ of Orgagna, at Pisa, from which it was partly imitated), and in marble in the Minerva Church at Rome; and,

the Virgin as the female ideal in the belief and the devotion of Christendom, was a consecration or an expression of the new value that was attached to the feminine virtues.

The general superiority of women to men in the strength of their religious emotions, and their natural attraction to a religion which made personal attachment to its Founder its central duty, and which imparted an unprecedented dignity and afforded an unprecedented scope to their characteristic virtues, account for the very conspicuous position they assumed in the great work of the conversion of the Roman Empire. In no other important movement of thought was female influence so powerful or so acknowledged. In the ages of persecution female figures occupy many of the foremost places in the ranks of martyrdom, and Pagan and Christian writers alike attest the alacrity with which women flocked to the Church, and the influence they exercised in its favour over the male members of their families. The mothers of St. Augustine, St. Chrysostom, St. Basil, St. Gregory Nazianzen, and Theodoret, had all a leading part in the conversion of their sons. St. Helena, the mother of Constantine, Flacilla, the wife of Theodosius the Great, St. Pulcheria, the sister of Theodosius the Younger, and Placidia, the mother of Valentinian III., were among the most conspicuous defenders of the faith. In the heretical sects the same zeal was manifested, and Arius, Priscillian, and Montanus were all supported by troops of zealous female devotees. In the career of asceticism women took a part little if at all inferior to men, while in the organisation of the great work of charity they were

on the other hand, by the frescoes of Perugino, at Perugia, representing the great sages of Paganism. The figure of Cato, in the latter, almost approaches as well as I remember, the type of St. John.

pre-eminent. For no other field of active labour are women so admirably suited as for this; and although we may trace from the earliest period, in many creeds and ages, individual instances of their influence in allaying the sufferings of the distressed,[1] it may be truly said that their instinct and genius of charity had never before the dawn of Christianity obtained full scope for action. Fabiola, Paula, Melania, and a host of other noble ladies devoted their time and fortunes mainly to founding and extending vast institutions of charity, some of them of a kind before unknown in the world. The empress Flacilla was accustomed to tend with her own hands the sick in the hospitals,[2] and a readiness to discharge such offices was deemed the first duty of a Christian wife.[3] From age to age the impulse thus communicated has been felt; there has been no period, however corrupt, there has been no Church, however superstitious, that has not been adorned

[1] In that fine description of a virtuous woman which is ascribed to the mother of King Lemuel, we read, 'She stretcheth out her hand to the poor; yea, she reacheth forth her hands to the needy.' (Proverbs xxxi. 20.) I have already quoted from Xenophon the beautiful description of the Greek wife tending her sick slaves. So, too, Euripides represents the slaves of Alcestis gathering with tears around the bed of their dying mistress, who, even then, found some kind word for each, and when she died, lamenting her as their second mother. (Eurip. *Alcest.*) In the servile war which desolated Sicily at the time of the Punic wars, we find a touching trait of the same kind. The revolt was provoked by the cruelties of a rich man (named Damophilus) and his wife, who were massacred with circumstances of great atrocity; but the slaves preserved their daughter entirely unharmed, for she had always made it her business to console them in their sorrow, and she had won the love of all. (Diodor. Sic. *Frag.* xxxiv.) So, too, Marcia, the wife of Cato, used to suckle her young slaves from her breast. (Plut. *Marc. Cato.*) I may add the well-known sentiment which Virgil puts in the mouth of Dido, 'Haud ignara mali miseris succurrere disco.' There are, doubtless, many other touches of the same kind in ancient literature, some of which may occur to my readers.

[2] Theodoret, v. 19.

[3] See the beautiful description of the functions of a Christian woman in the second book of Tertullian, *Ad Uxorem.*

by many Christian women devoting their entire lives to assuaging the sufferings of men, and the mission of charity thus instituted has not been more efficacious in diminishing the sum of human wretchedness than in promoting the moral dignity of those by whom it was conducted.

Among the Collyridian heretics, women were admitted to the priesthood. Among the orthodox, although this honour was not bestowed upon them, they received a religious consecration, and discharged some minor ecclesiastical functions under the name of deaconesses.[1] This order may be traced to the Apostolic period.[2] It consisted of elderly virgins, who were set apart by a formal ordination, and were employed in assisting as catechists and attendants at the baptism of women, in visiting the sick, ministering to martyrs in prison, preserving order in the congregations, and accompanying and presenting women who desired an interview with the bishop. It would appear from the evidence of some councils, that abuses gradually crept into this institution, and the deaconesses at last faded into simple nuns, but they were still in existence in the East in the twelfth century. Besides these, widows, when they had been but once married, were treated with peculiar honour, and were made the special recipients of the charity of the Church. Women advanced in years, who, either from their single life or from bereavement, have been left without any male protector in the world, have always been peculiarly deserving of commiseration. With less strength, and commonly with less means, and less knowledge of the world than men, they are liable to contract certain peculiarities

[1] See, upon the deaconesses, Bingham's *Christian Antiquities*, bock ii. ch. 22, and Ludlow's *Woman's Work in the Church*. The latter author argues elaborately that the 'widows' were not the same as the deaconesses.

[2] Phœbe (Rom. xvi. 1) is described as a διάκονος.

of mind and manner to which an excessive amount of ridicule has been attached, and age, in most cases, furnishes them with very little to compensate for the charms of which it has deprived them. The weight and dignity of matured wisdom which make the old age of one sex so venerable, are more rarely found in that of the other, and even physical beauty is more frequently the characteristic of an old man than of an old woman. The Church laboured steadily to cast a halo of reverence around this period of woman's life, and its religious exercises have done very much to console and to occupy it.

In accordance with these ideas, the Christian legislators contributed largely to improve the legal position of widows in respect to property,[1] and Justinian gave mothers the guardianship of their children, destroying the Pagan rule that guardianship could only be legally exercised by men.[2] The usual subservience of the sex to ecclesiastical influence, the numerous instances of rich widows devoting their fortunes, and mothers their sons, to the Church, had no doubt some influence in securing the advocacy of the clergy, but these measures had a manifest importance in elevating the position of women who have had in Christian lands, a great, though not, I think, altogether a beneficial influence, in the early education of their sons.

Independently of all legal enactments, the simple change of the ideal type by bringing specially feminine virtues

[1] A very able writer, who takes on the whole an unfavourable view of the influence of Christianity on legislation, says, 'The provision for the widow was attributable to the exertions of the Church, which never relaxed its solicitude for the interests of wives surviving their husbands, winning, perhaps, one of the most arduous of its triumphs when, after exacting for two or three centuries an express promise from the husband at marriage to endow his wife, it at last succeeded in engrafting the principle of dower on the customary law of all Western Europe.'—Maine's *Ancient Law*, p. 224.

[2] See Troplong, *Influence du Christianisme sur le Droit*, pp. 308–310.

into the fore front, was sufficient to elevate and ennoble the sex. The commanding position of the mediæval abbesses, the great number of female saints, and especially the reverence bestowed upon the Virgin, had a similar effect. It is remarkable that the Jews, who, of the three great nations of antiquity, certainly produced in history and poetry the smallest number of illustrious women, should have furnished the world with its supreme female ideal, and it is also a striking illustration of the qualities which prove most attractive in woman, that one of whom we know nothing except her gentleness and her sorrow should have exercised a magnetic power upon the world incomparably greater than was exercised by the most majestic female patriots of Paganism. Whatever may be thought of its theological propriety, there is, I think, little doubt that the Catholic reverence for the Virgin has done much to elevate and purify the ideal of women, and to soften the manners of men. It has had an influence which the worship of the Pagan goddesses could never possess, for these had been almost destitute of moral beauty, and especially of that kind of moral beauty which is peculiarly feminine. It supplied in a great measure the redeeming and ennobling element in that strange amalgam of religious, licentious, and military feeling which was formed around women in the age of chivalry, and which no succeeding change of habit or belief has wholly destroyed.

It can hardly, I think, be questioned that in the great religious convulsions of the sixteenth century, the feminine type followed Catholicism, while Protestantism inclined more to the masculine type. Catholicism alone retained the Virgin worship, which at once reflected and sustained the first. The skill with which it acts upon the emotions by music, and painting, and solemn architecture, and imposing pageantry, its tendency to appeal to the imagination rather than to the reason, and to foster modes of feeling rather than modes of thought, its assertion of absolute and infallible certainty, above all, the manner in which it teaches its votary to throw himself perpetually on authority, all tended in the same direction. It is the part of a woman to lean, it is the part of a man to stand. A religion which prescribed to the distracted mind unreasoning faith in an infallible Church, and to the troubled conscience an implicit trust in an absolving priesthood, has ever had an especial attraction to a feminine mind. A religion which recognised no authority between man and his Creator, which asserted at once the dignity and the duty of private judgment, and which, while deepening immeasurably the sense of individual responsibility, denuded religion of meretricious ornaments, and of most æsthetic aids, is pre-eminently a religion of men. Puritanism is the most masculine form that Christianity has yet assumed. Its most illustrious teachers differed from the Catholic saints as much in the moral type they displayed as in the system of doctrines they held. Catholicism commonly softens, while Protestantism strengthens the character; but the softness of the first often degenerates into weakness, and the strength of the second into hardness. Sincerely Catholic nations are distinguished for their reverence, for their habitual and vivid perceptions of religious things, for the warmth of their emotions, for a certain amiability of disposition, and a certain natural courtesy and refinement of manner that are inexpressibly winning. Sincerely Protestant nations are distinguished for their love of truth, for their firm sense of duty, for the strength and the dignity of their character. Loyalty and humility, which are especially feminine, flourish chiefly in the first; liberty and self-assertion in the second. The first are most prone to superstition, and the second to fanaticism. Protestantism, by purifying and dignifying marriage, conferred a great benefit upon women ; but it must be owned that neither in its ideal type, nor in the general tenor of its doctrines or devotions, is it as congenial to their nature as the religion it superseded.

Its complete suppression of the conventual system was also, I think, very far from a benefit to women or to the world. It would be impossible to conceive any institution more needed than one which would furnish a shelter for the many women who, from poverty, or domestic unhappiness, or other causes, find themselves cast alone and unprotected into the battle of life, which would secure them from the temptations to gross vice, and from the extremities of suffering, and would convert them into agents of active, organised, and intelligent charity. Such an institution would be almost free from the objections that may justly be urged against monasteries, which withdraw strong men from manual labour, and it would largely mitigate the difficulty of providing labour and means of livelihood for single women, which is one of the most pressing, in our own day one of the most appalling, of social problems. Most unhappily for mankind, this noble conception was from the first perverted. Institutions that might have had an incalculable philanthropic value were based upon the principle of asceticism, which makes the sacrifice, not the promotion, of earthly happiness its aim, and binding vows produced much misery and not a little vice. The convent became the perpetual prison of the daughter whom a father was disinclined to endow, or of young girls who, under the impulse of a transient enthusiasm, or of a transient sorrow, took a step which they never could retrace, and useless penances and contemptible superstitions wasted the energies that might have been most beneficially employed. Still it is very doubtful whether, even in the most degraded period, the convents did not prevent more misery than they inflicted, and in the Sisters of Charity the religious orders of Catholicism have produced one of the most perfect of all the types of womanhood. There is, as I conceive, no fact in modern history more deeply to be deplored than that the Reformers, who in matters of doctrinal innovations were often so timid, should have levelled to the dust, instead of attempting to regenerate, the whole conventual system of Catholicism.

The course of these observations has led me to transgress the limits assigned to this history. It has been, however, my object through this entire work to exhibit not only the nature but also the significance of the moral facts I have recorded, by showing how they have affected the subsequent changes of society. I will conclude this chapter, and this work, by observing that of all the departments of ethics the questions concerning the relations of the sexes and the proper position of women, are those upon the future of which there rests the greatest uncertainty. History tells us that as civilisation advances, the charity of men becomes at once warmer and more expansive, their habitual conduct both more gentle and more temperate, and their love of truth more sincere; but it also warns us that in periods of great intellectual enlightenment, and of great social refinement, the relations of the sexes have often been most anarchical. It is impossible to deny that the form which these relations at present assume has been very largely affected by special religious teaching, which, for good or for ill, is rapidly waning in the sphere of government, and also, that certain recent revolutions in economical opinion and industrial enterprise have a most profound bearing upon the subject. The belief that a rapid increase of population is always eminently beneficial, which was long accepted as an axiom by both statesmen and moralists, and was made the basis of a large part of the legislation of the first and of the decisions of the second, has now been replaced by the directly opposite doctrine, that the very highest interest of society is not to stimulate but to restrain multiplication, diminishing the number of marriages and of children. In consequence of this belief, and of the many factitious wants that accompany a luxurious civilisation, a very large and increasing proportion of women are left to make their way in life without any male protector, and the difficulties they have to encounter through physical weakness have been most unnaturally and most fearfully aggravated by laws and customs which, resting on the old assumption that every woman should be a wife, habitually deprive them of the pecuniary and educational advantages of men, exclude them absolutely from very many of the employments in which they might earn a subsistence, encumber their course in others by a heartless ridicule or by a steady disapprobation, and consign, in consequence, many thousands to the most extreme and agonising poverty, and perhaps a still larger number to the paths of vice. At the same time a momentous revolution, the effects of which can as yet be but imperfectly descried, has taken place in the chief spheres of female industry that remain. The progress of machinery has destroyed its domestic character. The distaff has fallen from the hand. The needle is being rapidly superseded, and the work which, from the days of Homer to the present century, was accomplished in the centre of the family, has been transferred to the crowded manufactory.[1]

The probable consequences of these things are among the most important questions that can occupy the moralist or the philanthropist, but they do not fall within the province of the historian. That the pursuits and education of women will be considerably altered, that these alterations will bring with them some modifications of the type of character, and that the prevailing moral notions concerning the relations of the sexes will be subjected in many quarters to a severe and hostile criticism, may safely be predicted. Many wild theories will doubtless be propounded. Some real ethical changes may perhaps be effected, but these, if I mistake not, can only be within definite and narrow limits. He who will seriously reflect upon our clear perceptions of the difference between purity and impurity, upon the laws that govern our affections, and upon the interests of the children who are born, may easily convince himself that in this, as in all other spheres, there are certain eternal moral landmarks which never can be removed.

[1] The results of this change have been treated by Miss Parkes, in her truly admirable little book called *Essays on Woman's Work,* better than by any other writer with whom I am acquainted.

# INDEX.

# INDEX.

# LIST OF WORKS

# PUBLISHED BY D. APPLETON & COMPANY,

## 90, 92 & 94 GRAND STREET, NEW YORK.

*A Descriptive Catalogue, with full titles and prices, may be had gratuitously on application.*

About's Roman Question.
Adams' Boys at Home.
—— Edgar Clifton.
Addison's Spectator. 6 vols.
Adler's German and English Dictionary.
—— Abridged do. do. do.
—— German Reader.
—— " Literature.
—— Ollendorff for Learning German.
—— Key to the Exercises.
—— Iphigenia in Tauris.
After Icebergs with a Painter.
Agnel's Book of Chess.
Aguilar's Home Influence.
—— Mother's Recompense.
—— Days of Bruce. 2 vols.
—— Home Scenes.
—— Woman's Friendship.
—— Women of Israel. 2 vols.
—— Vale of Cedars.
Ahn's French Method.
—— Spanish Grammar.
—— A Key to same.
—— German Method. 1 vol.
Or, separately—First Course. 1 vol.
Second " 1 vol.
Aids to Faith. A series of Essays, by Various Writers.
Aikin's British Poets. From Chaucer to the Present Time. 3 vols.
Album for Postage Stamps.
Albums of Foreign Galleries; in 7 folios.
Alden's Elements of Intellectual Philosophy.
Alison's Miscellaneous Essays.
Allen's Mechanics of Nature.
Alsop's Charms of Fancy.
Amelia's Poems.
American Poets (Gems from the).
American Eloquence. A Collection of Speeches and Addresses. 2 vols.
American System of Education:
1. Hand-Book of Anglo-Saxon Root-Words.
2. Hand-Book of Anglo-Saxon Derivatives.
3. Hand-Book of Engrafted Words.
Anderson's Mercantile Correspondence.
Andrews' New French Instructor.
—— A Key to the above.
Annals of San Francisco.
Antisell on Coal Oils.
Anthon's Law Student.
Appletons' New American Cyclopædia of Useful Knowledge. 16 vols.
—— Annual Cyclopædia, and Register of Important Events for 1861, '62,' 63, '64, '65.
—— Cyclopædia of Biography, Foreign and American.

Appletons' Cyclopædia of Drawing.
The same in parts:
Topographical Drawing.
Perspective and Geometrical Drawing.
Shading and Shadows.
Drawing Instruments and their Uses.
Architectural Drawing and Design.
Mechanical Drawing and Design.
—— Dictionary of Mechanics and Engineering. 2 large vols.
—— Railway Guide.
—— American Illustrated Guide Book. 1 vol.
Do. do., separately:
1. Eastern and Middle States, and British Provinces. 1 vol.
2. Southern and Western States, and the Territories. 1 vol.
—— Companion Hand-Book of Travel.
Arabian Nights' Entertainments.
Arnold's (S. G.) History of the State of Rhode Island. 2 vols.
Arnold's (Dr.) History of Rome.
—— Modern History.
Arnold's Classical Series:
—— First Latin Book.
—— First and Second Latin Book and Grammar.
—— Latin Prose Composition.
—— Cornelius Nepos.
—— First Greek Book.
—— Greek Prose Composition Book, 1.
—— Greek Prose Composition Book, 2.
—— Greek Reading Book.
Arthur's (T. S.) Tired of Housekeeping.
Arthur's (W.) Successful Merchant.
At Anchor; or, A Story of our Civil War.
Atlantic Library. 7 vols. in case.
Attaché in Madrid.
Aunt Fanny's Story Book.
—— Mitten Series. 6 vols. in case.
—— Night Cap Series. 6 vols. in case.

Badois' English Grammar for Frenchmen.
—— A Key to the above.
Baine's Manual of Composition and Rhetoric.
Bakewell's Great Facts.
Baldwin's Flush Times.
—— Party Leaders.
Balmanno's Pen and Pencil.
Bank Law of the United States.
Barrett's Beauty for Ashes.
Bartlett's U. S. Explorations. 2 vols.
—— Cheap edition. 2 vols. in 1.
Barwell's Good in Every Thing.
Bassnett's Theory of Storms.

Baxley's West Coast of America and Hawaiian Islands.
Beach's Pelayo. An Epic.
Beall (John Y.), Trial of.
Beauties of Sacred Literature.
Beauties of Sacred Poetry.
Beaumont and Fletcher's Works. 2 vols.
Belem's Spanish Phrase Book.
Bello's Spanish Grammar (in Spanish).
Benedict's Run Through Europe.
Benton on the Dred Scott Case.
—— Thirty Years' View. 2 vols.
—— Debates of Congress. 16 vols.
Bertha Percy. By Margaret Field. 12mo.
Bertram's Harvest of the Sea. Economic and Natural History of Fishes.
Bessie and Jessie's Second Book.
Beza's Novum Testamentum.
Bibles in all styles of bindings and various prices.
Bible Stories, in Bible Language.
Black's General Atlas of the World.
Bloomfield's Farmer's Boy.
Blot's What to Eat, and How to Cook it.
Blue and Gold Poets. 6 vols. in case.
Boise's Greek Exercises.
—— First Three Books of Xenophon's Anabasis.
Bojesen's Greek and Roman Antiquities.
Book of Common Prayer. Various prices.
Boone's Life and Adventures.
Bourne's Catechism of the Steam Engine.
—— Hand-Book of the Steam Engine.
—— Treatise on the Steam Engine.
Boy's Book of Modern Travel.
—— Own Toy Maker
Bradford's Peter the Great.
Bradley's (Mary E.) Douglass Farm.
Bradley's (Chas.) Sermons.
Brady's Christmas Dream.
Breakfast, Dinner, and Tea.
British Poets. From Chaucer to the Present Time. 3 large vols.
British Poets. Cabinet Edition. 15 vols.
Brooks' Ballads and Translations.
Brown, Jones, and Robinson's Tour.
Bryan's English Grammar for Germans.
Bryant and Stratton's Commercial Law.
Bryant's Poems, Illustrated.
—— Poems. 2 vols.
—— Thirty Poems.
—— Poems. Blue and Gold.
—— Letters from Spain.
Buchanan's Administration.
Buckle's Civilization in England. 2 vols.
—— Essays.
Bunyan's Divine Emblems.
Burdett's Chances and Changes.
—— Never Too Late.
Burgess' Photograph Manual. 12mo.
Burnett (James R.) on the Thirty-nine Articles.
Burnett (Peter H.), The Path which led a Protestant Lawyer to the Catholic Church.
Burnouf's Gramatica Latina.
Burns' (Jabez) Cyclopædia of Sermons.
Burns' (Robert) Poems.
Burton's Cyclopædia of Wit and Humor. 2 vols.
Butler's Martin Van Buren.
Butler's (F.) Spanish Teacher.
Butler's (S.) Hudibras.
Butler's (T. B.) Guide to the Weather.
Butler's (Wm. Allen) Two Millions.
Byron Gallery. The Gallery of Byron Beauties.
—— Poetical Works.
—— Life and Letters.
—— Works. Illustrated.

Cœleb's Laws and Practice of Whist.
Cæsar's Commentaries.
Caird's Prairie Farming.
Calhoun's Works and Speeches. 6 vols.
Campbell's (Thos.) Gertrude of Wyoming.
—— Poems.
Campbell (Judge) on Shakespeare.
Canot, Life of Captain.
Carlyle's (Thomas) Essays.
Carreno's Manual of Politeness.
—— Compendio del Manual de Urbanidad.
Casseday's Poetic Lacon.
Cavendish's Laws of Whist.
Cervantes' Don Quixote, in Spanish.
—— Don Quixote, in English.
César L'Histoire de Jules, par S. M. I. Napoleon III. Vol. I., with Maps and Portrait. (French.)
Cheap Edition, without Maps and Portrait.
Maps and Portrait, for cheap edition, in envelopes.
Champlin's English Grammar.
—— Greek Grammar.
Chase on the Constitution and Canons.
Chaucer's Poems.
Chevalier on Gold.
Children's Holidays.
Child's First History.
Chittenden's Report of the Peace Convention.
Choquet's French Composition.
—— French Conversation.
Cicero de Officiis.
—— Select Orations.
Clarke's (D. S.) Scripture Promises.
Clarke's (Mrs. Cowden) Iron Cousin.
Clark's (H. J.) Mind in Nature.
Cleaveland and Backus' Villas and Cottages.
Cleveland's (H. W. S.) Hints to Riflemen.
Cloud Crystals. A Snow Flake Album.
Cobb's (J. B.) Miscellanies.
Coe's Spanish Drawing Cards. 10 parts.
Coe's Drawing Cards. 10 parts.
Colenso on the Pentateuch. 2 vols.
—— On the Romans.
Coleridge's Poems.
Collins' Amoor.
Collins' (T. W.) Humanics.
Collet's Dramatic French Reader.
Comings' Physiology.
—— Companion to Physiology.
Comment on Parle a Paris.
Congreve's Comedy.
Continental Library. 6 vols. in case.
Cooke's Life of Stonewall Jackson.
Cookery, by an American Lady.
Cooley's Cyclopædia of Receipts.
Cooper's Mount Vernon.
Copley's Early Friendship.
—— Poplar Grove.
Cornell's First Steps in Geography.
—— Primary Geography.
—— Intermediate Geography.
—— Grammar School Geography.
—— High School Geography and Atlas.

Cornell's High School Geography.
—— " " Atlas.
—— Map Drawing. 12 maps in case.
—— Outline Maps, with Key. 13 maps in portfolio.
—— Or, the Key, separately.
Cornwall on Music.
Correlation and Conservation of Forces.
Cortez' Life and Adventures.
Cotter on the Mass and Rubrics.
Cottin's Elizabeth; or, the Exiles of Siberia.
Cousin Alice's Juveniles.
Cousin Carrie's Sun Rays.
—— Keep a Good Heart.
Cousin's Modern Philosophy. 2 vols.
—— On the True and Beautiful.
—— Only Romance.
Coutan's French Poetry.
Covell's English Grammar.
Cowles' Exchange Tables.
Cowper's Homer's Iliad.
—— Poems.
Cox's Eight Years in Congress, from '57 to '65.
Coxe's Christian Ballads.
Creasy on the English Constitution.
Crisis (The).
Crosby's (A.) Geometry.
Crosby's (H.) Œdipus Tyrannus.
Crosby's (W. H.) Quintus Curtius Rufus.
Crowe's Linny Lockwood.
Curry's Volunteer Book.
Cust's Invalid's Book.
Cyclopædia of Commercial and Business Anecdotes. 2 vols.

D'Abrantes' Memoires of Napoleon. 2 vols.
Dairyman's (The) Daughter.
Dana's Household Poetry.
Darwin's Origin of Species.
Dante's Poems.
Dasent's Popular Tales from the Norse.
Davenport's Christ. Unity and its Recovery.
Dawson's Archaia.
De Belem's Spanish Phrase-Book.
De Fivas' Elementary French Reader.
—— Classic French Reader.
De Foe's Robinson Crusoe.
De Girardin's Marguerite.
—— Stories of an Old Maid.
De Hart on Courts Martial.
De L'Ardeche's History of Napoleon.
De Peyrac's Comment on Parle.
De Staël's Corinne, ou L'Italie.
De Veitelle's Mercantile Dictionary.
De Vere's Spanish Grammar.
Dew's Historical Digest.
Dickens's (Charles) Works. Original Illustrations. 24 vols.
Dies Irae and Stabat Mater, bound together.
Dies Irae, alone, and Stabat Mater, alone.
Dix's (John A.) Winter in Madeira.
—— Speeches and Addresses. 2 vols.
Dix's (Rev. M.) Lost Unity of the Christian World.
Dr. Oldham at Greystones, and his Talk there.
Doane's Works. 4 vols.
Downing's Rural Architecture.
Dryden's Poems.
Dunlap's Spirit History of Man.
Dusseldorf Gallery, Gems from the.
Dwight on the Study of Art.
Ebony Idol (The).
Ede's Management of Steel.
Edith Vaughan's Victory.

Egloffstein's Geology and Physical Geography of Mexico.
Eichhorn's German Grammar.
Elliot's Fine Work on Birds. 7 parts, or in 1 v.
Ellsworth's Text-Book of Penmanship.
Ely's Journal.
Enfield's Indian Corn; its Value, Culture, and Uses.
Estvan's War Pictures.
Evans' History of the Shakers.
Evelyn's Life of Mrs. Godolphin.
Everett's Mount Vernon Papers.
Fables, Original and Selected.
Farrar's History of Free Thought.
Faustus.
Fay's Poems.
Fénelon's Telemaque. The same, in 2 vols.
—— Telemachus.
Field's Bertha Percy.
Field's (M.) City Architecture.
Figuier's World before the Deluge.
Fireside Library. 8 vols. in case.
First Thoughts.
Fiji and the Fijians.
Flint's Physiology of Man.
Florian's William Tell.
Flower Pictures.
Fontana's Italian Grammar.
Foote's Africa and the American Flag.
Foresti's Italian Extracts.
Four Gospels (The).
Franklin's Man's Cry and God's Gracious Answer.
Frieze's Tenth and Twelfth Books of Quintilian.
Fullerton's (Lady G.) Too Strange Not to be True.
Funny Story Book.

Garland's Life of Randolph.
Gaskell's Life of Brontë. 2 vols.
The same, cheaper edition, in 1 vol.
George Ready.
Gerard's French Readings.
Gertrude's Philip Randolph.
Gesenius' Hebrew Grammar.
Ghostly Colloquies.
Gibbes' Documentary History. 3 vols.
Gibbons' Banks of New York.
Gilfillan's Literary Portraits.
Gillespie on Land Surveying.
Girardin on Dramatic Literature.
Goadby's Text-Book of Physiology.
Goethe's Iphigenia in Tauris.
Goldsmith's Essays.
—— Vicar of Wakefield.
Gosse's Evenings with the Microscope.
Goulburn's Office of the Holy Communion.
—— Idle Word.
—— Manual of Confirmation.
—— Sermons.
—— Study of the Holy Scriptures.
—— Thoughts on Personal Religion.
Gould's (E. S.) Comedy.
Gould's (W. M.) Zephyrs.
Graham's English Synonymes.
Grandmamma Easy's Toy Books.
Grandmother's Library. 6 vols. in case.
Grand's Spanish Arithmetic.
Grant's Report on the Armies of the United States 1864–'65.
Granet's Portuguese Grammar.
Grayson's Theory of Christianity.
Greek Testament.
Greene's (F. H.) Primary Botany.
—— Class-Book of Botany.
Greene's (G. W.) Companion to Ollendorff.

Greene's (G. W.) First Lessons in French.
—— First Lessons in Italian.
—— Middle Ages.
Gregory's Mathematics.
Griffin on the Gospel.
Griffith's Poems.
Griswold's Republican Court.
——— Sacred Poets.
Guizot's (Madame) Tales.
Guizot's (M.) Civilization in Europe. 4 vols.
—— School edition. 1 vol.
—— New Edition, on tinted paper. 4 vols.
Gurowski's America and Europe.
——— Russia as it is.

Hadley's Greek Grammar.
Hahn's Greek Testament.
Hall's (B. H.) Eastern Vermont.
Hall's (C. H.) Notes on the Gospels. 2 vols.
Hall's (E. H.) Guide to the Great West.
Halleck's Poems.
—— Poems. Pocket size, blue and gold.
—— Young America.
Halleck's (H. W.) Military Science.
Hamilton's (Sir Wm.) Philosophy.
Hamilton's (A.) Writings. 6 vols.
Hand-Books on Education.
Hand-Book of Anglo-Saxon Root-Words.
Hand-Book of Anglo-Saxon Derivatives.
Hand-Book of the Engrafted Words.
Handy-Book of Property Law.
Happy Child's Library. 18 vols. in case.
Harkness' First Greek Book.
——— Latin Grammar.
——— First Latin Book.
——— Second "
——— Latin Reader.
Hase's History of the Church.
Haskell's Housekeeper's Encyclopædia.
Hassard's Life of Archbishop Hughes.
——— Wreath of Beauty.
Haupt on Bridge Construction.
Haven's Where There's a Will There's a Way.
—— Patient Waiting no Loss.
—— Nothing Venture Nothing Have.
—— Out of Debt Out of Danger.
—— Contentment Better than Wealth.
—— No Such Word as Fail.
—— All's Not Gold that Glitters.
—— A Place for Everything, and Everything in its Place.
—— Loss and Gain.
—— Pet Bird. [in case.
—— Home Series of Juvenile Books. 8 vols.
Haven (Memoir of Alice B.).
Hazard on the Will.
Hecker's Questions of the Soul.
Hemans'. Poems. 2 vols.
—— Songs of the Affections.
Henck's Field-Book for Engineers.
Henry on Human Progress.
Herbert's Poems.
Here and There.
Herodotus, by Johnson (in Greek).
Herodotus, by Rawlinson (in English). 4 vls.
Heydenreich's German Reader.
Hickok's Rational Cosmology.
—— Rational Psychology.
History of the Rebellion, Military and Naval, Illustrated.
Hoffman's Poems.
Holcombe's Leading Cases.
——— Law of Dr. and Cr.
——— Letters in Literature.

Holly's Country Seats.
Holmes' (M. A.) Tempest and Sunshine.
——— English Orphans.
Holmes' (A.) Parties and Principles.
Homes of American Authors.
Homer's Iliad.
Hooker's Complete Works. 2 vols.
Hoppin's Notes.
Horace, edited by Lincoln.
Howitt's Child's Verse-Book.
—— Juvenile Tales. 14 vols. in case.
How's Historical Shakspearian Reader.
—— Shakspearian Reader.
Huc's Tartary and China.
Hudson's Life and Adventures.
Humboldt's Letters.
Hunt's (C. H.) Life of Livingston.
Hunt's (F. W.) Historical Atlas.
Huntington's Lady Alice.
Hutton's Mathematics.
Huxley's Man's Place in Nature.
—— Origin of Species.

Iconographic Encyclopædia. 6 vols.—4 Text and 2 Plates.
Or, separately:
The Countries and Cities of the World. 2 vols.
The Navigation of all Ages. 2 vols.
The Art of Building in Ancient and Modern Times. 2 vols.
The Religions of Ancient and Modern Times. 2 vols.
The Fine Arts Illustrated. 2 vols.
Technology Illustrated. 2 vols.
Internal Revenue Law.
Iredell's Life. 2 vols.
Italian Comedies.

Jacobs' Learning to Spell.
—— The same, in two parts.
Jaeger's Class-Book of Zoology.
James' (J. A.) Young Man.
James' (H.) Logic of Creation.
James' (G. P. R.) Adrien.
Jameson's (Mrs.) Art Works.
——— Legends of Saints and Martyrs. 2 vls.
——— Legends of the Monastic Orders.
——— Legends of the Madonna.
——— History of Our Lord. 2 vols.
Jarvis' Reply to Milner.
Jay on American Agriculture.
Jeffers on Gunnery.
Jeffrey's (F.) Essays.
Johnson's Meaning of Words.
Johnson's (Samuel) Rasselas.
Johnston's Chemistry of Common Life. 2 v.

Kavanagh's Adele.
——— Beatrice.
——— Daisy Burns.
——— Grace Lee.
——— Madeleine.
——— Nathalie.
——— Rachel Gray.
——— Seven Years.
——— Queen Mab.
——— Women of Christianity.
Keats' Poems.
Keep a Good Heart.
Keightley's Mythology.
Keil's Fairy Stories.
Keith (Memoir of Caroline P.)
Kendrick's Greek Ollendorff.

Kenny's Manual of Chess.
Kinglake's Crimean War. Vols. 1 and 2.
Kirke White's Poems.
Kirkland's Life of Washington.
A Cheaper Edition, for Schools.
Knowles' Orlean Lamar.
Kœppen's Middle Ages.
—— Separately—Middle Ages, 2 vols.
—— Atlas.
Kohlrausch's History of Germany.
Kuhner's Greek Grammar.

Lafever's Beauties of Architecture.
Lady Alice.
Lamartine's Confidential Disclosures.
—— History of Turkey. 3 vols.
Lancelott's Queens of England, and their Times. 2 vols.
Landon's (L. E.) Complete Works.
Latham's English Language.
Layard's Nineveh. Illustrated.
—— Cheap edition. Without Illustrations.
Learning to Spell.
Le Brun's Telemaque.
Lecky's Rise & Influence of Rationalism. 2 v.
Le Sage's Adventures of Gil Blas. 1 vol.
—— Gil Blas, in Spanish.
Letter Writer.
Letters from Rome.
Lewes' (G. H.) History of Philosophy. 2 vls.
—— In 1 vol.
—— Physiology of Common Life.
Library of Travel and Adventure. 3 v. in case.
Library for my Young Countrymen. 9 vols. in case.
Libro Primario de Ortografia.
Liebig's Laws of Husbandry.
Life of Man Symbolized by the Months of the Year.
Light and Darkness.
Lights and Shadows of New York Picture Galleries.
Lindsay's Poems.
Linn's Life and Services.
Little Builder.
Little Engineer.
Livy, with English Notes.
Logan's Château Frissac.
Looking Glass for the Mind.
Lord's Poems.
—— Christ in Hades; a Poem.
Louise.
Lunt's Origin of the Late War.
Lyell's Elements of Geology.
—— Principles of Geology.
Lyra Americana.
Lyra Anglicana.

Macaulay's Essays. 1 vol.
—— Essays. 7 vols.
—— Essays. A New and Revised Edition, on tinted paper. 6 vols.
Mackintosh's (Sir James) Essays.
Madge.
Mahan's Answer to Colenso.
—— Numerals of Scripture.
Mahon's England. 2 vols.
Maiu's Novum Testamentum Græce.
Mandeville's New Series of Readers.
1. Primary Reader.
2. Second Reader.
3. Third Reader.
4. Fourth Reader.
5. Fifth Reader.

Mandeville's Course of Reading.
—— Reading and Oratory.
—— First Spanish Reader.
—— Second Spanish Reader.
—— Third Spanish Reader.
Magnall's Historical Questions.
Man's Cry and God's Gracious Answer.
Manners' At Home and Abroad.
—— Sedgemoor.
Manning's Temp. Mission of the Holy Ghost.
—— The Reunion of Christendom.
Manual of Matrimony.
Markham's History of England.
Marrayat's Africa.
—— Masterman Ready.
—— Popular Novels. 12 vols.
—— A New and Revised Edition, printed on tinted paper 12 vols.
Marryat's Settlers in Canada.
Marshall's (E. C.) Book of Oratory.
—— First Book of Oratory.
Marshall's (T. W.) Notes on Episcopacy.
Marsh's Double Entry Book-keeping.
—— Single Entry Book-keeping.
—— Bank Book-keeping.
—— Book-keeping (in Spanish).
—— Blank Books for Double Entry. 6 books in set.
—— Do. for Single Entry. 6 books in set.
Martha's Hooks and Eyes.
Martineau's Crofton Boys.
—— Peasant and Prince.
Mary Lee.
Mary Staunton.
Mathews on Whist.
Mayhew's Illustrated Horse Doctor.
May's Bertram Noel.
—— Louis' School Days.
—— Mortimer's College Life.
—— Sunshine of Greystone.
McCormick's Visit to Sebastopol.
McIntosh's Aunt Kitty's Tales.
—— Charms and Counter Charms.
—— Evenings at Donaldson Manor.
—— Lofty and Lowly. 2 vols.
—— Maggie and Emma.
—— Meta Gray.
—— Two Lives.
—— Two Pictures.
—— New Juvenile Library. 7 vols. in case.
McLee's Alphabets.
McWhorter's Church Essays.
Meadows' Italian Dictionary.
Memoirs of Catharine II.
Merchant of Venice.
Merivale's History of the Romans. 7 vols.
Conversion of the Roman Empire.
" " Northern Nations.
Merry Christmas Book.
Michelet's France. 2 vols.
Milhouse's Italian Dictionary. 2 vols.
Mill's Political Economy. 2 vols.
Milledulcia.
Milton's Poems.
—— Paradise Lost.
Miniature Library. 27 vols.
Ministry of Life.
Minturn's Travels in India.
Modern British Essayists. 8 vols.
Modet's Light.
Moore's Revolutionary Ballads.
Moore's (George H.) Notes on the History of Slavery in Massachusetts.
Moore's (Thos.) Irish Melodies.

Moore's (Thos.) Memoirs and Journal. 2 vls.
—— Lallah Rookh.
—— Poems. 1 vol., cheap edition.
—— Do., on fine tinted paper.
Morales' Spanish Reader.
Moran on Money.
More's Practical Piety. 2 vols.
—— Private Devotions.
—— Domestic Tales.
—— Rural Tales.
—— Village Tales. 2 vols. in 1.
Morin's Practical Mechanics.
Morphy's Chess Games.
—— Triumphs.
Mulligan's English Grammar.
My Cave Life in Vicksburg.

Napoleon Bonaparte, by F. de l'Ardeche.
Napoleon Correspondence. 2 vols.
New Fairy Stories.
Newcomb on Financial Policy.
Newman's Apologia Pro Vita Sua.
—— Sermons.
New Testament, with engravings on wood from designs by the ancient masters. 1 vol.
New Testament, with Comment by E. Churton and W. B. Jones. 2 vols.
New York City Banks.
New York Picture Galleries.
Nightcap Series of Juveniles. 6 vols. in case.
Nightingale on Nursing.
Novum Testamentum, interprete Beza.
Nueva Biblioteca de la Risa.
Nuovo Tesoro di Schergos.
Nursery Basket.

O'Callaghan's New Netherlands. 2 vols.
Œhlschlager's German Reader.
Ogilby on Lay Baptism.
Oldfellow's Uncle Nat.
Oliphant's Katmandu.
Ollendorff's Eng. Grammar for Spaniards.
A Key to the Exercises.
—— English Grammar for Germans.
A Key to the Exercises.
—— French Grammar, by Jewett.
A Key to the Exercises.
—— French Grammar, by Value.
A Key to the Exercises.
—— French Grammar for Spaniards.
Key to the same.
—— German Grammar.
A Key to the Exercises.
—— Italian Grammar.
A Key to the Exercises.
—— Spanish Grammar.
A Key to the Exercises.
Ortografia.
Ordronaux' Hints on Health.
Oriental Library. 5 vols. in case.
Osgood's Hearthstone.
—— Mile Stones.
Ostervald's Nouveau Testament.
Otis' Landscapes. 1 vol.
—— The same, in 6 parts.
—— Studies of Animals. 1 vol.
—— Studies of Animals. 6 parts.
Overman's Metallurgy.
Owen's (Jno. J.) Acts of the Apostles.
—— Greek Reader.
—— Homer's Odyssey.
—— Homer's Iliad.
—— Thucydides.

Owen's (Jno. J.) Xenophon's Anabasis.
—— Xenophon's Cyropædia.
Owen's Penmanship. 3 books.

Paez' Geografia del Mundo.
Pages and Pictures. From the writings of James Fenimore Cooper.
Paine's Tent and Harem.
Palenzuela's Gramatica Inglesa.
Key to the same.
Palmer's Book-keeping.
Parker's Critical and Miscellaneous Writings.
—— Speeches and Addresses. 3 vols.
—— Additional Speeches. 2 vols.
—— Sermons of Theism.
—— Ten Sermons.
—— Trial and Defence.
—— Two Christmas Celebrations.
—— Works. 2 vols.
—— (Life of Theodore). 2 vols.
Parley's Faggots for the Fireside.
—— Present for all Seasons.
Parley's Wanderers by Sea and Land.
Patton's History of the United States.
Paul and Virginia.
Pearson on the Creed.
Perkins' Primary Arithmetic.
—— Elementary Arithmetic.
—— Practical Arithmetic.
—— The same, in Spanish.
—— A Key to Practical Arithmetic.
—— Higher Arithmetic.
—— Algebra.
—— Higher Algebra.
—— Geometry.
—— Higher Geometry.
—— Plane Trigonometry.
Perry's Americans in Japan.
—— Expedition to the China Seas and Japan.
Petit's Household Mysteries.
Peyrac's Comment on Parle à Paris.
Phelan on Billiards.
Phœnixiana.
Picture Gallery, in Spanish.
Pickell's Narrative. History of the Potomac Company.
Planches' Lead Diseases.
Plato's Apology.
Poetical Gems. Blue and Gold. 6 vls. in case.
Poets' Gallery.
Pollok's Poems.
Pomeroy's Municipal Law.
Pope's Poems.
Porter's Scottish Chiefs.
Portraits of my Married Friends.
Practical Cook Book.
Pratt's Dawnings of Genius.
Prince Charlie.
Pulpit Cyclopædia & Minister's Companion.
Punch's Pocket-Book of Fun.
Punchinello.
Pure Gold.
Pusey's Eirenicon.
Putz's Ancient Geography.
—— Mediæval Geography.
—— Modern Geography.

Quackenbos' First Book in Eng. Grammar.
—— English Grammar.
—— First Lessons on Composition.
—— Advanced Course of Composition and Rhetoric.
—— Natural Philosophy.
—— Primary History.

www.ingramcontent.com/pod-product-compliance
Lightning Source LLC
LaVergne TN
LVHW021137110826
845150LV00005B/1054

* 9 7 8 1 4 2 5 5 4 8 3 8 4 *